A CLINICIAN'S GUIDE TO SYSTEMIC SEX THERAPY

The second edition of *A Clinician's Guide to Systemic Sex Therapy* has been completely revised, updated, and expanded. This volume is written for beginning psychotherapy practitioners in order to guide them through the complexities of sex therapy and help them to be more efficient in their treatment. The authors offer a unique theoretical approach to understanding and treating sexual problems from a systemic perspective, incorporating the multifaceted perspectives of the individual client, the couple, the family, and the other contextual factors.

Both beginning and experienced sex/relationship therapists will broaden their perspectives with the Intersystem approach and gain information rarely seen in sex therapy texts such as: how to thoroughly assess each sexual disorder, the implementation of various treatment principles and techniques, how to incorporate homework, dealing with ethical dilemmas, understanding different expressions of sexual behavior, and addressing the impact of medical problems on sexuality. Aside from bringing the diagnostic criteria up-to-date with the DSM 5, this new edition contains a new chapter on sensate focus, an expanded section on assessment, more information about development across the lifespan, and more focus on diversity issues throughout the text.

Gerald R. Weeks, PhD, APBB, CST, is a certified sex therapist with 30 years of practice experience and is a professor at the University of Nevada, Las Vegas. He is among a handful of individuals to be given the "Outstanding Contribution to Marriage and Family Therapy" award in 2009 from the American Association of Marriage and Family Therapy, and was named the "2010 Family Psychologist of the Year." He has published over 20 books in the fields of individual, couple, family, and sex therapy.

Nancy Gambescia, PhD, CST, is a certified sex therapist with 35 years of practice experience, and is the Director of the postgraduate sex therapy program at Council for Relationships in Philadelphia, Pennsylvania. She also maintains a private practice specializing in relationship and sex therapy in Rosemont, PA. Dr. Gambescia has published numerous book chapters, journal articles, and 6 books in couple and sex therapy.

Katherine M. Hertlein, PhD, is a professor and Program Director of the marriage and family therapy program at the University of Nevada, Las Vegas. She has published over 50 articles, 7 books, and 25 book chapters over the course of her career. She presents nationally and internationally on sex, technology, and couples.

"Written by master sex therapy clinicians, this second edition surpasses its predecessor by offering up-to-date research and clinical insight, making a compelling case for its use for systemic sex therapy with couples experiencing sexual problems. This text will serve as an outstanding resource for all clinicians, particularly those heavily entrenched in working with individuals and couples. It is an invaluable text for both beginners and seasoned practitioners. I applaud the authors on producing a masterful work and strongly recommend it."

—**Frank M. Dattilio, PhD, ABPP**, works in the department of psychiatry at Harvard Medical School

"It is a pleasure to endorse such a strongly resourced, credible, and contemporary resource for the practicing sexual and relationship therapist. Throughout the text, the authors emphasize the crucial awareness yet problematic dichotomy between psychological and physiological states alongside relational and other factors that contribute to sexual functioning. The text offers practical tips, guidance and tools from a strong clinical background with clear emphasis to systemic practice. Key signposting throughout the text makes this especially meaningful to the audience of modern society with key literature sharing space with other media resources."

—**Professor Kevan Wylie, MD FRCP FRCPsych FRCOG FECSM**, is a consultant in sexual medicine, Sheffield, and President, World Association for Sexual Health

"There are three reasons why you should read *A Clinician's Guide to Systemic Sex Therapy*. It is the only book that places sex therapy squarely within a family systems approach. In other words, it focuses not only on the mechanics and biology but also on the couple relationship. Second, it is among the most comprehensive books on sex therapy with sections on diversity, diagnosis and ethics. Finally, as the title suggests, it is the most practical text available with cutting edge techniques described in detail and updated for DSM-V. Every clinician working with couples needs this book."

—**Mark E. Young, PhD**, works at the Marriage and Family Research Institute at the University of Central Florida

"The only book you need to practice effective sex therapy. Drs Weeks, Gambescia, and Hertlein have improved on their original gem and expanded their integrated model to include the latest diagnostic categories of the DSM 5. The authors show how to treat sexual problems within the context of the couple relationship and not as an unconnected 'plumbing' problem. This easy-to-use guide that addresses the gamut of sexual and relationship issues belongs on every clinician's bookshelf."

—**Jon Carlson, PsyD, EdD, ABPP, CST,** is a Distinguished Professor of Adlerian Psychology at Adler University in Chicago

"This is much more than a 'Guide.' The term 'guide' is really a humble misnomer. This is in the true term of the word a veritable encyclopedia of all you want to know and need to do systemic sex therapy. Beginning students as well as seasoned professionals will be brought up to date in all the myriad of possible information that makes this humbly-called 'guide' a classic source of information and knowledge about sex therapy. I wish I had it when I first started doing couple therapy."

—**Luciano L'Abate, PhD, ABEPP,** is Professor Emeritus of Psychology at Georgia State University

A CLINICIAN'S GUIDE TO SYSTEMIC SEX THERAPY

Second Edition

Gerald R. Weeks, Nancy Gambescia, and Katherine M. Hertlein

Routledge
Taylor & Francis Group

NEW YORK AND LONDON

Second edition published 2016
by Routledge
711 Third Avenue, New York, NY 10017

and by Routledge
2 Park Square, Milton Park, Abingdon, Oxon, OX14 4RN

Routledge is an imprint of the Taylor & Francis Group, an informa business

© 2016 Taylor & Francis

First edition published by Routledge 2009

Library of Congress Cataloging-in-Publication Data
A catalog record has been requested for this title

ISBN: 978-0-415-73840-8 (hbk)
ISBN: 978-0-415-73839-2 (pbk)
ISBN: 978-1-315-81739-2 (ebk)

Typeset in Bembo
by Apex CoVantage, LLC

MIX
Paper from
responsible sources
FSC
www.fsc.org   FSC® C013056

Printed and bound in Great Britain by
TJ International Ltd, Padstow, Cornwall

To Nancy, for the love you bring to my life.
—GW
To Matt, Lauren and Michael, with love
—NG
To Adam, for filling my life with joy
—KH

CONTENTS

Preface   *xvi*
   Chapter Overview   xix
   References   xxi
Acknowledgments   *xxii*

1   The Intersystem Approach to Sex Therapy   1
   Theory and Integration in Couple Therapy   *1*
      Moving Toward Theoretical Integration   2
   Intersystem Theory and Application   *3*
      Intrapsychic Components   4
      Interactional Components   5
   Understanding Etiology and Treatment within
      the Intersystem Approach   *8*
      Individual/Biological   8
      Individual/Psychological   9
      The Dyadic Relationship   9
      Family-of-Origin Influences   11
      Contextual Factors   12
   Conclusion   *13*
   References   *14*

2   Diagnosis of Sexual Disorders   16
   Introduction   *16*

Diagnosing with the DSM-IV-TR and DSM-5   17
  Specifiers   18
Overview of Sexual Disorders in DSM-5   19
  Sexual Interest/Arousal Disorder   19
  Male Hypoactive Sexual Desire Disorder   20
  Erectile Disorder   20
  Premature (Early) Ejaculation   21
  Delayed Ejaculation   21
  Female Orgasmic Disorder   22
  Genito-Pelvic Pain/Penetration Disorder   22
Limitations of the DSM Diagnostic Categories   22
  Disorder versus Problem   23
  Etiology: Physiology versus Psychology   24
  Comorbidity with Other Conditions   24
  Individual or Relational Problems   25
  Clinical Judgment   26
Sexual Problems Not Currently in the DSM-5   27
  Sexual Compulsivity, Addiction or Hypersexuality   27
  Gender Nonconformity   28
  Persistent Genital Arousal Disorder   28
Diagnosis from the Intersystem Perspective   29
References   29

3 Intersystem Assessment of Sexual Disorders   32
  Introduction   32
  The Biphasic Assessment Process   33
  The Sexual History   35
  The Intersystem Sexual History   37
    Individual Physiological   41
    Individual Psychological   42
    The Relationship   42
    Intergenerational Factors   43
    Contextual   43
  Guidelines for Taking a Sexual History   44
    Promote Comfort and Ease   44
    Provide a Safe Environment   45
    Therapist Considerations   45
    Understand One's Own Sexuality   46
    Avoid Shaming   47
    Adopt a Stance of Both Never Assuming
      and Always Assuming   47

Normalize Sex Talk 48
Think Systemically 48
Conducting the Clinical Interview 49
Interviewing for Specific Disorders 49
Assessing for Sexual Desire Disorders 50
Male Hypoactive Sexual Desire Disorder and
Female Sexual Interest/Arousal Disorder 50
Sexual Aversion Disorder 53
Hyperactive Sexual Desire/Sexual Compulsivity 54
Erectile Disorder 55
Female Sexual Arousal Disorder (FSAD) 56
Persistent Genital Arousal Disorder 58
Assessing for Orgasm and Ejaculation Disorders 58
Premature (Early) Ejaculation 58
Female Orgasmic Disorder 60
Genito-Pelvic Pain/Penetration Disorder 61
Conclusion 63
References 64

4 The Sexual Genogram in Assessment 66
Introduction 66
Function of the Sexual Genogram 66
Constructing the Sexual Genogram 69
Organization 70
Potential Genogram Questions 71
General Questions 71
Gender Questions 72
Sexual Timeline 72
Timeline Questions 73
References 74

5 Measures of Sexual Function and Dysfunction 75
Introduction 75
Behavioral Assessment 76
Physiological Measures 76
Psychological Measures 77
Collections of Assessments 78
References 80

6 General Treatment Principles, Strategies and Techniques 83
General Treatment Considerations 83

Beginning Treatment   *84*
  Initial Contact   84
  The Initial Session   85
The Triage Tree   *86*
Presenting Problem versus Other Clinically Relevant Problems   *87*
  Medical Problems   87
  Significant Individual Psychopathology   88
  Severe Relational Discord   88
Multiple Dysfunctions in an Individual   *88*
Sexual Dysfunctions in Both Partners   *89*
Keeping Treatment Systemic   *91*
  Treatment Planning   92
  Beginning Treatment   93
  Readiness for Sex Therapy   94
The Importance of Principle, Techniques and Process   *94*
References   *95*

7 Treating Absent or Low Sexual Desire in
   Men and Women   96
   Definitional Issues   *97*
     Male Hypoactive Sexual Desire Disorder   97
     Female Sexual Arousal/Interest Disorder   97
   Strategies and Techniques   *98*
     Providing Bibliotherapy and Education   98
     Overcoming Pessimism and Skepticism   99
     Addressing Relationship Considerations   99
     Reducing Response Anxiety   99
     Conducting Cognitive Work   100
     Defining Oneself as a Sexual Person   101
     Increasing Sexual Fantasies   101
     Using Therapeutic Reframes   102
     Working with Intimacy Fears   102
     Promoting Communication   102
     Assessing for Other Sexual Disorders   103
     Considering Medical Issues   103
     Assigning Appropriate Homework   104
   References   *105*

8 Treatment Principles, Strategies and
   Techniques Specific to Men   106
   Treating Erectile Disorder   *106*

Strategies and Techniques   107
  Promote Systemic Thinking   107
  Provide Bibliotherapy and Education   108
  Dissipate Performance Anxiety   108
  Conduct Cognitive Work   109
  Use of Medical Treatment   110
  Assign Appropriate Homework   111
  Nongenital Touch   112
  Focused Genital Touch   112
  Ejaculation   113
  Penetration   113
  Free Form Intercourse   114
  Final Issues in Treating ED   115
Treating Premature (Early) Ejaculation   115
  Medical Treatment for PE   116
  Behavioral Strategies and Techniques   117
Treating Delayed Ejaculation   120
  Assessment   122
  Relationship Issues   123
  Strategies and Techniques   124
References   128

9 Treatment Principles, Strategies and
  Techniques Specific to Women   131
  Treating Female Orgasmic Disorder   131
    Individual Medical Issues   132
    Intergenerational Factors   133
    Individual Psychological Factors   133
    Relational Issues   133
    Strategies and Techniques   134
  Treatment of Genito-Pelvic Pain/Penetration Disorder 141
    Terms Used to Describe Pain   143
    Strategies and Techniques   146
  References   149

10 The New Sensate Focus Technique   152
  The Role of Cognitive-Behavioral Homework   153
  Promoting Compliance   154
  Pessimism and Skepticism   154
  Commitment   155
  The Systemic Perspective   155

Sensate Focus Exercises	*156*
Understanding Sensate Focus	*156*
Nine Functions of Sensate Focus	*158*
Readiness for Sensate Focus Assignments	*163*
Structure and Application of Sensate Focus	*164*
Using Metaphors	*165*
Proscribing Intercourse	*167*
Creating a Sensual Environment	*167*
Touching and Sensual Pleasuring	*167*
Sensual Pleasuring with Erotic Stimulation	*171*
Transitioning to Intercourse	*172*
Conclusion	*173*
References	*174*
11 Factors That Complicate Treating Sexual Disorders	176
Introduction	*176*
Sexual Ignorance	*176*
Sexual Mythology	*176*
Faulty Cognitions	*177*
Sexual Guilt, Anxiety and Shame	*178*
Dealing with Sexual Mythology	*179*
Dealing with Common Intimacy Fears	*179*
Fear of Intimacy	180
Fear of Anger	182
Fear of Feelings	182
Fear of Losing Control	183
Fear of Rejection/Abandonment	184
Fear of Dependency	185
References	*187*
12 Principles of Homework	189
Introduction	*189*
Homework	*189*
Common Structural Elements	190
Case Illustration	193
Processing an Assignment	194
Reading Assignments	*195*
References	*195*
13 Psychoeducation in Sex Therapy	197
Introduction	*197*
Bibliotherapy	*197*

Videos/Multimedia   *202*
Internet Resources   *204*
Other Internet Sources   *205*
References   *207*

14   Physical/Medical Issues in Sex Therapy   208
    Introduction   *208*
    Sexuality and Clients with Physical Illness   *209*
      Neurological Ailments   209
      Cardiovascular Illness   210
      Cancer   211
      Diabetes   213
    Sexuality and Disability   *214*
    Sexuality and Aging   *215*
      Health Issues   216
      Men   217
      Women   217
      Sexual Scripting   217
      Changing Roles   217
      Partner Availability   218
      Sexually Transmitted Illnesses   218
      Sexual Assessment   218
    Treatment Strategies for Special Populations   *219*
      Keeping a Systemic Focus   219
      Collaborate with Medical Providers   219
      Psychoeducation   221
      Reducing Anxiety, Misinformation and Myths   222
      Addressing Relationship Issues in the Context of Illness   223
      Attending to Sexual Scripting   224
      Expanding the Sexual Repertoire   224
      Enhance Couple Communication   226
      Attend to Issues in the Therapist   226
    References   *227*

15   Diversity in Sexual Expression   231
    Introduction   *231*
    Queer Clients   *232*
    Kinky Clients   *232*
      Treatment Implications   233
      Kink Resources   233
    Lesbian, Gay and Bisexual Clients   *234*
      LGB Issues   234

Treatment Issues 235
Therapist Competency 236
Nonmonogamous Intimate Relationships 237
Types of Consensual Nonmonogamy 237
Rules and Agreements 238
What Works, What Doesn't 238
Countertransference Issues 239
Transgender 240
Gender Dysphoria 241
Transgender Issues 241
Treatment Implications 241
Therapist Competency 242
Paraphilias 243
Treatment Implications 244
Asexuality 245
Is Asexuality an Orientation? 245
Distinguishing from the Lack of Sexual
Interest/Arousal or Desire 245
Assessment and Treatment Issues 246
Countertransference Issues 247
Tantric Sex 247
Therapeutic Application 247
Therapist Competency with Diversity in Sexual Expression 248
Countertransference Issues 248
Recognizing Transference Issues 249
Reference 250

16 Ethics in Sex Therapy 254
Introduction 254
The Process and Structure of Treatment 254
Client Identification 254
Problem Definition 256
Goal Setting 256
Range of Sex Therapy Practice 257
Referrals and Consultations in Sex Therapy 258
Collaboration 258
Identifying Ethical Dilemmas in Sex Therapy 259
Gender Bias 259
Religious Issues in the Therapist and Client 261
Secrets in Therapy 262
Boundaries in Sex Therapy 263

Managing Ethical Dilemmas   *264*
  Organizations and Guidelines for
    Ethical Issues in Sex Therapy   265
  Sex Therapy Surrogates   265
Summary   *266*
References   *267*

About the Authors   *269*
Index   *271*

PREFACE

The second edition of *A Clinician's Guide to Systemic Sex Therapy* is a companion volume to *Systemic Sex Therapy* (Hertlein, Weeks, & Gambescia, 2009) or may be used as a stand-alone book. This book is the first major popular text to propose that sexual problems must be considered within the context of the couple system. The book is based on several assumptions, which make it highly compatible with the field of marriage and family therapy or for those therapists who view problems from a systemic perspective. We assume (1) sexual problems may reflect problems at many different levels in the couple; (2) the resolution of many couple-related problems must precede work on the sexual difficulty; (3) unconscious factors in the couple's relationship may sabotage the sex therapy; (4) sexual problem(s) in one partner may serve to mask sexual problems in the other partner; (5) sexual problems may be unconsciously maintained by the couple in order to avoid intimacy in other parts of the relationship; (6) homework assignments must always actively involve both partners such that each derives benefit; and (7) couple and sexual problems may reciprocally maintain and exacerbate each other. Thus, this text is an ideal choice for marriage and family therapy programs because it is practical and has a systemic orientation.

With the first edition of *A Clinician's Guide to Systemic Sex Therapy*, we noticed that therapists we were training often carried the book to and from sessions, paging through it to read descriptions of specific disorders, or to find a plan for conducting their next session. We also noted that postgraduate interns consulted the book during classes in which *Systemic Sex Therapy* (Hertlein, Weeks & Gambescia, 2009) was used as a textbook. In the preparation of the second edition, we focused on topics that every therapist needs to know about when doing psychotherapy, specifically when integrating couple and sex therapy. We refined it so it would be more of a guide, a reference, a quick source of information for the clinician. Accordingly, we added chapters on conducting a sex history; using the sexual genogram and timeline; and incorporating sensual touch exercises, commonly known as sensate focus (but in our chapter, a much more refined approach is presented).

The second edition of *A Clinician's Guide to Systemic Sex Therapy* is truly a companion to the larger text, *Systemic Sex Therapy, Second Edition* (Hertlein, Weeks, & Gambescia, 2015). It covers such topics as the new *DSM-5* (American Psychiatric Association, 2013) diagnostic categories, assessment strategies and treatment issues. It also offers a road map for the experienced therapist dealing with a sexual disorder or for the therapist-in-training who might be meeting a couple for the first time. This book is different from many psychotherapy texts because of the inclusion of essential topics such as a triage tree, conducting a sexual interview, and multilayered diagnosis formulations.

The core chapters of this book are lengthy and highly detailed chapters on clinical assessment and treatment. These chapters blend our extensive experience from training sex therapists and being practitioners. We offer general guidelines for assessment and treatment and then proceed with offering very specific guidelines about how to assess and treat. In the assessment chapter, we list questions that provide the essential information for the therapist to have in order to construct a treatment plan. The treatment chapter is very specific about the general principles and the steps to intervention. We discuss not only the technique but also the proper implementation of the technique. The purpose of this book is to provide readers with an integrative and comprehensive theory in guiding their clinical practice. Most of this text is pragmatically oriented. We inform the therapist about diagnosing and treating sexual problems with many resources, such as tables, graphs, flow charts, treatment plans, and implementation strategies. The use of this information needs to be guided by a theory that can be translated into practice. The Intersystem Approach that we have developed gives the clinician this guide.

As with all of our texts, the overarching theory is the Intersystem Approach, a unique contribution to the field of couple and sex therapy developed by Gerald Weeks in 1977 with some of the fundamental concepts, and refined and developed continuously since that time. This approach has produced a major paradigm shift in the field of sex therapy, expanding the focus of treatment beyond the individual partner to include several contexts in the person's life, such as the relationship, family of origin, medical issues and contextual factors.

In general, the field of sex therapy started with an emphasis on behavioral therapy, then psychodynamic/behavioral therapy, followed by cognitive-behavioral therapy, next the integration of medical treatments with sex therapy and finally with an emerging use of mindfulness as an adjunctive treatment. Each movement in sex therapy has advocated for the use of a singular perspective, such as cognitive-behavioral therapy, psychodynamic approaches or the medicalization of sex therapy, with the *individual always being the basic unit of treatment* and the spouse as a cotherapist. The Intersystem Approach is distinctive because it is a *comprehensive* and *integrative* paradigm that empowers the therapist to draw from multiple approaches simultaneously while addressing all components of the couple system. These components or domains of behavior include the individual, the couple, the intergenerational system and larger contextual factors such as culture and religion. In summary, the following factors make *Systemic Sex Therapy, Second Edition* (Hertlein, Weeks, & Gambescia, 2015) unique from other texts:

• **Grounded in Systems Theory**

The basic assumptions regarding sexual problems are compatible with a systems approach. This means the individual is not the sole unit of treatment, but one part of a larger system.

• **The Intersystem Approach**

The meta-framework for this volume is the Intersystem Approach. This approach transcends all specific therapeutic modalities and techniques and focuses on several domains of behavior that should be evaluated and possibly used in the treatment for every sexual problem.

• **The Integration of Sex and Couple Therapy**

We view these two approaches as inseparable. The sexual problem is embedded within the couple relationship, and the couple relationship may be contributing to the sexual problem or the sexual problem may be creating or exacerbating couple problems.

• **Clinical Innovation**

This text represents over a century of clinical experience from a systems perspective and the integration of the latest research findings. The assessment and treatment protocols blend practice and research.

• **Focus on Implementation**

Many of the prior books on sex therapy described techniques without providing a context or suggestions as to how to sequence and implement the techniques.

A technique is likely to fail without proper implementation. This text offers suggestions on how to create treatment plans and implement the techniques.

Chapter Overview

A Clinician's Guide to Systemic Sex Therapy, Second Edition, contains many chapters that deal specifically with issues that arise in sex therapy:

Chapter 1. The Intersystem Approach to Sex Therapy establishes the foundation for the entire book by introducing the Intersystem paradigm we have been using for years in couple and marital therapy. This approach enables assessment and treatment of sexual and marital problems through five domains: (1) individual/biological; (2) individual psychological; (3) the dyadic relationship; (4) family of origin influences; and (5) contextual factors such as society, culture, history, religion and so on. This chapter addresses the theoretical stagnation that has been discussed by several other authors in the field of sex therapy and emphasizes the need to integrate couple and sex therapy.

Chapter 2. Diagnosis of Sexual Disorders begins with a review of the *DSM-5* diagnostic criteria for sexual dysfunctions, comparing the differences between the last two editions of *DSM* and some sexual issues not included in the *DSM-5,* such as sexual compulsivity, ego-syntonic gender nonconformity, and consensual kink. Diagnosis from an Intersystemic perspective is described as a way to bring the various diagnoses together.

Chapter 3. Intersystem Assessment of Sexual Disorders is presented as a comprehensive, continuous and fluid process that can be comingled with treatment throughout the duration of therapy. Guidelines for conducting a sex history, assessment for specific sexual disorders and related questions for inquiry are offered. A review of how to assess each domain of the system provides guidelines for different methods of evaluation.

Chapter 4. The Sexual Genogram in Assessment is a relatively new and efficient way to assess sexual function and dysfunction from an intergenerational perspective. The functions, construction and use of the different sexual/ gender/attachment genograms is discussed with their implications for treatment. Follow-up questions to the genogram and the use of a sexual timeline are offered.

Chapter 5. Measures of Sexual Function and Dysfunction reviews a number of ways of objectively collecting information about sexual functioning. These methods include behavioral, physiological and psychological measures that are objective and have known validity and reliability.

Chapter 6. General Treatment Principles, Strategies and Techniques covers some of the basic considerations when beginning treatment for sexual problems. Issues such as how to begin treatment, how to conceptualize the sequencing of treatment and how to keep treatment systemic (couple-oriented) are discussed. The assessment and treatment of each domain of behavior is reviewed. Each one is a multifactorial disorder requiring the combination of multiple techniques of treatment. A number of new and innovative treatment techniques are offered for these disorders.

Chapter 7. Treating Absent or Low Sexual Desire in Men and Women combines the diagnosis and treatment of low/absent desire in men and women. Although *DSM-5* splits these diagnoses, the etiology and treatment are so similar that combining them in one chapter was more reasonable.

Chapter 8. Treatment Principles, Strategies and Techniques Specific to Men gives a detailed description of the techniques, methods and strategies for treating erectile disorder, premature ejaculation, and delayed ejaculation. The assessment and treatment of each domain of behavior is reviewed. A guideline for the sequence of treatment for each disorder is laid out, with a focus on effective implementation.

Chapter 9. Treatment Principles, Strategies and Techniques Specific to Women gives a detailed description of the techniques, methods and strategies for treating female orgasmic disorder and a newly defined disorder in *DSM-5* called genito-pelvic pain disorder. The latter diagnosis is a combination of several disorders that produce pain with touch and/or penetration. A guideline for the sequence of treatment for each disorder is laid out, with a focus on effective implementation.

Chapter 10. The New Sensate Focus Technique is a special application of incremental sensual touch exercises within an Intersystem framework. Although we still call these sensate focus exercises, our conceptualization of the functions of this technique and their implementation is radically different from traditional approaches. For the first time since the publication of our first volume, sensate focus is described within a systemic framework. This change represents a significant advance over the traditional use of sensate focus.

Chapter 11. Factors That Complicate Treating Sexual Disorders reviews topics such as sexual ignorance, incorrect mythological information, faulty cognitions, sexual guilt and shame. It also highlights specific treatment strategies for these factors. Much of the chapter describes underlying fears of intimacy in the couple that can manifest as sexual problems.

Chapter 12. Principles of Homework illustrates many of the cognitive and behavioral assignments we design in session that must be practiced outside of the therapy office in order for lasting change to occur. The chapter provides an overview of the basic principles of how to design homework assignments. The structural elements of a homework exercise are outlined along with principles of how to increase compliance. The collaborative process of creating homework assignments is thoroughly described.

Chapter 13. Psychoeducation in Sex Therapy describes the numerous ways of providing clients with psychoeducational information. The text gives the clinician a number of resources that can be used with clients from books, to videos/multimedia, to Internet resources, and so on.

Chapter 14. Physical/Medical Issues in Sex Therapy offers suggestions for working with clients dealing with medical issues such as cardiovascular illness, neurological disorders, cancer, diabetes and other illnesses or disabilities that affect sexual functioning. Changes associated with ageing that typically affect sexual functioning are also described.

Chapter 15. Diversity in Sexual Expression addresses the needs of gay, lesbian, queer, kinky, gender-variant, nonmonogamous and asexual clients and other groups. The therapeutic treatment of these groups has been under-emphasized in the literature on sex therapy. Particular attention is given to countertransference issues.

Chapter 16. Ethics in Sex Therapy reviews specific obligatory concerns in sex therapy treatment, such as the responsibility of the therapist to understand his or her own ethical vulnerabilities that could obstruct treatment and inter-fere with a safe environment for the sex therapy. Some of the specific topics covered are how to refer and collaborate with other professionals, especially physicians, several common ethical dilemmas in sex therapy, the use of sexual surrogates, and suggestions for the ethical management of all of these issues.

References

American Psychiatric Association. (2013). *Diagnostic and statistical manual of mental disorders* (5th ed.). Arlington, VA: Author.

Hertlein, K.M., Weeks, G.R., & Gambescia, N. (Eds.) (2009). *Systemic sex therapy.* New York: Routledge.

Hertlein, K.M., Weeks, G.R., & Gambescia, N. (Eds.) (2015). *Systemic sex therapy* (2nd ed.). New York: Routledge.

ACKNOWLEDGMENTS

A book is always the effort of many different people. First, we would like to thank George Zimmar, the senior editor at Routledge/Taylor & Francis and Marta Moldvai, the editor for this volume. We wrote this second edition at Marta's request because the first edition of this book was one of their most important texts in the field of sex therapy. Marta was always available to guide us and answer questions. She also did a superb job of editing the final manuscript. Of course, many other staff at Routledge helped to bring this book to publication.

Second, we want to thank our own partners, who showed infinite patience and support when we spent weekends, weeknights and parts of holidays working on the book rather than spending time with them. Their understanding and tolerance were invaluable in our finding the seemingly endless hours to work on this project. They truly understood how important this project was to us.

Third, we had assistance from a small army of extremely helpful students who performed literature reviews and made editorial comments on the chapters. These graduate and postgraduate students were interested in the field of sex therapy and willing to devote hours in helping with this text. Their feedback helped to ensure the book would be more understandable to the beginning sex therapist and would be user friendly. These students tediously performed multiple reference checks. Paige Espinosa, the lead graduate assistant (GA) on the project, helped coordinate the work of the GAs and did more than her share of editing, searching for references and reading for the flow of content. Kiera McGillivray, another research assistant, also did much of the final proofreading and meticulous editing. Other GAs and postgraduate students also provided invaluable assistance: Nedka Klimas, Dawn Canty, Diane Caldas, Jenna

DiLauro, Claire Wertz and Mary Chen. Their personal interest in our writing about sex therapy was another source of inspiration for us.

Finally, a book that presents an alternative paradigm to the traditional paradigm would be of no value unless we had an audience of readers interested in doing sex therapy in a different way. We are gratified that so many readers found value in this new approach in the first volume of *A Clinician's Guide to Systemic Sex Therapy*. Without their interest, this second volume would not exist.

1

THE INTERSYSTEM APPROACH TO SEX THERAPY

Theory and Integration in Couple Therapy

The field of couple therapy has experienced a significant evolution over the last several decades, particularly in terms of its theoretical development (Gurman & Fraenkel, 2002). The earliest theoretical phase of couple therapy was described as "atheoretical," and the concepts were drawn from the psychoanalytic theories of the time. As the field evolved, the theories used for couple therapy began to incorporate the family therapy models, heavily influenced by the work of Jackson, Satir, Bowen and Haley (Gurman & Fraenkel, 2002). With the idea that multiple frameworks might/can be combined into one treatment, many books and papers were published in the 1970s and 1980s describing how one might integrate theories (Weeks, 1989, 1994). Over time, couple therapy has shifted from what Olson described as a field without a strong theoretical base (as cited in Gurman & Fraenkel, 2002) to its present state, described as theoretical refinement and integration (Gurman & Fraenkel, 2002).

We also believe that it is absolutely essential the fields of couple and sex therapy be fully integrated theoretically and pragmatically. We consider sex therapy a subset of couple therapy and agree with Binik and Meana's (2009) analysis that the techniques that are typically defined as sex therapy are not unique, but are all part of the field of couple therapy. The shift toward integration in couple therapy and sex therapy is encapsulated in the Intersystem Approach. The Intersystem Approach was established by Gerald Weeks (1986), who used the term *Intersystem* to describe how individual and systems theories could be integrated in order to create a more comprehensive approach to assessment and treatment. In its application to couple and sex therapy, this metatheory or meta-framework provides a comprehensive perspective for understanding and improving the state of intimate, sexual relationships for clients and for the therapist trying to help them resolve their sexual problems in a larger context than previously undertaken. Prior to Al Gurman's death, he invited Weeks to write the chapter on sex therapy for the new *Handbook of Couple Therapy* (Gurman, Lebow, & Snyder, in press). Gurman believed the Intersystem Approach was the next step in the evolution of sex therapy. Weeks and Gambescia (in press) collaborated in writing a chapter on the application of the Intersystem Approach to all the major sexual disorders.

The Intersystem framework offers a method of approaching couple sex therapy from a dialectically grounded metatheoretical perspective as described by Riegel (1976). At its basis, the Intersystem application of Riegel's dialectics postulates a connection between an individual's inner and outer worlds, the intrapsychic processes that impact and are impacted upon by a variety of factors, including interpersonal dynamics, physiology, psychology, culture and social situation and other forces such as economics, politics, religion, physical environment, natural disasters and so on. The Intersystem framework incorporates all of these areas to enable therapists to understand and treat sexual problems and represents a true integration of these parts of a couple system. This framework emphasized the simultaneous consideration of the individual, dyadic and intergenerational aspects of any client system (an individual client, couple, or family).

Moving Toward Theoretical Integration

The Intersystem Approach is unique in that it is a truly integrative perspective. Many theories and frameworks, which purport to be integrative, are actually technically eclectic. This differs from theoretical integration in that technical eclecticism is composed of techniques or strategies from several theories being used by the clinician without a coherent theoretical foundation (Lebow, 1997). A therapist working from an integrative approach has an articulated theoretical foundation and a clear conceptual framework that informs diagnosis and treatment. As a result, the Intersystem Approach is a more thorough, sophisticated, responsible and ethical approach (Slife & Reber, 2001) than other so-called integrative therapies.

In addition to the lack of comprehensive theoretical integration in the practice of couple and sex therapy, there is also a lack of integration in the professional fields of sex therapy and couple therapy. For example, there are many professional organizations in the field of Marriage and Family Therapy with overlapping interests that operate in isolation of one another. The American Association for Marriage and Family Therapy (AAMFT) and the American Counseling Association (ACA) have established standards for the practice of couple therapy, yet there is little emphasis on sex therapy training for students as outlined in their training standards (COAMFTE 2014; CACREP, 2009). Also, although the American Association of Sexuality Educators, Counselors, and Therapists (AASECT) has established educational and supervisory standards for certification in sex therapy, very little training in couple or family therapy is required to become a certified sex therapist. Second, historically, there has been separation or fragmentation of these two fields at the theoretical level. Sex therapy, marital therapy and family therapy have had different historical theoretical trajectories. The texts in these fields show very little confluence or mixing of approaches. Finally, the literature in the field of sex therapy is lacking theory. Wiederman (1998) pointed out this deficiency over a decade ago and nothing has changed since that time. Given the evidence, it is not surprising that practicing clinicians are also plagued by an inability to be truly integrative because of the lack of a theory to guide their work.

The Intersystem Approach is the result of over 30 years of refinement through scholarly thought and clinical practice. Its development began after Weeks's (1977) initial writings on the dialectical approach to psychotherapy. This paper laid the foundation for the fact that psychotherapy was not using a dialectical framework that could allow for the integration of the individual-system dialectic. Weeks and Hof (1987) published the first book on the integration of sex and marital therapy, which moved the field of sex therapy away from a strictly individual and behaviorally oriented perspective toward a systems perspective. Subsequently, Weeks published several books demonstrating the practicality of the Intersystem Approach with a variety of clinical problems. Weeks and Hof (1994), for example, outlined the approach and demonstrated how it could be used in couple therapy in general, especially in cases of lack of desire. Weeks and Gambescia (2000, 2002) and Weeks, Gambescia, and Jenkins (2003) have also written several books utilizing the approach in the treatment of erectile dysfunction, hypoactive sexual desire, and infidelity.

As couple therapy moves more deeply into Gurman and Fraenkel's (2002) refinement/integration phase, couple therapists should continue to become more precise regarding the theories informing their practice. Further, clarity in one's epistemology results in an appropriate application of systemic frameworks and leads to integrative treatment (L'Abate, 2003, 2013). Therapists must understand what each theory or construct contributes to their overall treatment plan. The Intersystem Approach does exactly that without advocating for one particular theory or model of couple therapy. It helps therapists to identify an epistemology or philosophy from which they base their assumptions about people and change, and to specifically articulate how each of the theories selected within their clinical work is consistent with their overarching approach to treatment.

Intersystem Theory and Application

The Intersystem sex therapy paradigm is informed by three integrational constructs:

1. Sternberg's Triangular Theory of Love (Sternberg, 1986)
2. The Theory of Interaction (Strong & Claiborn, 1982)
3. Attachment Theory and Sexuality (Johnson & Zuccarini, 2010)

These constructs also encompass the emotions, cognitions and behaviors of the couple and address the couple's issues, including those related to sexuality. Effectively, they operate together to create a cohesive paradigm rather than a series of isolated and disconnected models of therapy.

Sternberg (1986), a social psychologist, developed a Triangular Theory of Love, discussing three components: commitment, intimacy, and passion. He asserted that each of these components interfaced with one another in relationships. While some therapists may attend to only one of the three sides of the triangle, we believe it is necessary to attend to all three, shifting emphasis as the case warrants. Focusing on each of these elements ensures that the etiology of the couple's problem as well as the particular sexual problem is addressed from an integrative perspective. All three elements of this triangle in roughly equal proportion constitute an adult loving relation. Couple therapists tend to focus on commitment and intimacy while sex therapists tend to focus on passion. A couple or sex therapist should be considering the interplay of all three parts simultaneously.

Strong and Claiborn's (1982) Theory of Interaction addresses the idea that both intrapsychic (the internal aspects of our behavior) and interactional (the way in which people relate to each other) components are active in all relationships. The Intersystem Approach has adopted this *interactional* theory as another *integrational* component in the understanding of what sexual difficulties mean to the couple and how each partner understands his or her role in the relationship. In the section to follow, we describe the six concepts of their theory as integrational constructs in the Intersystem Approach. The fact that these constructs cut across different theories makes it possible to decide which differential theory might be most useful. For example, the first construct to be described is interpretation or the meaning that is attributed to events. If the meaning is faulty, the therapist can choose to explore it at different levels using different models. A faulty interpretation could be explored from a cognitive or narrative perspective at the individual level, the effects of the old belief could be explored from a system perspective by focusing on faulty interpretations of each other's behavior as reciprocal and interlocking and, finally, the belief could be examined from a transgenerational perspective using the theory of attachment styles and how these early internalized interpretations set the stage for long-term patterns in relationships.

Intrapsychic Components

The intrapsychic components used within the Intersystem Approach include interpretation, definition, and prediction. Interpretation (meaning that is ascribed to an event, behavior or problem) refers to the extent to which one interprets his or her partner's behavior accurately or inaccurately. For example, a partner who suffers from hypoactive sexual desire disorder may have a partner who interprets this behavior as unloving and uncaring. The partner may interpret the behavior as an intentional withholding of sex out of anger or some other negative feeling.

This interpretation, though incorrect, will be that which underlines the partner's future behavior and shapes his or her views about the partner and the relationship.

Definition (the reciprocal arrangement of how the relationship defines each partner and how each partner defines the relationship) can infiltrate the couple's view of the relationship without awareness, influencing cognitions, affect and behavior. For instance, someone with more sexual experience might have different expectations of what constitutes a lot of sex or what is included in kinky sex than his or her partner. If this expectation is articulated, partners can come to some agreement on the frequency and types of behaviors that will constitute this part of their relationship. If these expectations are not articulated or are unconscious, problems may develop between the couple. It then becomes essential for the therapist to help the couple address the unspoken expectations or implicit definitions of their relationship. In another case, one partner may define the relationship as highly sexual while the other might define the relationship as highly romantic. The partners are not in agreement about how the relationship is to be defined sexually. They have different definitions of their relationship and therapists can assist them in obtaining clarity about (1) the progression of the definitions within the relationship, and (2) the definition of terms used without conscious understanding of their implications.

Prediction addresses the notion that to some degree, human beings have a tendency to try to predict each other's behaviors, thoughts or a particular outcome. Frequently, intimate partners believe once they know their partner well, they can predict the partner's behavior (and in many cases, believe that our partner knows us well enough to predict our reactions to their behaviors). Further, we tend to make positive predictions, such that the other person is loving, caring, generous, sensitive, wanting to meet our needs and so on. When the other person does not respond as expected or predicted, it can raise questions about the fundamental nature of the relationship. For example, a client, upon finding his partner using pornography stated, "I thought my partner had sexual thoughts about me and only me. Now that I know it isn't true, I don't know who this person is." The fact that *one* prediction turned out to be false now calls into question all other predictions about the partner. Sex therapists frequently see faulty prediction as it impacts homework completion. The therapist may begin the treatment with an assignment such as sensate focus exercises, thinking it an easy assignment with which the couple will readily comply. The clients, on the other hand, do not complete homework, predicting (consciously or not) that any attempt to connect physically will result in anger, disappointment, a sense of failure or any other negative feelings that have been associated with sexual interaction in the past.

Interactional Components

The interactional components include congruence, interdependence and attributional strategy. Congruence refers to the degree to which couples share or agree on how events are defined. For example, a husband may consider his wife's online chatting with other men as a form of infidelity while the wife does not. The definition of the event may be incongruent relationally because in his definition she is cheating, but in her mind she is having a friendly chat. The couple can also agree that they define infidelity differently, thus being congruent in their assessment of incongruence. They still face the dilemma of how they are both acting in accordance with their various and conflicting definitions of fidelity. Further, in many cases of low or absent sexual desire, one partner may believe that the couple is having sex often, but the other partner disagrees. The partner with the lower level of desire perceives that they are having sex more frequently than claimed by the partner who wants sex more frequently. The therapist will need to help the couple understand whether they have congruent definitions of salient behaviors and then help them reach a consensus. Each partner is defining some aspect of their sexuality and hoping that definition will become the relational definition in order to achieve definitional congruence. For example, if each partner thinks they have sex frequently and are creative lovers, they might say they are a highly sexual couple—and that they are in a state of congruence.

Interdependence includes partner perceptions of the other's ability to meet emotional and sexual needs and the extent to which partners believe they can depend on each other. For example, an individual may believe that he or she is meeting the partner's sexual needs, but the partner is desperate to explore sex with someone else, believing that satisfaction can only come from another person. This couple demonstrates a low level of interdependence. On the other hand, if both partners believe that the other wants to please and what they offer will fulfill their needs, then they have a high level of interdependence. In general, couples with high levels of interdependence typically proceed through treatment more quickly than couples with low levels. If the partners are highly interdependent, they typically will want to continue to fulfill each other's needs in hopes that the reciprocity of need fulfillment will continue unabated. Those who are less interdependent may be tentative about the continuation of the relationship and therefore less willing to change for the sake of the other or the relationship. In short, when the partner(s) does/do not believe the other can or will give them what they desire, treatment is compromised. When working with couples with lower levels of interdependence, it may be helpful to focus on a discussion of commitment. A common example of interdependence can be found in the desire for differing sexual activities. A man may wish to receive oral sex, but his partner refuses because she feels it to be perverted or disgusting. The wife might want more foreplay, but her partner spends little time in foreplay. Thus, neither may believe that the other will give them what they want.

Attributional strategy is the manner in which partners ascribe meaning to an event. In this book we focus on one aspect of attribution. This aspect views how the couple defines events in the relationship in linear or circular terms. In a linear attribution strategy, the behavior of one partner is viewed as causing the behavior of the other. They are thinking in terms of simple cause and effect. Blaming is a common linear strategy. A husband, for instance, might report that his wife makes him angry when she nags him about household chores, causing him to withdraw from her sexually. Since couples commonly use linear attributional strategies, therapists are wise to quickly redirect them to viewing the systemic or circular nature of the couple's dynamics. Circular attribution strategies are those in which partners examine the impact of their behavior on the other in a reciprocal or interlocking way. The partners are able to comprehend that they each affect the other and are affected by the other. The thinking is not linear, but rather circular and reciprocal (systemic). Reframing is the primary technique sex therapists can use to help the couple move from linear and blaming statements to circular and positive views of their dynamics (Weeks & Fife, 2014; Weeks & Gambescia, 2002).

For example, Rachael and Mike came to therapy because Rachel often had difficulty reaching orgasm during intercourse. She claimed the reason was because Mike sometimes lost his erection. She did not see that she had a role in her inability to reach orgasm; initially, she believed only he was to be blamed. Rachael typically needed about 20 minutes of stimulation to climax, but she started to become frustrated after about 10 minutes of intercourse if she had not yet reached orgasm. Prior to sex, she would direct Mike to thrust faster and longer, tell him what position she needed, and that he was obligated to keep a good erection throughout. Mike tried his best to please her, but he was very anxious about performing, which increased his performance anxiety and lead to erectile failure. Frequently, she told him he was doing something wrong during intercourse, making matters worse for Mike's ability to maintain an erection.

The therapist might address the attribution by demonstrating how much each liked sex and how clear it was that each one wanted to please the other. The therapist explained that Rachael's wish to orgasm quicker to make Mike's life easier, and Mike's desperate concern with Rachael's pleasure combined to create escalating anxiety on *both* sides. Mike's anxiety stemmed from sensing Rachael's pressure to orgasm quickly and his need to please her. This anxiety made it more difficult for her to reach orgasm and more difficult for him to maintain an erection. In addition to highlighting the circular nature of the problem, psychoeducation on male and female sexuality and different techniques to enhance Rachael's pleasure (thereby opening up other options for her orgasm) reduced the pressure on their relationship and changed their sexual patterns.

Attachment theory is the latest integrational construct to supplement the Intersystem approach. DeMaria recommended the addition of this integrational construct as it enhances the understanding of any client system (see DeMaria, Weeks, & Hof, 1999). Like all integrational constructs, attachment theory traverses the domains of the individual, couple and family. As such, individuals develop internal working models of attachment early in life, which are carried into adult relationships, specifically dyadic relationships; thus, the attachment style of each partner forms a unique and complex dynamic in the functioning of the couple system. The individual adult attachment styles of the couple are then transmitted to their children through the unique parental bonds that form with each child.

In this section of the chapter, we demonstrate the ways in which attachment style can affect each domain and the interaction among the domains, including sexual behavior.

Understanding Etiology and Treatment within the Intersystem Approach

The Intersystem Approach directs our attention to several aspects of the system. Each part of the system is given equal attention in terms of assessment. Once the clinician has examined each of these domains of the system, a treatment plan can be constructed that attends to each of the domains requiring intervention. This framework has five major domains:

1. Individual/biological
2. Individual/psychological
3. The dyadic relationship
4. Family-of-origin influences
5. Contextual factors (society/culture/history/religion and so on)

Each of these five parts of the system is examined in terms of the part it plays in the creation of the sexual problem. The parts that are relevant are then incorporated into a comprehensive treatment plan.

Individual/Biological

Each person's biology is different. Therefore, the therapist must consider the influence of each individual's overall health status and medical concerns of the relationship and their connections with the sexual problems. For example, in the treatment of erectile dysfunction, therapists are well advised to consider any medical problems or hormonal issues potentially contributing to the dysfunction. Certain psychological disorders with biological components such as bipolar disorder may also contribute to problems experienced by a couple. In addition, some medications can also impact one's sexual function. Serotonin-based antidepressants have significant sexual side effects, including diminished libido and delayed/absent orgasm (Phelps, Jones, & Payne, 2015). If a therapist develops a hypothesis that medications might be impacting sexual functioning, the client should contact an appropriate physician and discuss this issue.

A typical case involved a therapist seeing a couple who had been married for 18 years. The presenting problem was that the wife had been experiencing orgasm with intercourse only about 50% of the time, yet was always orgasmic when using other means of stimulation. She was now having trouble reaching orgasm through any means. The therapist discovered that her father had passed away recently and assumed that she was grieving and perhaps depressed. The therapeutic error involved the omission to ask about medications; thus, the therapist failed to realize the wife was taking an antidepressant. It is widely known that antidepressant medications, specifically those in the serotonin-based group, can make it difficult to orgasm. As a result, the interventions that were tried were unsuccessful, leading to greater frustration for the couple, increasing their frustration about treatment and future ability to orgasm on her part and complicating the sexual problem already occurring. The husband started to experience a lack of desire because he predicted another failure to give his wife an orgasm.

Individual/Psychological

The Intersystem Approach points to the importance of taking a comprehensive view of the aspects involved in an individual's psychological makeup. Individual-psychological factors to consider include (but are not limited to) the following:

- Personality (including personality disorders)
- Psychopathology
- Intelligence
- Temperament
- Developmental stages/deficits
- Attitudes
- Values
- Defense mechanisms
- Attachment style

An individual's psychological composition influences what one understands about sexuality and its manner of expression. There may be a history of depression, other psychological issues or covert messages about sexuality that are impacting the current relationship. For example, a person experiencing depression may not feel desire to engage in sexual activity, particularly if the depression is related to the relationship. One's sexual experience may also have been acquired in such a way (e.g., through sexual abuse) that elicits guilt or shame about particular sexual activities, thus inhibiting desire. Therapists can gather information about a client's psychological composition by taking an adequate history and utilizing the history-taking methods described in the clinical assessment chapter later in this volume.

The Dyadic Relationship

Though it is important to assess each individual's behavioral patterns, the Intersystem Approach also addresses how these individual behaviors manifest as interlocking patterns of behavior within the couple. For almost every couple in sex therapy there are relational factors that contribute to and maintain the sexual dysfunction. These dyadic issues include (but are not limited to) the following:

• Relationship defined in an incongruent way
• Negative attributions made about each other
• Regulation of intimacy
• Fears (of dependency, intimacy, etc.)
• Communication problems
• Conscious and unconscious expectations
• Conflict management

While acknowledging the contributions of each individual to the couple, the Intersystem Approach defines the relationship as the client because it is an elaboration of a systemic way of conceptualizing. In other words, the focus is on the couple's dynamics and how these dynamics may contribute to sexual problems. Consider the case of Martha and Jack, who had been married about 30 years when they entered therapy for a sexual problem. Martha did most of the talking in the session and wanted to set the agenda. Considering how the couple's behavior in a session was often isomorphic with how they behaved at home, the therapist started to explore how they communicated. Jack said he thought their communication was fine, but Martha said Jack never said much, was neither assertive nor expressive of his needs and never articulated any statements of feeling. Due to Jack's lack of communication, Martha had become resentful and withdrawn sexually. A traditionally trained sex therapist would have probably focused on their lack of sexual communication and given the couple instructions on how to better express sensual and sexual needs. An Intersystem therapist would explore Jack's lack of communication from his early years, his current lack of communication and Martha's unconscious collusion in this pattern.

The therapist first explored the family of origin and found that Jack's parents were verbally abusive to each other and toward Jack. He learned not to speak because he would be viewed as a troublemaker; he stayed away from home as much as possible in his youth. The therapist surmised that he was seeking a partner who would be quiet and nonconfrontational, and avoid conflict. Some exploration with Jack confirmed that this was his conscious motivation in marrying Martha but his unconscious motivation was to reproduce that with which he was familiar. He perceived Martha as verbally abusive toward him when she made reasonable requests that he communicate with her. On the other hand, Martha saw the good in Jack and expected he would open up after marriage. Martha had a history of caretaking in her family of origin. The therapist recognized her need for caretaking and confirmed Martha's desire to rescue Jack. Therefore, Martha would not confront his underlying issues because it would change the underlying dynamic and needs in their relationship. She would confront issues that were on the surface. The dynamic in the relationship fulfilled her unconscious need.

In this case example, the therapist redirected much of the initial therapy toward couple dynamics that emerged from family-of-origin issues and became the interlocking basis for their relationship rather than the sexual issue that they initially presented. This refocusing of the problem is critical to the Intersystem Approach: frequently, the therapist must persuade the couple that the real or underlying problem is to be found in their dysfunctional relationship. Sex therapy can proceed successfully with a couple such as this only after a convincing argument can be made for doing couple work. The argument may be made verbally or the therapist may work on improving some aspect of their relational function and help the couple see how it affects their sexual functioning. The couple is lead toward connecting the dots between different aspects of their relationship. The sexual problem is a manifestation of their relational issue.

In short, the sex therapist must be a well-trained couple therapist who knows how to assess issues that impact sexuality and treat the couple relationship. From a systemic perspective, the sexual problem is a symptom of a dysfunctional relationship and will resolve with help if the couple problem is resolved. In other cases, the relational problem was the impetus for the problem but the problem has become functionally autonomous. In these cases, the therapist will need to proceed to doing sex therapy.

Family-of-Origin Influences

Commonly, individuals learn about relationships and sexuality in their families of origin. Often, parents and other significant relatives demonstrate patterns and styles for demonstrating affection. Additionally, messages communicated about sexuality within one's family can be covert, overt, internalized and/or openly expressed in relationships. When sexuality in families is not openly discussed, children may interpret this silent avoidance to mean that sexuality is inherently bad and that expression of it should be minimized. As these children grow into adulthood, they may struggle with their emerging sexuality and tell themselves that they are bad for having such feelings, wanting to express their sexuality or communicate about any sexual thoughts. This impacts their sexual self-identity, self-esteem and inevitably their relationships.

Some parents are overt in their condemnation of sexual behavior, again resulting in internal struggles for their children as they grow into adulthood and develop intimate relationships. Research demonstrates that children from dysfunctional families (with or without sexual abuse) are more likely to develop sexual dysfunctions such as absent/low sexual desire (Kinzl, Mangweth, Traweger, & Biebel, 1996; Kinzl, Traweger, & Biebel, 1995). Sex therapists are wise to obtain information about family history via a relationship/sexual genogram. We discuss this genogram briefly in the chapter on clinical assessment and it is a major focus of attention in DeMaria, Weeks, and Blumer (in press). Another case example of how family of origin can affect sexual/relational functioning is exemplified in the following case.

Pat and Vincent entered therapy with an unusual presentation. Vincent claimed that Pat had always had too high a sex drive. If the therapist had accepted this presentation, then the strategy might have been to try to decrease her sexual drive and increase his. After a few sessions, the therapist had learned that Pat had been sexually abused by her father, but never sought any help. Although the typical pattern for a sexually abused woman is to present with diminished sex drive, Pat fell into the opposite category, as a small percentage of women do. For her it was a classic case of repetitive compulsion whereby the person reenacts some aspect of the trauma in order to feel mastery over it. Prior to marriage, the couple was hypersexual and Vincent enjoyed the sex. On their wedding night, Vincent refused to have sex with her, started finding faults in her behavior and brought up her sexual past in a highly negative way. Pat felt he was suggesting she was a slut. This behavior continued throughout an extended honeymoon trip with Pat reporting the honeymoon represented some of the worst days of her life. Once they settled into their lives, Vincent demonstrated little sexual interest. Pat was always initiating sex. The therapist learned that Vincent was having emotional affairs with a number of women. He would spend hours on the phone or text messaging multiple women he knew or found on cheating websites. He appeared to be using these other relationships as a way to emotionally distance himself from Pat. Exploration of his family of origin showed that he had an overbearing, smothering mother. Vincent was afraid that Pat might take on the same role, if he allowed her to do so, especially now that she was his wife. Moving from the status of partner to wife can change many underlying expectations regarding the roles and expectations that partners play. Thus, Vincent found ways to distance himself and justified it by blaming Pat for her sexual history of acting out prior to marriage and finding fault with her. No matter what Pat did, it was never good enough. The therapist helped the couple understand their current pattern of behavior, their underlying motivations and how these motivations stemmed from early life experiences in their families of origin. The initial phase of therapy was directed toward helping Pat understand the consequences of her sexual abuse and working through it. For Vincent, the work was more difficult. He could see the link intellectually, but he had trouble letting go of his self-protective behavior of distancing himself.

Contextual Factors

The last component is the couple's sociocultural environment and its effect on their relationship. Everything in the environment and one's context can affect one's ability to form a healthy sexual relationship, including one's beliefs, customs and values around sexuality and messages about appropriate sexual expression. For example, although some cultures or subgroups may prohibit masturbation, other cultures have greater sexual permissiveness. This becomes important in treatment planning, where some clients may be opposed to sexual self-exploration. Clients also feel the pressure of the external environment, which complicates their sexual problem. Hall and Graham (2013) have done an excellent job of documenting the societal/cultural influences on sexual beliefs and behaviors in their book. For example, one couple struggling with absent/low sexual desire reported how difficult their honeymoon was because they both expected that their honeymoon would be filled with great sex. Their families had kidded them about how they would be in a beautiful resort but probably never leave the bed. They believed everyone expected them to have great sex, which raised their expectation level beyond what was possible. Over time, values about sexual behaviors and preferences such as masturbation, positions, oral sex, premarital sex, anal sex and so on have changed significantly. As norms change, couples should work to understand the extent to which culture and contemporary society has played into their decision making, values and behaviors as a couple.

Terrance represents one case where cultural/societal background played a key role. He came to therapy individually because every time he tried to have sex he experienced back pain and would lose his erection. The therapist quickly learned that Terrance always used the missionary position and never considered another position that might take the stress off his back. The obvious solution was to suggest he try the male-on-bottom position; however, the therapist realized that something must have prevented him from implementing this rather obvious solution.

The therapist discovered that Terrance and his wife were fundamentalist Christians. They had grown up in the Bible belt and religion was a central part of their lives. The therapist needed to understand Terrance's religious beliefs about sex in order to gradually challenge them. Terrance believed that sex was only proper after marriage, and had been given very little information regarding much else in the realm of human sexuality. He had heard of the missionary position and assumed that it was the only proper position. The therapist gently challenged this belief as an assumption and asked if Terrance knew of any biblical verse that prescribed a particular sexual position. Terrance could not think of any. The therapist asked whether God had given man the ability to have sex in other positions, to which Terrance answered that He must have. At this point, Terrance spontaneously said that God must want man to try different positions and he had only been using one. The therapist could now suggest that Terrance try the female-on-top position with his wife to see if that would alleviate his back pain. He would, however, need to discuss this with his wife first and talk about the religious insight he had experienced. With all these things done, Terrance experienced a miracle cure within the first week.

Conclusion

In summary, the Intersystem Approach guides the clinician in integrating the individual, couple, transgenerational and other contextual factors that may be affecting sexual functioning. The drive toward integrative therapy begins with the assessment phase, leading to a case formulation (described fully in this text), and continues throughout therapy. The therapist may shift back and forth between or among the different elements of the Intersystem Approach in a flexible and fluid way that best serves the clients' needs (Althof, 2003). Although therapists are usually trained in several approaches to therapy nested within one or two modalities (individual, couple, family, group), therapists using the Intersystem Approach should be knowledgeable and proficient in the areas of individual, couple, family and sex therapy. This fact makes mastery of the Intersystem treatment approach one of the most ambitious and challenging approaches in the literature. Most training programs focus on one modality and limit the number of specific approaches that student clinicians must master. The challenge is to continue learning in order to master as many approaches to therapy as possible within as many modalities as possible. The Intersystem Approach offers a way to conduct a comprehensive assessment and provide flexible treatment that is uniquely designed for each couple. We believe that every couple is different; therefore, rather than making clients fit one specific modality, we are able to tailor the therapy to each specific client system.

References

Althof, S. (2003). Therapeutic weaving: The integration of treatment techniques. In S. Levine, C. Risen, & S. Althof (Eds.), *Handbook of clinical sexuality for mental health professionals* (pp. 359–376). New York: Brunner/Routledge.

Binik, Y., & Meana, M. (2009). The future of sex therapy: Specialization or marginalization? *Archives of Sexual Behavior, 38*(6), 1016–1027.

Commission on Accreditation for Marriage and Family Therapy Education [COAMFTE]. (2014). *Accreditation standards: Graduate & post-graduate marriage and family therapy training programs.* Retrieved from https://www.aamft.org/imis15/Documents/COAMFTE/COAMFTE_Accreditation_Standards_Version_12.pdf

Council for Accreditation of Counseling and Related Educational Programs [CACREP]. (2009). *CACREP 2009 Standards.* Retrieved from http://www.cacrep.org/wp-content/uploads/2013/12/2009-Standards.pdf

DeMaria, R., Weeks, G., & Blumer, M. (in press). *Focused genograms.* New York: Routledge.

DeMaria, R., Weeks, G., & Hof, L. (1999). *Focused genograms: Intergeneration assessment of individuals, couples, and families.* New York: Routledge.

Gurman, A., Lebow, J., & Synder, D. (in press). *Clinical handbook of couple therapy* (5th ed.). New York: Guilford Press.

Gurman, A., & Fraenkel, P. (2002). The history of couple therapy: A millennial review. *Family Process, 41*(2), 199–260.

Hall, K., & Graham, C. (Eds.). (2013). *Cultural context of sexual pleasure and problems.* New York: Routledge.

Johnson, S., & Zuccarini, D. (2010). Integrating sex and attachment in emotionally focused couple therapy. *Journal of Marital and Family Therapy, 36,* 431–445.

Kinzl, J., Traweger, C., & Beibel, W. (1995). Sexual dysfunctions: Relationship to childhood sexual abuse and early family experiences in a nonclinical sample. *Child Abuse and Neglect, 19*(7), 785–792.

Kinzl, J., Mangweth, B., Traweger, C., & Beibel, W. (1996). Sexual dysfunction in males: Significance of adverse childhood experiences. *Child Abuse and Neglect, 20*(8), 759–766.

L'Abate, L. (2003). *Family psychology III: Theory building, theory testing, and psychological interventions*. Lanham, MD: University Press of America.

L'Abate, L. (2013). *Beyond the systems paradigm: Emerging constructs in family and personality psychology*. New York: Springer.

Lebow, J. (1997). The integrative revolution in couple and family therapy. *Family Process, 36*, 1–17.

Phelps, K., Jones, A., & Payne, R. (2015). The interplay between mental health and sexual health. In K. Hertlein, G. Weeks, & N. Gambescia (Eds.), *Systemic sex therapy* (2nd ed.) (pp. 255–275). New York: Routledge.

Riegel, K. F. (1976). The dialectics of human development. *American Psychologist, 31*, 689–700.

Slife, B. D., & Reber, J. S. (2001). Eclecticism in psychotherapy: Is it really the best substitute for traditional theories? In B. Slife, R. Williams, & S. Barlow (Eds.), *Critical issues in psychotherapy: Translating new ideas into practice* (pp. 213–233). Thousand Oaks, CA: Sage Publications.

Sternberg, R. (1986). A triangular theory of love. *Psychological Review, 93*(2), 119–135.

Strong, S., & Claiborn, C. (1982). *Change through interaction: Social psychological processes of counseling and psychotherapy*. New York: John Wiley.

Weeks, G. R. (1977). Toward a dialectical approach to intervention. *Human Development, 20*, 277–292.

Weeks, G. R. (1986). Individual-system dialectic. *American Journal of Family Therapy, 14*(1), 5–12.

Weeks, G. R. (Ed.). (1989). *Treating couples: The intersystem model of the marriage council of Philadelphia*. New York: Brunner/Mazel.

Weeks, G. R. (1994). The intersystem model: An integrative approach to treatment. In G. Weeks & L. Hof (Eds.), *The marital-relationship therapy casebook: Theory and application of the intersystem model* (pp. 3–34). New York: Brunner/Mazel.

Weeks, G., & Fife, S. (2014). *Couples in treatment*. New York: Routledge.

Weeks, G., & Gambescia, N. (2000). *Erectile dysfunction: Integrating couple therapy, sex therapy, and medical treatment*. New York: W.W. Norton.

Weeks, G., & Gambescia, N. (2002). *Hypoactive sexual desire: Integrating couple and sex therapy*. New York: W.W. Norton.

Weeks, G., & Gambescia, N. (2015). Couple therapy and the treatment of sexual problems: The intersystem approach. In A. Gurman, J. Lebow, & D. Snyder (Eds.), *Clinical handbook of couple therapy* (5th ed.) (pp. 635–658). New York: Guilford Press.

Weeks, G., Gambescia, N., & Jenkins, R. (2003). *Treating infidelity*. New York: W. W. Norton.

Weeks, G., & Hof, L. (Eds.). (1987). *Integrating sex and marital therapy: A clinical guide*. New York: W. W. Norton.

Weeks, G., & Hof, L. (Eds.). (1994). *The marital-relationship therapy casebook: Theory and application of the intersystem model*. New York: Brunner/Mazel.

Wiederman, M. (1998). The state of theory in sex therapy. *Journal of Sex Research, 35*, 88–99.

2

DIAGNOSIS OF SEXUAL DISORDERS

Introduction

The latest volume of the *Diagnostic and Statistical Manual of Mental Disorders* (*DSM-5*) (American Psychiatric Association, 2013) was released just prior to the publication of the first edition of *A Clinician's Guide to Systemic Sex Therapy*; therefore, almost all the research cited in that volume and in *Systemic Sex Therapy, Second Edition* (Hertlein, Weeks, & Gambescia, 2015) is based on *DSM-IV-TR* diagnostic criteria (American Psychiatric Association, 2000). There are numerous changes in the classification and criteria for sexual disorders in the *DSM-5* (American Psychiatric Association, 2013) and we address these changes throughout this text.

Diagnosis of sexual disorders may seem straightforward in that clients may describe difficulties that could be matters of desire, arousal, pain or orgasm; nonetheless, diagnosis is never quite as simple as it appears. Even in cases such as erectile disorder, understanding how the problem occurred (etiology) is just as important as discerning the diagnostic label that is most appropriate (the differential diagnosis). As such, a diagnosis that incorporates individual (both mind and body) as well as interpersonal and contextual elements is crucial to the treatment of sexual disorders from the Intersystem perspective.

This chapter begins with a review of the diagnostic criteria for sexual dysfunctions (now called Disorders in the *DSM-5*) as outlined by the American Psychiatric Association in the two most recent Diagnostic and Statistical Manuals: *DSM-IV-TR* (American Psychiatric Association, 2000) and the *DSM-5* (American Psychiatric Association, 2013), replete with etiology and risk factors. Next, we provide a brief overview of each disorder. Finally, we present limitations of and debates surrounding the *DSM* categories as a way to guide clinicians through the complexities of diagnosis.

Diagnosing with the *DSM-IV-TR* and *DSM-5*

The *DSM-5* (American Psychiatric Association, 2013) serves as the basis for research given that a standard definition and clinical criteria are major components of research. Research studies also inform the clinician about etiology and treatment; nonetheless, the clinician must understand how the new terminology may affect the meaning or interpretation of these studies. The current role of the *DSM-5* (American Psychiatric Association, 2013) in sex therapy is to help clinicians make treatment decisions about sexual and other mental disorders, which include the nature of the problem, identification of other problems that coexist with the sexual problem (comorbidity), expectations for improvement (prognosis) and numerous factors that should be considered when planning treatment strategies. In the *DSM-5* (American Psychiatric Association, 2013) new diagnoses appear, some of the diagnostic categories from the prior *DSM* disappear or are combined and in some cases the same basic diagnosis may be preserved but with different clinical criteria.

Prior to the *DSM-5* (American Psychiatric Association, 2013), the linear models of the human sexual response cycle were used as a basis for so-called normal sexual functioning and also for the diagnostic criteria for sexual disorders (Kaplan, 1974; Masters & Johnson, 1966, 1970). Masters and Johnson (1966) described a purely physiologic linear model with four components (excitement, plateau, orgasm and resolution). Kaplan's model emphasizes a triphasic sexual response including sexual desire (libido), arousal (excitement) and orgasm. In *DSM-IV-TR*, Sexual Disorders are "characterized by a disturbance in the processes that characterize the sexual response cycle or by pain associated with sexual intercourse" (American Psychiatric Association, 2000, p. 535).

Nonlinear or circular models provide the basis for assessing and treating sexual disorders in the *DSM-5*. These models treat the sexual response as complex and dependent on a variety of partner and contextual variables. Additionally, sexual interest or desire is treated differently for men and women. In the *DSM-5*, Sexual Disorders are viewed as "a heterogeneous group of disorders that are typically characterized by a clinically significant disturbance in a person's ability to respond sexually or to experience sexual pleasure" (American Psychiatric Association, 2013, p. 423). We will compare the diagnostic categories of each of the *DSM*s. Remember, even though some terms may be the same, the clinical criteria may be quite different.

- The *DSM-IV-TR* described disorders of desire: Hypoactive Sexual Desire Disorder (HSDD) and Sexual Aversion Disorder (SAD). In *DSM-5*, Sexual Aversion Disorder was eliminated and Hypoactive Sexual Desire Disorder was split into two diagnoses—one for men and one for women. The new terms are Male Hypoactive Sexual Desire Disorder and Female Sexual Interest/Arousal Disorder. These last two terms are basically characterized by absent/low desire.

- The *DSM-IV-TR* itemized disorders of sexual arousal: Female Sexual Arousal Disorder (FSAD) and Male Erectile Disorder (ED). In *DSM-5*, Female Sexual Arousal Disorder was combined with Female Sexual Interest. The classification Erectile Disorder remained the same.
- In the *DSM-IV-TR* there were categories for disorders of orgasm: Female Orgasmic Disorder, Male Orgasmic Disorder and Premature Ejaculation (PE). In *DSM-5*, the term Female Orgasmic Disorder was retained; Male Orgasmic Disorder was eliminated and essentially replaced by Delayed Ejaculation. Also, the term Premature Ejaculation became Premature (early) Ejaculation.
- *DSM-IV-TR* contained categories for Sexual Pain Disorders: Dyspareunia and Vaginismus. These terms do not appear anywhere in *DSM-5*. In *DSM-5*, the term Genito-Pelvic Pain/Penetration Disorder is used to describe any type of pain associated with the genital area, including pain with penetration.

In *DSM-5*, three new diagnostic categories were added:

- Substance/Medication-Induced Sexual Disorder, which refers to a sexual disorder resulting from substance abuse or prescribed medications.
- Other Specified Sexual Disorders. These are disorders that do not meet full criteria and cause distress, but can be added with a specifier, a specific reason such as sexual aversion.
- Unspecified Sexual Disorder. These are disorders that do not meet full criteria and cause distress, but the clinician has insufficient information to make any specifications about the disorder.

DSM-IV-TR was based on the multiaxial system of diagnosis, allowing the clinician to make a diagnosis in several different categories. *DSM-5* does not use a multiaxial system but does allow for several different specifications that are similar to what was used in *DSM-IV-TR*.

Specifiers

In addition to diagnostic criteria, the clinician must be aware of the following three major specifiers in the *DSM-5*:

1. Lifelong versus acquired
2. Generalized versus situational
3. Mild, moderate or severe distress

For Sexual Disorders to be specified as *Lifelong*, the condition must have been present since the client's earliest sexual activity. For the specifier *Acquired*, the client must have previously had nonproblematic sexual functioning in the area that is now problematic. For example, a client who had been able to delay ejaculation with previous partners, but is unable to do so with his new partner, would be diagnosed with *Premature Ejaculation, Acquired*. In Acquired Sexual Disorders, it is important to note the context of onset, such as any changes in physical or mental health, job or relationship status and so on. The second specifier, *Generalized* or *Situational*, indicates whether the disorder is considered global—the problem occurs in every situation, or it only occurs in certain situations. For example, in one of our cases, a husband experienced Erectile Disorder (moderate) with his wife but never had a problem when acting out sexually with prostitutes and other women. For these types of problems, the sexual disorder implies a psychological etiology. Moreover, it is important to note if the sexual problem may be an adaptive response to current or past trauma or stress. In the example of the man who had perfect erectile ability with prostitutes, his father validated him for having sex with women other than his primary partner and with prostitutes. Since the father also acted out sexually, he provided a strong male sexual script for his son.

Overview of Sexual Disorders in *DSM-5*

Sexual Interest/Arousal Disorder

The criteria for a diagnosis of Sexual Interest/Arousal Disorder in the *DSM-5* (American Psychiatric Association, 2013) take into account biological, psychological and contextual factors that influence sexual arousal and interest (Brotto & Luria, 2014). Sexual Interest/Arousal Disorder does not manifest itself the same way in all diagnosable women. For a diagnosis of Sexual Interest/Arousal Disorder, a minimum of three of the following symptoms must be present:

1, Absent/reduced interest in sexual activity
2, Absent/reduced sexual/erotic thoughts or fantasies
3, No/reduced initiation of sexual activity
4, Typically unreceptive to a partner's attempts to initiate
5, Absent/reduced sexual excitement/pleasure during sexual activity in all or almost all (approximately 75%–100%) sexual encounters
6, Absent/reduced sexual interest/arousal in response to any internal or external sexual/erotic cues
7, Absent/reduced genital or nongenital sensations during sexual activity in all or almost all (approximately 75%–100%) sexual encounters. (American Psychiatric Association, 2013, p. 433)

Brotto and Luria (2014) highlight the fact that the diagnostic criteria for this disorder refer to desire being responsive to a stimulus. This definition assumes that sexual desire is less spontaneous for women than men and more related to contextual and relational variables. In adjusting the criteria in this way, the authors recognize that sexual motivation is complex, particularly for women (Basson, 2002). Variations in sexual expression and reactivity, both among women and throughout the life of the same woman, are accounted for and thereby depathologized for women lacking so-called spontaneous desire, particularly considering the requirement that the changes are present for at least 6 months in almost all sexual experiences. The new criteria for diagnosis require examining the overall situation instead of the sexual behavior alone, specifically with respect to the level of emotional intimacy between partners, and the overall variability of the sexual response. Additionally, situational stressors, financial worries and other hassles of daily living can affect desire and arousability for women (Hamilton & Julian, 2014). Since sexual arousal and desire can occur simultaneously, this diagnosis requires focusing on more than issues with vaginal lubrication.

Male Hypoactive Sexual Desire Disorder

Very little is known about low sexual desire in men. Moreover, it is rarely the primary presenting concern (Meana & Steiner, 2014; Hall, 2015). Some men with concerns about low desire are engaging in activities other than intercourse with their established partner to fulfill their sexual needs, such as masturbation or sex outside the primary relationship. Their desire, therefore, may be hidden from the primary partner and not hypoactive. It is important to assess if the man is complaining about his lack of desire or if it is more of a problem for the partner. Variations in desire between men and across the lifetime of a single man are important to keep in mind when making this diagnosis. Additionally, although most men experience spontaneous desire, small percentages actually prefer responsive desire (Štulhofer, Carvalheria & Traeen, 2012).

For a diagnosis of Male Hypoactive Sexual Desire Disorder, the individual must present with "persistently or recurrent deficient (or absent) sexual/erotic thoughts or fantasies and desire for sexual activity" (American Psychiatric Association, 2013, p. 440). Additionally, the clinician should be mindful of physiologic factors such as age, and the man's relationship and contextual variables such as stressors, worries, finances and the overall circumstances of his life.

Erectile Disorder

For a diagnosis of Erectile Disorder (ED), the individual must have at least one of the following three symptoms (American Psychiatric Association, 2013, p. 426):

1.   Marked difficulty in obtaining an erection during sexual activity
2.   Marked difficulty in maintaining an erection until the completion of sexual activity
3.   Marked decrease in erectile rigidity

The prevalence of ED increases in men as they age because of the increase in organic factors associated with aging. As with all of the sexual diagnoses,

ED can be linked to unknown physical conditions such as cardiovascular disease or diabetes mellitus. The presentation is often more psychogenic for younger men and mixed (psychogenic and organic) as the man ages, making him less resilient to the impact of emotional factors on the resilience of erectile capacity (Rosen, Miner, & Wincze, 2014). Thus, medical screenings are essential unless the clinician is certain that ED occurs only under conditions of emotional distress. One way of distinguishing the etiology is to inquire about the level of tumescence during self-stimulation versus partnered sex. Additionally, Fisher et al. (2004) report that frequently older men with erectile disorder also experience difficulties with sexual desire, ejaculation and orgasm.

Premature (Early) Ejaculation

A diagnosis of Premature Ejaculation (PE) requires "a persistent or recurrent pattern of ejaculation occurring during partnered sexual activity within approximately 1 minute following vaginal penetration and before the individual wishes it" (American Psychiatric Association, 2013, p. 443). Thus, the diagnostic criteria for PE are not stated for noncoital sexual activity. Nonetheless, the man should be asked about how much stimulation occurs prior to orgasm during oral, anal, manual and other forms of sexual activity. He should be asked to express the degree of distress he suffers over PE. As mentioned earlier, symptoms of premature ejaculation and ED are often co-occurring. Performance anxiety is common among individuals with either disorder. Men with ED may try to rush intercourse, thereby putting themselves at greater risk of developing premature ejaculation (Althof, 2014). Most cases of PE are considered lifelong; only one third of men with PE have the acquired type (Althof, 2014). The clinician should determine the conditions under which the man is more likely to experience PE. For a more detailed description of this disorder, see Betchen (2015).

Delayed Ejaculation

A diagnosis of Delayed Ejaculation (DE) requires that the individual experience either "marked delay in ejaculation or marked infrequency or absence of ejaculation," and the individual must desire ejaculation (American Psychiatric Association, 2013, p. 424). Though DE may be related to preferences for sexual activity other than partnered sex, it may occur in nonpartnered sexual activities as well. Stress related to delayed ejaculation is frequently in the form of anticipated negative reactions from partners. Some partners may enjoy the duration, but prolonged sexual activity may lead to physical discomfort for partners, sexual dissatisfaction and/or negative beliefs or questions about the relationship (Perelman, 2014). Negative reactions from partners or fear of negative reactions may lead to an avoidance of sexual activity or to faking orgasm. See Foley and Gambescia (2015) for greater elaboration on this distressful condition.

Female Orgasmic Disorder

The diagnostic criteria for Female Orgasmic Disorder (FAD) are as follows: "Marked delay in, marked infrequency of or absence of orgasm or markedly reduced intensity of orgasmic sensations" (American Psychiatric Association, 2013, p. 429). When a lack of orgasmic response is reported for partnered intercourse, but not with direct clitoral stimulation, a diagnosis of FOD is not appropriate (American Psychiatric Association, 2013). The clinician is responsible for determining if the woman is receiving adequate stimulation in intensity, duration and focus (Graham, 2014). Moreover, there is variance among women in terms of preference, physiological responses to stimulation and overall experience. Women who have never had an orgasm may question whether their sexual experience constituted an orgasm. Some women who report an inability to reach orgasm are not distressed by it; they enjoy the physical and emotional closeness to their sexual partner. Therefore, it is essential to assess for levels of distress (Laan, 2011; McCabe, 2015; Shifren, Monz, Russo, Segreti, & Johannes, 2008). Criterion C in the new diagnostic system states the woman must experience significant distress from the problem.

Genito-Pelvic Pain/Penetration Disorder

For a diagnosis of Genito-Pelvic Pain/Penetration Disorder, the individual must experience persistent or recurrent difficulties with one (or more) of the following (American Psychiatric Association, 2013, p. 437):

1. Vaginal penetration during intercourse
2. Marked vulvovaginal or pelvic pain during vaginal intercourse or penetration attempts
3. Marked fear or anxiety about vulvovaginal or pelvic pain in anticipation of, during or as a result of vaginal penetration
4. Marked tensing or tightening of the pelvic floor muscles during attempted vaginal penetration

Bergeron, Rosen, and Pukall (2014) stress the importance of exploring the physiological, cognitive, emotional, behavioral and interpersonal factors that have a potential impact and influence on the pain symptoms. Numerous factors may simultaneously contribute to the symptoms; thus a multidisciplinary approach is necessary to determine the extent of organic, psychogenic, and mixed etiologies.

Limitations of the DSM Diagnostic Categories

Although *DSM-5* provides the information necessary to assign a diagnosis that meets insurance or other third-party payer needs, it may not provide a full enough understanding of the factors that precipitate, maintain, contribute to or follow from a sexual problem. The *DSM* assumes normal sexual functioning to include the facility to experience desire and satisfaction (that is, receptivity to sexual activity), with the experiencing of orgasm under suitable circumstances (Sugrue & Whipple, 2001). This has led to what some believe is sexology's pre-occupation with coitus and orgasm (Tiefer, 2001, 2002). This section reviews some of the limitations of the current DSM categories and definitions in order to provide clinicians with a better understanding of how sexual problems arise and impact other areas of functioning. Such information is presented to help with a more accurate diagnosis and treatment plan.

Disorder versus Problem

Many of our clients, especially women, report a lack of sexual pleasure, enjoyment and satisfaction, despite being able to respond sexually in terms of having an adequate sex drive, becoming aroused and being able to achieve orgasm; nevertheless, sexual dissatisfaction is not a diagnosable disorder. In addition, many clients will report dissatisfaction with the amount of foreplay and after play; the partner choosing an inconvenient time or a time of day to have sex; a difference in preferred sexual practices, including positions; and a crude way of initiating sex. As a sex therapist, you will likely see many cases involving individual or dyadic sexual issues that may or may not qualify as diagnosable Sexual Disorders by the *DSM* standards. Sexual Disorder implies that normal functioning is impaired and that this impairment causes personal and/or inter-personal distress; however, many sexual problems do not qualify as a Sexual Disorder, yet produce similar, if not greater, levels of distress for clients. We encourage clinicians to consider those sexual problems as well. For example, a woman may present for treatment because of persistent genital arousal or a high level of sexual desire that troubles her. This could be understood in a number of ways, none of which the *DSM-5* addresses with a specific diagnostic category. It could be a case of what some researchers term *Persistent Sexual Arousal* (Facelle, Sadeghi-Nejad, & Goldmeier, 2013; Goldmeier, Sadeghi-Nejad, & Facelle, 2014; Leiblum & Seehuus, 2009) (discussed later) or the condition could result from gender socialization patterns and sexual scripting that do not allow the woman to admit her sexual desire. When a woman has physiological responses or urges, she may, for lack of a better understanding, interpret or read these responses as problematic. *DSM-5* does not provide an easy category of diagnosis for this type of situation, yet it is vital that the therapist take the woman's distress seriously.

A far more common sexual problem, which does not fit within the *DSM* qualification of Sexual Disorder, is incongruence of sexual desire between sexual partners; this is a very common presentation, called desire discrepancy. It is often difficult to determine whether the problem is based on perception or lack of knowledge, or if it stems from other, more serious issues, either individual or relational. One interesting case involved a woman who expressed that she had low sexual desire and believed she had what was then called Hypoactive Sexual Desire Disorder. She was a therapist and had self-diagnosed. On further examination, the therapist learned that her husband wanted to have sex three or four times a week while she only desired sex one or two times a week. Her level of desire was within normal limits, but she believed the discrepancy to be indicative of her having low desire because she thought that she must always please her husband and should share his level of desire.

Etiology: Physiology versus Psychology

From the Intersystem perspective, there is a problematic dichotomy between physiological and psychological causes of a disorder. This dichotomy suggests that treatment should be binary: some problems should be treated from a strictly medical perspective and others from a psychotherapeutic perspective. Regardless of the source of the cause or the combination of etiologic factors, sexual symptoms will always have psychological/couple consequences. Sexual problems are embedded in relationship dynamics and vice versa. Treatment from just one perspective is simplistic. For example, a man may have ED stemming from a medical problem and will require medical treatment. Additionally, the ED will have psychological consequences for the man and consequences for the couple that need to be recognized and become part of the overall treatment program. Sexual problems, even those with a purely physiological basis, are best treated with an approach that combines medical and psychotherapeutic approaches (Gambescia & Weeks, 2015). In cases where clinicians have conducted a thorough Intersystem assessment and suspect a physiological component of sexual disorder, a good clinical practice requires consultation/ collaboration with a physician who has expertise in the area of sexual disorders and an assessment of normal physical sexual responses.

Comorbidity with Other Conditions

Sexual Disorders often cooccur with physical health issues, other sexual disorders, and other mental health problems, including substance-related, mood, and anxiety disorders. Although the connection between anxiety disorders, performance anxiety and premature ejaculation is complex and far from universal, more and more researchers are finding a bidirectional correlation between sexual disorder and depressive, eating and anxiety disorders, as well as physical health problems. Frequently, clients will present with a combination of physiological and psychological disorders that are impacting their sexual functioning. For example, a woman with breast cancer may experience absent/low desire, partially due to the physical aspects of her medical condition, but also as a consequence of changes in her own body image and sense of self brought about by her health status (Pillai-Friedman & Ashlinea, 2014). Here, it is important to view and treat the disorder within the context of her health status—not as disorder independent of it, nor as a strict and direct consequence of her cancer. For a better understanding of how chronic illness and impaired physical functioning can impact sexual functioning, and specific interventions for such cases, clinicians should review Chapter 11.

Clients frequently present with more than one sexual disorder. Although the *DSM-5* allows for as many diagnoses as necessary, there is no way to indicate the interactional quality of a dual or multiple diagnoses within the couple. Quite frequently, for example, ED may serve to mask and/or exacerbate male hypoactive sexual desire, as described in our companion volume (Hertlein, Weeks, & Gambescia, 2015). Generally in such cases, it is important to triage, discern etiology and attempt to treat the most pressing sexual concern first. Certain problems, however, must be treated first in the individual and the couple as described in the triage tree in our treatment chapter (Chapter 6). Restoring erectile ability alone may not cure the man of a low libido, just as increasing a man's sexual desire without addressing the diminished erectile functioning will only produce frustration. Thus, the interaction of problems must be considered in designing a treatment plan, including all sexual problems in both partners and how they interact with each other.

Individual or Relational Problems

One common presentation is a couple seeking treatment for Erectile Disorder (ED). On one hand, the problem is physiologically/psychologically an *individual* one. On the other, both partners can feel the distress caused by the erectile disorder and the ED may be a result of relationship problems. Another common presentation is an individual seeking treatment for an incompatibility in the couple's levels of sexual desire, which is often framed as *her* being the one with the lack of sexual desire. On an individual level, the woman may report that she is fine with her sexual drive, and that the problem is only in relation to her husband's greater or more frequent desire for sex. A diagnosis of Female Sexual Interest/Arousal Disorder may or may not be warranted; yet it is important to include both partners in the treatment, particularly as the discrepancy in levels of desire is the real problem in the relationship. The husband may be behaving in ways that would reduce or eliminate desire in most any partner. Thus, a problem that appears to be in the women may stem from the man's sexual approach to her.

A distinct limitation of an individual diagnosis is that there is frequently comorbidity within the couple. We have observed numerous cases where sexual problems are the consequence of relationship conflict and difficulty. We have also observed numerous cases where the sexual problems precipitated or exacerbated a more general lack of intimacy in and satisfaction with the relationship. In these cases, determining cause and effect of the sexual disorder may not be easy, so treating both the couple and the sexual difficulties simultaneously or planning to treat both in a stepwise fashion becomes important. In fact, to simply consider cause and effect implies linear or nonsystemic thinking. We view the problem as reciprocal or interlocking in the couple's relationship or in relationships.

Diagnosing relational problems, whether the problem is primarily about the couple, about sex or about the circular interactional patterns is a central part of developing interventions and treatments from the Intersystem perspective. As shown in the chapter on assessment (Chapter 3), the level of severity and degree to which nonsexual aspects of a relationship are disrupted by the sexual problem greatly influence the perception, and hence treatment, of the problem. The *DSM-5* allows for relational diagnosis through the T and Z codes, which are ways of noting relationship issues that are either a focus of clinical attention in the absence of other disorders or relationship issues that are risk factors for negative outcomes in treatment (APA, 2013). Some of the following are codes that a sex therapist might want to use:

- Z63.0 Relationship Distress with Spouse or Intimate Partner
- ZZ63.5 Disruption of Family by Separation or Divorce
- Z63.8 High Expressed Emotion Level within Family
- T74.11XA Initial Encounter (physical violence, confirmed)
- T74.01XA Initial Encounter (spouse or partner neglect, confirmed)
- T74.31XA Initial Encounter (spouse or partner psychological abuse, confirmed)
- Z72.9 Problem Related to Lifestyle

These codes are just a small sampling of possible codes that can help contextualize sexual problems. Unfortunately, there are currently no set criteria for any of the T or Z codes and interpreting when and how to use the codes is left up to the clinician's discretion. *DSM-5* gives only broad descriptions for each category of T and Z codes. As can be seen from the listing included here, the problems are vague and the categories quite broad, which can be difficult for beginning sex therapists to apply appropriately. A thorough assessment of the individual's dyadic patterns or current couple interactions will help ascertain which T or Z code is applicable and when to use it.

Clinical Judgment

Finally, the *DSM-5* (following previous versions of the DSM) includes one key criterion for diagnosing many of the sexual dysfunctions: clinical judgment. This may be considered the most flexible of all criteria. The clinician is given the freedom to use good clinical judgment based on his or her knowledge and experience in deciding the most accurate diagnosis.

Sexual Problems Not Currently in the *DSM-5*

The current sexual nosology that is used in the *DSM-5* is an evolving document. Sexual disorders have never been given much attention in the diagnostic manual and are underresearched compared to other common psychological problems. Sex therapy is a relatively new field and innovative knowledge about how to classify and define disorders is being actively researched for some problems and not for others. Some of the common problems that have been identified still do not appear in the classification system. The following subsections review some of these problems.

Sexual Compulsivity, Addiction or Hypersexuality

Sexual compulsions mask or can be a symptom of numerous psychiatric disorders. For this reason, there has been considerable dispute about giving a psychiatric label to a disorder that has so much comorbidity. Sexual compulsivity refers to an excessive involvement in sex with a high potential for damaging consequences for the financial stability and physical health of the individual and his or her partner (Reid, Carpenter, & Lloyd, 2009). The distinction between a sexual compulsion and a manic episode is that in extreme cases of mania, the mood disturbance is sufficiently severe to necessitate hospitalization to prevent harm to self or others. Additionally, acting-out may not necessarily be sexual. In sexual compulsion, hospitalization may result as consequence of risky, out of control or criminal sexual acts or the need to remove oneself from the environment that allows for acting-out. Psychiatric hospitalization for sexual compulsivity is increasing as treatment facilities are becoming more equipped to handle these cases. Most hospitalizations for sexual compulsivity are voluntary, though usually forced by an intimate other. Another example of comorbidity is the degree of narcissism and sociopathy in persons suffering from sexual compulsivity.

The major debate in the field of sexual compulsivity is the use of the label or what to call it. Many believe the term *sex addiction* is not a psychological correlate of a physical addiction. Others argue that there is extreme variability in sexual preferences and appetites. Why pathologize? Nonetheless, agreement must be achieved about a clinical diagnosis, which is derived from a standardized set of criteria, in order to inform treatment (Reid, 2013). Labels such as sexual addiction, sexual compulsivity, sexual impulsivity or hypersexuality can affect how and what treatments are provided. The terms also influence the client's perception of the problem and his or her partner's perception of the problem. Regardless of comorbidity, the clinician must utilize a hierarchy when establishing a diagnosis and seek the most appropriate treatment for the most pressing problems as long as they are appropriately sequenced.

Gender Nonconformity

DSM-5 has gratified many people who engage in nonnormative, kinky sexual behavior. The text is significantly more accepting of sexual variation such as consensual sexual masochism, sexual sadism, fetishism, cross-dressing and gender dysphoria, which used to be labeled Gender Identity. The fundamental assumption guiding whether a behavior should be diagnosed as a paraphilia is only if the behaviors are leading to distress or impairment, or if these behaviors cause personal harm/risk or are a risk to others (American Psychiatric Association, 2013). For example, we have frequently seen couples in our practice who engage in consensual BDSM (bondage, discipline, sadism, masochism). In the past, this behavior would have automatically been diagnosed as pathological. Under the new guidelines, if the partners enjoy or are satisfied with this activity, it is not a diagnosable mental disorder. The main point is for the therapist to be sensitive to issues of gender variance and keep countertransference issues in check.

Persistent Genital Arousal Disorder

Another sexual problem not found in *DSM-5* involves unrelenting female genital arousal. Persistent Genital Arousal Disorder (PGAD) is a persistent genital arousal not caused by any feelings of sexual desire and that frequently does not diminish with orgasm. The following are the most common characteristics of PGAD (Goldmeier, Sadeghi-Nejad, & Facelle, 2014):

- Persists for an extended period of time (i.e., at least several hours)
- Does not subside spontaneously or with ordinary orgasmic experience (i.e., may require multiple orgasms over hours or days in order to gain some relief)
- Causes a clinically significant degree of distress (p. 268).

In some, but not all circumstances, PGAD is accompanied by genital swelling. This suggests a physiological, typically neurological, basis to this newly discovered phenomenon (Facelle, Sadeghi-Nejad, & Goldmeier, 2013; Goldmeier, Sadeghi-Nejad, & Facelle, 2014; Leiblum, 2007; Leiblum & Seehuus, 2009). Recent research proposes that some cases of PGAD are linked to Tarlov (sacral) cysts that form on the S2 and S3 dorsal ganglia in the sacral spine region (Langdown, Grundy, & Birch, 2005). The S2 and S3 dorsal roots direct sensory information to pelvic nerves, which affects the internal and external genitalia. It is suggested that Tarlov cysts produce the genital sensory disturbances and abnormal sensations in some women who suffer from PGAD (Komisaruk & Lee, 2012). Because of the shame associated with this disorder, it is likely that the prevalence is underreported, but still rare. A validated treatment approach has yet to be discovered, but Leiblum (2007) reported success in one case with a client using self-monitoring, massage and stretching exercises. Goldmeier, Sadeghi-Nejad, and Facelle (2014) suggest a combination of approaches, including mindfulness-based cognitive behavioral therapy, medication and pelvic floor physical therapy.

Diagnosis from the Intersystem Perspective

Although the sexual disorders are listed as separate disorders, only a complex assessment considering all the domains of the Intersystem Approach will give a full diagnostic picture. Specifically, the Intersystem Approach will require the clinician to consider the individual-biological-psychological, interpersonal/couple, intergenerational (family-of-origin) and environmental contexts of the client's life, including comorbidity, factors that may complicate treatment and ways the sexual problem may be serving to mask intimacy or other issues in a couple.

An Intersystem-informed diagnosis would probably lead to the use of several F codes as well as a number of T and Z codes. Clinicians utilizing the relevant relational T and Z codes will begin to address the couple system, which would include significant refinements to the catch-all Partner Relational Problem that was used in *DSM-IV-TR* (APA, 2000). The ways relational processes become intertwined with individual psychopathology generally and with sexual disorders specifically are complex and poorly understood. Assessment of the couple system will shed light on how emotional contracts, communication styles, attachment styles and patterns of couple interaction both reflect and reinforce sexual problems.

Finally, some of the T and Z codes also allow for noting significant social and contextual stressors that warrant clinical attention. These codes may reflect the intergenerational and environmental systems in the Intersystem approach. Internalized messages about sexuality from the families of origin are learned with and within the subcultures of ethnicity, race, religion and so on. Sex therapists should ascertain the level of discord regarding sexual messages, attitudes and beliefs between partners, discordance of belief systems within an individual and the sociocultural environment of each partner.

References

Althof, S.E. (2014). Treatment of premature ejaculation: Psychotherapy, pharmacotherapy, and combined therapy. In Y.M. Binik & K.S.K. Hall (Eds.), *Principles and practices of sex therapy* (5th ed.) (pp. 112–137). New York: Guilford Press.

American Psychiatric Association (APA). (2000). *Diagnostic and statistical manual of mental disorders* (4th ed., text rev.). Washington, DC: Author.

American Psychiatric Association (APA). (2013). *Diagnostic and statistical manual of mental disorders* (5th ed.). Arlington, VA: Author.

Basson, R. (2002). Women's sexual desire: Disordered or misunderstood? *Journal of Sex and Marital Therapy, 28,* 17–28.

Bergeron, S., Rosen, N.O., & Pukall, C.F. (2014). Genital pain in women and men: It can hurt more than your sex life. In Y.M. Binik & K.S.K. Hall (Eds.), *Principles and practices of sex therapy* (5th ed.) (pp. 159–177). New York: Guilford Press.

Betchen, S. (2015). Premature ejaculation: An integrative, intersystem approach for couples. In K.M. Hertlein, G.R. Weeks, & N. Gambescia (Eds.), *Systemic sex therapy* (2nd ed.) (pp. 90–106). New York: Routledge.

Brotto, L., & Luria, M. (2014). Sexual interest/arousal disorder in women. In Y.M. Binik & K.S.K. Hall (Eds.), *Principles and practices of sex therapy* (5th ed.) (pp. 17–41). New York: Guilford Press.

Facelle, T.M., Sadeghi-Nejad, H., & Goldmeier, D. (2013). Persistent genital arousal disorder: Characterization, etiology, and management. *Journal of Sexual Medicine, 10*(2), 439–450.

Fisher, W., Rosen, R.C., Eardley, I., Niederberger, C., Nadel, A., Kaufman, J., & Sand, M. (2004). The multinational men's attitudes to life events and sexuality (MALES) study phase II: Understanding PDE5 inhibitor treatment seeking patterns, among men with Erectile Dysfunction. *Journal of Sexual Medicine, 1*(2), 150–160.

Foley, S., & Gambescia, N. (2015). The complex etiology of delayed ejaculation: Assessment and treatment. In K.M. Hertlein, G.R. Weeks, & N. Gambescia (Eds.), *Systemic sex therapy* (2nd ed.) (pp, 107–124). New York: Routledge.

Gambescia, N., & Weeks, G.R. (2015). Systemic treatment of Erectile Disorder. In K.M. Hertlein, G.R. Weeks, & N. Gambescia (Eds.), *Systemic sex therapy* (2nd ed.) (pp. 72–89). New York: Routledge.

Goldmeier, D., Sadeghi-Nejad, H., & Facelle, T.M. (2014). Persistent genital arousal disorder. In Y.M. Binik & K.S.K. Hall (Eds.), *Principles and practices of sex therapy* (5th ed.) (pp. 262–279). New York: Guilford Press.

Graham, C.A. (2014). Orgasm disorder in women. In Y.M. Binik & K.S.K. Hall (Eds.), *Principles and practices of sex therapy* (5th ed.) (pp. 89–111). New York: Guilford Press.

Hall, K. (2015). Male hypoactive sexual desire disorder. In K.M. Hertlein, G.R. Weeks, & N. Gambescia (Eds.), *Systemic sex therapy* (2nd ed.) (pp. 55–71). New York: Routledge.

Hamilton, L.D., & Julian, A.M. (2014). The relationship between daily hassles and sexual function in men and women. *Journal of Sex & Marital Therapy, 40*(5), 379–395. doi: 10.1080/0092623X.2013.864364

Hertlein, K.M., Weeks, G.R., & Gambescia, N. (2015). *Systemic sex therapy* (2nd ed.). New York: Routledge.

Kaplan, H.S. (1974). *The new sex therapy: Active treatment of sexual dysfunctions.* New York: Brunner/Mazel.

Komisaruk, B.R., & Lee, H.J. (2012). Prevalence of sacral spinal (Tarlov) cysts in persistent genital arousal disorder. *International Society for Sexual Medicine, 9,* 2047–2056.

Laan, E.H. (2011). Can we treat anorgasmia in women? The challenge to experiencing pleasure. *Sexual & Relationship Therapy, 26,* 329–341.

Langdown, A.J., Grundy, J.R., & Birch, N.C. (2005). The clinical relevance of Tarlov cysts. *Journal of Spinal Disorders and Techniques, 18,* 29–33.

Leiblum, S. (2007). *Principles and practice of sex therapy* (3rd ed.). New York: Guilford Press.

Leiblum, S.R., & Seehuus, M. (2009). FSFI scores of women with persistent genital arousal disorder compared with published scores of women with Female Sexual Arousal Disorder and healthy controls. *Journal of Sexual Medicine, 6*(2), 469–473.

Masters, W.H., & Johnson, V. (1966). *Human sexual response.* Boston: Little, Brown.

Masters, W.H., & Johnson, V. (1970). *Human sexual inadequacy.* Boston: Little, Brown.

McCabe, M. (2015). Female Orgasmic Disorder. In K.M. Hertlein, G.R. Weeks, & N. Gambescia (Eds.), *Systemic sex therapy* (2nd ed.) (pp. 171–190). New York: Routledge.

Meana, M., & Steiner, E.T. (2014). Hidden disorder/hidden desire: Presentations of low sexual desire in men. In Y.M. Binik & K.S.K. Hall (Eds.), *Principles and practices of sex therapy* (5th ed.) (pp. 42–60). New York: Guilford Press.

Perelman, M.A. (2014). Delayed Ejaculation. In Y.M. Binik & K.S.K. Hall (Eds.), *Principles and practices of sex therapy* (5th ed.) (pp. 138–158). New York: Guilford Press.

Pillai-Friedman, S., & Ashline, J.L. (2014). Women, breast cancer survivorship, sexual losses, and disenfranchised grief: A treatment model for clinicians. *Sexual and Relationship Therapy, 29*(4), 436–453. doi:10.1080/14681994.2014.934340

Reid, R.C. (2013). Personal perspectives on hypersexual disorder. *Sexual Addiction & Compulsivity, 20*(1–2), 4–18.

Reid, R.C., Carpenter, B.N., & Lloyd, T.Q. (2009). Assessing psychological symptom patterns of patients seeking help for hypersexual behavior. *Sexual and Relationship Therapy, 24*(1), 47–63. Retrieved from http://dx.doi.org/10.1080/14681990802702141

Rosen, R.C., Miner, M.M., & Wincze, J.P. (2014). Erectile Dysfunction: Integration of medical and psychological approaches. In Y.M. Binik & K.S.K. Hall (Eds.), *Principles and practices of sex therapy* (5th ed.) (pp. 61–88). New York: Guilford Press.

Shifren, J.L., Monz, B.U., Russo, P.A., Segreti, A., & Johannes, C.B. (2008). Sexual problems and distress in United States women. *Obstetrics and Gynecology, 112,* 970–978.

Štulhofer, A., Carvalheira, A.A., & Træen, B. (2012). Is responsive sexual desire for partnered sex problematic among men? Insights from a two-country study. *Sexual and Relationship Therapy, 28*(3), 246–258. doi:10.1080/14681994.2012.756137

Sugrue, D., & Whipple, B. (2001). The consensus-based classification of female sexual dysfunction: Barriers to universal acceptance. *Journal of Sex Marital Therapy, 27,* 221–226. doi:10.1080/00926230152052030

Tiefer, L. (2001). Feminist critique of sex therapy: Foregrounding the politics of sex. In P.J. Kleinplatz (Ed.), *New directions in sex therapy: Innovations and alternatives* (pp. 29–49). New York: Routledge.

Tiefer, L. (2002). Sexual behaviour and its medicalisation: Many (especially economic) forces promote medicalisation. *BMJ, 325*(7354), 45. doi:10.1136/bmj.324.7342.896

3

INTERSYSTEM ASSESSMENT OF SEXUAL DISORDERS

Introduction

The assessment of sexual problems is a comprehensive, continuous and fluid process that can be masterfully comingled with treatment throughout the duration of therapy. It begins with the initial contact, continues during the preliminary interviews and ends with the last session. Intersystem assessment is particularly comprehensive because all facets of the client system are evaluated, including individual characteristics, relationship patterns, intergenerational factors, contextual and sociocultural constituents and so on. Assessment can be used to direct areas of inquiry and eventually contribute to establishing sexual, relational or individual diagnoses. Ultimately, assessment helps in the formulation or conceptualization of a case and provides the basis for treatment planning and modifications. With any assessment, it is important to determine the following:

- The couple's perception of the problem(s)
- Current baseline of individual and relational functioning
- Physical status of each partner
- The couple's expectations or goals at the end of treatment
- Realistic treatment goals
- Level of sexual desire for each partner
- Perceived degree of sexual satisfaction
- Level of distress experienced because of the sexual problem
- Impact on the intimate relationship
- The functions of sex in their relationship

As treatment progresses, the assessment should inform treatment of how the sessions will be structured (when to use individual or conjoint). Finally, as therapy culminates, assessment is used to more precisely determine treatment outcomes and, toward the end of therapy, relapse-prevention strategies. For sex therapists, assessment of sexual problems typically relies on information originating from a variety of sources, including self and partner reports, inventories, structured interviews and collaborative data from medical and psychological practitioners.

The Biphasic Assessment Process

The first phase of Intersystem assessment is designed to obtain general information about the presenting problem and the health histories of each partner. The therapist may initiate assessment by asking about the nature of the sexual problem. Most couples feel embarrassed talking about sexual issues; thus, the therapist must use sensitivity in eliciting information, beginning with broad, open-ended, general questions about sexual satisfaction and dissatisfaction. It is helpful to use normalizing statements in order to help reduce anxiety and to gain more information. The subsequent questions can be more specific, such as asking about difficultly with sexual desire, problems getting or keeping an erection, trouble ejaculating, difficulty in reaching orgasm, pain with intercourse and so on. Depending on the information gathered, the therapist can ask about other aspects of sexual functioning, such as adequate foreplay, creating an environment favorable to sex, preferences and disfavors and so on. The therapist should assume that sexual complaints are often underreported; some couples might be reluctant to reveal one or more sexual problems and others simply do not recognize a problem as a problem.

The second phase of the assessment process enlarges the perspective to include questions about the couple's overall relationship and broader contextual material such as environmental stressors and religious, historical, financial or other sociocultural factors. Additionally, in the second phase, the therapist gathers more detailed information about the specific presenting problems, particularly with respect to etiologic factors and how the sexual difficulties are impacting the partners and the couple. These focused questions are essential, but certainly not all inclusive or exhaustive of the information that needs to be gathered. In the present discussion, we include only the most common sexual problems the therapist is likely to see. Fundamentally, the therapist is going through a checklist of possible sexual difficulties in order to rule them out. The following areas of concentration should be addressed during the assessment:

- *The who, what, where, when and duration of the sexual problem*

This information can be acquired through a series of questions or conversations between the therapist and partners. How do they view the problem? Is there agreement? What measures have they taken to resolve the problem on their own?

Do not ask "why" questions. Why questions are of little value and often answers are created to explain what they cannot really explain.

- *Level of distress on the individual and the relationship*

How are the partners feeling about the problem? Who is more upset? Are they able to discuss their feelings about the sexual difficulty? Pessimism is a common emotion that results from attempting to deal with sexual problems. Are the partners skeptical, anxious, angry or giving up hope?

- *History of the problem*

Did the problem begin prior to or during the current relationship? Was the onset sudden or gradual? When did they first notice the symptoms? How have the couple managed the sexual issue and their feelings related to it?

- *The overall couple relationship*

The therapist acquires an overview of how the couple perceives strengths and weaknesses in their relationship (Weeks & Fife, 2014; Weeks & Treat, 1992). Some of the most common relationship issues present as intimacy fears, anger, communication problems and so on. These conflicts can have a direct and indirect influence on sexual satisfaction. Determine if the couple recognizes a connection between their sexual and relationship problems and vice versa. Many couples cannot comprehend that sexual and relational issues are often comingled and each impacts the other. In many cases of heterosexual couples, it is the woman who believes that sexual and relational satisfaction affects sexual functioning, whereas the man believes that such issues do not or should not affect her ability to participate in sex. The therapist must encourage the couple to think systemically by explaining that most sexual problems do not occur in a vacuum and that sex affects the relationship and vice versa (Mark & Jozkowski, 2013). It is critical to make these connections in order for the partners to believe the therapist is working on the correct issues and in the proper sequence.

- *Level of affection in the relationship*

Many couples with sexual concerns view affection as a precursor to sex; therefore, expressions of affection are eventually avoided. Ask the couple to work together to compile a list of behaviors that they define as affectionate and whether they view each of these behaviors as a precursor to sex. Specifically, couples develop a pattern of avoiding sexual contact. If they believe an exchange of affection must lead to sex, they will begin to avoid affection too in many cases. Do the partners believe they share the same level of affection in the relationship? Is sharing the same level of affection important?

- *The level of sensuality in their relationship*

Sensuality should not be confused with sexual expression. Sensuality involves giving and receiving physical pleasure involving the senses. How sensual does each partner feel the relationship is? Does the level of sensuality change when other factors in the relationship fluctuate, such as with stress on one or both partners? Does one partner generally have a tendency to be more sensual than another? If so, does the more sensual partner expect a certain level of reciprocity with regard to sensual behaviors?

- *Communication skills*

Do the partners talk to each other about sex and/or express themselves nonverbally?
    How do they talk to each other about sex? Can they ask for what they want to give and get from each other during a sensual and sexual encounter? Do they cease communication during sex or express themselves in ways that sabotage the experience?

- *Is there anything else the therapist needs to know?*

Couples may have other significant problems they do not want to discuss, other than the sexual problem. For example, an alcoholic man may not want to discuss his drinking, but just focus on his erectile problems. The therapist must provide opportunities for partners to share secrets such as previous sexual abuse, Internet compulsivity, addictions or affairs that they do not want to reveal in the presence of the partner. Moreover, the therapist must be vigilant for undisclosed secrets that will interfere with treatment.

The Sexual History

The sexual history/assessment provides the information needed to construct a treatment plan using the Intersystem Approach to treatment. Treatment must be comprehensive and detailed, including all facets of the couple's life (physical issues, psychological concerns in each partner, relational dynamics, history of sexual experiences, religion, culture and environment) (Hamilton & Julian, 2014; Ramlachan & Campbell, 2014; Weeks & Gambescia 2000, 2002). Some therapists prefer to use formal assessment instruments such as questionnaires and intake forms to collect sexual information, and we believe written inventories can be useful. Interviewing of the partners, however, provides the greatest opportunity to build a rapport in a relatively safe environment. The observation of how the information is presented and the reactions of the partners when this information is revealed are invaluable.

We prefer to use a flexible treatment format that incorporates individual and conjoint sessions when conducting the sexual history. Conjoint sessions provide an opportunity for clarification of the presenting problem and other issues in the relationship. Individual sessions, on the other hand, can give the partners a chance to talk without the pressures and worries about reactions or judgments from the other.

We recommend that the sex history be conducted in a flowing and relaxed manner. It is always important to attend to the presenting problem first and spend time discussing it. Additionally, the therapist will want to explore and investigate other areas of sexual functioning. Although it is important to give nonurgent sexual information an opportunity to surface naturally, the therapist will gently direct the conversation toward the information needed. The key to providing clients with meaningful answers to their problems lies in asking the right questions. The main objective in gathering a sex history is to gain an accurate representation of a client's sexual past and current behavior in order to screen for the presence of sexual problems, provide insight into possible etiology and indicate the treatment most likely to be efficacious. The therapist needs to explain why he or she is asking the question and how that question might be relevant. Doing so allows the therapist and clients to connect the dots if the couple views a sexual problem in isolation when it is embedded in a much larger problematic context.

A good way to begin the sex history is to use general and open-ended questions. One way to start is to ask, "Are you in a relationship?" if this information is not obvious initially. It is possible some clients are in closeted gay relationships, some are having affairs (a side relationship), some are seeing prostitutes (for straight sex, BDSM, etc.) and some are having gay sex on the down low: they are in a heterosexual relationship but having gay liaisons. There are any number of possibilities that could be occurring. The question "Are you in a relationship?" is a good place to start; in the individual session, ask about any other current sexual relationships, whether steady or intermittent. Alternately, the therapist can ask about the client's intimate relationship or sex life. If the questions are general enough, the answers will help direct the line of inquiry. As the sexual history progresses, the queries become more specific, including asking for extremely sensitive information such as the composition of one's sexual fantasies, masturbatory preferences and history of sexual abuse. The therapist would be remiss if any of these areas are overlooked, as discussed in Berthelot,

Godbout, Hébert, Goulet, and Bergeron (2014). Additionally, information obtained in a sex history can reveal material about overall physical health. For instance, erectile dysfunction might be an early symptom of cardiovascular disease. Lack of desire might be an indicator of depression, anxiety or hormonal imbalance.

Since the therapist is actually controlling the pace of the session, clients can be helped to explore sensitive sexual areas if the timing is right for the situation. It is often helpful to explain the rationale for seeking sexual information so that it makes sense to the couple and eases their anxiety. Be sure to ask if they have any questions or concerns. Additionally, the therapist should use language that is comfortable and understood by the couple. It is important that the therapist never hesitates to ask for details into the meaning of slang or particular subcultural terms a client may use. Clarification of the client's meaning promotes an expectation for description and signals that the therapist is interested in the client's experiences. The therapist simultaneously provides a role model for the client in how to ask about unfamiliar or difficult sexual matters. If the therapist chooses to use the client's language, he or she must first establish a mutual understanding for the terms that are being used.

A variety of structures are commonly used when taking a sex history. Some medical practitioners begin by focusing on purely physical details such as preventing sexually transmitted infections and planning pregnancies before asking about sexual problems. This approach can have obvious limitations because sexual intimacy is an important component of individual and relational satisfaction. Others tend to take a lifespan approach to the sexual history, gathering information as it pertains to each stage of the person's development. Many therapists structure their questions according to a psychiatric model, using the recent *DSM-5* sexual diagnoses (American Psychiatric Association, 2013) to elicit information about current and past sexual functioning and the presence of sexual disorders in each partner. This approach will incorporate issues of gender identity, sexual preferences and the presence of consensual or nonconsensual paraphilias.

The sexual history can cover many areas as mentioned earlier. For the clinician seeking a general outline of areas of inquiry Table 3.1 may be of some help. The clinician should use the guidelines reviewed previously and this table as general references or reminders of the kinds of questions to ask.

The Intersystem Sexual History

Our approach to the sexual history incorporates all of the previously mentioned information and is considerably more comprehensive since it incorporates sexual feelings, beliefs, behaviors and the meaning of sexual intimacy to the couple.

TABLE 3.1 Typical Sexual History Areas of Assessment

Category	Areas of Focus
Individual History	
Personal Background	• Sex
	• Age
	• Level of education
	• Employment
	• Relationship with parents
	• Social relationships (siblings, other relatives, friends)
	• Marital/relationship status
	• Parenthood (number of children, quality of relationships)
	• Religious commitment
	• Moral values
	• Interests and hobbies
	• Sports activities
	• Psychological disorders
Mental State	• Feel depressed or anxious?
	• More irritable recently?
	• Crying lately?
	• Difficulty in getting to sleep?
	• Waking in the early hours of the morning?
	• Poor appetite at present?
	• Changes in weight recently?
	• Has your sexual drive been reduced recently?
	• Do you have any special fears or phobias?
	• Have you ever heard voices or noises that you think other people cannot or have not heard?
	• Is your concentration good?
	• Is your memory reasonable for your age?
Medical History	• Any hospitalizations? When? For what?
	• Are you taking any medications? If yes, what? What dosages? For how long?
	• Illnesses?
	• How much do you drink daily or use recreational drugs?
	• How many cigarette do you smoke a day?
Interpersonal History and Other Factors	
Family-of-Origin Factors	• What were the ideas communicated to you by your family about sex?
	• How did your family communicate affection?
	• Family structure?
	• Messages about sex?
	• Relationship with siblings?
	• History of mental illness within the family?

(*Continued*)

TABLE 3.1 Continued

Category	Areas of Focus
Marital History (if any history)	• How long have you been married to your present partner? • How long (if at all) did you live together before marriage? • How many children do you have in the present marriage? • Did you have these children by choice? • Have you at any time separated from your present spouse? • Have you been married before? Please give details, reasons for ending the relationship, number and ages of children and who is now looking after them. • Have you, or your partner, ever had a pregnancy terminated (aborted) for any reason? • Have you had any infertility problems? • Have you had any sexual problems in past marriages? If so, what kind? • Did you ever have sex outside your marriage or committed relationship (usually asked in an individual session)?
Couple Factors	• What is your definition of intimacy? • Do the two of you talk openly about sex? • Do you look at one another in the eyes when having sex? • How important is sex to you in this relationship? • Have you been able to get what you wanted from sex? • What is communication like within the relationship? • How is conflict managed in the relationship? • How do you spend your leisure time as a couple?
Sex Education	• What sexual information was received? When? From whom? Under what circumstances? • What were the meanings associated with sex based on this early information? • Did you receive any sex education in school? If so, what did you learn? • Have you sought out other sources of sex information such as books or Internet sites?

(Continued)

TABLE 3.1 Continued

Category	Areas of Focus
Masturbation, Fantasy and Dreams	• How often do you engage in solo sex? • How often do you have sexual fantasies or dreams? • Do you share these with your partner? • How do you feel about your fantasies? • Do you try to act out some of your fantasies or role-play them? • Please tell me about the nature of your fantasies? (usually done in a private session, but can be done with the couple if they are comfortable sharing).
Sexual Experience with Others	• What was your initiation into sex? How did you feel about your first and early sexual experiences? • Obtain a history of past sexual experiences. • When and with whom did these experiences occur? How often did you have sex? Who initiated? What was the overall nature of your relationship? • Did you ever feel forced into having sex? • Did you ever experience rape, including date rape? • Did you ever feel any of your partners were inappropriate, such as a much older person, teacher, relative? • Did you experiment with any homosexual or nontraditional forms of sexuality? With whom, what age, how long, what degree of satisfaction? • How do you think your earlier sexual experiences affect you today?
Use of Contraceptive Methods (if at all)	• When did you begin to use birth control? • What method(s) did you use? • How long did you use them? Obtain history of usage? • Did a parent ever talk to you about birth control? Was your parent involved in your obtaining birth control? • Did you ever have any adverse effects from using birth control? • How satisfied have you (and your partners) been with using birth control?
Sex and Money	• Have you ever paid or been paid for having sex? When, for how long and what were the circumstances? • Were you forced into this experience by someone else or by circumstances beyond your control? • What was the experience like? • How do you feel about this experience?

(Continued)

TABLE 3.1 Continued

Category	Areas of Focus
Sexual Violence	• Victim or/and perpetrator? How often? When? Where? Who? Under what circumstances?
Sexual Problems and Dysfunctions	• What kind of sexual problems have you had in the past? In the present? These could be small or large problems. • When and for how long did they last? • Did you seek treatment? • Were you able to find a solution to the problem? If so, how and what was the solution? • To what extent did the problem affect how you feel about and function as a sexual person now? • What is your overall level of sexual satisfaction? Is there anything you would like to see improved?
Precipitating Factors	• What do you think lead to the sexual problem? • Medical-physiological changes • Acute stress • Relationship problems or crisis in relationship • Why are you seeking treatment at this particular time (especially when the problem has been long-term)? • How did you (the two of you) cope with this problem (for so long)?
Positive Aspects of Sex	• In what ways do you see sex as positive? • How has sex been a positive force in your relationship? • How much do you enjoy sex? • How free or creative are you in expressing your sexuality. • What is the best thing you like about sex individually, in your relationship?

Individual Physiological

The initial step is for the therapist to gain an accurate assessment of organic (physical) illnesses in each partner and how these conditions may affect their overall functioning and sexual performance. Always inquire about recreational, prescription and/or nonprescription medication use, including alcohol and marijuana. Ask about the reasons for taking medications, and keep in mind the client might not comprehend the nature of an illness or the action of a prescription drug on his or her sexual functioning. Inquire about dosage and length of time taking every medication. It is incumbent upon the therapist to understand the action and common side effects of medications, particularly those that may adversely affect the sexual system (see Phelps, Jones, & Payne, 2015; Crenshaw & Goldberg, 1996).

Individual Psychological

The therapist should establish the client's current levels of stress and coping mechanisms; general affect and cognitive functioning, history of mental disturbances; and previous emotional, mental or sexual trauma. You will want to know about the clients' perceptions of self and others, especially significant others, lovers, parents and authority figures. You should also address psychosexual issues, including the ability to fantasize, sexual self-schemas and conceptions about sex internalized from early experiences and family-of-origin messages. Of utmost importance is determining the level of distress the clients are experiencing from the sexual problem and how they manage that distress.

Clients can vary greatly regarding how personally distressed they are about a problem. Is there a discrepancy between the level of sexual functioning the client couple is experiencing and what they want? Always look for a discrepancy in level of distress between partners as well. Sometimes, the clients' responses will indicate the need to assess further for substance abuse or mood and/or anxiety disorders, particularly depression, because these disorders are common and linked to sexual problems. For example, a man might have an erection problem and know that it is probably related to his long-term use of alcohol. He does not want to stop drinking so he minimizes the distress produced by his inability to get an erection.

Our clients present with varied individual preferences, tendencies, likes and dislikes and other factors that dominate the sexual template. It is important to assess for the gender identity of the client, comfort with assigned gender, gender orientation and its relationship to sexual attraction and behavioral sexual preferences. A therapist may develop anxiety or judgmental feelings toward clients who do not conform to binary gender identities. Additionally, the therapist might be intimidated by the client's physical presentation, sexual orientation or choice of sexual behaviors. The therapist is obligated to anticipate, understand and deal with countertransference issues that could impede treatment, especially when helping gender nonconforming or other kinky clients (Nichols, 2006). The gender, age, attractiveness of the therapist and many other issues can also play into transference issues. Note whether one client requests more individual sessions, flirts or dresses up for the session. It is interesting that virtually little literature exists on transference and countertransference issues in sex therapy. These issues are about sexual attraction yet we deny that these issues exist when we are explicitly discussing sex, but not when we might be discussing other issues in other contexts.

The Relationship

The relationship, or context in which the sexual problem is embedded, is also important to evaluate. Commonly, sexual problems are created within or maintained by the relationship. Risk factors including anger, resentment, fear of intimacy, conflict management styles and power struggles will predispose a couple to sexual problems (Gambescia & Weeks, 2015; Weeks & Gambescia, 2000, 2002). For example, an overriding negative emotion (such as anger) would probably contribute to negative emotions about the relationship, and thus result in sexual impairment. As negative incidents build and remain unresolved, the sexual relationship becomes a place where these problems are expressed. For example, some clients experiencing lack of sexual desire attribute it to power imbalances in the relationship, acknowledging that withholding sex gives them at least some power in the relationship (Weeks & Gambescia, 2002).

We have found that there is often a sexual problem in the partner who is presenting without a sexual problem. The problem could be in reaction to, separate from or triggering the sexual dysfunction in the identified partner or a combination. An obvious problem in one partner often masks and distracts us from looking for a sexual/relational problem in the other partner. Always assess for sexual problems, expectations, disappointments and level of satisfaction/dissatisfaction in both partners. Since sexual satisfaction and relational satisfaction are correlated, inquiries about both areas are essential elements of the sexual history. Additionally, the therapist should ask about discrepancies in sexual styles or drives; levels of physical, sexual, and other attraction to the partner; and the ability to get sexual and intimacy needs met within the relationship.

Intergenerational Factors

Sexual information is transmitted within the family of origin through words, actions and other intimate exchanges. In many cases, this information is positive. Often, however, sexual information can be secretive, inaccurate or traumatic, leading to sexual ignorance, guilt or shame in the adult (Rellini & Meston, 2011). Internalized negative messages about sexuality, the absence of expressions of affection and unrealistic expectations of a partner can be damaging to adult sexual relationships. Intergenerational factors must be a part of the overall sexual history.

Couples with sexual problems often do not see any connection between their early life experiences and what they are experiencing today. Thus, they may think the therapist is bringing up old painful issues for no reason. Nonetheless, specific sexual messages originating from the family of origin that may have been covert and overt, spoken directly or indirectly and/or modeled through a parent's behavior need to be carefully explored. One client, who had been unfaithful, was amazed to recognize the intergenerational legacy of infidelity in both parents. Although he was extremely bright, he had never put the pieces together until he found himself in a similar position.

Contextual

An Intersystem approach to sex therapy recognizes that culture, religion, environment and so on are central to a person's life; thus, it is the obligation of the clinician to collect specific information that will inform therapy and help to customize treatment. Sexuality is interpreted through the filter of sociocultural beliefs, customs and values, affecting the ability to form nourishing sexual relationships. As such, the sexual history will include any contextual factor, regardless of how trivial, that can contribute to sexual problems. An interesting example is the impact of daily stressors on sexual functioning. Hamilton and Julian (2014) found that financial stressors, stressors related to low socioeconomic status and environmental daily stressors adversely affect sexual functioning (and contributed to anxiety and depression) for women more than men. Nonetheless, this research underscores the importance of inquiring about environmental considerations when assessing problems with sexual functioning.

Begin by asking about daily contextual stressors; gender roles in the initiation of sexual activity; gendered expectations regarding sexuality; and beliefs about the role and function of sex, pleasure, procreation and contraception. Be sure to look for particular ethnic, cultural or religious mandates about adherence to societal sexual scripts. When assessing the broader sociocultural impact, it is wise to honor the individuality of the client, maintaining the not-knowing stance that prevents premature identification of the problem, as well as stereotyping and labeling of the client. In addition, what the client has internalized from his or her culture may also vary from the cultural norm. In short, moving too quickly on some issues may be threatening to the clients, leading them to terminate therapy.

Guidelines for Taking a Sexual History

Promote Comfort and Ease

Promoting comfort begins with the physical arrangement of furniture in the office, including arranging chairs so that the couple can look at each other when they speak. If both partners sit on the same sofa, it can sometimes be difficult for them to speak to each other, and they direct conversation through the therapist. The therapist does not want the clients to develop the habit of talking to him or her or through them, but talking to each other and the therapist all at the same time. The point is to facilitate communication between the partners and when they feel uncomfortable, to help them through those points.

The couple should be comfortable in telling their story in their own way and time. Interruptions by the therapist can disrupt the client's process and concentration, and have the potential to elicit denials in behavior. Instead, the couple can be gently guided to remain on topic if they seem to be having difficulty discussing the sexual problems in their intimate relationship. The therapist should also attend to pauses, silences, gestures, tone of voice and other nonverbal cues of embarrassment or anxiety or other emotions. In such cases, the therapist is advised to routinely check in with a client and frequently ask how he or she is feeling. Another case we treated involved a professional couple referred for sex therapy. As soon as they began to talk, the wife covered her entire face with her hand.

The therapist stopped the interview to discuss her discomfort. A few minutes later she was much more comfortable discussing their sexual problem.

Fears about confidentiality may also reduce a client's comfort and level of disclosure. Reassurance about confidentiality should be offered if indicated. Moreover, the therapist needs to make every effort to understand the partners' personal and sexual self-schemas and scripts. Some clients may be reluctant to discuss sexual problem that have led to public embarrassment or being arrested in the past, such as prostitution, voyeurism or exhibitionism. These are all serious issues that must be fully addressed in session. Every effort should be made to increase clients' comfort through validation and reassurance of confidentially, unless the therapist is ethically bound to report behaviors that are coercive and compromise the safety of one partner. Even then, the therapist can join with clients in a frank discussion of the situation and potential outcomes.

Provide a Safe Environment

Set the tone by allowing and promoting an open, affirming discussion of all aspects of sexuality. Remember that sexuality is often experienced with coexisting feelings of shame, guilt and uncertainty. Create the opportunity for discovering, normalizing and reframing attractions, thoughts, feelings, fantasies and sensations. Be aware that sexuality is fluid, not binary, and individuals and couples can be distressed about variance from gender norms and roles. As Iasenza (2010) explains, sexuality is filled with unexpected incongruities and paradoxes and the therapist must allow for the safe exploration of these contradictions. Explore the meaning of the queer experience as it changes over time and within individuals and the culture. Examine your own reactions to unanticipated stories you may hear. Probably the most important factor is to provide a nonjudgmental stance. Clients frequently believe their sexual behavior is inappropriate, abnormal or deviant. The therapist should be able to listen to their statements without judgment, provide accurate information when inaccurate information is stated and explore the meaning of behaviors that cause the clients distress.

Therapist Considerations

Many elements can interfere with therapist efficacy, such as the lack of adequate comfort levels and insufficient knowledge base. Maurice (1999) contends that the main reason therapists do not ask questions about sex is because they are unprepared to deal with the answers. Additionally, fear of offending clients or prying into sensitive areas can be barriers to seeking information (Maurice, 1999; Risen, 2007). Other therapist limitations that can interfere with the adequate completion of the sex history include fear of one's own feelings, lack of self-awareness, awkwardness with sexual language, sexual ignorance and other inhibitions.

Therapist considerations such as age, gender and sexual orientation can factor into the dynamics of a sex history. For instance, therapists who experience disparity with regard to age or sexual orientation of the clients might spend too much energy managing their own anxiety instead of instilling confidence in the couple. The gender of the therapist might add to a dynamic of perceived triangulation in the therapy setting. If the therapist suspects that this is happening, it must be addressed. We often hear that therapists feel "too young" or "too different" when dealing with older or gay clients. As stated, countertransference reactions abound when working with people who have newly divergent sexual interests, emerging sexual identities or consensual kinky practices (see Iasenza, 2010). Therapists must be aware of heteronormative assumptions and biases. With information, self-awareness and experience, the therapist can expect to become comfortable discussing sexual and intimacy issues.

In providing a safe environment for the exploration of sexual feelings and behaviors, the therapist must be respectful and nonjudgmental. Nonjudgmental means being aware of one's own internal dialogue and arbitrations regarding sexual matters. The therapist must work to be self-aware and able to control the need to interject a personal bias. The therapist should expect to feel some degree of discomfort, surprise or confusion, especially when dealing with unexpected expressions of sexual behavior. If the therapist's issues are interfering with the process of attaining a client's sex history, then therapist self-reflection, supervision and sometimes psychotherapy are indicated (Ramlachan & Campbell, 2014; Risen, 2007).

Moreover, boundaries need to be constructed and enforced especially when dealing with sexual information. This might seem counterintuitive because the therapist is encouraging clients to open up and talk about sexual material; however, the therapist needs to be mindful about how much and what kind of sexual material he or she is pursuing. The clients' response must also be constantly monitored and discussed before moving from one subject to the next. Finally, the therapist must know and abide by the code of ethics proposed by his or her certifying associations (Fairburn & Cooper, 2011).

Understand One's Own Sexuality

As stated, being comfortable about one's own sexuality may be the most important aspect of talking about sex with clients. A therapist needs not have personal experience in the sexual activity under discussion in order to provide support. The therapist should be open minded and educated in order to understand and appreciate a variety of sexual experiences and acts. The therapist can gain cultural competency in sexual matters simply by being receptive to others and actively seeking out points of view from a variety of individuals. Attending a SAR (Sexual Attitude Reassessment) or other educational or experiential workshop can help the therapist become desensitized to sexual material and learn about his or her own sexuality. A Google search of unknown sexual expressions can help educate the therapist, and looking for examples of these sexual behaviors on the top 10 pornography sites can show what the behavior looks like.

Avoid Shaming

Assessment questions should be stated neutrally, without judgment, and in a matter-of-fact manner. Compare these questions: *"Have you been unfaithful?"* and *"Do you have sexual or emotionally intimate relations with others in addition to your primary partner?"* The first question has been phrased in such a way that may not be clear to the clients (what is meant by unfaithful? Do emotional affairs or cyber infidelity count?). The first question could prompt a socially preferred answer because few people believe being unfaithful is acceptable. The second question gets information that is far more accurate and does not imply a certain way to answer, thereby normalizing the client's sexual experiences. Similarly, do not suggest answers. When a client reports that his erections last "less than normal," be sure not to suggest an answer by saying something like "so, about 3 and a half minutes?" In such a case, you might be signaling that erections *should* last a particular length of time, when the reality is what is normal sexual behavior varies from person to person and with an individual over time.

Adopt a Stance of Both Never Assuming and Always Assuming

Never assume a client's sexual orientation. The use of gender-neutral language early on, such as partner instead of husband or boyfriend, will signal an openness to hear a variety of answers. Also, keep the focus on the client's sexual behaviors, not sexual orientation. For instance, men who identify as straight may also have sex with men. Once the individual feels safe in treatment, he or she will usually declare a sexual orientation, at which point the therapist should use the terms the client uses in referencing sexual partners. Additionally, do not assume the nature of a client's sexual problem based on a general demographic profile. For example, do not anticipate that a woman going through menopause is suffering from a decrease in libido or that a young man's primary problem is premature ejaculation because he says he is not able to last long enough to satisfy his partner.

Conversely, therapists should always assume that everyone does everything, even though they may not talk about it. One couple we treated appeared very conservative and came to treatment because of an affair. Later, it was learned that they were polyamorous, and he had gone off with a partner without his wife's knowledge. The earliest sex researcher, Alfred Kinsey, mastered the technique of expecting a wide variety of sexual behaviors in all of his subjects in the phrasing of his questions. By asking "How frequently do you masturbate?" as opposed to "Do you masturbate?" allows the therapist to normalize the behavior, which puts the clients at greater ease. In the event that clients are offended by a question, use the situation as an opportunity to join with them by seeking information as to what was offensive.

Finally, never assume that just because a client may be highly educated that he or she also knows much about sex or sexual problems. Two of the authors are sex therapists who have worked in a prestigious medical school and treated a number of physicians. They very quickly learned that physicians may have an excellent knowledge of the physiological features of one or more aspects of sexuality, but they generally can lack sound information regarding the psychological and emotional facets of sexuality.

Normalize Sex Talk

Taking a client's sexual history can be an opportunity for discovery and relationship building. The therapist can begin the session with a statement that he or she knows the couple is coming in to improve their sexual life and understands that getting started is difficult for most clients. The therapist can ask the couple how they feel about coming to therapy for help with a sexual problem, thus normalizing their feelings, and work to help the couple become more comfortable talking about sexual matters. Normalizing sex talk at the very beginning through a gentle, accepting, matter-of-fact style will help the clients feel more comfortable and increase their willingness to disclose sensitive information. The therapist may provide an overview of the therapeutic process at this point, allowing the clients to adjust to the situation and surroundings.

One technique that we frequently use is to simply say to the couple, "The hardest part is getting started. Talking about sex with a stranger is difficult, but it will get easier over time."

Think Systemically

As stated earlier, the therapist may experience greater success in treatment when partners are interviewed independently in addition to the conjoint sessions. Individual interviews should be conducted only for particularly sensitive areas, not for the full clinical history, and typically only if secrets or severe discomfort in disclosing information is suspected. Other circumstances such as infidelity require that the client be allowed individual time to express anger with the unfaithful partner or sadness about giving up an affair partner. See Weeks, Gambescia, and Jenkins (2003) for greater elaboration about handling secrets. Even when interviewing individually, it is important to ask about the systemic impact of the client's problems. The most basic question—"What impact has this problem had on your relationship?"—is usually the most effective. At this point, it is important for the therapist to listen for signs of criticism, defensiveness, contempt, stonewalling or disengagement, for they are strong indicators of a dysfunctional relationship (Gottman, 1994).

Typically, we interview partnered couples together for the first few sessions. As a matter of routine, the therapist can ask if they think they need individual sessions, or decide to offer individual sessions. We have learned that one area that is particularly sensitive to discuss in a conjoint format is lack of sexual desire. The partner who lacks desire may be unwilling to say how strongly they experience their lack of desire. In another case, the need to interview and treat was quite clear although the partners did not see lack of desire as their primary issue. The husband often had erectile difficulty with his wife but could have multiple escorts and other women at his home when his wife was away and never have erectile problems. He was clear that he needed to work on his sexually compulsive behavior with women and pornography before working on his sexual relationship with his wife. He lacked desire for his wife but did not perceive that to be his problem.

Finally, the client may have a disability, illness or other medical health issue, which complicates the sexual problem. For example, one client needed to take an antipsychotic medication in order to control a mental illness that resulted from Lyme's Disease. He was very distraught about the adverse effects on sexual desire and performance caused by the medication. The man and therapist had many frank discussions about the costs and benefits of reducing the medication. Eventually, a sensitive psychopharmacologist interviewed the client and we collaborated on a gradual reduction of the antipsychotic medication with the addition of a medication that augmented erections. The message here is to frankly and sensitively discuss all health related issues and be knowledgeable about your client's physical history (Weeks & Gambescia, 2000).

Conducting the Clinical Interview

Review any intake forms or other written assessment information before meeting with the clients. Next, allow each partner to talk about the problem, using the first few questions provided here. Be sure to get the most essential information before asking questions that are specific to the particular sexual dysfunction. Essential questions include the following:

- What are the reasons you are coming in? What seems to be the problem?
- Why are you seeking treatment at this time?
- What treatments or strategies have you tried already to fix this problem on your own?
- What was the result? Did some things work better than others?
- What are your goals for this therapy?
- What is your theory about this problem? (This question provides information about how each partner frames the problem. It is not intended as a factual question.)
- To what extent does this problem distress each of you?
- What impact has it had on your relationship?

Next, begin to explore more deeply the factors surrounding the main sexual problems as identified by the clients. Then, begin to elaborate on pertinent issues in each of the five domains of the Intersystem Approach (see the discussion in Chapter 1, Understanding Etiology and Treatment within the Intersystem Approach).

Interviewing for Specific Disorders

One aspect of the sex history is the attempt to uncover the presence of any problems within the individual or relationship that impact sexual functioning or satisfaction. Typically, the therapist includes questions about sexual or nonsexual *DSM-5* (American Psychiatric Association, 2013) disorders or the presence of a comorbid disorder in either partner. In such cases, it is important to determine if the symptoms have biological, organic or mixed etiologies. Additionally, are the symptoms secondary to another psychological disorder? Chapter 2 provides details on the features of each disorder; however, in this chapter we discuss specific questions that can be used to make a diagnosis and begin the process of developing a case formulation for each dysfunction.

Assessing for Sexual Desire Disorders

Male Hypoactive Sexual Desire Disorder and Female Sexual Interest/Arousal Disorder

The *DSM-5* (American Psychiatric Association, 2013) departed from previous editions in that disorders affecting sexual desire are treated differently for men and women. The term *Hypoactive Sexual Desire Disorder* was retained for men, but the terminology and diagnostic criteria for women were broadened and comingled. As such, the term *Female Sexual Interest/Arousal Disorder* addresses the fact that for women, desire and arousal are often concurrent. In this discussion we will refer to both diagnoses as *absent/low desire* for both men and women. See Gambescia and Weeks (2015) and Hall (2015) for greater elaboration on Female Sexual Interest/Arousal Disorder and Male Hypoactive Sexual Desire Disorder respectively. Weeks and Gambescia (2002) and Gambescia and Weeks (2015) proposed that positive sexual thoughts and/or fantasies are essential components of sexual desire. Another measure of sexual desire is the individual's interest in sexual activity, whether partnered or alone. For women, the process of igniting and sustaining sexual desire is more complex and dependent on numerous individual and relational variables. Nonetheless, for both genders, sexual desire is usually experienced in conjunction with sex-positive cognitions and fantasies.

Absent/low sexual desire is one of the most difficult of all sexual dysfunctions to assess and treat. A number of psychological factors are usually working together to suppress sexual desire, making the assessment of this problem time consuming, complex and involving many questions over the course of several sessions. Instead of experiencing sexual desire, the person with this problem is burdened by negative sexual thoughts, the absence of sexual fantasies, or distracting nonsexual thoughts. The negative cognitions could result from relationship discord, comorbid psychopathology, the presence of another sexual dysfunction that dampens the person's interest in sex, a history of misinformation, secrecy, trauma or other factors.

One of the most common factors identified in absent/low desire is the presence of negative sexual thoughts about the sexual partner. Once the thoughts have been identified, it will be fairly clear that they fall within two categories:

one requires individual treatment and the other, which is the result of relationship issues, necessitates couple therapy.

Another key part to the assessment of sexual desire is to ask the clients about the five domains of sexual desire described in Table 3.2. These domains of behavior give us an overview of how desire and affectional/sensual/sexual behaviors related to desire manifest in the relationship or may be absent in the relationship. The therapist inquires about five general aspects of each partner's desire:

1. Frequency of sex
2. Frequency of sexual desire
3. Degree of sexual interest
4. Context of sexual desire
5. Presence of other sexual dysfunctions of difficulties

Some typical questions to ask in order to assess these areas are these:

• Roughly, how often do you actually have sex in a week, month or year?
• How often do you feel like having sex?
• Do you believe your level of desire is too low? Too high?
• When did you first notice that you were losing your sexual desire?
• What was happening at the time that might account for the loss of desire?
• Did you lose your desire suddenly or gradually?
• What was your level of desire early in the relationship, over the course of the relationship and now?
• What medications are you taking now/since losing your desire?
• Any changes in your health?

Table 3.2 is provided as a quick reference guide for assessing the five domains of behavior regarding lack of sexual desire.

In addition to the five domains of behavior to assess for sexual desire, we also like to ask questions about the level of desire. These questions are framed in terms of a hypothetical scale from −10 to +10, with minus 10 indicating no desire or an active avoidance of sex and plus 10 being as much desire as a client can imagine (see Figure 3.1). We might ask this question regarding the client's level of desire: Do you feel desire most of the time, when the partner makes an advance or during the process of having sex?

The following questions give the clinician a more complete description of how desire or lack thereof is experienced.

• If you feel desire and it is suddenly lost, what are the circumstances? What are you thinking at the moment it is lost?
• Do you feel a lack of desire for your partner or is it for everyone?
• To what extent does your sexual desire distress you/your partner?
• What are your theory and your partner's theory for your lack of desire?

TABLE 3.2 Domains of Sexual Desire Assessment

Domain	Assessment Items
Frequency of Sex	• How often do you engage in affectionate or sexual behaviors (cuddling, kissing, holding hands, back rubs, etc.) in a week, month, or year? • How often do you actually have sex in a week, month, or year?
Frequency of Sexual Desire	• How often do you feel like having sex? • Do you feel the frequency of your wanting to have sex is a problem?
Context of Sexual Desire	• Do you ever feel sexy or sexually desirous? How often? When? With whom? • Do you ever feel desire for your partner? For someone else you know? For people you don't know personally, such as movie stars or fictional characters? • Do you feel desire for sex without it being attached to anything or any person? • What was your level of desire early in the relationship, over the course of the relationship, now? • When did you first notice that your sexual desire had changed?
Degree of Sexual Arousal and Satisfaction	• Are you happy with how often you have sex? • Do you usually enjoy having sex? Do you orgasm? • Do you feel as though you can become easily aroused (for women that would include lubrication, for men the ability to obtain and maintain an erection)? • How much time do you devote to sexual activity, including foreplay? • What do you find most pleasurable?
Presence of Other Sexual Dysfunctions or Difficulties	• Do you wish your lovemaking could be different? How so? • Does your partner seem to enjoy sex? • Do you have concerns or worries regarding sex about you or your partner? Do you think your partner has a sexual problem?

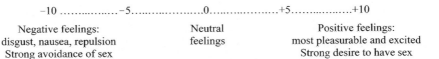

FIGURE 3.1 Sexual Desire Assessment Scale

Sexual Aversion Disorder

In *DSM-IV-TR* (American Psychiatric Association, 2000) Sexual Aversion Disorder was listed as a major sexual dysfunction. It is also listed as a major sexual dysfunction in *DSM-5* (American Psychiatric Association, 2013) but it is grouped under a diagnostic category called *Other Specified Sexual Dysfunctions*. An individual with this disorder has a strong repulsion to any kind of genital contact with a partner. Sexual Aversion Disorder (SAD) frequently has a similar etiology to absent/low desire and is more commonly seen in women than in men (Kaplan, 1987). The distress experienced is typically interpersonal, in that a client will present for treatment only after being told by a partner that there is something wrong with him or her. In short, clients with SAD usually avoid sex therapy and only come when the partner insists. The client with the aversion may be distressed by it but is so fearful of sexual contact that he or she is unlikely to seek treatment without the partner's prodding. In interviewing suspected cases of SAD, it is of utmost importance to work at the pace set by the client and build trust, for there may be a history of emotional or sexual abuse. We recommend using a scale ranging from −10 to +10 to assess both motivations for sexual encounters and feelings of aversion, disgust or repulsion when the client thinks of a sexual encounter. Depending upon the information obtained previously, the therapist would ask the client the following questions:

- Where would you generally place yourself/your partner on this scale?
- Where would you place yourself/your partner just prior to initiation of sex?
- Where would you place yourself/your partner when your partner initiates any sexual activity?
- Where would you place yourself/your partner when you think about/imagine having sex?
- Where would you place yourself/your partner during or if you engaged in sexual activity?
- Where would you place yourself/your partner when your relationship is going well?
- Where would you place yourself/your partner when your relationship is not working?
- How distressed do you feel when a sexual interaction is being initiated? How would you describe how you feel? How much anxiety, repulsion or panic do you feel, if any?

- Where would you place yourself on this scale prior to, during and after solo sex or masturbation?
- When did you notice having such strong negative feelings about sex?
- What kinds of negative messages did you receive about sex?
- What kind of traumatic, hurtful or painful experiences have you had around sex?

Hyperactive Sexual Desire/Sexual Compulsivity

Neither *DSM-IV-TR* (American Psychiatric Association, 2000) nor *DSM-5* (American Psychiatric Association, 2013) recognizes the existence of sexual addiction or sexual compulsivity despite the body of literature that exists on this topic (see the journal *Sexual Addiction and Compulsivity*). Sexual addiction is often difficult to diagnose because it may be masked by other psychiatric disorders such as anxiety, depression, bipolar illness, hypomania, obsessive-compulsive personality, narcissistic personality disorder and so on. Further, it is often comorbid with other forms of addiction such as drug and alcohol abuse and gambling. Additionally, posttraumatic stress disorder as a result of childhood or other forms of sexual abuse is often a part of the sexual compulsivity etiology.

At the basis of this classification is a presentation of out-of-control sexual thoughts, feelings and behaviors, including chronic fantasy, masturbation, recurrent infidelity, frequenting strip clubs, sex in exchange for money, extensive use of pornography, Internet-based pornography, chat room hook-ups and others. Moreover, this disorder (whatever it will be called) is extremely damaging to the individual, family, finances (due to loss of job or excess spending on the addiction), health and health of partner (due to sexually transmitted illnesses), legal consequences and so on. See Reid, Carpenter, and Lloyd (2009) for an interesting discussion of the psychological symptoms associated with hypersexual behavior. There are numerous screening tests for sexual compulsivity, many based on the work of Carnes (1991, 2005). The following questions can be used when beginning to assess for sexual addiction:

- Do you often find yourself preoccupied with sexual thoughts?
- Have bad things happened because of your sexual behavior?
- Do you try unsuccessfully to manage your sexual behavior?
- When you have sex, do you feel depressed afterward?
- Do you enjoy doing risky things such as speeding, doing drugs or stealing?
- Do you practice safe sex in every sexual encounter?
- When you are stressed or worried, do you find yourself thinking about sex or rehearsing a sexual fantasy in your mind?
- Have you increased the number or degree of risk of your sexual acts over time?
- Have you engaged in unsafe or risky sex even though you knew it could cause harm?

- How much time would you say you spend thinking about or pursuing sexual encounters?
- Have you neglected important social, occupational or recreational activities because you were thinking about or pursing sex?
- How much time do you spend viewing pornography? Are you or your partner concerned about this amount of time? Is watching pornography done in secret?
- Do you feel you are constantly seeking sex in some form?
- How often have you used sexual services such as a strip club, online chatting about sex, massage parlors, swingers club, escorts, prostitutes or anything else that fulfills your need for sex? Does your established partner know about any of these activities?

Erectile Disorder

The term Erectile Disorder (ED) has replaced Erectile Dysfunction in the *DSM-5* (American Psychiatric Association, 2013). Erectile disorder (ED) is the persistent inhibition of a man's sexual arousal and erectile capacity, precluding his ability to engage in satisfying sexual experiences. The psychological consequences of ED are considerable, impeding the man's self-esteem, confidence and overall quality of life. Over time, this disorder can contribute to relationship dissatisfaction and the avoidance of sexual activity. Partners of men with ED often report diminished sexual interest, confidence and satisfaction.

The etiology of ED can include multiple layers of psychogenic, relational and situational elements. Moreover, as the man ages, organic factors progressively influence the clinical presentation; thus, a comprehensive bio-psychosocial assessment is essential. All aspects of the man's life, including his intimate relationship, need to be considered when treating ED.

In assessing for ED, it is important to have the results of a recent physical examination by a physician or urologist who specializes in the etiology of sexual dysfunction. As men grow older, the chances of medical problems and medication causing greater interference with erectile ability increase, so establishing the etiology is critical. The following questions help the therapist begin to understand some of the fundamental causes.

The diagnostic criteria for ED specify that at least one of following must be present on almost all or all (75%–100%) occasions of sexual activity (American Psychiatric Association, 2013):

1. Distinct difficulty in obtaining an erection during sexual activity
2. Noticeable difficulty in maintaining an erection until the completion of sexual activity
3. A marked decrease in erectile rigidity

A thorough description of etiology and assessment has been described in Gambescia and Weeks (2015) and Weeks and Gambescia (2000). Initial questions would include these:

- How long have you had problems with erections?
- Describe the erectile difficulty.
- How often are you able to get an erection during sexual activity?
- How confident are you that you can get and keep an erection to the completion of sex?
- Do you have erectile difficulty in particular situations?
- Are you satisfied with the hardness of your erection?
- Are you satisfied with the overall sexual experience?
- Are your erections hard enough for penetration?
- Is sexual stimulation with your partner adequate?
- Was the onset of problems sudden or gradual?
- Do you have erections in the morning, upon awakening or during sleep?
- Do you have erectile difficulties during solo sexual activity?
- Is it easier to maintain an erection in certain positions?
- During penetration, how difficult is it to maintain the erection to completion?
- Are you sometimes able to get a firm erection but then lose it shortly after penetration?
- Have you seen a doctor or urologist for this problem?
- Do you have any problems with your heart or circulation?
- Any diabetes or neurological problems?
- Has there been any trauma to your pelvis (including extensive bike riding)?
- Are you taking any medications?

Once etiology has been determined, the following questions will assist in assessing the level of performance anxiety and any related dysfunctions:

- Do you try to will yourself to have a strong erection? What happens when you do this?
- What thoughts do you now have about being able to keep an erection?
- Do you feel anxious about losing it?
- How do you react to losing your erection? How does your partner react?
- Has this problem lead to avoiding sex with your partner?

Female Sexual Arousal Disorder (FSAD)

The category, Female Sexual Arousal Disorder (FSAD), used in *DSM-IV-TR* (American Psychiatric Association, 2000) was eliminated in the *DSM-5* (American Psychiatric Association, 2013). In its place, two diagnostic categories were combined to form the diagnosis of *Female Sexual Interest/Arousal Disorder*. This new disorder was developed because of more recent information about the female sexual response. In particular, sexual appetite and fantasy are present for some women but not necessarily prior to sexual activity; thus, interest and arousal can occur *during* sexual activity. Additionally, sexual desire and arousal can occur simultaneously for women. Finally, the intensity of sexual desire is not necessarily the most compelling aspect of sexual engagement for all women. Relational sex is dependent on contextual and interpersonal variables that can create interest in or receptivity to sexual activity.

In this volume, we have kept the discussion of these diagnoses separate because the majority of clinical literature on these disorders has been separate until now. As such, there is a body of information about desire and another about arousal. It will take some time before articles begin to appear which do not separate the two.

With FSAD, the desire for sexual intimacy is present, yet there is a persistent or recurrent inability to attain or to maintain sexual arousal until completion of the sexual activity.

The clinician must be sensitive to relational and organic factors, such as menopause, that can potentially interfere with sexual arousal. FSAD causes personal and/or interpersonal distress.

Most women, as well as most clinicians, have difficulty differentiating problems of arousal from problems of desire. Furthermore, lack of sufficient sexual arousal may be the result of inadequate intensity, focus and duration of physical or psychological stimulation (Graham, 2009).

FSAD is highly age related, frequently occurring in menopausal and post-menopausal women and arising from both physiological as well as psychological conditions (Sims & Meana, 2010). It can be comorbid with absent/low desire and anorgasmia, as well as a range of diagnosable conditions, particularly depression. As such, it is important to assess for hormonal, cardiovascular, neurological and psychiatric conditions. Also important is a detailed understanding of why the woman is currently seeking treatment; often, her level of distress over the problem may be less than her partner's level of distress, complicating her motivation to undergo treatment. In addition to the questions listed for absent/low desire, the following questions probe the client's subjective understanding of her state of arousal:

- Are you taking any medications or using any nonprescription substances?
- When did your arousal problem begin? What was different then?
- What sexual activities or kinds of touching do you find sexually arousing?
- If your partner provided more of the kinds of touching that you enjoyed, would you still have a problem with sexual arousal?
- Do you become excited or turned on mentally as well as physically during sexual stimulation?
- Do you have difficulty staying focused during sexual activity? If yes, what interferes?
- Do you experience changes in your pulse rate and respiration when stimulated sexually?

- Do you experience pleasurable sensations (feelings of warmth, tingling, and increased sensitivity) in your clitoris and vagina with sexual stimulation?
- Do you become lubricated or wet with sexual stimulation?
- How often is intercourse difficult or painful because your vagina feels dry and tight?
- Do you need to use a vaginal lubricant for intercourse?
- What kinds of stimulation (hand-genital, mouth-genital, genital-genital, sex toy-genital) are most pleasurable?
- Do you feel comfortable talking with your partner about what you like?
- When you feel wet, do you also feel sexually aroused?
- When did you first start noticing that you didn't feel sexually aroused?
- What kinds of negative sexual messages and/or traumatic, hurtful or painful sexual experiences have you had?

Persistent Genital Arousal Disorder

Persistent Genital Arousal Disorder (PGAD) is a rare, complex and perplexing condition characterized by high levels of intrusive, undesired and spontaneous genital arousal in the absence of sexual interest. The arousal can be unrelenting or intermittent, accompanied by genital engorgement and not relieved through orgasm (Goldmeier & Leiblum, 2008). This disorder is extremely frustrating and distressing to women. Many physicians are not aware of PGAD and there are no empirically validated treatments, although physicians often attempt to remedy the symptoms through pelvic floor physiotherapy, pudendal or clitoral nerve blocks, local anesthetics, medications or surgery. The etiology is believed to be mostly organic and treatment is dictated by the nature of the cause (Komisaruk & Lee, 2012). The symptoms can be triggered by physical stimulation, sexual activity or anxiety. See Goldmeier, Sadeghi-Nejed and Facelle (2014) for a thorough discussion of assessment and treatments for PGAD.

Assessing for Orgasm and Ejaculation Disorders

Premature (Early) Ejaculation

Premature Ejaculation (PE) is the most commonly reported male sexual disorder in every country of the world (Namavar & Robati, 2011). According to the *DSM-5*, there are three diagnostic criteria:

1. Consistent ejaculation occurs within 1 minute or less of vaginal penetration
2. PE has persisted for at least six months and has been experienced 75%–100% of the time
3. PE results in clinically significant distress, sexual frustration, dissatisfaction or tension between partners (Graziottin & Althof, 2011)

Most often, men experience PE as a result of excitement, inexperience and penile hypersensitivity. PE can become a conditioned response. Anxiety about climaxing too quickly and over-focusing on the woman's pleasure can perpetuate the sexual dysfunction. The diagnostic criteria for PE involve endurance during intercourse and not other sexual activities. Another way to define PE is if ejaculation happens before it is desired. Since PE involves the inability to control when ejaculation occurs, assessment should focus more on the subjective experience of controlling one's ejaculation rather than the actual length of time between penetration and ejaculation.

PE may begin from the first sexual experience or be acquired later in life. Some of the psychological factors involved can include anxiety disorders, especially social phobias. Genetic and physiological factors may include a genetic predisposition, dopamine and serotonin transportation, thyroid disease, prostatitis and so on. PE can become comorbid with ED if frequent attempts at sexual activity are disappointing and anxiety provoking, particularly if the partner is distressed. Some assessment questions include the following:

- Do you think you ejaculate too quickly? Does your partner share your belief?
- How often do you or your partner think you ejaculate too quickly?
- Does your partner pressure you to last longer during intercourse? Has she or he ever compared you to other men?
- When did you first notice you had a problem with ejaculatory control?
- Do you usually ejaculate within 1 minute of penetration during intercourse?
- Have there been times when your control has been better? If so, under what conditions?
- When did your inability to delay ejaculation first become a problem?
- Have you had any significant health changes?
- Do you believe that the force and volume of your ejaculate are appropriate?
- Do you ever have pain or discomfort upon ejaculation?
- How do you react when you ejaculate too quickly? How does your partner react?
- Have you ever become panicked at the thought of ejaculating too quickly? Are there other times when you feel panicky?
- How much pressure do you put on yourself to not ejaculate so quickly?
- Are you/your partner less satisfied with sexual experiences that culminate too quickly?
- Do thoughts that you won't last long enough keep you from engaging in sexual activity?
- Does your partner's belief that you won't last long enough stop your partner from engaging in sexual activity with you?
- How long does your partner wish to have intercourse? Does your partner have orgasms with intercourse? If so, about how long does it take?
- Have you had this problem with every partner with whom you have had sex?

- Do you think you ejaculate too quickly during masturbation or when your partner is stimulating you orally or with her or his hand?
- What do you try to do to slow down how quickly you ejaculate?
- Do you actually try to ejaculate quickly in order to end the experience?
- What medications or substances are you using?

Female Orgasmic Disorder

In Female Orgasmic Disorder (FOD), the woman is unable to experience orgasm even though she receives adequate sexual stimulation (intensity, focus and duration). Another presentation of FOD is the decrease of pleasure or sensation, or increased difficulty in reaching orgasm. These symptoms are distressing; they must be present most of the time when sexual activity occurs and they have been present for at least 6 months (American Psychiatric Association, 2013). FOD can be lifelong as opposed to acquired and generalized as opposed to situational.

FOD is often comorbid with other sexual disorders, such a lack of interest or arousal. The etiologic factors associated with FOD are varied and related to the woman's self-esteem, capacity for experiencing pleasure, comfort with her body and knowledge of what is pleasing to her. Relational issues can interfere with a woman's ability to be vulnerable and sexually expressive with her partner. For instance, the lack of trust or anger can interfere with a woman's ability to relax and experience orgasm (Goldhammer & McCabe, 2011). As with all sexual difficulties, a sexual problem in the partner may contribute to FOD. Negative introjects from the family of origin and a negative sexual script will predispose a woman to experiencing sexual inhibitions that will adversely impact her capacity for orgasm. Contextual, cultural, religious, socioeconomic and other hassles of daily living can inhibit and interfere with a woman's sexual capacity, particularly her capacity to experience orgasm. Some cases of FOD may have an organic basis, such as diabetes, vaginal atrophy, multiple sclerosis, spinal cord injuries or medication usage of substances such as serotonin-based antidepressants. In many cases of FOD, the etiology can be a mix of organic and psychogenic factors. It is useful to assess the cognitive-affective and sensory elements of sexual pleasure, not just the physiological responses women may believe are necessary for orgasm (McCabe, 2015). Assessment questions that provide a more detailed and subjective picture of the woman's sexuality include these:

- How did you learn to experience sensual or sexual sensations?
- Do you typically enjoy sensual/sexual experiences?
- When and how did you learn to engage in solo sexual activity?
- Have you ever in your life experienced an orgasm?
- In the past could you have orgasms more easily or at all?
- How has your orgasmic ability changed over time?

- What forms of stimulation do you use to become aroused and achieve orgasm?
- How difficult is it for you to achieve orgasm through manual stimulation (vibrator, with hand, oral) and during intercourse?
- How much stimulation and what type of stimulation do you typically need to become sexually aroused? To orgasm? What do you feel with this form of stimulation? What are your subjective sensations?
- Do you feel sexually satisfied if you don't orgasm?
- Do you feel you are disappointing your partner if you don't orgasm?
- Do you feel that you sometimes get close to orgasm but can't quite get there or that you are stopping an orgasm from happening?
- Has the level of sexual pleasure you experience changed over time?
- When you have intercourse, about how long does it last? Do you feel you must have an orgasm for yourself? For your partner?
- If you can achieve orgasm, what percent of the time can you do so if that is what you want?
- Do you pressure yourself to orgasm? Does your partner pressure you to have an orgasm?
- Do you feel your orgasm is yours or is it for the sake of your partner?
- What is your goal for this therapy? How would you like to be able to orgasm if that is your goal?
- At what age did you begin to stimulate yourself? Did you have an orgasm?
- If you have never had an orgasm, what do you imagine will happen when you do? What do you imagine it will feel like?
- What are your beliefs about self-touch or bringing yourself to orgasm?
- Have you ever tried using a vibrator to produce an orgasm?
- Do you find that you can orgasm with some partners and not with others? What makes it different?
- In your culture, are women expected to experience sexual pleasure and have orgasms?
- Do you simply lack sexual desire?
- Did you receive any negative sexual messages about orgasm? Have you had any traumatic, hurtful or painful sexual experiences?
- What's your theory about why you don't have orgasms?
- Are you taking any medications or have any medical problems? Do you know if your hormonal levels are normal?

Genito-Pelvic Pain/Penetration Disorder

Roughly 15% of American women report recurrent pain during intercourse (American Psychiatric Association, 2013). Skin conditions, menopausal changes in the vagina, infections, irritations and other factors can cause pain in the vulva (external genital organs of the female) or the vaginal opening. There are numerous terms used to describe vulvar pain. *Provoked Vestibulodynia* refers to pain around the opening of the vagina in response to touch (whether it is sexual or nonsexual touch). In some cases, pelvic floor tension contributes to the pain. The term used to describe the tensing of the vaginal muscles and pelvic floor is *Vaginismus*. Another term used to describe painful intercourse is *Dyspareunia*. The diagnosis Genito-Pelvic Pain/Penetration Disorder (GPPPD) incorporates these conditions and others into a general category. The diagnostic criteria for GPPPD include persistent or recurrent difficulties for at least 6 months with one or more of the following:

- Inability to have vaginal intercourse/penetration
- Marked vulvovaginal or pelvic pain during vaginal intercourse/penetration attempts
- Marked fear or anxiety either about vulvovaginal or pelvic pain during vaginal penetration
- Marked tensing or tightening of the pelvic floor muscles during attempted vaginal penetration
- Clinically significant distress or impairment

The pain wreaks havoc on sex, causing or reinforcing sexual dysfunction, negative attitudes, avoidant behaviors, relationship discord and a decline in self-esteem. The factors discussed previously augment the experience of pain (Sims & Meana, 2010). Readers should consult the chapter on this topic by Meana, Maykut, and Fertel (2015) in the recent publication of *Systemic Sex Therapy*. Typically, the etiology is a combination of physical and psychological factors. Appropriate questions for women experiencing these factors include the following:

- When did you first notice pain with intercourse?
- Do you experience genital pain at other times?
- Was anything out of the ordinary happening at the time, such as depression, anxiety, grief, stress and so on?
- Describe what happens when you attempt any type of penetration.
- What do you feel with digital penetration (a finger), tampon, a penis or other object?
- What exactly do you feel? Is it a burning, stretching, tearing or other type of sensation?
- Where do you feel the sensation? Is it around the vaginal opening or deep inside?
- Have you seen a gynecologist for this problem? If not, why not? What did he or she find? Have you had vaginal infections, an accident causing pain or any other kind of pain in the genital region that didn't result from penetration?
- How long have you had this problem? Has it changed over time?
- Have you ever experienced any kind of sexual trauma, especially rape or incest?

- Can you sometimes have intercourse without pain or other types of penetration without pain or discomfort?
- To what extent are you afraid your partner will hurt you during sex?
- Have you had sex with anyone else without pain?
- On a scale of 1 to 10, with 1 being little pain and 10 being great pain, how fearful do you feel before engaging in some type of penetration (specify types)?
- Are you able to become less anxious or relax after penetration?
- Are you usually lubricated prior to penetration? Have you used lubricants? What types?
- Do you find that you avoid sexual interactions because of the fear of pain?
- Can you think of any negative consequence of having intercourse (e.g., fear of pregnancy, getting diseases, losing control, religious reason)?
- What impact has this problem had on your relationship?
- Does your partner have a sexual/medical problem? Are you afraid that having sex will make the problem worse?
- What is sexual communication like in your relationship?
- Does your partner want you to have sexual pleasure?
- Does your partner want sex much more than you? Has your partner pressured you into having sex frequently?
- How do you feel about your body? Do you think you are sexually attractive? Do you feel your partner is attracted to you?
- Did you receive negative messages about having intercourse?
- Why are you coming to treatment at this particular time?

Most general gynecologists are not well trained in making a differential diagnosis and the therapist can only guess what might be the actual problem. The therapist will need to find a specialist in the treatment of GPPPD. Additionally, a pelvic floor physiotherapist may be incorporated into the treatment team.

Conclusion

Intersystem assessment is a multifaceted and flowing procedure. There is an initial assessment designed to give an overview of the problem. As treatment proceeds, additional questions are asked based on what appear to be missing pieces of the puzzle, reactions to homework and other sensual and sexual activities. Remember that all the disorders described in this chapter are much more complex than the questions reflect. Additionally, the questions mentioned are only a portion of those that can and should be used. The therapist can use more general questions to initiate a trail of inquiry, probing further with further questions that derive from the replies in order to obtain as complete a picture of the presenting problem as possible. The client's answers to the questions provided in this chapter are best seen as a point of departure for additional questions. Once you have an idea about the primary factors involved in the disorder, you can refer to *Systemic Sex Therapy* (Hertlein, Weeks, & Gambescia, 2015) in order to develop additional questions related to those etiological concerns. Additionally, you may need to search the literature and refer to the other major texts in the field of sex therapy.

References

American Psychiatric Association (APA). (2000). *Diagnostic and statistical manual of mental disorders* (4th ed., text rev.). Washington, DC: Author.

American Psychiatric Association (APA). (2013). *Diagnostic and statistical manual of mental disorders* (5th ed.). Washington, D.C.: Author.

Berthelot, N., Godbout, N., Hébert, M., Goulet, M., & Bergeron S. (2014). Prevalence and correlates of childhood sexual abuse in adults consulting for sexual problems. *Journal of Sex & Marital Therapy, 40*(5), 434–443.

Carnes, P. (1991). *Don't call it love: Recovery from sexual addiction.* New York: Bantam.

Carnes, P. (2005). *Out of the shadow: Starting sexual and relationship recovery* (2nd ed.). Carefree, AZ: Gentle Path Publishing.

Crenshaw, T., & Goldberg, G. (1996). *Sexual pharmacology.* New York: W.W. Norton.

Fairburn, G.F., & Cooper, Z. (2011). Therapist confidence, therapist quality, and therapist training. *Journal of Behavior Research & Therapy, 49*(6–7), 373–378.

Gambescia, N., & Weeks, G.R. (2015). Systemic treatment of Erectile Disorder. In K. Hertlein, G. Weeks, & N. Gambescia (Eds.), *Systemic sex therapy* (2nd ed.) (pp. 72–89). New York: Routledge.

Goldhammer, D., & McCabe, M. (2011). A qualitative exploration of the meaning and experience of sexual desire among partnered women. *The Canadian Journal of Human Sexuality, 20*, 19–29.

Goldmeier, D., & Leiblum, S. (2008). Interaction of organic and psychological factors in persistent genital arousal disorder in women: A report of six cases. *International Journal of STD and AIDS, 19*, 488–90.

Goldmeier, D., Sadeghi-Nejed, H., & Facelle, T.M. (2014). Persistent genital arousal disorder. In K. Hall and Y. Binik (Eds.), *Principles and practice of sex therapy* (5th ed.) (pp. 263–279). New York: Guilford Press.

Gottman, J.M. (1994). *What predicts divorce? The relationship between marital process and marital outcomes.* Hillsdale, NJ: Erlbaum.

Graham, C. (2009). The DSM diagnostic criteria for Female Sexual Arousal Disorder. *Archives of Sexual Behavior, 39*(2), 240–255. doi:10.1007/s10508-009-9535-1

Graziottin, A., & Althof, S. (2011). What does premature ejaculation mean to the man, the woman, and the couple? *The Journal of Sexual Medicine, 8*(4), 304–309.

Hall, K. (2015). Male hypoactive sexual desire disorder. In K. Hertlein, G. Weeks, & N. Gambescia (Eds.), *Systemic sex therapy* (2nd ed.) (pp. 55–89). New York: Routledge.

Hamilton, L.D., & Julian, A.M. (2014). The relationship between daily hassles and sexual function in men and women. *Journal of Sex & Marital Therapy, 40*(5), 379–395.

Hertlein, K., Weeks, G., & Gambescia, N. (Eds.). (2015). *Systemic sex therapy* (2nd ed.). New York: Routledge.

Iasenza, S. (2010). What is queer about sex? Expanding sexual frames in theory and practice. *Family Process, 49*(3), 291–308.

Kaplan, H.S. (1987). *Sexual aversion, sexual phobias and panic disorder.* New York: Brunner/Mazel.

Komisaruk, B., & Lee, H. (2012). Prevalence of sacral spinal (Tarlov) cysts in persistent genital arousal disorder. *Journal of Sexual Medicine, 9,* 2047–2056. doi:10.1111/j.1743-6109.2012.02765.x

Mark, K.P., & Jozkowski, K.N. (2013).The mediating role of sexual and nonsexual communication between relationship and sexual satisfaction in a sample of college-age heterosexual couples. *Journal of Sex & Marital Therapy, 39*(5), 410–427. doi:10.1080/00 92623X.2011.644652

Maurice,W.L. (1999). *Sexual medicine in primary care.* St. Louis: Mosby.

McCabe, M.P. (2015). Female orgasmic disorder. In K. Hertlein, G.Weeks, & N. Gambescia (Eds.), *Systemic sex therapy* (2nd ed.) (pp. 171–190). New York: Routledge.

Meana, M., Maykut, C., & Fertel, E. (2015). Painful intercourse: Genito-Pelvic Pain/ Penetration Disorder. In K. Hertlein, G. Weeks, & N. Gambescia (Eds.), *Systemic sex therapy* (2nd ed.) (pp. 191–210). New York: Routledge.

Namavar, M.R., & Robati, R. (2011). Removal of foreskin remnants in circumcised adults for treatment of premature ejaculation. *Urology Annals, 3*(2), 87–92. doi:10.4103/0974-7796.82175

Nichols, M. (2006). Psychotherapeutic issues with "kinky" clients: Clinical problems, yours and theirs. *Journal of Homosexuality, 50*(2/3), 281–300.

Phelps, K.W., Jones, A.B., & Payne, R.A. (2015). The interplay between mental and sexual health. In K. Hertlein, G. Weeks, & N. Gambescia (Eds.), *Systemic sex therapy* (2nd ed.) (pp. 255–276). New York: Routledge.

Ramlachan, P., & Campbell, M.M. (2014). An integrative treatment model for patient with sexual dysfunctions. *South African Medical Journal, 104*(6), n p.

Reid, R., Carpenter, B., & Lloyd, T. (2009). Assessing psychological symptom patterns of patients seeking help for hypersexual behavior. *Sexual and Relationship Therapy, 24*(1), 47–63. http://dx.doi.org/10.1080/14681990802702141

Rellini, A.H., & Meston, C.M. (2011). Sexual self-schemas, sexual dysfunction, and the sexual responses of women with a history of childhood sexual abuse. *Archive of Sexual Behaviors, 40,* 351–362.

Risen, C. (2007). How to do a sexual health assessment. In L. VandeCreek, F. Peterson, & J. Bley (Eds.), *Innovations in clinical practice: Focus on sexual health* (pp. 19–33). Sarasota, FL: Professional Resource Press.

Sims, K., & Meana, M. (2010). Why did passion wane? A qualitative study of married women's attributions for declines in sexual desire. *Journal of Sex and Marital Therapy, 36*(4), 360–380.

Weeks, G., & Fife, S. (2014). *Couples in treatment.* New York: Routledge.

Weeks, G., & Gambescia, N. (2000). *Erectile dysfunction: Integrating couple therapy, sex therapy, and medical treatment.* New York: W.W. Norton.

Weeks, G., & Gambescia, N. (2002). *Hypoactive sexual desire: Integrating couple and sex therapy.* New York: W.W. Norton.

Weeks, G.R., Gambescia, N., Jenkins, R. (2003). *Treating infidelity.* New York: W.W. Norton.

Weeks, G., & Treat, S. (1992). *Couples in treatment: Techniques and approaches for effective practice.* Philadelphia, PA: Brunner/Mazel.

4

THE SEXUAL GENOGRAM IN ASSESSMENT

Introduction

A genogram is a graphic illustration of a family map or tree portraying family members and the relationships among them. Typically, the diagram involves three or four generations and uses symbols and other codes to depict domestic patterns. Specifically, the genogram tracks the intergenerational transmission of relationship themes. Since the genogram's introduction into family therapy, other clinicians and authors have adapted it to focus on specific areas in a client's life, including genograms that focus on patterns of money through the family (Mumford & Weeks, 2003), spirituality (Frame, 2000; Hodge, 2001) and cultural issues (Shellenberger et al., 2007).

Function of the Sexual Genogram

The sexual genogram is a focused version of the genogram that specifically relates to gender, romantic love, attachment, intimacy, communication, gender orientation and other themes associated with sexuality (DeMaria, Weeks, & Hof, 1999). It is an extremely useful assessment tool because individual patterns regarding love, sex and intimacy can be viewed within the larger contexts of the couple's relationship, families of origin, previous relationships and so on. Often, family secrets such as hidden pregnancies, affairs, abortions, sexual trauma and sexual compulsivity are chronicled. Additionally, children from the present or prior partnerships are included, with a concentration on how intergenerational legacies can affect them.

Frequently, couples that present with sexual issues are caught in a cycle of blame, disappointment, helplessness and pessimism. The sexual genogram is a therapeutic tool that increases the informational lens beyond the individual or couple to incorporate an understanding of the intergenerational forces behind the current issue. The greater background provides history and opportunity for continued exploration of sexual behavior, sexual attraction, sexual self-identification and sexual preferences, among others. The sexual genogram is embedded within the larger theory of Intersystem assessment, which emphasizes motivation to change, empathy and optimism.

Hof and Berman's (1986) original conceptualization included several areas of concentration; among these was the transmission of overt and covert messages regarding sex, gender roles and intimacy. The therapist concentrates on how partners communicate about intimacy and sex, and facilitates discussions with open-ended questions. There is always dialogue about missing family information and sexual secrets. Partners are encouraged to discuss their reactions to the other's portion of the genogram or to embellish or refine the final product—although it is never really finished. Finally, use of the genogram allows clients to explore wishes about how their sexual histories could be different. In Table 4.1, we offer clusters of questions related to gender as proposed by Hof and Berman (1986).

TABLE 4.1 Gender Genogram Questions

	Assessment Items
Family Beliefs about Being a Man or a Woman	• What does the family believe about what men and women should do in the world? • Does this change over the life cycle? • What are family beliefs about the roles of men and women in marriage? • What defines masculinity and femininity? • What do you have to do or be to become an adult man or woman in the family? • What are the family beliefs about money? Who earns it? Who controls it? Who spends it? Who saves it? • Is one gender considered superior to the other? On what basis?
Family Patterns of Relationships	• What are the patterns of relationships in your family in terms of closeness or distance; showing emotions; taking, giving or sharing power? • Do men and women show their needs for closeness and distance differently? • Do relationships generally tend to be equal?
Couple Relationship Patterns	• What are the patterns of affairs, divorces, abandonment, loyalty and sacrifice by men and women in the family? • Discuss family honor and shame. • Who are the family heroes and heroines? For what are they honored? Are there more men or women who are honored? • Are the family villains male or female? What are their crimes?

(Continued)

TABLE 4.1 Continued

	Assessment Items
Family Impact on Current Gender Behavior	• How close do you come to fulfilling your family's expectations for your gender? • How have you tried to conform or rebel against these expectations? • What positive or negative effects have these expectations had on your life? • How have you struggled to overcome the negative effects? • If you are married or in a serious relationship, how close do you and your partner come to meeting expectations of marriages, of being a husband or wife? • How have family expectations of men and women affected your relationship? • Under what circumstances do you have the most positive image of yourself in your relationship? The most negative? • In what ways does your partner live up to your ideal wife, husband or partner?
Peer Expectations	• How have the standards of your peer group concerning male and female roles affected your life? • Have there been different peer groups with different standards over the years to which you have related? How have you dealt with the pressure to conform to these standards? • Which standards do you consider desirable or undesirable? • How is your self-image affected if you fail to attain these standards?
Cultural Expectations	• How has your culture affected your sexual expression? • Who were your idols growing up (real or fictional)? • What did they model as desirable male or female qualities? • What effect did these models have on your expectations of relationships? • What impact are they having on your current relationships? • What is the effect of mass media on your ideas about male and female roles and your current relationship?

Issues related to romantic love, attachment and culture could also be assessed through the sexual genogram. Romance involves physiologic arousal, sexual longing, intense focus on the loved one and a particular kind of idealization. The question of how in the family one knew one was loved and what one was loved for may be central to a greater understanding of the complexity of the couple relationship. Culture provides the lens through which expectations, feelings and other dimensions of sex and intimacy are expressed. Attachment behaviors and styles are initially formed in the family of origin and later consolidated in adulthood. Only recently have researchers started to investigate the relationship between attachment style and sex drive, sexuality, fidelity, infidelity and sexual problems (Burchell & Ward, 2011; Treger & Sprecher, 2011).

Belous, Timm, Chee, and Whitehead (2012) expanded the scope of the sexual genogram to incorporate more contemporary issues about the diversity of gender expression; sexual attraction; sexual orientation; privilege of one group over another; and gay, lesbian, bisexual and transgender issues. Additionally, they emphasize the use of a sexual timeline, which is a graphic illustration listing important sexual events for successive years within a person's life. Creating this chronology allows each partner to track consistencies and changes in sexual development over time.

Constructing the Sexual Genogram

Therapists and clients can (and should) work collaboratively in the psychotherapy setting to develop and discuss the genogram. In part, the generation of a genogram in clinical practice with the therapist present creates more opportunity for joining, since the disclosures made about one's family will likely place a client in a vulnerable position (Beck, 1987). Additionally, each partner can continue to expand the genogram at home, compare and discuss additions and changes and return to the therapy setting with an edited document.

The therapist works from a sexual genogram outline or a sequence of carefully constructed questions that move from open ended to closed ended, and from least threatening to most threatening. By threatening we mean questions that might be more embarrassing, shameful, secretive and so on. The clients and therapist may elect to write on a large writing tablet or take notes on a smaller genogram form for use during sessions. Additionally, the couple might prefer working together at home and/or refining the genogram in the office. The sexual genogram should be developed, updated or changed over time.

Frequently, the therapist will encourage the partners to discuss sexual genogram material with family members, ask questions for clarification or initiate conversations about content relevant to their situation. Clinicians should allow for discussion of fears and apprehensions during the therapy session about how to approach other family members around such a sensitive topic. It should be suggested that the client approach sexual material gradually and respectfully after explaining the rationale for the conversation. Processing of the information gained from family contacts should occur during conjoint therapy sessions so that information, insights and new perspectives gained from the conversations with family members can be reflected on and assimilated. It is also useful to note the other partner's reaction to the new information.

It is also essential for therapists in training to construct and understand their personal sexual genograms. This sexual exploration and self-understanding is crucial for anyone working with individuals, couples and families around sexual issues. In addition to greater self-knowledge, the therapist will gain an in vivo appreciation of the complexity of this project, especially as it involves other family members, and the feelings that can emerge. Unresolved problems can be discussed with the supervisor and may require referral to a therapist.

Organization

Hof and Berman (1986) suggest a stepwise approach to conducting a sexual genogram:

Step 1

Discuss the role of the intergenerational process in fostering early learning and the development of attitudes and beliefs about sexuality, family scripts and loyalties. As partners perceive the importance of considering the impact of the family of origin on their interpersonal relationships and sexual behavior, they will begin to see how intergenerational messages have hindered or disabled their sexual functioning. As a result of this awareness, motivation to change increases, blaming is decreased, empathy increases and optimism is fostered.

Step 2

Introduce the family genogram (which covers three generations) as a way to map cross-generational behavioral concerns and patterns.

Step 3

Create the sexual genogram, showing the names and ages of all family members and citing specific dates of significant life events. Make marginal notations regarding significant life events, feelings, thoughts and dreams. Use lines, symbols and colors to identify feelings, alliances, boundaries, closeness, distance and other relevant factors. Personal creativity is encouraged along with the use of resources such as family pictures to tap into early and forgotten memories.

Step 4

Ask each partner to discuss the sexual genogram and answer the questions (provided in the next section) in a free-flowing manner. After exploring meanings, insights and ideas gained, decide which issues will benefit from further explorations directly with other family members.

Step 5

After working on the sexual genogram in sessions, the partners are helped to prepare to discuss some of the genogram material with family members. Talking to family members about sensitive material can generate fear and apprehension; for that reason, clients should be given the opportunity to discuss these feelings prior to making contact with family members. If possible, face-to-face meetings are preferable, with the caveat that sexual material should be approached gradually and respectfully after covering other historical issues. The emphasis is on enabling family members to tell and hear each other's stories, gather information and discover family scripts or legacies of an intergenerational nature. This new knowledge may facilitate a new understanding of current behavior.

After family contact, clients meet in a conjoint therapy session to integrate meanings, insights and ideas from the exercises. Invite the partners to engage in a reflective review of the total process, as well as the couple's sexual genogram and the sexual intergenerational genogram, to see what new perspectives have emerged that may foster greater appreciation, empathy and objectivity regarding their current sexual beliefs, feelings and behaviors.

Potential Genogram Questions

The following questions are grouped into three broad content areas. The questions are structurally designed to be general, open ended, and lead to further, more focused inquiry into a particular content area, depending on the client's response. Many inquiries can be asked in the conjoint format but some questions should be discussed in private sessions. It is likely that because of the sensitive content, a person might not be honest and forthcoming in the presence of the partner.

General Questions

This group of queries is designed to generate information about general sexuality, sexual scripting, love maps, re-creating parents' patterns, romantic love, family messages, reproductive issues and cultural messages. See Hof and Berman (1986) and Berman (1999) for further elaboration.

- How did you learn about sex? Parents? School? Friends? Media?
- What were the hidden or unspoken messages regarding sex in your family?
- What was your parent's relationship like? How close did they appear to be? What did affection between your parents look like?
- Who in your life most influenced your views about sexuality?
- What was discussed about conception, pregnancy or abortion?
- What role did religion/culture play in shaping your sexual values? Did anyone else influence the development of your sexual values?
- What were the secrets in your family regarding sexuality or intimacy (e.g., having sex, sexual abuse, incest, unwanted pregnancies)? Who knew the secrets?
- Do you still have secrets as an adult?
- How did you learn about self-stimulation (masturbation)? What were the messages, if any, about sex and pleasure in your family?

- Were you ever caught during self-stimulation? How did you feel?
- Did anything upsetting ever happen to you regarding sex?
- What was your first sexual experience like?
- What would you like to change about your sexual history?

Gender Questions

The next group of questions focuses on gender, gender roles, sexual attraction, sexual orientation, comfort and discomfort with sexual orientation, gender variance, sexual environment and related issues. The work of Belous, Timm, Chee, and Whitehead (2012) significantly expanded the original version of the sexual genogram through the inclusion of more contemporary gender issues.

- How do you define yourself as a sexual person?
- How do you view the term *gender*? How do you describe yourself with respect to gender?
- Are you comfortable in your gender?
- Are you attracted to persons of the same, different or other gender?
- Do you have a partner(s)? Like your partner? Feel safe with your partner?
- What sexual behaviors do you enjoy most/least? How do you feel about them?
- Are you uncomfortable with some of the things you do sexually or completely avoid certain sexual behaviors?
- Do you feel you have to hide a part of your sexual self?
- Are you content with your body? How do you feel about your genitalia (sex organs)?
- How do you feel about your sexual thoughts/fantasies? How often do you have sexual thoughts/fantasies? About what and whom? Do you share your thoughts and fantasies with anyone?
- Is sexually related information still missing that I should know about your family, partner or yourself?

Sexual Timeline

A sexual timeline is a graphic representation of events in one's life, beginning with birth and extending to the current time. This assessment tool is recommended in addition to the sexual genogram because it accesses important information that may be missed in the sexual genogram (Belous, Timm, Chee, & Whitehead, 2012). Additionally, the timeline provides opportunities to further connect the assessment process with specific treatments. Typically, the timeline is recommended as a homework assignment to be discussed in session. Each partner is asked to record significant sexual events in his or her life. During the process of treatment, meaningful memories and feelings associated with them

FIGURE 4.1 Genogram Timeline of Significant Life Events

will arise and can be addressed. These events can be added to the timeline, providing an ever more comprehensive picture of sexual development. Some of the genogram questions mentioned previously can be used in the timeline. A thorough selection of sexual timeline questions is offered by Belous, Timm, Chee, and Whitehead (2012). Above is a brief example of part of a timeline with notches for events.

Timeline Questions

This category of questions reveals information about the first time hearing about masturbating, first time masturbating, first romantic relationship, first sexual experience, first intercourse and so on. The timeline may need to be extended into several content areas covering different dimensions of sexuality over time, such as fantasy, behavior and feelings. Again, we offer a few examples that can serve as starting points that will lead to more specificity and refinement of questions.

- What is your first memory of sex?
- When was your first menstrual period and how did you react?
- Did you have a family member or friend to talk to about sexual questions or activities?
- At what age did you first have orgasm during sleep or have a wet dream? Did you know what was happening? How did you feel about it?
- When did you first fall in love? How long, with whom, who broke up with whom?
- When and how did you first have a sexually related experience (e.g., touching, masturbating, oral, vaginal intercourse, anal)? Was the experience more positive/negative?
- When and how many causal sexual experiences would you guess you have had? (Were you sober, drinking, doing drugs, etc.?)
- What did it mean not to be a virgin?
- When was the first time you got pregnant? Tell me about it. Second time, and so on.
- When and how did you learn to explore your body in a sexual way?
- How has your definition of sex changed throughout your lifetime?
- When did you notice/feel sexual attraction toward others?
- Has your enjoyment of sex changed over time?

- Have you ever exchanged sex for money, favors, goods, promotions or things that weren't related to sex with an intimate partner?
- What personal meaning does sex have to you now?

Even though these three content areas are addressed during the couple's course of therapy, the sexual genogram does not need to conclude. The partners might want to continue to revisit expectations, disappointments, uncovered information, wishes and areas of desired change.

References

Beck, R.L. (1987). The genogram as process. *The American Journal of Family Therapy, 15*(4), 343–351. doi:10.1080/01926188708250694

Belous, C.R., Timm, T.A., Chee, G., & Whitehead, M.R. (2012). Revisiting the sexual genogram. *The American Journal of Family Therapy, 40*(4), 281–296.

Berman, E. (1999). Gender, sexuality and romantic love: Genograms. In R. DeMaria, G. Weeks, & L. Hof (Eds.), *Focused genograms: Intergenerational assessment of individuals, couples and families* (pp. 145–146). Philadelphia, PA: Brunner/Mazel.

Burchell, J., & Ward, J. (2011). Sex drive, attachment style, relationship status and previous infidelity as predictors of sex differences in romantic jealously. *Personality and Individual Differences, 51*, 657–661.

DeMaria, R., Weeks, G., & Hof, L. (1999). *Focused genograms: Intergenerational assessment of individuals, couples and families.* Philadelphia, PA: Brunner/Mazel.

Frame, M.W. (2000). The spiritual genogram in family therapy. *Journal of Marital and Family Therapy, 26*(2), 211–216. doi:10.1111/j.1752-0606.2000.tb00290.x

Hodge, D.R. (2001). Spiritual genograms: A generational approach to assessing spirituality. *Families in Society, 82*(1), 35–48.

Hof, L., & Berman, E. (1986). The sexual genogram. *The Journal of Marital and Family Therapy, 12*, 39–47.

Mumford, D., & Weeks, G.R. (2003). The money genogram. *Journal of Family Psychotherapy, 14*, 33–44.

Shellenberger, S., Dent, M.M., Davis-Smith, M., Seale, J.P., Weintraut, R., & Wright, T. (2007). Cultural genogram: A tool for teaching and practice. *Families, Systems, & Health, 25*(4), 367–381. doi:10.1037/1091-7527.25.4.367

Treger, S., & Sprecher, S. (2011). The influences of sociosexuality and attachment style on reaction to emotional versus sexual infidelity. *Journal of Sex Research, 48*, 413–422.

5

MEASURES OF SEXUAL FUNCTION AND DYSFUNCTION

Introduction

In 2013 the American Psychiatric Association released the newest version of the *Diagnostic and Statistical Manual*, the *DSM-5*. In this version, there are numerous changes regarding psychiatric diagnoses and diagnostic criteria. Many of the sexual dysfunctions (now called disorders) were reconfigured, merged or deleted. To date, most of the existing literature and research on sexual disorders is grounded in the *DSM-IV-TR* (American Psychiatric Association, 2000) classifications. Accordingly, the objective assessment tools described in this chapter were based on *DSM-IV-TR* (American Psychiatric Association, 2000). Many of these assessment instruments will need to be revised in order to conform to *DSM-5* (American Psychiatric Association, 2013). Given the timing of the release of *DSM-5* (American Psychiatric Association, 2013) and the writing of this text, it is impossible to review or list the new and/or revised instruments that will be developed. The reader should be cognizant that the research that grounds current assessment tools will lead to a new series of studies based on newly developed surveys and other assessment tools that will conform to the new definitions and criteria.

Assessment in sex therapy is a critical part of research and the therapeutic process. This chapter focuses on formal assessment in clinical and research contexts. Assessments guide decisions about who participates in treatment, how sessions will be structured and which interventions will be used. Assessment in sex therapy can be formalized via the use of specific measures or instruments or it can be more informal, such as through getting a psychosocial history or by simply observing behavior. This chapter provides an overview of a variety of assessments, both physiological and psychological. Also, the reliability, validity, strengths and weaknesses of current scales are discussed.

Behavioral Assessment

In addition to the information gained during a clinical interview, the therapist might also want to use some behavioral measures. These differ from the psychological measures in that the therapist relies on observations of the client. In order to conduct a behavioral assessment, it is necessary to identify specific behaviors of interest. Additionally, the therapist will want to evaluate which dynamics or factors are maintaining those behaviors (Gudjonsson, 1986). For example, the therapist can glean information regarding the couple's commitment, intimacy level and passion toward one another from observations of how the couple interacts together in the session. The therapist can determine the necessity of a behavioral assessment based on the presenting problem, the severity of the problem, the couple's dynamics and the goals of such an assessment.

Physiological Measures

There are a variety of physiological measures used by physicians, sexuality researchers and clinicians. For example, to monitor penile tumescence and degree of erectile dysfunction, penile circumference can be measured by the use of penile plethysmography (Simon & Schouten, 1991), of which there are two types. One is the volumetric air chamber, which measures changes through an assessment of the displacement of air around the penis. Another is the circumferential transducer, which measures changes in the circumference of the penis through a strain gauge placed around the shaft of the penis. Sexuality researchers have primarily used the circumferential transducer. Although the physiological measures are intended to infer one's subjective state, more recent research has indicated that this is not always the case. For example, Delizonna, Wincze, Litz, Brown, and Barlow (2001) examined the physiological and subjective arousal indicators of 28 men without sexual dysfunction under two arousal conditions. They found that although there was evidence of penile tumescence, this was not necessarily accompanied by a subjective state of arousal. For further discussion of the nocturnal penile tumescence method, see Schiavi (1992).

In women, the complimentary physiological measure is the vaginal photoplethysmography, which measures the amount of vasocongestion in the vaginal wall by inserting a tampon-shaped object with a light source and a photocell. The amount of light that is produced is converted into electrical impulses and interpreted as an estimate of blood flow. Other researchers (i.e., Rogers, Van de Castle, Evans, & Critelli, 1985) have utilized an assessment of vaginal pulse amplitudes (measuring genital vasodilation) using the same device.

Another way that researchers have measured arousal physiologically is through assessing reaction time in study participants (Letourneau, 2002; Williams, 2003). For example, Koukounas and McCabe (2001) assessed the interaction of sexual and emotional variables that influenced the physical response to erotic material.

They measured how much time each participant spent to activate a switch after hearing a tone, while also monitoring eye-blinking behavior as recorded by electromyography (EMG) activity. The EMG records the electrical activity produced within muscle cells, and how rapidly the muscular activity occurs. The graphed values can also reveal abnormalities in the conduction of the electrical activity, which can interfere with physiological performance. Another physiological measure of sexual arousal is the skin conductance (SC) test. When measuring SC, electrodes are placed in specific locations of the hands and feet in order to measure fluctuations in sweat activity in response to sexual arousal (Quinsey, Steinman, Bergersen, & Holmes, 1975). SC is often used in conjunction with penile circumference measurements to determine sexual arousal because SC alone is often a measure of nonspecific physical arousal.

Psychological Measures

Researchers make wide use of standardized assessment instruments in the screening of sexual dysfunctions for clinical trials and in measuring treatment outcome during the medical and psychological treatment of sexual dysfunctions. These instruments generate scores for a respondent's perception of, satisfaction with or pain during the various phases of the sexual response (Derogatis, 2008). These types of instruments are frequently designed for research; thus, many do not have a strong application in clinical practice. That said, there might be times when a formalized assessment is defensible in clinical practice. Ideally, standardized instruments will allow therapists to identify and diagnose quickly, easily and accurately by utilizing more or less agreed-upon measures of sexual functioning.

This section begins by addressing issues in the administration of standardized instruments in the private practice of sex therapy. Also included is a brief overview of a variety of assessment tools that address both individual and couple sexual dysfunction. Sources for instruments are reviewed. A clinically useful chart is provided, which lists the application (gender or issue), domains assessed, number of items and method of scoring and psychometric properties for a variety of instruments.

Pion and Wagner (1971) reported that the use of a questionnaire "is not to usurp the importance of data collection by the interview technique but rather to enhance this objective" (p. 3). The therapist should convey to the client that there is no right or wrong answer, and should encourage honesty in the client's responses.

Burg and Sprenkle (1996) advised that sexuality measures should be assessed from many perspectives (client, therapist, partner). In order to achieve this goal, self-report questionnaires are the most frequently used. Clinicians can frequently find complete inventories in journal articles or in books of collections of formalized assessments. Bancroft (1990) reported that some advantages of questionnaires include the potential for anonymity, standardization and the amount of time saved.

Wincze and Carey (2001) outlined strategies for clinicians to use when evaluating questionnaires. First, it is important to examine the psychometric properties of a questionnaire. Questionnaires that are used should have some evidence of adequate reliability and validity. Secondly, only questionnaires that are clinically relevant should be selected. For example, there are some questionnaires that are devoted to assessing many dimensions of sexuality, while other instruments measure only a few dimensions of sexual behavior. The key is to have a clear understanding of the clinicians' needs as well as the purpose of the inventory. Another consideration is the practicality of an inventory. In some cases, the reading level of the scale surpasses that of the client (Wincze & Carey, 2001). Two final considerations include comparability (i.e., your clients' scores compared to those of others who have taken the test) and cost.

Conte (1983) divided the assessments into two classes: Guttman-type scales and scales looking at a wider range of behavior. Guttman-type scales, as defined by Conte (1983), are those that are described as "cumulative and unidimensional" (p. 557). Typically, these scales are short in length (10–20 items). The second class of assessments are multidimensional, typically are composed of more items and measure a wider scope of behavior. Conte (1983) suggested that unidimensional scales are useful for assessing behavior throughout the course of treatment, but admits such scales may have a higher degree of utility in research than in clinical settings; multidimensional scales are typically more comprehensive and might have greater utility in clinical settings in terms of treatment planning and outcomes.

Conte (1983) also provided two tables summarizing such scales. There has not been further classification in the literature of these scales in spite of the fact that this article was published over two decades ago.

Collections of Assessments

There are several ways to find psychological measures related to sexuality: in journal articles, in collections of sexual or dyadic assessments or in works that focus on the treatment of a particular sexual dysfunction. For example, Schiavi, Derogatis, Kuriansky, O'Connor, and Sharpe (1979) summarized the assessment tools, lists and descriptions of a variety of sexual assessment instruments. Although this article is nearly 30 years old, it provides detailed information about many of the tests and assessments that are still in use, including information on obtaining the scale, method of administration and reliability and validity. Further, Talmadge and Talmadge (1990) also specify a review of assessments in sexuality geared toward clinical practice. They reviewed 14 different scales, including the Sexual Interaction Inventory, the Derogatis Sexual Functioning Inventory, the Sexual Functioning Questionnaire for Heterosexuals, the Sexual Orientation Method and Anxiety and the Guttman Scale of Sexual Experience.

Another comprehensive review of the measures assessing one's quality of sex life is from the authors Arrington, Cofrancesco, and Wu (2004). The authors found over 160 sexuality assessments that assessed quality of sexual life. They further divided the articles into three groups: articles with no reliability/validity listed; those that listed reliability, but whose reliability was inadequate (below .70); and those with adequate reliability and validity. Further, the articles were divided into whether the inventory was a unidimensional measure (i.e., whether the scale was only intended to measure sexual quality of life) or multidimensional, where only one subscale intends to measure sexual quality of life. The findings indicate that there were 62 instruments representing six areas of sexual functioning: attitude, arousal, interest/desire, satisfaction and relationship qualities. Yet after sifting through the analysis, the authors found that only 9 of the 60+ measures displayed adequate validity and reliability.

Many of the sexual assessments are described in the most recent edition of the *Handbook of Sexuality-Related Measures* (Fisher, Davis, Yarber, & Davis, 2010). The text, which is approximately 600 pages, describes over 200 measures that cover a variety of areas in sexual functioning, including measures to assess attitudes and beliefs about sexually charged topics, the presence of sexual dysfunctions, gender identity, masturbation, orgasm and so on. This study might create the impression that the field is rich with assessment tools: however, Meana, Binik, and Thaler (2008) disagree.

Indeed, our own investigation revealed that the body of literature contains many assessment instruments that do not give adequate reliability and validity estimates. Those interested in reading descriptions on the wide body of instruments available may consult the *Handbook of Sexuality-Related Measures* (Fisher, Davis, Yarber, & Davis, 2010), Meana, Binik, and Thaler's (2008) chapter in *A Guide to Assessments That Work*, Schiavi, Derogatis, Kuriansky, O'Connor, and Sharpe's (1979) article, and Talmadge and Talmadge's (1990) article.

Meana, Binik, and Thaler (2008) have written an extremely useful critique and review of assessment instruments. Their chapter discusses various methods to measure subjective and physiological sexual phenomena related to global sexual function. They describe each of the sexual dysfunctions in the *DSM-IV-TR* (American Psychological Association, 2000) and review global sexual function measures that are appropriate for diagnosis, case conceptualization, treatment planning, treatment monitoring and outcome. Their review focuses on scales that have adequate psychometric properties. The authors critique and evaluate the scales' norms, various types of reliability and validity and internal consistency, and provide an evaluation of clinical utility. The scales they investigated were divided into different groupings. For example, some inventories were specific to dysfunctions while others were specific to gender, and so on. Some widely used scales are the Derogatis Interview for Sexual Functioning (DISF; Derogatis, 1997, 1998) and the Golombok-Rust Inventory of Sexual Satisfaction (GRISS; Rust & Golombok, 1985, 1986, 1998). These scales assess global functioning and are appropriate for either men or women. The inventories reviewed for use for assessment of men were the Brief Male Sexual Function Inventory (BMSFI; O'Leary et al, 1995), the International Index of Erectile Function (IIEF; Rosen et al., 1997), and the Male Sexual Health Questionnaire (MSHQ; Rosen et al., 2004). Of these three, the IIEF was highly recommended by Meana, Binik, & Thaler (2008). The scales reviewed in order to assess women are the Brief Index of Sexual Functioning for Women (BISF–W; Rosen, Taylor, & Leiblum, 1998; Taylor, Rosen, & Leiblum, 1994), Female Sexual Function Index (FSFI; Rosen et al., 2000), McCoy Female Sexuality Questionnaire (MFSQ; McCoy & Matyas, 1998), Sexual Function Questionnaire (SFQ; Quirk, Heiman, & Rosen, 2002; Quirk, Haughie, & Symonds, 2005), and the Structured Diagnostic Method (SDM; Utian et al., 2005). Of these, the scales most highly recommended by Meana, Binik, & Thaler (2008) were the FSFI, the SFQ and the MSFQ. Of the two dysfunction-specific scales (the Sexual Aversion Scale [SAS] and the IIEF), the IIEF was highly recommended by the authors, seemingly because of its norms, validity and generalizability.

Assessments in clinical practice and research have different aims. The clinician needs an inexpensive, nonthreatening, focused and somewhat reliable method to begin understanding a sexual problem. The clinician would continue assessment throughout a clinical interview and continue to collect assessment data as therapy unfolds.

References

American Psychiatric Association. (2000). *Diagnostic and statistical manual of mental disorders* (4th ed., text rev). Washington, DC: Author.

American Psychiatric Association. (2013). *Diagnostic and statistical manual of mental disorders* (5th ed.). Arlington, VA: Author.

Arrington, R., Cofrancesco, J., & Wu, A.W. (2004). Questionnaires to measure sexual quality of life. *An International Journal of Quality of Life Aspects of Treatment, 13*(10), 1643–1658.

Bancroft, J. (1990). Sexual behaviour. In D.F. Peck & C.M. Colin (Eds.), *Measuring human problems: A practical guide* (pp. 339–373). Oxford, England: John Wiley & Sons.

Burg, J.E., & Sprenkle, D.H. (1996). Sex therapy. In F.P. Piercy, D.H. Sprenkle, & J.L. Wetchler (Eds.), *Family therapy sourcebook* (2nd ed.) (pp. 153–180). New York: Guilford Press.

Conte, H.R. (1983). Development and use of self-report techniques for assessing sexual functioning: A review and critique. *Archives of Sexual Behavior, 12*(6), 555–576.

Delizonna, L.L., Wincze, J.P., Litz, B.T., Brown, T.A., & Barlow, D.H. (2001). A comparison of subjective and physiological measures of mechanically produced and erotically produced erections (or, is an erection an erection?). *Journal of Sex and Marital Therapy, 27*(1), 21–31.

Derogatis, L.R. (1997). The Derogatis Interview for Sexual Functioning (DISF/DISF-SR): An introductory report. *Journal of Sex & Marital Therapy, 23*, 291–304.

Derogatis, L.R. (1998). The Derogatis Interview for Sexual Functioning. In C.M. Davis, W.L. Yarber, R. Bauserman, G., G. Schreer, & S.L. Davis (Eds.), *Handbook of sexuality-related measures* (pp. 268–269). Thousand Oaks, CA: Sage Publications.

Derogatis, L.R. (2008). Measures of sexual dysfunction and disorders. In J.A. Rush Jr., M.B. First, & D. Blacker (Eds.), *Handbook of psychiatric measures* (2nd ed.) (pp. 601–620). Arlington, VA: American Psychiatric Publishing.

Fisher, T.D., Davis, C.M., Yarber, W.L., & Davis, S.L. (2010). *Handbook of sexuality-related measures* (3rd ed.). New York: Routledge.

Gudjonsson, G.H. (1986). Sexual variations: Assessment and treatment in clinical practice. *Sexual and Marital Therapy, 1*(2), 191–214.

Koukounas, E., & McCabe, M.P. (2001). Sexual and emotional variables influencing sexual response to erotica: A psychophysiological investigation. *Archives of Sexual Behavior, 30*(4), 393–408.

Letourneau, E.J. (2002). A comparison of objective measures of sexual arousal and interest: Visual reaction time and penile plethysmography. *Sexual Abuse: Journal of Research and Treatment, 14*(3), 207–223.

McCoy, N. L., & Matyas, J.R. (1998). McCoy Female Sexuality Questionnaire. In C.M. Davis, W.L. Yarber, R. Bauserman, G. Schreer, & S.L. Davis (Eds.), *Handbook of sexuality related measures* (pp. 249–251). Thousand Oaks, CA: Sage Publications.

Meana, M., Binik, Y.M., & Thaler, L. (2008). Sexual dysfunction. In J. Hunsley & E. Mash (Eds.), *A guide to assessments that work* (pp. 464–487). New York: Oxford University Press.

O'Leary, M.P., Fowler, F.J., Lenderking, W.R., Barber, B., Sagnier, P.P., Guess, H.A., et al. (1995). A brief male sexual function inventory for urology. *Urology, 46*, 697–706.

Pion, R.J., & Wagner, N.N. (1971). Diagnosis and treatment of inadequate sexual responses. In J.J. Rovinsky (Ed.), *Davis' gynecology and obstetrics* (pp. 1–17). Hagerstown, MD: Harper & Row.

Quinsey, V.L., Steinman, C.M., Bergersen, S.G., & Holmes, T.F. (1975). Penile circumference, skin conductance, and ranking responses of child molesters and "normals" to sexual and nonsexual visual stimuli. *Behavior Therapy, 6*(2), 213–219.

Quirk, F.H., Heiman, J.R., Rosen, R.C. (2002). Development of sexual function questionnaire for clinical trials of female sexual dysfunction. *Journal of Women's Health & Gender-Based Medicine, 11*(3), 277–289.

Quirk, F.H., Haughie, S., & Symonds, T. (2005). The use of the Sexual Function Questionnaire as a screening tool for women with sexual dysfunction. *Journal of Sexual Medicine, 2*, 469–477.

Rogers, G.S., Van de Castle, R.L., Evans, W.S., & Critelli, J.W. (1985). Vaginal pulse amplitude response patterns during erotic conditions and sleep. *Archives of Sexual Behavior, 14*(4), 327–342.

Rosen, R., Brown, C., Heiman, J., Leiblum, S., Meston, C., Shabsigh, R., Ferguson, D., & D'Agostino, R. (2000). The Female Sexual Function Index (FSFI): A multidimensional self-report instrument for the assessment of female sexual function, *Journal of Sex and Marital Therapy, 26*, 191–208.

Rosen, R.C., Catania, J., Pollack, L., Althof, S., O'Leary, M., & Seftel, M.D. (2004). Male Sexual Health Questionnaire (MSHQ): Scale development and psychometric validation. *Urology, 64*(4), 777–782.

Rosen, R.C., Riley, A., Wagner, G., Osterloh, I.H., Kirkpatrick, J., & Mishra, A. (1997). The International Index of Erectile Function (IIEF): A multidimensional scale for assessment of erectile dysfunction. *Urology, 49*, 822–830.

Rosen, R.C., Taylor, J.E., Leiblum, S. (1998). Brief index of sexual functioning for women. In C.M. Davis, W.L. Yarber, R. Bauserman, G. Schreer, & S.L. Davis (Eds.), *Handbook of sexuality-related measures* (pp. 251–255). Thousand Oaks, CA: Sage Publications.

Rust, J., & Golmbok, S. (1985). The Golombok-Rust Inventory of Sexual Satisfaction (GRISS). *British Journal of Clinical Psychology, 24*(1), 63–64.

Rust, J., & Golombok, S. (1986). The GRISS: A psychometric instrument for the assessment of sexual dysfunction. *Archives of Sexual Behavior, 15,* 153–165.

Rust, J., & Golombok, S. (1998). The GRISS: A psychometric scale and profile of sexual dysfunction. In C.M. Davis, W.L. Yarber, R. Bauserman, G. Schreer, & S.L. Davis (Eds.)., *Handbook of sexuality-related measures* (pp. 192–194). Thousand Oaks, CA: Sage Publications.

Schiavi, R.C. (1992). Laboratory methods for evaluating erectile dysfunction. In R.C. Rosen, & S.R. Leiblum (Eds.), *Erectile Disorders: Assessment and treatment* (pp. 141–170). New York: Guilford Press.

Schiavi, R.C., Derogatis, L.R., Kuriansky, J., O'Connor, D., & Sharpe, L. (1979). The assessment of sexual function and marital interaction. *Journal of Sex and Marital Therapy, 5*(3), 169–224.

Simon, W.T., & Schouten, P.G. (1991). Plethysmography in the assessment and treatment of sexual deviance: An overview. *Archives of Sexual Behavior, 20*(1), 75–91.

Talmadge, L.D., & Talmadge, W.C. (1990). Sexuality assessment measures for clinical use: A review. *American Journal of Family Therapy, 18*(1), 80–105.

Taylor, J.F., Rosen, R.C., & Leiblum, S.R. (1994). Self-report assessment of female sexual function: Psychometric evaluation of the Brief Index of Sexual Functioning for Women. *Archives of Sexual Behavior, 23*(6), 627–643.

Utian, W.H., McLean, D.B., Symonds, T., Symons, J., Somayaji, V., & Sisson, M. (2005). A methodology study to validate a structured diagnostic method used to diagnose female sexual dysfunction and its subtypes in postmenopausal women. *Journal of Sex and Marital Therapy, 31,* 271–283.

Williams, K.M. (2003). Two techniques for assessment of sexual interest: A discussion of the clinical utility of *penile plethysmography* and visual reaction time. *The Forensic Examiner, 12*(1–2), 35–38.

Wincze, J.P., & Carey, M.P. (2001). *Sexual dysfunction: A guide for assessment and treatment* (2nd ed.). New York: Guilford Press.

6

GENERAL TREATMENT PRINCIPLES, STRATEGIES AND TECHNIQUES

General Treatment Considerations

Assessment and treatment are overlapping processes. The therapist wants to obtain information about the onset, duration and impact upon the couple, and then proceeds directly with specific treatment strategies. Too much initial history taking may cause the couple to feel frustrated or pessimistic, or to lose interest in treatment. They must have the impression that the therapist is offering solutions in addition to collecting information. As the psychotherapy continues, the therapist can always (and usually will) obtain new information about the presenting problem as well as different struggles that almost always emerge. In other words, the couple will search for information about one problem while another issue is being concurrently treated. The key task for the therapist is to flexibly shift back and forth between assessment and treatment.

- The *treatment goal* is the overarching concept that drives therapy. It represents the outcome that successful treatment should provide.
- The *treatment strategy* is the general method the clinician uses to implement the treatment. The strategy is derived from the theoretical understanding of the problem and will later be used in goal development.
- The *techniques* are the specific interventions used to implement treatment strategies.

As sex therapists, we need to address individual, relational, family, contextual and environmental factors that contribute to a couple's sexual problems. Then, we need to rely on careful integration of a variety of treatment approaches and theoretical perspectives for treatment. Unlike strictly individually oriented behavioral approaches so common in sex therapy, in systemic treatment, the role of the partner is considered in the creation, continuation and correction of the problem. For example, this perspective is crucial during the homework component of treatment because assignments have to be shared so that each partner receives some kind of emotional, affectional, sensual or sexual pleasure. The systemic viewpoint further considers how each partner feels about the problem, their opinions about the impact the problem has had on their relationship, coexisting problems in each partner, how to work together to solve the issues eventually uncovered and so on.

Beginning Treatment

This guide is useful for those therapists who are inexperienced in how to begin the process of working with a couple. As soon as you have a particular impression about the problem you will be treating, you should follow up by gaining more information from the resources listed later in this chapter; you should also become familiar with the overview chapter in our companion volume so that you are prepared to conduct and complete the appropriate initial assessment, then offer the couple some understanding about the nature of the problem and initiate an effective treatment plan.

Initial Contact

Typically, the initial phone call is the clinician's first contact with the client(s). Sometimes, Internet websites or email requests are used to inquire about treatment. The therapist should respond as quickly as possible in a telephone conversation. Usually, this is when the reason for seeking treatment is stated, often accompanied by client distress when describing it. Sometimes clients will say that they have tried to solve the issue on their own or have worked with other clinicians without successful resolution. The therapist must demonstrate understanding and acknowledge their concerns in this first contact. Some preliminary information, such as scheduling and fee structure can also be discussed at this time. Not returning phone calls, calling days later or rushing the conversation are all recipes for losing the client. We have found these basic steps to work well:

- Ask the client if he or she has the time and privacy to speak for a few minutes. If not, schedule a follow-up telephone call.
- Control the time limit of the first phone contact. Some individuals will want to spend too much time discussing the reason for the referral, especially if distressed. The therapist must be sensitive yet mindful of time boundaries.
- Inquire about how the client heard about you, for this information can reveal what is expected from treatment.
- Request a brief description about the nature of their problem, stating that you want to make sure they are beginning with the right therapist.

- Ask if they have seen a physician within the past year for this or any other problems. Request that they bring a list of medications and dosages to the first meeting.
- Question relationship status. Are they married or partnered? Explain that sex therapy works best when both partners come to the sessions. Ask if the partner is willing to come. If not, then say you will discuss it in the first session.
- Discuss your hours, fees, location and other details.
- Make an appointment if they are ready. If not, ask if there is any way you can help them.
- Ask if they have any questions.

The fact that you take 5–10 minutes to talk with them on the phone indicates your interest in working with the client(s). Rarely does any provider spend this much time doing an initial phone screening. Clients immediately appreciate the attention or service they receive from the initial contact. It is one of the common factors that helps create an alliance with the couple and improves outcome (Weeks & Fife, 2014).

The Initial Session

The initial session is one of relationship building and discovery. In sex therapy cases, most clients are ashamed, embarrassed, uncomfortable, or have some difficulty talking openly. Additionally, they can feel pessimistic due to previously failed attempts to resolve the problem. The therapist can open the session with a statement acknowledging the couple is attempting to improve their sexual life and that getting started is difficult for most clients. The therapist can ask the couple (assuming the couple is the unit of treatment) how they feel about coming to therapy for help with a sexual problem. The therapist can normalize the feelings, if appropriate, and work to help the couple become more comfortable. He or she may explain that in most cases the couple needs to be seen together; however, if there is a need for some individual sessions or work, and everyone agrees to the plan, the therapist may see one or usually both individually. If the therapist chooses to later conduct some individual sessions, the rules of how to do so and the rules of confidentiality have been carefully described by Weeks and Fife (2014).

The initial session is also a time to follow up with questions about medical and psychiatric histories, focusing on medications and organic conditions that can affect psychological or physical functioning. Once the couple appears ready to proceed with an assessment of the problem, the therapy can begin. It is advisable to ask permission to proceed with more sensitive assessment questions, explaining that you will need very specific information in order to help them. They can also be told that if a question is too awkward or anxiety provoking, they should tell the therapist in order to talk about how to proceed.

The Triage Tree

The treatment of each of the presenting issues described in the next sections involves making complex decisions about the proper selection of techniques in handling specific sexual difficulties; thus, it is essential for the therapist to know the sequence in which the problems are treated. Research suggests that the presence of a single sexual dysfunction is rare. In fact, multiple sexual problems often exist within the individual and the couple. In our practices, it is quite common to see more than one coexisting sexual difficulty and disorder as well as relational issues, even though the couple may present with an awareness or focus on just one sexual issue. Accordingly, the clinician must make decisions about which problems to treat first and how to work with problems

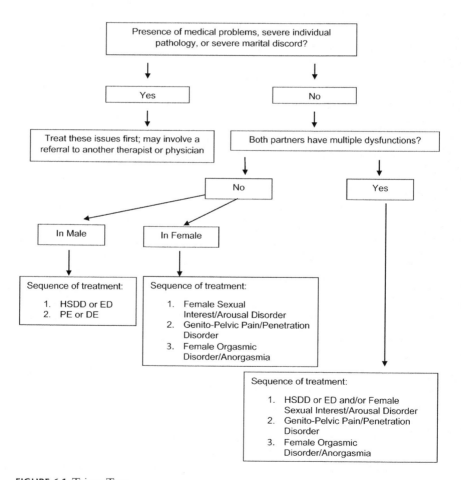

FIGURE 6.1 Triage Tree

concurrently. We have generally found that the decision-making principles presented in the Treatment Algorithm work to ensure effective treatment by providing the logic of when to begin treating a specific dysfunction and how to triage comorbidity within an individual and within the couple system.

Of course, not every couple will present with the same constellation of problems, so the therapist needs to understand the underlying logic more than the specific ordering. In general, we suggest the triage options for the following situations:

1. Treating presenting problems first versus other problems that warrant clinical attention.
2. Treating a comorbid problem first. Comorbidity reflects the effect of all of the client's illnesses, not just the presenting problem. For example, untreated depression takes precedence over the treatment of sexual problems.
3. Treating multiple sexual dysfunctions in the couple in a logical and sequenced way rather than being pressured to work on a specific problem the couple thinks should be solved first. The couple needs to understand the rationale for the sequencing of treating multiple problems.

The triage tree should be seen as a heuristic device rather than a fixed set of rules about which issue(s) to treat first.

Presenting Problem versus Other Clinically Relevant Problems

In many cases, there is more than one diagnosis that warrants clinical attention. We have generally found that it is best to treat the presenting problem first. This is true unless any of the following exist: medical problems, significant individual pathology or severe relational discord.

Medical Problems

The biogenic component of any dysfunction must be addressed first before beginning relational sex therapy. This category includes medical problems or medication-induced sexual dysfunction. Although medical intervention takes precedence, full resolution of the biomedical issues is not necessary before some preliminary sex therapy can be started. The couple should be told that progress will be limited during this phase, but that relational sex therapy is foundational to fully resolve their sexual problems, especially in terms of preparing the couple to regain sexual intimacy. During this time, the therapist should complete the sexual history for each partner, prescribe bibliotherapy and facilitate improved sexual communication. For many couples, it is possible to begin the incremental first stages of sensate focus without the medical issues being resolved.

Significant Individual Psychopathology

Psychological interventions have been demonstrated to have a robust effect in treating women with reduced desire, more so than in women in orgasmic disorder (Frühauf, Gerger, Schmidt, Munder, & Barth, 2013). Untreated mood or thought disorders or substance abuse are just two examples of individual psychopathology that will interfere with success in any form of sex therapy. In these cases, the sex therapy must be delayed while the individual issues are treated.

Severe Relational Discord

Severe couple conflict, such as the presence of intimate partner violence, is contradicted in all types of sex therapy. In these cases, therapy should focus on the couple's relational dynamics, moving only to sexual issues when there is a strong enough relational foundation for the two individuals to become sexually intimate with each other. The presence of an active affair or unresolved affair must also be attended to first before beginning sex therapy.

In short, any problem that is severe enough to impede progress in sex therapy must be worked through first. The problem may not need to be fully resolved, but the couple must be able to work cooperatively in carrying out the homework assignments and be ready for some kind of physical interaction.

Note that in establishing a system for triage, an understanding of the level of severity of the items mentioned previously is vital. In cases of mild to moderate individual pathology and couple discord, it may be possible to conduct the sex therapy. The litmus test is whether the couple can successfully begin the exercises that are assigned to them for the sexual problem. If individual or relational issues preclude successful progression through the stages of treatment, then the therapist must decide to address the interfering issues. Doing so requires a thorough explanation of the treatment rationale to the couple. Additionally, some therapists may want to refer the client to another therapist to treat individual psychopathology or for conflict management issues. The couple needs to understand that progress will be much slower when individual and couple issues are interfering with beginning sex therapy, or when they fail to understand or agree with the treatment plan.

Multiple Dysfunctions in an Individual

The general sequencing of treatment for men follows this decision tree:

1. Male Hypoactive Sexual Desire Disorder
2. Erectile Disorder (ED)
3. Premature (early) Ejaculation (PE)/Delayed Ejaculation (DE)

We believe it is best to approach comorbidity in an individual from the idea that desire is paramount. A man with little to no sexual desire will not be interested in resolving any other sexual problems. If he suffers from PE or DE, he will need to be able to achieve an erection of sufficient quality in order to work on the premature or delayed ejaculation. Of course, as one problem is being solved, it may be possible to phase in work on the next problem in the sequence. There may be exceptions to this sequence depending on the case. For a large number of men, a direct relationship has been shown between ED and Male Hypoactive Sexual Desire Disorder. Corona et al. (2004) found that men with ED also experienced a lack of sexual desire. Although the direction of causality may not be clear for every case, the clinician should try to determine which came first; if the ED appeared to contribute to the lack of desire, then treating the ED first might be advisable. The idea is that once the man has confidence that he can maintain an erection and some of the common accompanying feelings such as depression, low sex esteem, anxiety and so on have been resolved, his feeling of desire may return (McCabe & Connaughton, 2014).

Likewise, the general sequencing of treatment for women is as follows:

1. Female Sexual Interest/Arousal Disorder
2. Genito-Pelvic Pain/Penetration Disorder
3. Female Orgasmic Disorder

A woman with no desire will probably not be interested in the treatment of any of the other sexual problems. Women with sexual pain disorders may have a number of issues around fear of pain and anxiety that interfere with becoming orgasmic either through masturbation and especially intercourse. However, with some women, the treatments can overlap after the initial fear of sex and anxiety has been overcome. In addition, a woman with a pain disorder may have lost the desire for sex due to the pain. In these particular cases, it may be more useful to treat the pain disorder first.

Sexual Dysfunctions in Both Partners

As stated, it is crucial to recognize and treat multiple sexual dysfunctions in the couple simultaneously. In order to work systemically, the number of problems, types of problems and severity of the issues need to be considered. Additionally, the couple's readiness to engage in overlapping treatment must be assessed. In many cases, therapeutic work can begin with both partners and advance to a point where one partner will move forward before the other can proceed. For example, in treating a heterosexual couple where the male has ED and the woman experiences anorgasmia, the man will need to be able to sustain an erection during intercourse by the time the woman is ready for coitus.

In same-sex couples, the therapist can work to identify which person will be able to move forward first.

In sequencing the treatment of multiple sexual problems in the couple, it is advisable to treat absent/low desire first in the man or woman. In cases of gay or lesbian couples, the triage tree can be applied based on the gender of the couple only. The therapist can assess whether desire was present prior to the onset of other problems. Even if desire was present prior to these other problems, however, it may not return on its own and may require specific treatment. If the clinician believes the desire problem is a result of genito-pelvic pain or ED, for instance, the therapist explains to the couple that they lost their desire as a result of pain or ED and it may return once these problems are resolved; however, the therapist should make it clear that there is also the possibility that the lack of sexual desire may require specific treatment.

Genito-Pelvic/Penetration Disorder is usually the second problem that needs attention in the relationship if it is present. The woman's fear and anxiety will make it difficult to work on any other problem in her own sexual functioning, let alone her partner's. ED would be the next problem in the sequence. Without an erection, for example, the man cannot work on premature or delayed ejaculation. However, if the absent/low sexual desire appears to be a result of ED or genito-pelvic pain, then those problems may take priority. Likewise, the treatment of the male partner may be limited if there is no possibility of intercourse and his performance anxiety is negatively impacting the couple's sexual dynamics. The pelvic pain or penetration problem cannot be fully resolved until the man is capable of achieving an erection. However, if a couple presents with ED and Genito-Pelvic Pain/Penetration Disorder, both problems could be treated concurrently up to the point of penetration. At that time, the Genito-Pelvic Pain/Penetration Disorder would take priority and the treatment of ED will be suspended until it appears penile penetration is possible. This particular combination of problems is difficult to treat because it is still unknown whether penile penetration is possible and the man may fear causing pain, which increases his anxiety and thereby reduces erectile ability. If the ED is psychogenic, using a medication may be useful for the short-term. If it is psychogenic/biogenic, then finding the right medication and dose can be useful in helping him develop confidence that he can have a sustainable erection.

Another example of the treatment of concurrent sexual dysfunctions is PE in the man and the lack of coital orgasms in the woman. As the duration of coitus increases in the treatment of premature ejaculation, there become more opportunities for extended intercourse in addition to noncoital sexual stimulation. In order for the woman to work on having coital orgasms, the male partner will need to be able to sustain intercourse to a duration that meets the needs of the female. Of course, this is not to say that coitus of more extended duration will or should produce an orgasm with intercourse. Many women require additional stimulation during intercourse in order to reach orgasm. Thus, timing and sequencing of homework are very important when addressing multiple sexual dysfunctions in the couple.

Keeping Treatment Systemic

In the section that immediately follows, we explain the specific treatment plans for particular sexual dysfunctions in each partner. These may directly overlap or be somewhat sequential. Throughout the process, we are in search of ways the partner may be contributing to the problem in the identified client (the one who presented with the sexual problem), particularly ways the partner might sabotage treatment.

The treatment sections that follow focus only on the partner with the problem and what to do for him or her. Our general principle is that in every exercise, the experience must be balanced so the partners derive some sense of connection, physical touch, sensual or sexual pleasure or arousal. Recall that in nonsystemic approaches to sex therapy, the symptomatic person is the recipient of treatment while the partner is a surrogate therapist in the home. When we assign homework for the person who is working on a problem, we also discuss what each person will receive from the experience. The couple is encouraged to define the possible ways both partners might receive something, provided it is a reasonable expectation given the sexual problem. In most cases, the partner without the sexual problem will opt for several possible experiences. We further discuss this issue in the chapter on sensate focus in this volume as well as in the first volume of *Systemic Sex Therapy*. Sometimes, sexual experiences occur during the homework and other times the homework might be limited to time together, affection, or something sensual. Obviously, a woman cannot ask for intercourse from a man being treated for ED, but she might ask for doing something together, holding, affection or manual or oral sex leading to orgasm. The therapist needs to monitor two tasks. First, ensure that the partners always feel the experience is reciprocal and they receive something they want. Second, during the homework session make sure to attend to the needs of the nonidentified partner and help that person gain something he or she wants from the exercise. In the traditional approach to sex therapy, the therapy was one-sided. The partner was expected to provide whatever type of stimulation was needed for the symptomatic partner without receiving anything. At least, it was not part of the treatment protocols described in early and behaviorally oriented sex therapy. Whatever the asymptomatic partner states he or she might like in the homework must be reasonable and not interfere with the treatment of the symptomatic partner, and the symptomatic partner must agree to provide what is requested. The female partner of a man with ED might request that one thing she might want are orgasms produced by manual or oral stimulation. Obviously, this is not balanced in terms of the degree of sexual pleasure that will be experienced. Many men we have treated will gladly provide this stimulation, especially since they know there is no demand for them to have an erection; however, some may think it is unfair for the female partner to orgasm when the man cannot. Instead, he might agree to some of the other activities described earlier.

Keeping the treatment systemic has to be a priority. In the Intersystem Approach, multiple systems are considered concurrently in assessing and treating the couple/sexual problems. The therapist must also consider the possibility that the nonsymptomatic partner has contributed to or helped maintain the sexual problem as we pointed out in the companion editions of *Systemic Sex Therapy*. The nonsymptomatic partner may also undermine treatment in order to avoid having to deal with his or her own sexual problem or a relationship problem. For example, a woman who lacks sexual desire may subconsciously not want her partner to overcome his ED. The erectile symptoms lead him to avoid sex and perhaps lose his desire, and therefore she does not have to confront her problem. A man may be content that his partner is not interested in trying to become coitally orgasmic because he is a premature ejaculator. Furthermore, the duration of intercourse may be unimportant to the woman because she is not interested in having a coital orgasm or may be disinterested in sex and be thankful that it is over quickly. He does not see a problem in ejaculating quickly since it will not make a difference to his partner. Finally, there may be relationship and family-of-origin issues that prevent the couple from being successful. For instance, a couple where each partner has an avoidance attachment style will unconsciously not want the closeness that derives from a fully functioning and intimate sexual relationship. The presence of a sexual disorder helps them maintain the distance they require.

Treatment Planning

Treatment planning in sex therapy is just as important as in any other type of treatment. The treatment plan itself is a dynamic document, which serves to direct and organize the treatment process. In the case of sex therapy, the Intersystem therapist is attending to a number of areas: the sexual problem, the couple factors, biology, context and more. In addition, by the time a couple generally decides to seek sex therapy, they are at a place where they are nearly desperate for change. Therefore, it is important for the therapist to be able to keep track of the various aspects of treatment as well as demonstrate to the client the direction of treatment to avoid premature drop out. One way to accomplish this is through a treatment planning grid (see Table 6.1). This table assists therapists in outlining the vulnerabilities for each couple and can be provided to clients as a way to communicate to them the way in which treatment will be organized.

TABLE 6.1 Sample Treatment Plan

	Vulnerability	Goal	Specific Strategies to Achieve Goals
Individual Biology			
Individual Psychology			
Dyadic			
Family of Origin			
Sociocultural			

Beginning Treatment

Many couples with sexual problems have not had sex for an extended period of time prior to entering treatment. This fact means the therapist cannot just begin to intervene without attending to the fact that the partners have developed a pattern of sexual avoidance. Moreover, due to the avoidance of sexual interactions, they may have started to circumvent any physical relations, including sharing affection, touching and any type of sensual experience. Their anxiety over having sex and failing or having a problem leads them to avoid sex based on the learning principle of negative reinforcement. By avoiding any physical/sexual encounters, they can keep their anxiety turned off or minimize that which is reinforcing the anxiety. Anxiety is an unpleasant feeling. Whatever one does to avoid anxiety is reinforcing of that behavior. The therapist needs to ask about the extent to which the couple has avoided any physical/sexual contact and their level of anxiety, and explain the principle of negative reinforcement in simple terms. For example, the therapist might say, "When you think about having sex, you feel anxious and then you avoid it and everything you associate with it, such as kissing or touching. It is a self-perpetuating cycle. Avoidance begets avoidance; the more you avoid, the stronger the feeling to avoid becomes." The therapist attempts to interrupt the avoidance cycle by suggesting the following: "You must start somewhere. I am going to give you some touching exercises to do that will help you become physically connected again in a low-anxiety environment. It is important that you not avoid these touching exercises because that will keep you stuck." Then, the therapist explains the rationale for the suggestion: "At this point, any physical interaction is better than no physical interactions. As you become more comfortable with each other again and we move through the exercises, the feeling of avoiding these exercises will decrease." The therapist must monitor the level of anxiety when talking about a particular sexual topic in session and especially when giving homework. The couple is asked about their level of anxiety regarding the homework, and the assignment is modified until both partners agree that it does not engender too much anxiety and they think they will be able to do it.

Readiness for Sex Therapy

A related issue is whether the couple is really ready to begin sex therapy. In other words, are they ambivalent about their commitment to treatment? We have found that basic motivational interviewing questions can help to clarify how ready and capable they feel. Motivational interviewing assumes a basic innate tendency for personal growth and psychological integration. A directive therapeutic style promotes readiness for change by helping persons explore and resolve ambivalence (Miller & Rollnick, 2012).

- How motivated are you to solve this sexual problem on a scale from 1–10?
- How confident are you that you will be able to solve the problem on a scale from 1–10?

The answers to these questions provide a foundation for beginning treatment. Depending on their answers, the couple may not be ready to begin treatment, which needs to be discussed using some of the techniques of motivational interviewing. If the clients believe they lack confidence or skill to solve the problem, the therapist can work on their negative, self-defeating beliefs from a cognitive perspective. In addition, the therapist should ask the questions about readiness in the context of an individual session because the answers provided in this context may be different (and more accurate) than the answers provided in conjoint sessions.

The Importance of Principle, Techniques and Process

Many of the strategies and techniques of sex therapy seem very simple and straightforward. Kaplan (1987) published a manual with brief descriptions of the steps for treating the major sexual dysfunctions. It was a simple cookbook of sex therapy and a vast departure from her earlier work where she discussed the complexity of sex therapy from a behavioral and psychodynamic perspective (Kaplan, 1979). Our experience, however, in supervising clinicians over many years has shown us that the therapist must not only know which technique to use, when to use them and how to use them, but also the underlying principles on which a technique is based. Many authors in the field of sex therapy assume the therapist is familiar with behavioral principles, especially systematic desensitization. The training standards for becoming a sex therapist do not stress an understanding of the principles of behavioral psychology or learning theory, which has been the foundation of traditional sex therapy and is a key element in Intersystem sex therapy. Effective implementation is absolutely crucial to sex therapy and can only be learned through further reading, extensive practice and supervision. We have treated many failed sex therapy cases of other sex therapists because the previous therapist, and sometimes physicians, did not know how to properly implement the techniques. Moreover, sex therapy techniques are deceptively simple. This book is not designed as a substitute for proper clinical training in sex therapy, which includes extensive reading of current empirical literature, grounding in behavioral/learning and systems theory, understanding of systemic psychotherapy, a strong background in general psychotherapy and clinical supervision by an experienced certified sex therapist. This companion book to both editions of *Systemic Sex Therapy* offers a more in-depth understanding of how to work systemically and gives the reader more information about implementation.

References

Corona, G., Mannucci, E., Petrone, L., Giommi, R., Mansani, R., Fei, L., Maggi, M. (2004). Psycho-biological correlates of hypoactive sexual desire in patients with erectile dysfunction. *International Journal of Impotence Research, 16,* 275–281.

Frühauf, S., Gerger, H., Schmidt, H.M., Munder, T., & Barth, J. (2013). Efficacy of psychological interventions for sexual dysfunction: A systematic review and meta-analysis. *Archives of Sexual Behavior, 42*(6), 915–933. doi:10.1007/s10508-012-0062-0

Kaplan, H.S. (1979). *Disorders of sexual desire.* New York: Brunner/Mazel.

Kaplan, H.S. (1987). *The illustrated manual of sex therapy* (2nd ed.). New York: Brunner-Routledge.

McCabe, M.P., & Connaughton C. (2014). Psychosocial factors associated with male sexual difficulties. *Journal of Sex Research, 51*(1), 31–42.

Miller, W.R., & Rollnick, S. (2012). *Motivational interviewing: Helping people change* (3rd ed.). New York: Guilford Press.

Weeks, G.R., & Fife, S.T. (2014). *Couples in treatment: Techniques and approaches for effective practice* (3rd ed.). New York: Routledge.

7

TREATING ABSENT OR LOW SEXUAL DESIRE IN MEN AND WOMEN

This category includes two gender-based diagnoses: Male Hypoactive Sexual Desire Disorder and Female Sexual Interest/Arousal Disorder. In the *DSM-5*, desire disorders were bifurcated according to gender, a change that received much attention and criticism in the literature. The diagnosis for women merges the stages of desire and sexual arousal and uses the term "interest" to denote receptivity to sex. In fact, the word "desire" was not used in the classification for women as it was for men. Although there may be a few differences between the two diagnoses in terms of etiology and treatment, we noted in our companion volume that most of the research about the etiology of absent/low desire has been focused on women. This is because desire problems are significantly more common in women; thus, there is very little research about etiology with men, and virtually nothing about gender differences in treatment (Weeks & Gambescia, 2015). One exception is a study by McCabe and Connaughton (2014) examining biopsychosocial factors and their influences on sexual functioning in men. Medical, psychological and lifestyle factors are associated with the lack of desire in men and should be considered in the assessment. Thus, in light of the fact that little research has demonstrated the need for different treatment protocols for men and women, we have combined treatment in this section and simply refer to the diagnostic categories as absent or low sexual desire in both genders.

Absent/low sexual desire is the most complex of all problems to treat because so many factors may contribute to it, thus making it difficult to outline a specific course of treatment. An individual may have never felt desire, may have a lack of desire for only his or her established partner, may have felt desire at one time but lost it or may not feel desire for any person. Clients who have never felt desire and have no interest in experiencing sexual desire are by far the most difficult to treat. Generally, they come to treatment at the urging, sometimes threat of divorce, by the partner or as a result of their guilt about not being interested in pleasing their partner. The principle of treatment is (1) to identify the individual, relational, lifestyle and contextual factors suppressing desire, (2) to move them through the appropriate treatment modalities and strategies and (3) simultaneously to promote elements that enhance sexual desire.

It is always important to understand the meaning or interpretation of absent/low desire by the partner with the greater desire. When women experience lack of desire, their male partners generally accept it as something that happens to women. Alternately, men can become angry because they interpret that the partner is withholding affection or believe she should try harder. However, women generally assume that a man always has desire and men generally believe they should always feel desire. If the man presents with a lack of desire, this fact is confusing to the partner. She may attribute his lack of desire to her lack of youth, imperfect body or sexual desirability, sexual boredom and other factors. One viewpoint that we have never seen in the literature is that women may question whether the man is getting sex elsewhere, is having an affair or could be gay or has "turned gay," as one client put it. Women almost never bring up these concerns with their partners, especially their husbands, but may bring it up in an individual session spontaneously or if asked by the therapist if they have any ideas about why the male partner is so turned off to sex. A surprising number of women will say they have thought about these possibilities. The expectation is that men are sex machines and should always experience sexual desire. From a clinical perspective, we have seen only a small percentage of cases where either of these factors was true for men.

Definitional Issues

In this section, we review the current diagnostic criteria for absent or low sexual desire in men and women documented in the *Diagnostic and Statistical Manual of Mental Disorders* (*DSM-5*) (American Psychiatric Association, 2013).

Male Hypoactive Sexual Desire Disorder

- Deficient or absent sexual thoughts or fantasies
- Deficient or absent desire for sexual activity
- Must be of 6 months duration or longer
- Must cause clinically significant distress

Female Sexual Arousal/Interest Disorder

- Absent or reduced interest in sexual activity
- Absent or reduced sexual or erotic thoughts or fantasies

- Absent or reduced initiation of sexual activity and typically being nonresponsive to the partner's attempts to initiate sexual activity
- Absent or reduced sexual excitement or pleasure during sexual activity 75%–100% of the time during sexual activity
- Absent or reduced sexual interest or arousal in response to internal or external sexual or erotic stimuli (e.g. written, verbal, visual)
- Absent or reduced genital or nongenital sensations during sexual activity in 75%-100% of sexual encounters
- Must have persisted for a minimum duration of 6 months
- Must cause significant distress to the individual.

In both diagnoses, the therapist must specify if the disorder is lifelong or acquired, generalized or situational and whether it is causing mild, moderate or severe distress (American Psychiatric Association, 2013).

Strategies and Techniques

As stated, we have combined treatment in this section and simply refer to the diagnostic categories as absent/low sexual desire in both genders. With some disorders, the treatment plan is fairly standardized. Absent/low sexual desire requires a great deal of flexibility on the part of the therapist. Here, we present an outline of treatment roughly based on our book on absent/low sexual desire and our chapter in the companion book (Weeks & Gambescia, 2002, 2015). Assessment is key in determining how treatment is approached. Depending upon the factors present that suppress desire, the order of some of these treatment steps may need to be altered. The number of factors is staggering; thus, the therapist must remember that desire problems usually result from a combination of issues rather than a single factor.

Providing Bibliotherapy and Education

Information reduces anxiety and can be the antidote for pessimism. The couple needs general information about sexuality and specific information about the nature of their sexual problem. Psychoeducational strategies are discussed in Chapter 10. A lack of education can result in the adoption of a number of sexual myths, which tend to increase sex guilt and anxiety. In turn, these factors may heighten anxiety or guilt to the point that feeling desire is difficult. The therapist must always be diligent in listening for misinformation or sexual mythology. For example, in one case a man in his 40s believed that when he was nude with his partner, he should spontaneously get a firm erection and she believed the same thing. Of course, an erection did not occur under these conditions and he felt embarrassed and inadequate. She felt disappointed and criticized him. Over time, he lost desire for sex.

Overcoming Pessimism and Skepticism

Most couples presenting with absent/low desire have had the problem for some time, years in fact, and wonder whether talking about their issues can ever make it better. The therapist needs to inquire about their level of commitment to the relationship and to treatment. According to our experience, absent/low desire can lead to severe marital disruption and in some cases divorce. Their feelings of pessimism and hopelessness need to be addressed. It is imperative that the therapist demonstrates an optimistic attitude, which the couple can use to feel hopeful. Normalizing also instills hope. They need to know this problem is very common, even in men, and that treatment is usually effective if they are willing to make the commitment to therapy and to their relationship. Treatment needs to become the top of their hierarchy in order to devote time and effort to correcting the number of potential factors suppressing desire.

Addressing Relationship Considerations

The higher desire partner may be feeling frustrated, angry, and may think the absent/low sexual desire partner is deliberately withholding sex. The therapist needs to assess the impact on the relationship; educate the couple; and discuss other ways they can connect emotionally, affectionately, sensually and in some limited ways sexually, if possible. In the chapter on etiology of sexual problems in our companion volume, *Systemic Sex Therapy* (Hertlein, Weeks, & Gambescia, 2015), we offer a very long list of reasons why absent/low desire can result from relationship discord or problems. These reasons need to be carefully assessed and incorporated into the treatment plan. If relationship problems are fueling the sexual dysfunction, the couple will need to work on identifying, reducing or eliminating these issues in order to be able to feel desire. In our experience, couple dissatisfaction is typically present and must be worked through for the therapy to be successful.

Reducing Response Anxiety

Response anxiety is a term used to refer to the subjective preoccupation about not feeling enough or any desire, not getting aroused quickly enough or often enough and not feeling enough or any desire in sexual contexts. Often, partners have unrealistic expectations regarding their sexual abilities. When they feel they do not have enough desire in sexual situations, response anxiety further suppresses their motivation. It distracts them from the pleasurable aspects of physical intimacy and causes them to focus on something nonsexual. For example, a woman might suggest making love on a particular night and the man with absent/low need might begin to feel anxious that he is not going to bring enough or any desire to the evening's plans. He might assume that her offer of sex *should* turn him on. Therefore, couples need to be educated that response anxiety is nearly universal in cases of absent/low desire.

Of course, the therapist should verify whether one or both partners do in fact feel response anxiety. If so, they can be educated about what it is and what it does. The therapist gives the absent/low desire partner permission to feel only the desire he or she feels and not to try to force feeling more than he or she is ready to do. The more one partner tries to force desire, the less likely he or she is to experience it. The therapist will want to employ cognitive techniques such as thought stopping and thought substitution. First, the client must learn to recognize the intervening catastrophic antisexual thoughts that are causing response anxiety, such as "my partner will leave me if I cannot get turned on." They can use thought stopping to control this idea and use another self-statement about how pleasurable it feels to be touched or other phrases.

Conducting Cognitive Work

In the previous paragraph, we demonstrated the use of cognitive therapy in the treatment of absent/low desire. In our chapter in the companion volume (Weeks & Gambescia, 2015), we reviewed the literature showing that researchers have now demonstrated that one of the major factors in lack of desire is having negative thoughts about sexuality and experiencing distracting thoughts during sex. Thus, the therapist helps each partner to compile a list of negative sexual thoughts during the assessment phase. We ask both partners to list their negative sexual/relational thoughts about self, partner, the relationship and anything else. This process continues throughout therapy because new negative thoughts will emerge, especially as the couple begins to engage in touching exercises and sexual activities. During treatment, the therapist works with these thoughts in several ways. The overall strategy is to develop thoughts that both counter the negative thoughts and develop positive sexual thoughts. Of course, when the negative thoughts are reviewed with the couple, the first decision to be made (with the couple's help) is which thoughts are just unfounded negative thoughts and which ones represent the need for a real change in the sexual/couple relationship. For example, if the thoughts are "we fight all the time" or "he never gives me any foreplay and is rough and abusive sexually" were part of the list, the therapist would first want to determine whether these thoughts were true and then conduct couple therapy to work on changing the couple/sexual behavior.

Cognitive changes could be directed toward unfounded thoughts. For the unrealistic, irrational or distorted thoughts, the therapist will want to help the absent/low desire partner find one or more neutralizing or counter thoughts and develop a list of positive thoughts. The positive thoughts should be in the categories mentioned earlier of self, other or partner, relationship and family of origin. Typically, there are a number of thoughts in each category and this assignment continues in order to capture more negative thoughts. The therapist can expect that at the beginning of therapy, the list of negative thoughts may be relatively short; thus, the number of positive thoughts will be limited.

The therapist helps the person with absent/low desire develop a three-column list. One column would be the negative thoughts; the second would be counter-thoughts to the negative thoughts; and the third would be unconditionally posi-tive thoughts or positive thoughts from the past, what he or she wants to think in the future or "as if" thoughts. The client with the absent/low desire is told to mentally rehearse all the positive thoughts at least once a day until he or she can think about them automatically.

The underlying reasons for cognitive distraction need to be discerned. They can reflect internalized negative cultural or religious beliefs from the family of origin. The interfering thoughts can be about partner resentment or lack of trust or comfort. The individual might not feel comfortable with his or her body or lack the self-esteem needed for enjoyment of pleasure. The source could be any-thing from ADHD/ADD to other thought disorders to the habit of avoidance of thinking positive thoughts. The underlying reason for negative sexual thinking must be removed in order to focus on and rehearse positive sexual thoughts.

Defining Oneself as a Sexual Person

In our experience, many absent/low desire clients do not see themselves as sexual beings, especially women. As long as this self-perception is true, they are not going to have any sexual feelings. Thus, we developed a technique known as the *Sexual Bill of Rights*. The therapist asks the client to write about what he or she is entitled to feel sexually, to experience, to receive and to give. Most clients present a weak statement at first and are asked to work on strengthening the statement over the course of 3–4 weeks or until they have been able to develop a strong sense of their sexual entitlement. In many cases, they do not see themselves as sexual persons due to early negative messages from the family of origin, sexual secrecy or, in some cases, overt or covert sexual trauma.

Increasing Sexual Fantasies

In the list of criteria for absent/low desire, one criterion is that sexual fantasies and/or erotic thoughts are missing in the absent/low desire partner. We have, however, seen no treatment programs for absent/low desire that include the use of sexual fantasies. The primary function of sexual fantasies is to increase a person's sexual desire or to help maintain desire. Ask about whether the absent/low desire client has sexual fantasies and to what extent. If fantasy life or erotic thinking is nonexistent or very low, the therapist can discuss the importance of increasing both thoughts and fantasies. The client needs to be given permission to have fan-tasies and discuss the meaning of fantasies in the context of his or her relationship and personal belief system. Erotic literature, visual erotica and other materials may be used to help prime the client to develop a few fantasies and erotic thoughts he or she can use to trigger sexual desire.

Using Therapeutic Reframes

Reframing is a strategy used to change the meaning of a problem or situation, usually from something viewed as negative to positive and from an individual to systemic perspective. In the case of reframing sexual problems, there are a variety of techniques that can be used (Weeks & Fife, 2014). In some cases the therapist may want to reframe the absent/low desire as a couple's problem when the etiology suggests that a major factor in lack of desire is relational. For example, the therapist might say, "Your wife is the one who lacks sexual desire, but both of you have underlying fears of intimacy that motivate you to find some symptom to keep you from becoming too emotionally connected. At the present time, your wife is the one manifesting the symptom and protecting the two of you from having to deal with your underlying fears." Therapeutic reframes must be used judiciously with correct timing. The reframe will promote a shift from linear thinking, such as blaming, to a circular or systemic perspective.

Working with Intimacy Fears

The fears of intimacy that affect sex are the same as the underlying fears of intimacy, which distress the relationship (as described in Weeks & Fife, 2014). These fears include but are not limited to such phenomena as fear of exposure, loss of control or being controlled, fear of anger from the partner or losing control over one's own anger and fears of rejection or abandonment. It is common to encounter intimacy fears when working with absent/low desire. The therapist will need to spend a considerable amount of time identifying each underlying fear and then helping the client understand its origin and function, and how to move past the fear. Unfortunately, the fears are usually unconscious and must be inferred from the behavior and from the client's history in prior relationships and genogram work.

For example, a man lacked desire because he feared experiencing the sexual guilt, anxiety and shame from childhood when his mother had sexually abused him. In another case a woman grew up in a family that controlled her to the point of telling her how to function. The family did not encourage her to develop a sense of identity. Her lack of desire was a way of metaphorically saying that she was not going to be controlled sexually.

Promoting Communication

A lack of communication may affect the couple on two levels. If communication in the relationship is poor, the couple is likely to feel disconnected emotionally.

They may experience more conflict, and the ratio of positive to negative communications may be skewed toward the negative. All these factors and more may contribute to a lack of sexual desire. More specifically, lack of communication about and during sex may be a reflection of discomfort talking about sex, deriving from cultural norms and the family of origin. This lack of sexual communication will result in an inability to ask for what is and is not desired (sometimes expecting the partner to be a mind-reader), the avoidance of confronting or discussing a sexual problem and so on. As trivial as it may sound, in our experience, sexual communication in clinical couples is severely lacking. Couples who articulate what is desired and what feels good are more likely to have a better sexual relationship. Thus, we always inquire about their quality of communication at home, especially during the exercises, process any inhibitions of communication and encourage more communication related to all physical interactions. It usually takes a number of sessions before the couple can begin to communicate more freely about their sexual needs, wants and desires.

Assessing for Other Sexual Disorders

As we discussed in this section on the triage tree, other sexual disorders may be affecting levels of desire. Men with Erectile Disorder (Corona et al., 2004) frequently experience lack of desire. In our clinical experience, some women with Genito-Pelvic Pain/Penetration Disorder eventually lose desire because of the experience of pain and subsequently the anticipation of pain. It is possible that any other sexual disorder could produce a lack of desire depending on the salience of the problem. For example, if a woman could not achieve an orgasm with effective simulation, and having an orgasm is extremely important to her, she might develop a lack of desire for her partner. There are any number of possibilities when considering all the combinations of sexual problems, their etiology and their effect on desire.

Considering Medical Issues

There are no known or approved medical therapies for the treatment of absent/low desire. The therapist must determine that medical factors, medications and so on could be causing or contributing to the lack of desire; therefore, a medical examination should be recommended. Many clients today are taking several different medications, especially psychotropic medications for depression and anxiety. These medications are known to create sexual problems as extensively reviewed in a chapter in our companion book, *Systemic Sex Therapy* (Hertlein, Weeks, & Gambescia, 2015). The client is encouraged to talk with his or her doctor about these medications. Sometimes the doctors are not fully aware of the sexual side effects. If the physician is familiar with sexual side effects, he or she may be able to switch the client to a different medication that has fewer or no sexual side effects. The therapist must become knowledgeable about the sexual side effects of drugs and have resources available to suggest alternative medications (see our companion volume, Hertlein, Weeks, & Gambescia, *Systemic Sex Therapy*, 2015). Should the problem involve a psychotropic medication for a problem that can be treated with psychotherapy, the therapist is well advised to begin the psychotherapeutic treatment of the problem in order for the client to wean off the medication. The client should be informed about the sexual side effects since his or her doctor has probably not explained that the medication can affect desire, and most importantly that there is psychotherapy available for the problem so the client does not have to take a medication. The sex therapist can then treat for that problem prior to or concurrent with some sex therapy, delay sex therapy until the individual problems are resolved or refer the client to another therapist for treatment with these considerations in mind.

Assigning Appropriate Homework

Homework must be tailored for absent/low sexual desire in couples. Common homework exercises involve making time for dating and other enjoyable activities. Physical touch exercises are often recommended to help the couple reconnect physically, especially if they have been avoiding each other. We have described a new approach to sensate focus in Chapter 10 in this volume that can be used early in treatment. Another homework assignment that is often used later in treatment is the recommendation that if intercourse occurs, the absent/low desire partner should focus on the pleasant sensations without the pressure of having orgasm (Kaplan, 1979). This recommendation helps reduce response anxiety. Other assignments and strategies have been described in much more detail in one of our earlier books on absent/low desire (Weeks & Gambescia, 2002). These include such things as learning how to create a sensual environment, creating seduction rituals and becoming more comfortable with sexuality. Weeks and Gambescia (2015) also published a lengthy chapter in *Systemic Sex Therapy* with the latest information about etiology and treatment of absent/low sexual desire. In that volume, the focus was more on the techniques, whereas in this volume the focus is more on both techniques and their proper implementation.

The treatment of the sexual disorders reviewed in the following chapters is prepared within the context of the Intersystem approach. Note that the treatment protocols we have outlined are generic and must be tailored for each couple. The techniques are deceptively simple. The clinician will find they do not always work as intended; proper implementation is just as important as knowing the right strategy or technique to use. Adherence to the Intersystem Approach and experience will help the beginning therapist learn what to treat, when (our decision tree) and how to effectively implement the techniques. Supervision by a certified sex therapist is an invaluable tool in learning to do sex therapy effectively. Implementation and experience play such a critical role. It is well known that patients who need liver transplants or other complex surgeries, for example, do much better when they receive surgery from a doctor and a team who do these on a very consistent basis. Therapists who practice sex therapy must not only receive training, credentials and supervision, but they must be committed to making sex therapy a major component of their practices in order to acquire the continuing experience necessary to perfect their implementation skills.

References

American Psychiatric Association. (2013). *Diagnostic and statistical manual of mental disorders* (5th ed.). Arlington, VA: Author.

Corona, G., Mannucci, E., Petrone, L., Giommi, R., Mansani, R., Fei, L., & Maggi, M. (2004). Psycho-biological correlates of hypoactive sexual desire in patients with erectile dysfunction. *International Journal of Impotence Research, 16,* 275–281.

Hertlein, K.M., Weeks, G.R., & Gambescia, N. (2015). *Systemic sex therapy* (2nd ed.). New York: Routledge.

Kaplan, H.S. (1979). *Disorders of sexual desire.* New York: Brunner/Mazel.

McCabe, M.P., & Connaughton, C. (2014). Psychosocial factors associated with male sexual difficulties. *Journal of Sex Research, 51*(1), 31–42.

Weeks, G.R., & Fife, S.T. (2014). *Couples in treatment: Techniques and approaches for effective practice* (3rd ed.). New York: Routledge.

Weeks, G.R., & Gambescia, N. (2002). *Hypoactive sexual disorder: Integrating sex and couples therapy:* New York: Routledge.

Weeks, G.R., & Gambescia, N. (2015). A systemic approach to sensate focus. In K.M. Hertlein, G.R. Weeks, & N. Gambescia (Eds.), *Systemic sex therapy* (2nd ed.) (pp. 341–362). New York: Routledge.

8

TREATMENT PRINCIPLES, STRATEGIES AND TECHNIQUES SPECIFIC TO MEN

Treating Erectile Disorder

The psychiatric diagnosis of Erectile Disorder (ED) requires that at least one of the following three diagnostic criteria must be present on almost all or all (75%–100%) occasions of sexual activity:

1. Distinct difficulty in obtaining an erection during sexual activity
2. Noticeable difficulty in maintaining an erection until the completion of sexual activity
3. A marked decrease in erectile rigidity

Additionally, the symptoms will have persisted for a minimum duration of 6 months (American Psychiatric Association, 2013).

- Lifelong ED is an extremely rare presentation in which the man has always had this problem.
- Acquired ED occurs in men who have previously had satisfactory sexual activity and is more typical.
- The onset of acquired ED can be gradual or sudden.
- Generalized ED occurs in all situations, partnered or alone.
- Situational ED is more common, occurring only with certain partners and situations or during particular types of stimulation.

The psychological consequences of ED are substantial, for this disorder takes a toll on the man's self-esteem, confidence and overall quality of life. In this section the treatment of ED is described from a psychotherapeutic perspective; however, a therapist may also play a useful role when the problem has an organic basis and there is concurrent medical treatment.

The most common and basic principle of treatment is to lower performance anxiety and fear while creating small successes toward having a sustainable erection. Many advances have been made in the treatment of ED in the past decade (Gambescia & Weeks, 2006). It is now known that as men grow older, the chances of medical problems and greater use of medications, especially blood pressure medications, interfering with erectile ability increase. Thus, it is important that men undergo a medical examination by a general physician or more specialized evaluation by a urologist who is well trained in treating sexual dysfunction. Keep in mind that if the physician does not find physical causes, he or she may still prescribe medication for ED rather than refer the man and his partner for sex therapy. This is unfortunate because in our experience men, especially younger men, usually only need sex therapy. An erectile problem will have an effect on the relationship, which only a sex therapist can treat. As men age, the etiology of ED resulting from physical problems, such as cardiovascular disease, increases and can become comingled with anxiety. There are a variety of medical conditions that can produce ED, which may not be obvious and not diagnosable at the time of the initial evaluation. For example, sometimes ED is the first sign of emerging diabetes or cardiovascular disease, but it is possible that the physician is not able to diagnose the underlying cause. The following questions help the therapist begin to understand some of the fundamental causes. A thorough description of causes and assessment is available in Gambescia and Weeks (2015).

Strategies and Techniques

Promote Systemic Thinking

Couples usually think of ED as just the man's problem. After all, he is the one who cannot achieve an erection sufficient for intercourse. Looking at ED from a systemic perspective involves helping the couple understand how each partner may play a role in the development and maintenance of the sexual symptom. For example, if the woman tells the man he is taking too long to get an erection or if he loses it during intercourse, she might say intercourse is over, act very disappointed and not be willing to help him reestablish an erection so they could continue. In other cases, the man may be unconsciously responding to his partner's lack of interest or desire, and he might initially respond by trying to ejaculate as quickly as possible. Most men find that this approach doesn't work well because it increases anxiety, reduces pleasure and ultimately contributes to future occurrences of ED. Some couples believe the man should be able to develop spontaneous erections without any physical stimulation. In a clinical case, a wife wanted her husband to get an erection immediately and have rough sex with her by talking dirty, pounding her vigorously and so on. Although she enjoyed this sort of sexual role-playing, he felt this was treating his wife like a whore and was uncomfortable having sex with her in this fantasy mode. Moreover, he knew he was going to disappoint her. Deeper relational issues can also affect erectile ability. If a couple is fighting constantly and he is experiencing resentment, then ED might be the outcome. Some couples also need to avoid relational and sexual closeness as discussed in Chapter 7, this volume, so one partner develops a sexual symptom in order to facilitate this distance. Should this be the case, a therapist can use reframing to show how the symptom serves a positive function for the couple (Weeks & Fife, 2014).

Provide Bibliotherapy and Education

Psychoeducation for men with ED might include information about a variety of topics: the impact of psychological problems such as anxiety or depression on sexual functioning; the physiology of sex; and the impact of medications, aging and overall health on sexual functioning. The therapist may assign some readings, such as *The New Male Sexuality* (Zilbergeld, 1992), or have the client visit reliable websites dealing with ED. The therapist should listen carefully for any misinformation, mythology or lack of information regarding sexual functioning. Men often retain standards of sexual performance from their youth and do not understand that as men age, they need more physical and emotional stimulation and erections might be less robust. The therapist must challenge sexual mythology because misinformation leads to unrealistic expectations, which increase performance anxiety and lower a sense of self-worth. Some common misconceptions include the idea that any type of sexual arousal should automatically lead to an erection (Bullough & Bullough, 1995), that self-worth is related to erectile ability and that the only way to truly satisfy a woman is through intercourse with a firm erection.

The use of bibliotherapy and psychoeducational methods with the couple can also be helpful in enriching their communication skills. Both partners need to be able to express their feelings and desires about sex. Communication is the crucial mediating variable between relationship and sexual satisfaction (Byers, 2005; Mark & Jozkowski, 2013; Monteiro, de Santa, de Santa, & Narciso, 2014). We encourage couples to read about factual sexuality; talk about what they have read; talk about various points; and practice communicating affectional, sensual and sexual needs, wants and desires as well as stressors, worries and concerns.

Dissipate Performance Anxiety

Kaplan (1974) and Gambescia and Weeks (2015) have described the significant role that performance anxiety plays in ED. The formula is quite simple and should be described to the couple. Anxiety and fear about performance (getting and keeping an erection) significantly decreases the ability to acquire and maintain an erection. Men get caught in a vicious cycle of performance anxiety: the loss of an erection produces anxiety, which in turn makes getting an erection more difficult, which increases anxiety. Two techniques are useful in reducing performance anxiety after the man knows about the detrimental role it plays. First, the therapist *never* actually prescribes that the client should achieve an erection. The wording of the exercises should include "if" it happens. Second, we ask men to place themselves in a mental loop of focusing on the present. They are instructed to keep saying to themselves, "What is feeling good right now, and what would I like in order to continue feeling pleasurable sensation?" We explain that any time they start to think about the next moment or past experiences, they are inviting the anxiety back. For example, if they start thinking ahead, they will inevitability think about whether the erection will persist or be firm. This thought engenders anxiety that diminishes erectile ability.

Conduct Cognitive Work

Men with ED often have a number of negative thoughts about their erectile ability that generate fear and anxiety. They must be helped to identify and neutralize their negative thoughts, stop them and substitute positive cognitions. Men can become cognitively distracted with a myriad of catastrophic thoughts that interfere with keeping an erection: "It never works," "I don't want to fail again," "My wife must hate having sex with me," "It will be terrible if we begin to have intercourse and I lose the erection" and "I just know it isn't going to work so why try." Men with performance anxiety monitor their erections constantly while thinking negative thoughts. The man's preoccupation with his erection increases his performance anxiety. Getting and keeping the erection may become the only focus of the sexual interaction. When both partners get caught up in his erection or lack thereof, sex becomes a task, chore or performance. The interaction is no longer about being emotionally and physically connected and sharing a pleasurable experience. The partner may also participate in monitoring, assisting and reassuring to the point that the man believes he must perform because his partner is so invested in his erection. Overall, the couple loses sight of any other sexual activity. Their repertoire of sexual activities begins to shrink due to the exclusive focus on the erection or lack thereof. Rather than take advantage of other pleasurable activities and see those as a successful sexual experience, sexual success is measured in terms of erectile ability. The entire meaning of sex involves successful penetration. The meaning of sex needs to be broadly defined as any pleasurable physical interaction.

ED is usually the result of performance anxiety and treating this anxiety may produce significant improvement or complete recovery of erectile ability. Additionally, the therapist must also listen for hidden causes of ED, such as lack of desire for partner, individual psychopathology, fear of pregnancy, resentment of the partner, denial of self-pleasure, attraction to an affair partner, addiction to pornography and a host of other reasons mentioned previously in the Promote Systemic Thinking subsection of this chapter. One case illustrates this point. A man in his mid-30s had repeated affairs with strippers and prostitutes and was able to perform effortlessly with them. However, he could not maintain an erection with his wife, who was a polished and sophisticated woman who acted with integrity. In spite of the fact that he was well educated and successful, his father was mentally abusive and dismissive. This factor, in conjunction with other traumatic events in his childhood, let him to believe he was unworthy of his wife's love. Every time they attempted to make love, he made the unconscious association that he was unworthy. In particular, he remembered things his father had said to him, including one of his father's favorite sayings that he was a "small penis."

Use of Medical Treatment

Even though we stated this section would be about the psychotherapeutic treatment of men with ED, the therapist must be aware of medical options. Often, and particularly as the man ages, the probability of ED increases due to the underlying influence of organic disease states such as cardiovascular disease or diabetes. Additionally, a man's defense against anxiety is often less robust as he ages due to a confluence of organic and psychogenic factors. Thus, many cases of ED have mixed organic and psychogenic etiologies. Most of these men can be helped by erectogenic oral medications such as Viagra, Levitra or Cialis. These medications are mild vasodilators and each has a slightly different mode of action and duration of efficacy. Sometimes a man may not respond to the oral medications due to more severe neurological involvement, for instance. In these cases, an injectable treatment, where the vasodilator is directly injected into the spongy tissue of the penis, can be used. Several other options such as the penile vacuum pump and/or a tourniquet can be employed. Read more about these and other treatments as reviewed by Gambescia and Weeks (2015). In addition to augmenting the blood supply to the penis, medical treatments for ED can give the man confidence and better erectile ability when used in conjunction with psychotherapeutic exercises. There have even been some case reports of men who used an ED medication, regained confidence and were able to discontinue the medication and psychotherapy.

Although there are currently many medical alternatives to treating ED, our review of the rate of compliance with medical treatments shows that it is relatively poor regardless of the modality used (Gambescia & Weeks, 2015). It is understandable that the man and his partner will complain about the awkwardness while using a penile pump, physical discomfort related to the injection, the idea that the erection is not in response to his partner or the surgical implications of the penile prosthesis. The most common medical treatment for

ED is an oral medication called PDE-5 (phosphodiesterase type 5) inhibitors. which are reasonably safe, effective and easy to use; nonetheless, the discontinuation rate is roughly 50% (Carvalheira, Pereira, Maroco, & Forjaz, 2012). There are a number of reasons why men ceased using a drug that was working. Most of these involve unrealistic fears about the safety of the drugs, complaints about side effects such as flushing, embarrassment and relationship factors. All of these factors can be addressed in couple/sex therapy. For example, when a man is taking the oral medication, we often observe that he is still experiencing significant performance anxiety, self-monitoring and worry about his partner's response. Even when the medication is working, these issues may still reduce the effectiveness of the medication for the ED and the quality of the sexual experience for the couple. In short, men who use oral medications for ED can greatly benefit from sex therapy. In fact, the greatest benefit for those using an ED medication is learning how to incorporate a medication into their sexual lives, removing any obstacles to having sex and maximizing their sexual experience.

In our experience, men with ED have usually had the problem for an extended length of time, especially if the man is older. The couple nay have adapted or resigned themselves to not being sexual; alternatively, it might actually be a relief to a partner who is not interested. The restoration of the man's sexual ability may not be a welcome event for the partner—or for the man himself. Men who are prescribed ED medications or treatment by their physicians also need psychological help incorporating a medically enhanced erection into their sexual relationship.

Assign Appropriate Homework

A number of homework exercises are typically used in treating ED. These exercises are prescribed in session after careful discussion with the partners and are typically performed three times between weekly sessions. Always keep in mind that the partner should be receiving emotional or physical pleasure while doing the exercises. The following homework assignments for ED are based on the general principles of sensate focus (Weiner & Avery-Clark, 2014). However, we have significantly modified the practice of sensate focus as readers will see in Chapter 10 where a detailed discussion of the use of sensate focus is provided. The major directives for the sensual touch exercises are as follows:

- Pay attention to the sensations that accompany touch (temperature, pressure, etc.).
- Verbally or nonverbally communicate about what is pleasurable and what is not.
- Focus on one's own sensations, not those of the partner.
- Be mindful of sensations at the moment. Stay in the here and now.

- Do not try to force a feeling.
- Accept that the assignments are reciprocal so that the partner can give and receive sensual touch.

Each assignment should be incremental and designed for success. There is no uniform number of sessions for all couples. In the discussion that follows we provide an example of a typical course of assignments.

Nongenital Touch

The first exercise is a whole body caress with no genital stimulation with absolutely no expectation of the man getting an erection. The couple is told that this is a touching exercise that will allow them to begin to reconnect with his body. He is also told that with this beginning exercise and all that follow, he is to place himself in a mental loop that involves only thoughts about what is feeling good at the moment. He is directed to tell his partner what to do in order to maintain the pleasurable sensations. A number of such exercises are prescribed.

Genital Touch

Once the male client is free from anxiety from being touched nongenitally, the couple can move on to the next level of exercises: body and genital stimulation for the purpose of discovering what feels good. His partner is to do some bodily touching with some brief and light genital touching. The man is reminded that this exercise is to help him experience genital sensations without the pressure of getting an erection. It is useful to tell him that such a small amount of stimulation rarely if ever leads to an erection. The partner should use a dry hand for stimulation and it should be brief. As the man's performance anxiety decreases he will recognize the pleasurable aspects of genital sensations. In turn, he can focus on his partner nonsimultaneously to ensure the touch assignments are sensual for both.

Focused Genital Touch

After a number of successful trials of genital stimulation, the focus can become more intensive and lubrication can be used. This set of exercises should be a slow, steady process of increasing penile stimulation with no expectation of an erection. At some point during focused penile stimulation the man is probably going to get erections consistently. He is told not to hurry things but to enjoy getting the erection slowly and not to worry if it disappears. At some point the man is able to obtain an erection on a consistent basis. Remember, never prescribe or predict an erection should occur.

Once the man has gained *erectile consistency*, he is told to do something that he usually perceives as unusual. He is told to ask for stimulation and, if an erection occurs, to keep it for a while and then have his partner stop the stimulation in order to lose the erection. He is to get and lose the erection three times during the exercise should he find it is possible. If not, he is not to worry about it but just enjoy the sensations. This exercise gives him the experience of losing an erection, not worrying that it is gone, and then regaining it.

Ejaculation

Once the man is able to sustain an erection through the earlier exercises (even though it is never prescribed), the therapist tells him that if he is fully erect and stimulated enough, he may want to ejaculate. In the exercise just prior to this one the man has learned that if he loses an erection during a sexual interaction, he will be able to regain it. Also, he does not need to feel anxious about whatever happens during their interaction since the experience will always be fulfilling in some way for both partners. He is allowed to ejaculate if he desires while receiving manual or perhaps oral stimulation only. Penetration is still prohibited. It is also important that the partner receives some forms of sensual or sexual stimulation as well during this phase of treatment and into the next. The couple should agree on the menu of things each might desire and is willing to provide. After the successful completion of the exercise where the man gets and loses his erection, the man is beginning to feel much more confident that he has regained his erectile functioning.

Penetration

Moving to the next level, the homework assignment that is given would be brief penetration. Once the man is confident he can obtain and keep an erection, the couple is asked if they would like to try a penetration exercise. This discussion focuses on heterosexual couples but the exercises can be modified for same-sex couples. If they are ready, prescribe the following: The female partner prelubricates so penetration is easy and they work out how penetration will occur. Usually it works best if she stimulates the man while he is on his back and not tensing the muscles in his lower body, which has the effect of lowering penile blood pressure. The brief penetration exercise should only be done if he gets an erection through manual stimulation and he is to maintain it for a few minutes until he feels it is well established or not likely to quickly dissipate when stimulation stops. The woman is to briefly mount him for a few seconds of penetration guiding his penis inside. After a few seconds, they stop the penetration part of the exercise and go back to manual stimulation. This procedure is repeated a number of times, with the length of penetration becoming more and more extended. The man needs to be told that physically moving his body around and interrupting physical stimulation reduces his chances of keeping an erection. Men will sometimes get an erection but then fumble around, trying to find a position for intercourse or lubrication and lose their erection. Older men as well as men who have had ED problems generally need constant stimulation to the point of penetration. The couple can start with periods of penetration of 15 to 30 seconds, move back to manual stimulation and then back to penetration for 15 to 30 seconds again. The man is asked to try three penetrations and then to ejaculate with manual stimulation if he desires to do so. With each subsequent exercise the period of penetration becomes longer and longer until he can experience penetration without losing it. He is then given permission to ejaculate intravaginally.

The next step is to try a variety of positions. The man is instructed that should the erection disappear, he would try manual stimulation for a few minutes to see what happens; if nothing happens as far as regaining an erection, the couple is to create a sexual experience doing other activities. Should his performance anxiety reappear, he might need to go back to some of the earlier exercises. The therapist should closely monitor progress and never try to push the therapy any faster than what seems likely to happen naturally. It is important to create successes and avoid what the couple would perceive as failures. The therapist can also reassure the couple that sometimes the pacing of the therapy has been too fast and they may need to back up an exercise or two. This idea normalizes the fact that performance will not be consistent in a linear way; it is normal for a couple to simply need more time on an earlier exercise. The therapist must also constantly monitor the level of anticipatory anxiety and performance anxiety experienced.

In the exercises mentioned, there is the frequent use of manual stimulation. After the first few trials, the therapist will recommend that the stimulation may be performed using a lubricant. One problem with lubricants is that they dry out quickly and might need to be replenished with water or more lubricant. Petroleum-based lubricants should never be used because they trap bacteria and can clog the urethra. The therapist and couple should investigate the expanding literature on sexual lubricants and find one that does not dry out quickly and also leaves any tissue it is used on moisturized.

Free Form Intercourse

The couple has now learned enough to be able to move on to intercourse without specific instructions. They are reminded that if there is a problem, they will benefit by using the earlier strategies and techniques to help them. If they had been using a medication, the dosage may gradually be reduced to nothing or to the lowest dose possible since there is the possibility of some to significant organic involvement. For some couples, just having a medication available provides a safety net that reduces anxiety. The therapist should carefully monitor any use or reduction of erectogenic medications or devices.

Once the couple has completed the assignments, the therapist needs to help prevent relapses by monitoring progress, especially the return of performance anxiety. Every week you should ask the man about his level of performance anxiety about having sex and especially about having an erection. The sessions can begin to taper off to every 2 or 3 weeks. Should the couple feel the problem is returning, they should call the therapist and come back for a session as soon as possible.

Final Issues in Treating ED

Once the ED problem has been resolved, there are other issues to consider. Some men with ED also have premature ejaculation (PE). They would need to continue treatment to resolve their PE. The female partner who has not had sex for some time may experience Genito-Pelvic Pain/Penetration Disorder or may wish to work on having an orgasm coitally. The entire pattern of their sexual interaction should be reviewed to make sure the couple is able to experience sexual satisfaction. The simple resolution of ED does not in any way ensure a functional and satisfying sexual relationship. For some couples, it is merely the beginning of correcting other sexual problems and developing ways of having sex that are creative, flexible, not performance driven and mutually satisfying.

Treating Premature (Early) Ejaculation

Premature (early) Ejaculation (PE), the most common of all male sexual disorders (Namavar & Robati, 2011), is defined as the inability to control when ejaculation occurs or when ejaculation happens too early for the man's partner to orgasm; thus, for many, ejaculation happens in 1 minute or less of penetration as defined in *DSM-5* (American Psychiatric Association, 2013). Many sexologists delineate PE by measuring the intravaginal ejaculatory latency time (IELT), or the time between the start of vaginal penetration and the onset of intravaginal ejaculation (Waldinger et al., 2005). For men who engage in nonvaginal sex or penetration, duration criteria have not been established (American Psychiatric Association, 2013). Nonetheless, PE is a significant problem for heterosexual men and for men who have sex with men (MSM); thus, our treatment approach can be modified for all men. Fundamentally, we believe clients with PE have a very low threshold of stimulation needed for ejaculation. The most realistic goal for the treatment of PE is having ejaculatory control that is satisfactory to the man and his partner.

Clients with PE and their partners are distressed by it because they feel it diminishes their sexual pleasure, regardless of the nature of sexual activity. The principle of treatment is to enhance the man's ability to control when he ejaculates (or has an orgasm although they are actually different phenomena) through a series of graded exercises. In treating PE, the partner is very involved; therefore, it is important to keep the idea of receiving emotional/physical pleasure in mind when the partner is on the receiving end of the homework assignment.

Betchen (2009, 2015) discussed a variety of potential causes for PE in his review in our companion volumes. Waldinger (2010) believed that individuals with lifelong PE were poor candidates for any treatment, due to the fact that they must have significant psychological problems. This assertion has not been made elsewhere in the literature. A wide variety of causes for PE are contained in the clinical literature but most lack substantial empirical evidence:

- Organic factors (diminished neurotransmission of serotonin; neurological problems; hormonal problems having to do with testosterone, thyroid stimulating hormone and Prolactin; prostate problems, Type II diabetes)
- Other sexual disorders (Erectile Disorder [ED], lack of interest in the partner)
- Psychiatric problems (anxiety, depression, embarrassment and guilt, lack of confidence, negative body image, lack of knowledge)
- Lack of sexual experience
- Relational difficulties (power struggles, poor communication, fears of intimacy, unrealistic sexual expectations)
- Idiosyncratic masturbatory patterns
- Nonspecified family of origin problems resulting in internalized emotional conflicts (as reviewed by Betchen, 2015).

The client should be assessed medically and from an Intersystem viewpoint in order to determine all the factors that might underlie this problem. In the previous list, one of the most striking contributory factors was ED (Rowland et al., 2010). They hypothesized that in an effort to achieve firmer erections, men would overstimulate themselves and consequently ejaculate prematurely. Also, men who are afraid of losing their erections will become overwhelmed with anxiety and ejaculate prematurely to avoid the embarrassment of ED. As clinicians, we have seen a number of cases where the two were correlated. It has been reported that as many as 30% of men with PE experience some degree of ED (McMahon et al., 2004). The direction of causality is not always clear.

Medical Treatment for PE

Betchen (2009, 2015) provided an excellent review of medications used to treat PE; however, to date, there are no FDA-approved medications designated for this purpose. Physicians often use serotonin-based antidepressants off label that are taken continuously and often have a number of unpleasant side effects, including inhibited or absent ejaculation and loss/reduction of sexual desire. We do not advocate using any drug off label whose action is unpredictable and has significant side effects unless the client has tried a course of sex therapy and has failed or the problem is primary PE where drug treatment appears to be the treatment of choice. For years, drug companies have been trying to find a short-acting drug that will delay ejaculation. Thus far, all efforts have failed. Dapoxetine is a potent serotonin-based medication that is administered on demand 1–3 hours prior to planned sexual activity. It is rapidly absorbed and eliminated, and can be taken more than once within a limited time frame (McMahon, 2012). This drug is used extensively in Europe and Canada and holds promise for future use in the United States specifically for PE.

At this stage of medical treatment there are three basic options: daily treatment with serotonergic antidepressants; off-label use, as needed, of serotonin-based antidepressants; or topical local anesthetics, which have little to no efficacy. The only good news is that it has been found that using an antidepressant at a low dose 4–6 hours prior to intercourse is sometimes efficacious and well tolerated by most men and for men with secondary and situational PE. A course of medical treatment and then discontinuation may lead to a restoration of ejaculatory control. However, in men with primary PE, when drug therapy was discontinued, the problem was likely to return (McMahon et al., 2004).

Behavioral Strategies and Techniques

The first step in treating PE is to decide if the man will be treated alone or in conjoint sessions with a partner. In our clinical experience, the outcome is better if the partner is involved. The second step involves teaching the man and his partner about the physiology of orgasm in order for them to learn to cease stimulation prior to the point of ejaculatory inevitability.

Psychoeducation about Orgasm

The therapist explains that the two phases of the male orgasm, emission and ejaculation, typically occur simultaneously, but in reality they are distinct activities, regulated by separate neural pathways (Waldinger, 2010). Emission begins after physical/psychological stimulation with the closure of the urethra at the bladder neck to prevent the release of urine from the bladder during orgasm. The internal structures such as the vas deferens, seminal vesicles, prostate and ejaculatory ducts contract and deposit seminal fluid (sperm, semen and prostatic fluid) into the penile urethra. The man experiences ejaculatory inevitability; thus, the orgasm cannot be stopped during the emission phase because it is already in process. Ejaculation encompasses the continued movement of seminal fluid into the penile urethra and expulsion of fluid from the penis.

Treatment of PE involves the use of behavioral techniques that promote awareness of sensations as they build and how to stop or reduce stimulation before orgasm commences. There is little empirical evidence regarding the efficacy of the behavioral techniques commonly used to treat PE although clinical reports support the efficacy of behavioral treatments in increasing ejaculatory control.

Stop-Start and Squeeze Techniques

In cases where PE is about 2 minutes or less during intercourse, we begin with the squeeze technique. In our experience, men with less ejaculatory control benefit from the squeeze technique first and then graduate to the start-stop technique described by Kaplan (1979). Men who have more control may begin with the start-stop technique from the beginning. In this technique, the man is instructed to lie on his back and focus on his genital sensations. He directs his partner to stimulate his penis with a dry hand slowly and lightly until he has a firm erection. When he feels he is getting very aroused and is approaching ejaculation, the partner is instructed or signaled to stop stimulation until the ejaculatory urge dissipates. Men with PE frequently have very little awareness of the progression of arousal prior to orgasm, or ignore this awareness for some reason.

The squeeze technique is similar to the stop-start technique in that the man is focused on the gradually mounting sensations as he approaches orgasm. The partner provides stimulation with a dry hand; when the man feels he is about to ejaculate, he indicates that and the technique is applied immediately. The squeeze automatically inhibits ejaculation.

The couple repeats this process at least three times during a single session and can have as many sessions during the week as they like. At this stage in treatment, we discourage ejaculation with manual stimulation and prohibit intercourse throughout the first stage of treatment. If the man were to ejaculate at this time, there would be backward conditioning of rapid ejaculation, which is self-defeating.

The Stop-Slow Technique

No lubrication is used in the first few exercises. The partner uses a dry hand to deliver the stimulation. Stimulation should be slow with little pressure applied at first; over time stimulation becomes more rapid and pressure is applied as the man begins to gain more control. Once the man is able to delay ejaculation for a longer period of time, the therapist switches to the start-stop/start-slow technique as described by Kaplan (1979). The partner provides stimulation and when the man feels he is approaching ejaculation, he signals his partner to stop, allowing the ejaculatory urges to subside. He then prompts the partner to begin stimulation again. There are several variations of this technique. The couple may have at least three sessions a week with three starts and stops during each session with no concern for time. Another variation is to set a goal of 10–15 minutes of stimulation with as many starts and stops as necessary but keeping the stimulation low enough that only a few are needed. Our experience has been that the more times the partners practice this exercise during the week, the faster they move through the therapy. For example, for one couple where the man would always ejaculate in less than 1 minute, the couple practiced the exercise at least once a day. This type of motivation is very unusual. Within just a month he gained significant control, to his disbelief. Within two months he achieved complete control over ejaculation and then the couple worked on how they could maximize their sexual pleasure.

In general, we prefer setting a time span for the stimulation with 3–5 starts and stops. Once the man has been able to delay ejaculation for 10–15 minutes with only a few starts and stops, he may be permitted to ejaculate during the last stimulation. He is now delaying ejaculation for 10–15 minutes, so ejaculation is a useful backward conditioning reinforcement in delaying ejaculation. *Backward conditioning* is a concept in advanced learning theory. The principle is that whatever was occurring prior to the reinforcement is reinforced. If the man receives stimulation, is able to delay it, and then ejaculates, he has experienced an increase in control based on backward conditioning.

The next progression is for the man to be stimulated by his partner, but instead of asking that the stimulation stop, he asks his partner to switch to slow strokes that are light in order to reduce stimulation. He can always ask for a stop if he feels he is overstimulated. With the start-slow technique, the same recommendation is given for 10–15 minutes of stimulation with 3–5 slows. The couple moves to higher levels of stimulation when the man feels he can control ejaculation. During this process, he is learning to pay attention to his premonitory sensations and use those sensations to gauge when he needs less stimulation. Premonitory sensations are those sensations that the man feels just prior to ejaculation; by slowing down or stopping stimulation, he may be able to delay ejaculation. Doing so involves moving from being stimulated by a dry hand to having the partner use lubrication with just manual stimulation. Once the couple is satisfied with ejaculation control with high levels of stimulation, they can move on to the next exercise.

The Quiet Vagina Technique

In heterosexual couples, the woman provides some stimulation with a lubricant to produce an erection. She also prelubricates herself with ample lubrication in order to minimize friction. Once the man has an erection, she mounts from on top and does not move in order to gradually become accustomed to intravaginal stimulation without ejaculation. For physiological reasons, most men can control ejaculation better when on bottom than when on top. We also instruct the man to relax the large muscles in the buttocks and thighs since these muscles appear to be orgasm triggers when tense. If the man places one hand below his thigh muscle, he will notice there are times when he begins to become tense.

The quiet vagina technique is repeated several times with slowly increasing stimulation or movement. The man must monitor his sensations carefully and let his partner know when to stop or slow down. During the initial phase of this exercise, penetration should be deep and the movement minimal. This type of thrusting pattern means the most sensitive part of the penis is in the posterior portion of the vagina where there aren't muscles creating friction against the penis. Over the course of several exercises the pace and length of stroking can be increased such that the glands penis is now moving over the pubococcygeus muscle, which supports the external third of the vagina and experiences more friction. Once control is achieved using the female superior position, the man can try different positions. The next position is usually male on top, using plenty of lubrication. Once again, he should achieve full penetration and make only short thrusts, slowly increasing the rapidity of movement and length of stroke over time. He is to monitor his sensations and slow down or stop when needed. Over time his control will improve. The therapist constantly monitors the couple's progress, adjusting the exercises accordingly. The couple may need to slow down or proceed faster through these exercises. Always check to make sure the man is monitoring his sensations and telling his partner what he needs in order to delay ejaculation. Since the basic principles behind the exercises are described from the beginning, the couple can be good collaborators in setting up the next exercise or modifying the exercise at home without consulting the therapist.

Once ejaculatory control is obtained, it is usually stable. Should the man find it difficult to control ejaculation using the pacing method described above, he may practice some of the earlier exercises again. It is important to increase the time between sessions but not to discontinue treatment. Instead, we recommend that the couple check in periodically, perhaps monthly, until the therapist is certain that ejaculatory control is learned. Follow-up sessions will help maintain his progress.

A final note about treatment: a man with PE is often pessimistic about ever obtaining ejaculatory control through talking therapy, communication and homework exercises. When beginning treatment, the couple is told that there is a standard treatment that usually works and will improve ejaculatory control. However, if the man is told that it might be possible to gain complete ejaculatory control in 10–15 sessions over about 3 months, it is likely the therapist will not be perceived as credible. Once the couple has experienced some success, the therapist might discuss the possibility of complete control, but it is wise never to promise something so unpredictable.

Treating Delayed Ejaculation

Delayed Ejaculation (DE) is the least common sexual disorder in men, the most poorly understood and one of the most difficult to treat. Over the years DE has been identified in a number of ways, which reflects how misunderstood this condition has been: retarded ejaculation, inhibited ejaculation, ejaculatory incompetence, male orgasmic disorder and impaired orgasm, to mention a few. In *DSM-IV-TR* (American Psychiatric Association, 2000) it was called Male Orgasmic Disorder. In *DSM-5* the current term is Delayed Ejaculation (American Psychiatric Association, 2013). According to the current diagnostic criteria, the disorder must occur 75%–100% for a minimum of a 6-month duration. A man with DE wants to ejaculate but experiences marked delay, marked infrequency or the complete inability to ejaculate. The symptom causes distress for the man and is not better explained by another medical or psychological condition. Hartmann and Waldinger (2007) probably provided the most clinically useful working definition of DE. They stated that if a man wishes to ejaculate, has a good quality erection and adequate stimulation but finds it difficult or impossible to ejaculate, then it should be considered DE. Additionally, the physiological duration and ease of ejaculation are variable conditions among men; thus, psychological, cultural, relational and contextual factors are superimposed on the man's physical abilities. All factors must be considered when assessing and treating DE.

Delayed Ejaculation (DE) may be lifelong or acquired, although the former is extremely rare. The prevalence of DE among American men is less than 1% (American Psychiatric Association, 2013) although the worldwide incidence is reported to range from less than 1% to 10% depending on the age of the participant and the country in which the study was conducted (Perelman & Rowland, 2006; Waldinger, 2010).

DE may be underreported because it can co-occur with other sexual dysfunctions such as erectile dysfunction or low sexual desire. In fact, Apfelbaum (2000, 2001) concluded that DE is often a manifestation of low sexual desire. DE is also associated with aging. Although prevalence data are sparse, it is estimated that 7%–15% of men over the age of 50 will cope with secondary delayed ejaculation. This form of sexual dysfunction is characterized by an erratic manifestation—sometimes it is a problem and other times it is not (Waldinger, 2010). This may be because older men experience degeneration of the nerves supplying the penis as they age, producing less sensitivity. DE may also be underreported due to embarrassment or belief in the mythological notion that a man is supposed to sustain erections for long periods of time before ejaculating. It should be mentioned that prevalence data involve men in heterosexual relationships, although one recent study revealed no significant differences in the incidence of DE between heterosexual men and homosexual men (Jern et al., 2010).

A number of pharmacological agents are often associated with delayed ejaculation (Rowland et al., 2010). Common medications that can cause delayed ejaculation include anticholinergics, antiadrenergics, antihypertensives, psychoactive drugs, selective serotonin reuptake inhibitors (SSRIs) and other antidepressants, antipsychotics and medications associated with the treatment of obsessive compulsive disorder (Corona, et al., 2011). Alcohol can also contribute to delayed ejaculation, although a review of research indicates that alcohol and delayed ejaculation have not been systematically studied (Richardson, Nalabanda, & Goldmeier, 2006).

It is quite probable that as men age, they will need to take more medications for medical problems, many of which can affect ejaculation, such as serotonin-based antidepressants and antihypertensive medications to control blood pressure (Richardson, Nalabanda, & Goldmeier, 2006). Because there has been little research about this particular disorder, the clinician will have to be astute and comprehensive in assessing for it. It is sometimes necessary to collaborate with health care providers to rule out medical issues and then develop a treatment approach with the client(s).

Assessment

DE is a complex problem that can involve medical, psychological or combined etiologies (McMahon, Jannini, Waldinger, & Rowland, 2013; Perelman, 2013). Treatment must be driven by a thorough assessment of the etiology. The contributory factors associated with DE are the following:

1. Relationship problems, such as partner sexual problems or partner health status
2. Relationship factors, such as poor communication or desire discrepancies
3. Individual vulnerabilities, such as history of sexual abuse or other psychiatric comorbidities, including anxiety, depression or situational stressors
4. Cultural or religious factors that serve as inhibitors against sexual activity or negative attitudes toward sexuality
5. Medical factors relevant to the prognosis

These contributory factors mentioned in the *DSM-5* (American Psychiatric Association, 2013) are consistent with the domains of the Intersystem assessment. One way to conceptualize DE is to consider it as an outcome of a variety of bio-psychosocial influences.

Individual Factors

From an individual psychological perspective, there are a number of potential etiologic factors for DE. Apfelbaum (2000) theorized that these men are out of touch with their sensory experiences because they feel they need to control or attend to their partner's pleasure too much. If the man is focused only on his partner's pleasure and giving his partner an orgasm, he might delay ejaculation so long that he loses sensitivity and becomes fatigued. In these cases, the man's goal is to ejaculate but only after he perceives that he has completely pleasured his partner. He experiences performance anxiety over his partner's performance and later over his inability to ejaculate. Interestingly, some men have no difficulty ejaculating with self-stimulation but cannot ejaculate intravaginally. Perelman and Rowland (2006) also noted that some men with DE have unusual masturbatory patterns or masturbate frequently. For example, we treated a man who could only ejaculate by thrusting into his bed. He has never stimulated himself manually nor had a partner stimulate him manually. Other men have a very high frequency of masturbation. What appears to be happening is that masturbation produces a high level of stimulation to which the man adapts or becomes conditioned. Intercourse produces a much lower level of stimulation. In such cases, it is useful to recommend that the man masturbate less frequently and lower the amount of stimulation he provides for himself manually. Some men can only ejaculate in response to fetishistic behavior. For example, one man in his 40s could not ejaculate during coitus unless his wife wore a red scarf around her neck, red high heel shoes and bright red lipstick. He could then ejaculate easily and multiple times during a single sexual encounter.

A final individual problem may be anticipatory or performance anxiety. The man could be suffering from a generalized anxiety disorder (and taking medication that might interfere with ejaculatory ability). Common manifestations of anxiety with DE are the man's worries about his partner's response to him, or apprehension over his anticipated ejaculatory inability (Bancroft & Janssen, 2000).

Relationship Issues

In some cases the relationship may be the most important factor. It has been proposed that insufficient pleasure from the sexual interaction, holding back as a way to gain power, ambivalence about commitment, insufficient stimulation from the partner, poor communication and a lack of attraction to the partner as opposed to a fantasized partner could be contributors to DE (Apfelbaum, 2000; Perelman & Rowland, 2006; Shull & Sprenkle, 1980). For example, in one case, the man was not sure he wanted to be in a committed relationship with a woman. He could have intercourse with her but in his mind intravaginal ejaculation was equivalent to making a commitment to her; thus, he did not ejaculate. This process was unconscious when treatment began. Another possible factor could be the fear of impregnation or the desire to avoid a subsequent pregnancy.

Often, the couple will present for treatment of DE when conception is desired as a result of intercourse. The motivation for treatment in such cases is about a goal state of pregnancy rather than enjoyment of sexual activity. We have seen cases where there is considerable pressure on the man to ejaculate during coitus, unnatural or judgmental focus by the couple on his performance and extreme sexual and relational dissatisfaction for both partners.

One phenomenological study of only five men supported many of the proposed causes just mentioned. Robbins-Cherry, Hayter, Wylie, and Goldmeier (2011) found there were four major themes in the men with DE. First, the men had experienced low self-esteem from adolescence that carried over into adulthood. They described themselves as feeling inadequate and lacking in sexual confidence, knowledge and experience, all leading to performance anxiety. Second, the men described a history of negative and unhappy relationships that were characterized by problems in the area of power and control. Interestingly, a number of these men had extramarital affairs and did not experience DE in those relationships. These men also complained of sexual boredom and lack of communication in long-term relationships. Third, most of the men watched Internet pornography and had unrealistic expectations for sexual interactions. They also complained of their wives' lack of vaginal tightness during penetration following their wives giving (vaginal) birth. Not surprisingly, they stated that masturbation was easier and gave them firmer erections and they could provide themselves with more stimulation than during intercourse. Fourth, some of the men did not think DE was a problem and only attended therapy at the insistence of their partner. They either seemed to think their ejaculatory response time was acceptable, they were resigned to delayed ejaculation or they experienced high performance anxiety and avoided sex.

The response of the partner should also be kept in mind. Just as with ED, DE may become the single focus of a sexual interaction, thus increasing performance anxiety. Sometimes the partners do not feel they are attractive enough or have lost their attractiveness or that they are incompetent lovers (Hartmann & Waldinger, 2007). As with any sexual dysfunction, partners often blame themselves for the man's DE. Additionally, they may suffer from sexual anxiety, disappointment and lack of confidence.

Intergenerational and Contextual Factors

Foley's (2009) review of the literature found sparse support for intergenerational or sociocultural etiological factors. Some causes that have been suggested for assessment include lack of sex education, strict religious beliefs, early punitive experiences with masturbation or sex, having a sexual script involving being selfless or selfish, sexual trauma, being emotionally detached during sex (which could be interpreted as an attachment disorder), sexual messages about being independent (if you orgasm, you will be dependent on the other person) and having an unrealistic understanding of sex through education.

Strategies and Techniques

The fact that the number of strategies and techniques for the treatment of DE is limited in the literature may be due to the rarity of the disorder. Thus, this section will be shorter than many of the treatment sections for the other disorders. Treatment techniques generally involve three major areas (Foley, 2009):

- Cognitive behavioral therapy and homework assignments that increase competence
- Insight-oriented strategies that reduce self-blame and judgment and increase feelings of self-acceptance
- Couple-focused strategies that promote intimacy and mutuality as well as further sexuality education and positive sexual interaction for the couple

Assess Thoroughly

Prior to beginning any treatment program the therapist must thoroughly assess all the potential factors that might be contributing to the DE. The first step is to rule out potential physiological etiologies and refer the man to a physician to determine if he has structural, neurological or endocrine abnormalities. In cases of secondary DE, first determine when the condition started, circumstances under which it is most evident and any medical factors that could be contributing. The client will need to be told that the problem is sometimes medical or induced by medications or other substances. The therapist may collect some information about medical conditions and medications and make referrals to the appropriate physicians. The medical issues can be treated to the extent possible and medications may be switched to something with less severe sexual side effects. If medical issues and medications are ruled out as the problem, the therapist can begin the course of therapy.

Reduce Sensory Defensiveness and Anxiety

Sensory defensiveness refers to an aversion to certain smells, sounds, feelings, tastes or touch. A number of senses are engaged during intercourse. The man may not like the wetness of kissing, vaginal wetness, bodily secretions, the sound of thrusting and so on. In those cases, the therapist would employ progressive desensitization to help remove the aversion. In one extreme case, a man exclaimed that women's vaginas were like "meat grinders." When he had intercourse, he believed that his penis would literally be destroyed. He avoided having intercourse and when he did, he was so anxious and fearful that he could not ejaculate. His mother had sexually abused him when he was younger.

Use Sensual Touch Exercises

Sometimes both partners are experiencing anxiety over having sex with its emphasis on ejaculation and each one is experiencing his or her own anxiety.

The couple may need to start with sensate focus exercises in order to reconnect in a nondemanding/nonthreatening way. Once they begin to have intercourse, the man should focus on only his pleasure and not on performance as suggested by Apfelbaum (2000). He is learning that sex is a mutually reciprocal process of giving and receiving pleasure. He needs to also learn to become more mindful of the situation and not engage in any self-criticism or ongoing evaluation of his performance.

Explore Masturbatory Patterns and Fantasies

DE is associated with high frequency of masturbation. In fact, masturbation is often the preferred method of reaching orgasm. Additionally, men who have trouble ejaculating intravaginally frequently have unusual methods of masturbation or idiosyncratic masturbatory patterns (Kobori et al., 2012). Obviously, for the man who masturbates frequently, the meaning of this behavior should be explored and masturbation should be minimized. It is common for men to become fixed on a particular scenario and reinforce the intensity of this preference through the release of dopamine during orgasm and other physical processes. Treatment involves convincing the man to eliminate the use of pornography during masturbation after an initial period of abstinence whose duration is determined by the client and therapist. We recommend that eventually, each time the man masturbates, he should use less stimulation, and we advise a lubricant, which simulates the vaginal environment. Men who have unusual masturbatory patterns are helped to learn to stimulate themselves in more standard ways. This means eventually using manual stimulation with a hand. In one case, the man masturbated by rubbing himself on the floor to induce ejaculation, a procedure that could not be replicated with a partner. Treatment involved many trials of carefully designed exercises to increase his sensitization to human touch and eventually sex with a partner. Moreover, in conjoint therapy, the couple learned to communicate preferences, wishes and desires.

For some men with DE, the presence of fetishes and fixed fantasies that are the source of their arousal may interfere with the ability to focus on their own genital sensations, self and partner. Fetishistic fantasy is not easy to eradicate; thus, treatment might involve increasing the fantasy repertoire and reducing exclusive focus on one fetish. This was the case with a man who was aroused by focus on muscular bodies, masturbating to photos of women body builders, but experienced an inability to ejaculate when with a normal woman. This fantasy was extremely ego-dystonic (not congruent with his beliefs or values) for him; thus, he avoided having sex with body builders even though he was extremely attracted to them. After several months of attempting to understand the genesis of this ego-dystonic fetish, he agreed to cease masturbating to these scenarios and was instructed to begin to masturbate to body builders who were less massive. Over a course of several weeks he gradually reduced the muscularity of the women in the photographs to which he masturbated. Through progressive conditioning he was able to step down to women who were muscular but not massively muscular. These were women who looked more like fitness models than body builders. This strategy proved successful. Another man always fantasized about the first girl with whom he had sex. She happened to have red hair. His wife had blond hair; he resented this fact and found his arousal and ability to ejaculate were diminished. Treatment focused on the meaning of the first relationship and the fact that she had rejected him. He was instructed to fantasize about women with blond or dark hair while masturbating and having intercourse, especially at the moment of orgasm. The point was to condition him to become aroused by hair colors other than red. He was also encouraged to develop other sexual fantasies that involved his wife.

Examine the Couple Relationship

In the section on etiology, a number of possible relational factors were mentioned. The overall quality of the couple relationship should be addressed as well as their knowledge of sex, sexual competence or skill and willingness to please each other. In one case, a man expected to get an erection (his partner expected this as well) without any physical stimulation and be able to ejaculate on demand when his partner told him to do so. Of course, this created tremendous anxiety for him because he felt he was always failing. It seemed the harder he tried to ejaculate, the less he was able. Poor communication, conflict, unresolved resentment, commitment issues and problems in the area of power and control could affect other relationships. All these issues can be manifested in a number of sexual problems, including DE.

Other Issues

As stated earlier, messages and modeling from the family of origin and sociocultural messages could play a role in the development and maintenance of DE. These influences become a part of the man's sexual script. The therapist must underscore and treat any influences that are contributory to DE, such as contextual, financial and work-related stress factors. Treating DE appears to be much like treating absent/low desire. There may be a confluence of factors inhibiting ejaculation. The therapist begins with a treatment plan in collaboration with the client(s) once medical issues have been ruled out; as the therapy unfolds, so do other potential inhibiting factors. The client(s) need to understand that treatment may be of variable length and the factors initially identified for treatment may not be the only ones to which the therapist needs to attend. In all cases, we believe it is important to instill hope that once all the factors inhibiting or delaying ejaculation are resolved, there are chances of a good outcome. The last possible case would be that ejaculation does not occur for either medical or psychogenic reasons, is not improved by therapy and the couple still learns to adapt to this situation and enjoys all the other aspects of sexual intimacy.

References

American Psychiatric Association. (2000). *Diagnostic and statistical manual of mental disorders* (4th ed., text rev.). Washington, DC: Author.

American Psychiatric Association. (2013). *Diagnostic and statistical manual of mental disorders* (5th ed.). Arlington, VA: Author.

Apfelbaum, B. (2000). Retarded ejaculation: A much misunderstood syndrome. In S. Leiblum & R. Rosen (Eds.), *Principles and practice of sex therapy* (3rd ed.) (pp. 205–241). New York: Guilford Press.

Apfelbaum, B. (2001). What the sex therapies tell us about sex. In P. Kleinplatz (Ed.), *New directions in sex therapy: Innovations and alternatives* (pp. 5–28). New York: Brunner-Routledge.

Bancroft, J., & Janssen, E. (2000). The dual control model of male sexual response: A theoretical approach to centrally mediated erectile dysfunction. *Neuroscience & Biobehavioral Reviews, 24*(5), 571–579.

Betchen, S.J. (2009). Premature ejaculation: An integrative, intersystems approach for couples. In K. Hertlein, G. Weeks, & N. Gambescia (Eds.), *Systemic sex therapy* (pp. 131–152). New York: Routledge.

Betchen, S.J. (2015). Premature ejaculation: A systemic treatment model for couples. In K.M. Hertlein, G.R. Weeks, & N. Gambescia (Eds.), *Systemic sex therapy* (pp. 90–106). New York: Routledge.

Bullough, V.L., & Bullough, B. (1995). *Sexual attitudes: Myths and realities*. New York: Promethus Books.

Byers, E. (2005). Relationship satisfaction and sexual satisfaction: A longitudinal study of individuals in long-term relationships. *The Journal of Sex Research, 42*(2), 113–118.

Carvalheira, A.A., Pereira, N.M., Maroco, J., & Forjaz, V. (2012). Dropout in the treatment of erectile dysfunction with PDE5: A study on predictors and a qualitative analysis of reasons for discontinuation. *The Journal of Sexual Medicine, 9*(9), 2361–2369.

Corona, G., Jannini, E., Lotti, G., Boddi, V., De Vita, G., Forti, G., & Maggi, M. (2011). Premature and delayed ejaculation: Two ends of a single continuum influenced by hormonal milieu. *International Journal of Andrology, 34*, 41–48.

Foley, S. (2009). The complex etiology of delayed ejaculation: Assessment and treatment implications. *Journal of Family Psychotherapy, 20*(2–3), 261–282.

Gambescia, N., & Weeks, G. (2006). Erectile dysfunction. In J. Fisher & W. O'Donohue (Eds.), *Practitioner's guide to evidence based psychotherapy* (pp. 284–290). New York: Springer.

Gambescia, N., & Weeks, G. (2015). Systemic treatment of erectile disorder. In K.M. Hertlein, G.R. Weeks, & N. Gambescia (Eds.), *Systemic sex therapy* (2nd ed.) (pp. 72–89). New York: Routledge.

Hartmann, U., & Waldinger, M. (2007). Treatment of delayed ejaculation. In S. Leiblum & R. Rosen (Eds.), *Principles and practice of sex therapy* (4th ed.) (pp. 241–276). New York: Guilford Press.

Jern, P., Santtila, P., Johansson, A., Alanko, K., Salo, B., & Sandnabba, N. (2010). Is there an association between same-sex sexual experience and ejaculatory dysfunction? *Journal of Sex and Marital Therapy, 36*(4), 303–312. doi:10.1080/0092623X.2010. 488102

Kaplan, H. (1974). *The new sex therapy.* New York: Brunner/Mazel.

Kaplan, H.S. (1979). *Disorders of sexual desire.* New York: Brunner/Mazel.

Kobori, Y., Aoki, H., Nishio, K., Sato, R., Ashizawa, Y., Yagi, H., Arai, S., & Okada, H. (2012). Rehabilitation for severe delayed ejaculation (intravaginal ejaculation disorder) with use of a masturbation aid. *Asian Pacific Journal of Reproduction, 1,* 262–264.

Mark, K., & Jozkowski, K. (2013). Mediating role of sexual and nonsexual communication in a sample of college-age heterosexual couples. *Journal of Sex & Marital Therapy, 39,* 410–427.

McMahon, C. (2012). Dapoxetine: A new option in the medical management of premature ejaculation. *Therapeutic Advances in Urology, 4*(5), 233–251.

McMahon, C.G., Abdo, C., Incrocci, L., Perelman, M., Rowland, D., Waldinger, M., & Xin, Z.C. (2004). Disorders of orgasm and ejaculation in men. *The Journal of Sexual Medicine, 1*(1), 58–65.

McMahon, C.G., Jannini, E., Waldinger, M., & Rowland, D. (2013). Standard operating procedures in the disorders of orgasm and ejaculation. *The Journal of Sexual Medicine, 10*(1), 204–229.

Monteiro, P., de Santa, P., de Santa, I., & Narciso, B. (2014). What is sexual satisfaction? Thematic analysis of lay people's definitions. *Journal of Sex Research, 51*(1), 22–30.

Namavar, M.R., & Robati, R. (2011). Removal of foreskin in remnants in circumcised adults for treatment of premature ejaculation, *Urology Annals, 3,* 87–92. doi:10. 4103/0974-7796.82175

Perelman, M.A. (2013). Delayed ejaculation. *Journal of Sexual Medicine, 10*(4), 1189–1190. doi:10.1111/jsm.12141

Perelman, M.A., & Rowland, D.L. (2006). Retarded ejaculation. *World Journal of Urology, 24*(6), 645–652.

Richardson, D., Nalabanda, A., & Goldmeier, D. (2006). Retarded ejaculation: A review, *International Journal of STD & Aids, 17,* 143–150.

Robbins-Cherry, S.A., Hayter, M., Wylie, K.R., & Goldmeier, D. (2011). The experiences of men living with inhibited ejaculation. *Sexual and Relationship Therapy, 26*(3), 242–253.

Rowland, D., McMahon, C., Abdo, C., Chen, J., Jannini, E., Waldinger, M., & Ahn, T.Y. (2010). Disorders of orgasm and ejaculation in men. *Journal of Sexual Medicine, 7,* 1668–1686.

Shull, G.R., & Sprenkle, D.H. (1980). Retarded ejaculation: Reconceptualization and implications for treatment. *Journal of Sex and Marital Therapy, 6,* 234–246.

Waldinger, M. (2010). Premature ejaculation and delayed ejaculation. In S. Levine, C. Risen, & S. Althof (Eds.), *Handbook of clinical sexuality for mental health professionals* (pp. 267–292). New York: Routledge.

Waldinger, M., Quinn, B., Dileen, M., Mundayat, R., Schweitzer, D., & Bodell, M. (2005). A multinational population survey of intravaginal ejaculation latency time. *Journal of Sexual Medicine, 2,* 492–497.

Weeks, G. R., & Fife, S. T. (2014). *Couples in treatment: Techniques and approaches for effective practice* (3rd ed.). New York: Routledge

Weiner, L., & Avery-Clark, C. (2014). Sensate focus: Clarifying the Masters and Johnson's model. *Sexual and Relationship Therapy, 29*(3), 307–319.

Zilbergeld, (1992). *The new male sexuality*. New York: Bantam.

9

TREATMENT PRINCIPLES, STRATEGIES AND TECHNIQUES SPECIFIC TO WOMEN

Treating Female Orgasmic Disorder

Female Orgasmic Disorder (FOD) is the difficulty or inability to experience orgasm during sexual stimulation such as with a vibrator, hand or oral stimulation, or via intercourse (coital anorgasmia). *The DSM-5* (American Psychiatric Association, 2013) catalogues the diagnostic criteria for female orgasmic disorder as follows:

- Marked delay in orgasm
- Marked infrequency of orgasm
- Absence of orgasm
- Or low intensity of orgasmic sensations

These symptoms are experienced on almost all (75%–100%) occasions of sexual activity for a minimum duration of 6 months. Moreover, the orgasm problem is distressful to the woman (American Psychiatric Association, 2013).

Prevalence statistics for FOD are extremely varied and inconsistent. In a review of epidemiological surveys, Graham (2010) cited methodological inconsistencies in gathering data as reasons for inaccurate estimates. Graham (2010) reported a range of prevalence rates from 3% to 34%. It is also difficult to determine if FOD is more common in younger or older women in empirical investigations. In our clinical experience, we note that many younger women with FOD are sexually inexperienced or have not experimented with self-stimulation to orgasm. Pre- and postmenopausal women sometimes complain that the quality of orgasm had diminished over time or that they need to work harder to achieve orgasm.

Women vary in their ascribed importance of the relationship between having orgasm and overall sexual satisfaction. It should be noted that about 50% of women who have experienced orgasm difficulties are not distressed by it (Laan, 2011). Thus, it is clear that for many women who have not experienced orgasm, it is not important to them. Sometimes, if they do come for treatment, it may be at the insistence of their partner. In these cases, their motivation to reach orgasm may be very low. While anorgasmia may have an organic basis, it is most commonly an issue of lack of experience with masturbatory orgasms and other psychological factors that inhibit the woman with FOD. A detailed sex history, sexual genogram and sexual timeline are essential.

In assessing for anorgasmia, it is important to determine that the woman or her partner can provide adequate stimulation and communicate about what is desired. Next, it is imperative to gather information about the woman's levels of arousal, ability to focus on pleasurable sexual feelings, comfort with her sexual fantasies and so on. Finally, considering that there are different presentations of FOD, the clinician must assess for conditions under which the difficulty occurs. Some women have never had an orgasm; others have had an orgasm but are no longer able to. Some women can orgasm with solo sexual activity using a vibrator but not with manual stimulation. In other cases, some can have an orgasm with manual or oral stimulation, but not with penetration. Some women can attain adequate coital alignment with some partners and not others. As with all sexual dysfunctions, the clinician must determine if FOD is lifelong or acquired; situational or generalized; and if there is psychological distress, is it mild, moderate or severe?

Individual Medical Issues

Some medications, such as the serotonin-based antidepressants, can significantly diminish, delay or make orgasm impossible. The therapist should investigate all medications being taken and whether any of them have sexual side effects. Neurological problems such as spinal cord injuries, multiple sclerosis (MS) and other medical conditions and treatment can make orgasm difficult; thus, the woman's physician, usually an ob/gyn, should evaluate the woman if the therapist suspects a medical etiology. One client presented with MS and stated she had never had an orgasm and wanted to have one before she died. Her MS was at a point where she was having difficulty walking without a cane. After much experimentation, she was able to have an orgasm with vibratory stimulation of the clitoris, vagina and anus. The point is that aggressive treatment can sometimes overcome medically related problems even when the physician might say it is impossible.

Intergenerational Factors

The role of intergenerational factors in orgasm problems is not clear. It is commonly believed that misconceptions about sex, negative attitudes, sexual orientation issues and sexual identity problems may play a role, but the exact nature of the role is not clear (Basson et al., 2004; Graziottin & Leiblum, 2005). What is most interesting is that childhood sexual abuse does not appear to play a major role in anorgasmia, according to McCabe and Giles (2012). McCabe's review of the literature suggests that a range of individual factors may contribute to lack of orgasm but only two have been empirically verified. Others (Staples, Rellini, & Roberts, 2012) reported that avoidance of intimate relationships could be a mediating variable in women with orgasm difficulties and childhood sexual abuse. The connection between FOD and childhood sexual abuse remains unclear.

Individual Psychological Factors

Many women with FOD experience performance anxiety, which may be a cause or consequence of this condition. They worry about failing to have an orgasm; therefore, they are much less likely to experience orgasm. Some of these women also report response anxiety or the effort to force feelings of arousal and orgasm. The anxiety blocks the arousal and orgasm. High levels of stress are also associated with orgasmic dysfunction (McCabe & Giles, 2012). Although not empirically validated, women with FOD often appear to be unable to relax in numerous situations, including sex. They tend to be pleasure averse and might prefer to distract themselves with a nonsensual activity or project and derive fulfillment from those activities. They report focusing on nonsexual topics during sex, such as the laundry or grocery list. They are easily distracted from focusing on mounting feelings of pleasure. These women tend not to be self-indulgent or pleasure seeking in general although they are typically satisfied with their lives. It is difficult to convince them that experiencing orgasm is something they might want for their own pleasure. Finally, although there are no empirical data to support this clinical assertion, many women in our practices regarding FOD demonstrate fear of the loss of control in many contexts, especially partnered sexual activity (Meana, 2009).

Relational Issues

Relational factors may play the largest role in orgasm difficulties; thus, it is essential to assess for the women's level of current relationship satisfaction and history of previous intimate relationships. The quality of the relationship, enjoyment of sexual activities and level of affection may contribute to orgasm problems. McCabe's (2015) review of the literature showed that several studies had demonstrated that communication problems contribute to lack of orgasm. In assessment, it is clear that the focus should not be exclusively on issues such as the nature of the orgasm or lack thereof, but on all the potential intergenerational, individual and relational factors that might be involved. For example, a man who is sexually insensitive, shows no affection, initiates crudely, provides little to no foreplay and reaches orgasm quickly is very likely to have a partner who has orgasm problems.

Strategies and Techniques

The treatment program for FOD addresses all domains of the intersystem described previously (individual, couple, family-of-origin, relational, contextual, etc.) but focuses predominately on cognitive-behavioral interventions identified by Barbach (2000) and Heiman and Meston (1997).

Directed Masturbation

This approach has been shown to be an effective evidence-based form of cognitive-behavioral therapy for treating FOD. In fact, the success rate has been reported to be between 80% and 90% for primary anorgasmia (LoPiccolo & Stock, 1986) and between 10% and 75% for women with secondary anorgasmia (Kilmann, Boland, Norton, Davidson, & Caird, 1986). Directed masturbation (DM) begins with psychoeducation about sexual structures and functioning, and progresses through a series of self-exploration and self-pleasuring exercises to be practiced when alone. Self-stimulation is most effective because there is a built-in feedback loop telling the woman exactly what she needs. Sometimes women will need to begin with a higher level of stimulation than can be provided by self-stimulation. Vibratory stimulation may be required. The therapist will need to discuss the meaning and use of a vibrator and direct the woman to some resources. We have found the following online resources provide accurate information about sexuality, sex toys, G-spot stimulators, vibrators, dildos and so on. The therapist should carefully explore any website first before recommending it to a client. Some websites might be too direct for some clients.

- A Woman's Touch: http://a-womans-touch.com/sex_counselor.php?cat ID=355
- A Woman's Touch Sexuality Resource Center: http://www.sexualityresour ces.com
- Betty Dodson with Carlin Ross: http://dodsonandross.com
- Good Vibrations: http://www.goodvibes.com

Eventually, the progress made during the solo exercises can be transferred to partnered sexual activity. DM is often used in conjunction with other therapeutic modalities, such as sensate focus and communication skills, particularly with secondary anorgasmia. According to Hucker and McCabe (2013), the best combination of therapy involved DM, improved comfort with the body, communication skills training, couples therapy to attend to the issues in the relationship and mindfulness-based online treatment.

These findings are consistent with the Intersystem Approach to treatment. Moreover, these outcomes should suggest that with secondary orgasmic problems, masturbatory training is not sufficient due to psychological rather than conditioning problems. Intersystemic assessment and treatment combined with directed masturbation should produce better results. Additionally, we do not define anorgasmia as the inability to orgasm with intercourse. We view coital orgasms as an option that a woman may choose or not. Additionally, some women may not have the sensory threshold needed to reach orgasm with the minimal amount of stimulation that intercourse affords. The principle of treatment is to work through any psychological barriers to having an orgasm, systematically create enough stimulation for orgasm to occur consistently and then lower the threshold of orgasm to the lowest point possible.

The Use of Fantasy

Sexual fantasies are an essential element of sexual desire and arousal. It is important to appreciate the role of fantasy in continuing the arousal process as the woman approaches orgasm. Orgasm is not just a mechanical process; sexual fantasy promotes and heightens the level of excitement that leads to orgasm. Often, women inhibit their fantasies because they are uncomfortable with the subject matter. The therapist can ask about sexual fantasies when conducting the sex history. This topic often needs to be reexamined because women are typically too embarrassed to discuss what they think about when they are sexually aroused. The therapist needs to explain the role of fantasy and arousal in relation to orgasm and normalize that fantasies can be extremely varied. We have heard from some women that they cannot fantasize. In these cases we recommend female erotic literature or films. Additionally, we recommend books such as: *Arousal: The Secret Logic of Sexual Fantasies* (Bader, 2002) or *My Secret Garden: Women's Sexual Fantasies* (Friday, 1973).

Exploring Barriers to Orgasm

For the woman. What, if any, are the psychological obstacles to having an orgasm for the woman? Do these barriers involve negative associations for having an orgasm, such as losing control or being dependent on the partner? The therapist must carefully assess internalized fears, misattributions and misinformation, and work through those difficulties. Also, the therapist needs to explore messages originating within the family of origin, religion and culture. Many women have received negative religious messages about enjoyment of sexuality, or strong edicts about sex for procreation and not for pleasure. For some women, it is culturally inappropriate to enjoy sexuality or to act in a sexual way. For them sexual enjoyment is associated with undesirable attributes. Ask the woman about the negative internalized messages and the meanings connected to them. A sexual genogram and sexual timeline can help uncover these negative messages. This work can be done in the individual sessions but if the partner is available, the discussion can be enriched and embellished. In one case, a 50-year-old woman reported that she was never orgasmic with her husband. This woman was capable of orgasm when alone and, in fact, pleasured herself often. Although she offered a few complaints about her husband's personality, she reported that they were essentially fairly companionate. An exploration of her family of origin revealed that her parents had a very contemptuous marriage, punctuated by bitter arguments and negative comments about each other to the client. Effectively, she grew up being afraid of marriage. In treatment she learned that she held back a part of her sexual enjoyment from her husband in order to feel safe. This was a part of a larger issue of being afraid to be married, not necessarily fearing him.

For the relationship. Many heterosexual men carry cultural beliefs and expectations about the association between masculinity and pleasing the partner. Does her anorgasmia mean he is less of a man? Does the man believe he has to give her an orgasm because that's his role? Is there a control/power issue in the relationship? Explore the couple's dynamics around orgasm. Does the couple experience related problems that would prevent an orgasm, such as anger or resentment? Does the woman like her partner? Does she trust her partner? Work through the couple related problems. One of the most common negative messages is about self-stimulation or masturbation, thus preventing any experimentation that facilitates orgasm with a partner. As stated, masturbatory training is one of the most important factors in a woman becoming orgasmic. Transferring the experience of orgasm the woman has learned on her own to partnered sex requires considerable support from the therapist. These women are often too embarrassed to talk about sex, particularly their own sexual preferences. The therapist will need to support the couple in a series of conversations that should help them mutually enjoy what the woman has learned on her own. Also, the conjoint sessions provide an opportunity to dispel myths and fears the couple might be holding and not discussing. The therapist will also need to explore how comfortable the partner feels about using a vibrator during sex. While some men feel very comfortable with vibrators, others have a great degree of discomfort, particularly those who feel it is their responsibility to provide pleasure to the partner. In our practices we have found that lesbian women are considerably more comfortable with use of sex toys and vibrators. For the heterosexual women, education and permission giving within the couple are important for overcoming resistance to using devices that will provide the higher levels of stimulation that are sometimes needed.

Providing Bibliotherapy and Education

Bibliotherapy for anorgasmia can start by reviewing anatomical photographs with the client. In our practices we commonly use electronic devices such as iPads or computers to instantly present information to the woman when the time is right. This kind of bibliotherapy can be timed to occur concomitantly with the women's own self exploration of her genitals with a mirror during home assignments. The therapist might recommend websites or books that contain accurate information about the physiology of sex and the nature of the female sexual response. Always be mindful to recommend materials that the client can tolerate. Additionally, the therapist should read what the client is reading so that each will have the same understanding of the material. Bibliotherapy should include information on sexuality in general, becoming orgasmic, the experience of masturbation and orgasm and sexual fantasies. The therapist may wish to consult book *The Science of Orgasm* (Komisaruk, Beyer-Flores, Whipple, 2006), which contains information about orgasm, neuroanatomy, neurotransmitters and so on. Although this book might be too advanced for some clients, it is a necessity for the therapist. Many therapists tend to recommend books they are most comfortable with. Two examples are *For Yourself* and *For Each Other* (Barbach, 2000, 2001); these books have been long-standing favorites due to the sensitivity of the author about anorgasmia and the applicability of these books for the woman and her partner.

Assigning Appropriate Homework

With FOD, assignments to be performed at home are a critical component of treatment. The therapist should explore the woman's history with doing homework assignments in therapy and her feelings about doing homework assignments with herself and her partner. Additionally, the tasks should be carefully paced so that the woman does not become frustrated or overwhelmed. The homework exercises initially involve just the woman learning about her body and how to stimulate herself in order to receive as much pleasure as possible. In most cases, this will lead to experiencing an orgasm, but the therapist never prescribes that she must have an orgasm. The partner does not need to be involved unless the woman desires it. The majority of women in our experience are more comfortable doing these exercises alone.

The behavioral assignments are carried out three times a week. Later, the woman's partner will be providing her with stimulation; the woman is helped to direct her partner to give her any form of stimulation that feels good (except intercourse) to which they mutually agree. These exercises are a version of sensate focus and the partner should be able to receive pleasure also. Of course, stimulation of the partner occurs nonsimultaneously. Some couples will try to stimulate each other simultaneously, which is distracting. They must take turns and each must fully experience the sensations he or she is feeling while being stimulated. The therapist may accelerate or decelerate these steps or skip some entirely depending on the presentation of the problem. Begin the process of giving homework assignments, keeping these steps in mind throughout.

Beginning phase. Homework actually begins in the office with a discussion and examination of the reading materials the woman is going to use. Perhaps she will read the first chapter of an assigned book on her own and the therapist will review this chapter with the woman in session. If she is able to read the chapter and absorb it, the woman is instructed to continue reading and her partner may be invited to read the same text. They can then discuss what they are learning, which will have the indirect effect of helping them communicate about sexual issues and express themselves during sexual interactions. Next, the therapist recommends that the woman perform a self-genital examination. The details of this examination are thoroughly discussed in the session so that the woman is emotionally prepared for what she will do at home. The woman performs a genital examination with a mirror at home and uses a selected book with anatomical diagrams in order to identify all of the sexual parts. Once she has done the examination successfully, the process is repeated with the partner so he knows the structures and their functions. The genital examination helps the woman become more comfortable with her genitalia, improve communication, give the couple the language to discuss what needs to be stimulated and assure the woman that she has all the parts. We encourage the woman to take note of her feelings as she is doing the genital exam. Sometimes it is helpful for her to make brief notes about her feelings so that she can discuss them in session. We have seen a number of women who claim they cannot orgasm because they do not have a clitoris. They are always delighted to report back that after the mirror exam they have located the missing organ. Have the woman touch her genital area during the mirror exercises to connect the feeling of touch with the particular part of the structure she is touching, focusing on which parts are most sensitive. Process any resistance to touching the genital area.

Intermediate phase. The initial touching exercises with the mirror are designed to help the women feel the different structures and assess their sensitivity. Once this initial exploration has been successfully completed, the next exercise is to touch in order to explore which structures produce the most pleasurable sensations. The goal is not orgasm, but rather the discovery of the pleasure associated with particular anatomical parts. Tell the woman to focus on the clitoral area. Process her reactions and feelings. In subsequent sessions, homework involves the woman touching the clitoral area in order to produce as much pleasurable sensation as possible but not to worry about orgasm. Ask about what she felt and process her reactions and feelings. Continue to ask this question for the subsequent exercises in very carefully paced increments. The therapist wants to prescribe exercises that are going to have a good outcome. Continue this process until the woman wishes to try the exercises with a partner. Never prescribe an orgasm.

If the woman is feeling pleasurable sensations, move on with increased stimulation. (If she is not feeling sexual sensations, there is clearly a psychological barrier that needs work.) Some women will unconsciously cut off the sensations and thereby not be able to orgasm. Prescribe 10–20 minutes of self-stimulation, starting with slow, soft stimulation and moving to harder, faster stimulation later. Suggest that the woman use a lubricant to avoid irritation. Hopefully, doing this exercise will trigger an orgasm or move her closer to an orgasm. This exercise can be repeated a few times if the woman feels she is approaching an orgasm. If manual stimulation alone is not enough to produce an orgasm, then more intensity is needed. In the previous section, we discussed the use of vibrators. A vibrator can be incorporated at this stage of homework with instructions to focus on very gentle stimulation of the clitoral hood, clitoris and entire genital region. Some women can overstimulate themselves with the vibrator so the therapist should warn the woman in advance to use very gentle stimulation. In other words, the stimulation may be too strong initially. A lighter touch can be used or a cloth can be wrapped around the vibrator to reduce the level of stimulation. Additionally, a vibrator may also be used during intercourse if the woman wants to achieve an orgasm that way and she and her partner are accepting of this enhanced stimulation. A small vibrator will need to be used and the couple will need to use a position that will allow for both penetration and vibratory stimulation. One position that works well is the woman on top, sitting somewhat upright. The couple will need to be creative and experiment with several positions. They can do this as a practice exercise rather than wait until having intercourse for the purpose of experiencing being with each other and sharing sensations. Advances in vibratory technology are constantly being made. Therapists can keep up with this technology by attending the exhibits at AASECT (American Association of Sexuality Educators, Counselors and Therapists) as well as referring to some of the websites mentioned previously. Review with the couple all of the factual information related to vibrator use so that they are on the same page regarding its use. Essentially, be sure that the woman has communicated this information to her partner.

Using a vibrator almost always produces an orgasm within the first weeks of use. Some women fear becoming addicted to a vibrator or feel it is not natural. These beliefs will need to be processed. One woman used a vibrator for an extended length of time and every time she came close to an orgasm, she knew she was somehow stopping the process. It was clear she had a psychological block to experiencing an orgasm. If it is clear that an orgasm should have been the outcome of the exercise, but the woman feels she is doing something to stop it, then suspend the use of the vibrator or manual stimulation until the psychological block has been worked through. Otherwise, process the sensation of orgasm, how long it took and how the woman felt about using the vibrator. The initial sensation of an orgasm may be disappointing to a woman. We have found that the first few orgasms may be mild, but the intensity will increase with practice.

Advanced phase. Women who have never had an orgasm do not know what to expect or how an orgasm feels. They only know that other women have orgasms and that they should feel good. It may be useful to prescribe the book *The Hite Report* (Hite, 1976). The first couple of chapters normalize masturbation and women describe their experience of orgasm. These descriptions are useful in creating knowledge of how an orgasm can feel. Prescribe the use of the vibrator until the woman can achieve an orgasm quickly and consistently with this method. When *orgasm consistency* has been reached, begin to phase out the use of the vibrator. Have the woman use the vibrator until near orgasm and then switch to manual stimulation. Continue to phase out the use of the vibrator earlier and earlier during arousal so that eventually she can have an orgasm through manual stimulation alone. This is usually possible but may take a number of sessions. A few women may continue to need a higher level of stimulation that only a vibrator can produce.

The partner may become involved with these steps at any point, depending on the woman's desire. The couple then repeats some of the same steps with the partner providing the stimulation with the vibrator or manually with the woman giving instructions. The woman is to focus on what is feeling good in the moment and what she desires to maintain the pleasurable sensations. Explain the need for stimulation of sufficient *duration* (10–20 minutes), *focus* (clitoral), and *intensity* (how much pressure and rapidity of movement). Focus on facilitating communication and the man's willingness to cooperate. Is he doing things to sabotage the exercises? Eventually the woman should be able to orgasm with her partner providing the stimulation. This may take several exercises and, if needed, the couple can repeat these exercises with the male using the vibrator and then fading it out. By *fading it out* we mean using the vibrator for shorter periods of time or when the women reports that she feels she is close to the last time she achieved this level of stimulation and was then able to switch to manual stimulation or just intercourse.

Once the couple has reached a point where the woman can easily achieve an orgasm with manual stimulation, they are ready to move on to intercourse (or penetration with a dildo in lesbian couples) under prescribed conditions. Make sure they feel ready to move to the next step. The partner provides foreplay or stimulation to near orgasm. The couple quickly switches to intercourse with female on top. With female in the superior position the woman can press the clitoral area into his pubic area, thus maximizing stimulation. This procedure is called the coital alignment technique. This exercise is repeated a number of times to see if she can learn to have an orgasm this way. Some women do not prefer to be on top. The male-superior position can also be used with the coital alignment technique (Eichel, Eichel, & Kule, 1988). The male thrusts deep and with short strokes, pressing into her pubic/clitoral area to maximize stimulation. A technique that can be used before or after is to have the man provide manual/vibrator simulation during intercourse with the woman in the superior position. After a few sessions it will become clear whether the woman can achieve an orgasm only with manual stimulation/vibrator/oral sex, needs extra stimulation with intercourse or can have an orgasm though intercourse, with or without additional stimulation. The therapist processes whatever she is capable of doing and how the couple will incorporate her orgasmic potential into their lovemaking. It is important that they feel they have succeeded in achieving sexual satisfaction even though the goal of coital orgasms may not be met. Any final issues that may have been overlooked earlier can be discussed at this time.

The therapist can discuss the overall pattern of lovemaking and the couple can maximize their pleasure with each one's capabilities, levels of desire, pattern of initiation, frequency and so on. Although not part of treating anorgasmia, the therapist may also choose to help the woman learn to become multiorgasmic through the use of combined G-spot stimulation and clitoral stimulation. There are a number of popular books and articles on G-spot stimulation and extended orgasms for those couples who are interested. The basic principle is to switch between the stimulation of the G-spot digitally and the clitoris. When one area ceases to produce the orgasmic response, a switch is made to the other area. Extended orgasms require time in locating the G-spot, learning how to effectively stimulate it and practicing to master extended orgasms. Of course, extended orgasms are an optional addition to the therapy, require commitment on the part of both partners and occur after continued practice. A therapist wishing to teach a couple this procedure should be thoroughly familiar with the literature on this topic. In addition to the book mentioned previously, there are several other popular books on extended female orgasms (e.g., *ESO: Extended Sexual Orgasm* by Brauer and Brauer, 1983).

Treatment of Genito-Pelvic Pain/Penetration Disorder

Genito-Pelvic Pain/Penetration Disorder (GPPPD) is a new term used in *DSM-5* that refers to a complex sexual dysfunction that is characterized by pelvic or genital pain experienced primarily during intercourse (American Psychiatric Association, 2013). This term replaces the diagnoses of vaginismus and dyspareunia. In the past, intercourse that was painful was considered a sexual disorder. The reverse is now true. GPPPD is a pain disorder, which has significant effects on sexual functioning.

The diagnostic criteria are persistent or recurrent difficulties for at least 6 months with one or more of the following:

* Vaginal penetration during intercourse
* Marked vulvovaginal or pelvic pain during vaginal intercourse or penetration attempts
* Marked fear or anxiety either about vulvovaginal or pelvic pain in anticipation of, during or as a result of or vaginal penetration
* Marked tensing or tightening of the pelvic floor muscles during attempted vaginal penetration
* The problem causing clinically significant distress for the woman

The sexual dysfunction is not better accounted for by a nonsexual mental disorder, the effects of a substance or medication (American Psychiatric Association, 2013). GPPPD may be lifelong (present since the woman was sexually active) or acquired (the disturbance began after a period of relatively normal sexual function).

Prevalence

The latest data on prevalence of dyspareunia show that this problem occurs from 14% to 34% of the time in younger women and 6.5% to 45% in older women (van Lankveld et al., 2010). The prevalence rates for vaginismus range from 0.4% to 6% (ter Kuile & Reissing, 2014).

Individual Factors

Individual biological factors are believed to be a common cause of GPPPD. These causes may range from a chronic disease such as pelvic inflammatory disease, endometrioses, urinary tract infections, yeast infections, loss of vaginal elasticity, episiotomies and chemotherapy (Meana, 2012). The most common type of GPPPD appears to result in vestibulodynia (Harlow, Wise, & Stewart, 2001). The pain occurs when any attempt at penetration is made. Pelvic floor abnormalities are also associated with genital pain (Meana, 2015).

Individual psychological factors do not appear to play a major role. However, an unfortunate feedback loop is established in this disorder. The pelvic pain leads to hypervigilance, pain catastrophizing, fear of pain, negative sexual attitudes, anxiety and distraction from sexual cues and depressive symptoms (Brotto, 2012). Thus, attempts at intercourse produce pain, pain leads to an avoidance of sexual activity and the cycle continues.

Relational Factors

Relational causes are also not a direct cause of GPPPD. However, the partner may respond to the pain in a number of ways. The partner may press for intercourse even though it is painful, but more typically begins to avoid intercourse and all sexual activity entirely. This reaction means the couple loses all physical and sexual connection.

Intergenerational Factors

Intergenerational and sociocultural factors also appear to play a small role in GPPPD. It has been suggested that religious orthodoxy prohibiting premarital sex may play a role (ter Kuile & Reissing, 2014). The literature on GPPPD is virtually nonexistent. Researchers have had to extrapolate from the findings regarding the diagnoses of vaginismus and dyspareunia and other disorders that produce genital pain. Readers interested in learning more about this disorder will need to search these terms as well as the new diagnostic label.

Terms Used to Describe Pain

Vaginismus

Vaginismus has been defined as a disorder in which the woman has difficulty with penetration because the muscles surrounding the vaginal opening tighten or go into spasm. Historically, vaginismus has been viewed as a psychogenic disorder involving the pubococcygeus (PC) muscle surrounding the vagina tightening so that penetration is difficult, if not impossible. Women presenting with vaginismus are told a gynecologist should assess them first, one who is familiar with pelvic pain disorders and their proper evaluation (Meana, 2009). Generally speaking, women with vaginismus will present with a sensation of stretching, burning or tearing around the vaginal opening. In many instances, the woman has been unable to insert a tampon, a finger or any object into the vagina. Alternately, women can present individually or as a couple within unconsummated marriage or where sex is very infrequent due to the pain. Typically these women are able to experience sexual desire for their partners, arousal and orgasm. Often the couples engage in noncoital sexual activity. Sometimes they present because they want to get pregnant and realize that conception is impossible with this condition.

In the past literature, pain that is deeper, not localized in the vaginal opening and sharp usually represented a medical problem that may have been missed by the physician. Ideally, the physician should have an interest in sexual medicine. Assuming the problem is vaginismus, treatment consisted of several well-defined steps as described by Kaplan (1979). Some women do not have severe vaginismus so they may skip a number of the initial steps. The principle of treatment is to facilitate the relaxation (systematic desensitization) of the PC muscle so that penetration is comfortable.

Dyspareunia

Dyspareunia is a term that is generally used to describe genital pain that precludes intercourse. The term means painful sex. It is a nonspecific term that can be used for men and women. We are reviewing it here so that readers are familiar with its use. Women with dyspareunia often report pain during intercourse. They also experience fear, aversion to touch, avoidance of sex, impaired sexual functioning and personal distress, to name a few symptoms. The origin of the pain will need to be determined through a gynecologic examination. Many therapists use dyspareunia to describe pain from any number of regions within the vagina or vulva; thus, the specific origin of pain needs to be determined.

Vulvodynia

We briefly review here some anatomic terms that the therapist must understand when treating genital pain. The *vulva* refers to the external genital organs of the female. In colloquial speech, the term *vagina* is often used to refer to the female genitals, although this usage is anatomically incorrect. The vagina is a specific internal structure, whereas the vulva is the entire exterior genitalia. The vulva is comprised of major and minor anatomical structures, including the labia majora, labia minora, clitoris, urethra, vestibule of the vagina, greater and lesser vestibular glands and vaginal orifice.

Vulvodynia is a form of dyspareunia (painful sex). In the case of vulvodynia, the pain is within the vulva. Typically, the pain is described as soreness, burning and sometimes searing. This condition often causes limitation of activities, psychological distress and sexual dysfunction. Relationship problems can occur as the result of chronic frustration, disappointment and depression associated with the condition.

There are two forms of vulvodynia:

1. Dysesthetic vulvodynia: constant unprovoked vulvar pain
2. Vulvar vestibulitis syndrome (VVS): pain experienced only when pressure is applied to the vestibule, the area surrounding the entrance to the vagina. VVS is a type of vulvodynia that is a leading cause of dyspareunia in women. Inflammation and cutting pain at the vaginal vestibule occur, although the condition varies in persistence and location. Pain may be constant or intermittent, localized or dispersed. The pain is provoked by contact

or attempted penetration. Additionally, increased pelvic floor muscle tension (called hypertonicity) has recently been found to be a component of this condition.

The research reviewed in this section demonstrates that pelvic/penetration pain is most commonly a medical issue with significant effects on the woman's sexuality and the couple's sexual relationship. Treatment should be collaboration between a physician with specific training in pelvic/genital pain, the sex therapist and in many cases a physical therapist. The internal muscles supporting the vagina may become hypertonic (overly tense). They can be manipulated through trigger-point therapy by a physical therapist with special training. The physical therapist can teach the client and/or her partner how to go about manipulating the points that need to be released and how to do so. In order to find a physical therapist, readers can access the national database by going to the American Physical Therapy Association (www.apta.org).

Women with dyspareunia, vulvar vestibulitis syndrome, vulvodynia and clitorodynia (vulvodynia affecting the clitoris) need a different approach to treatment. The clinician unfamiliar with these disorders may confuse them with vaginismus and begin a course of treatment based on PC muscle relaxation, which is inappropriate. Due to the complexity of the disorder it will be difficult to tell whether a course of sex therapy should begin or whether medical treatment in conjunction with sex therapy would be most valuable. In cases where the problem has a biogenic cause, there have always been psychological consequences. For medically caused sexual pain problems, the therapist may help the couple adapt their sexuality to these conditions and help the woman with the chronic pain and encourage a change in sexual image.

Therefore, some sex therapy will be needed. Table 9.1 describes these conditions and their treatment:

TABLE 9.1 Resources for Information on Genito-Pelvic Pain Disorders in Women

Topic/Website	Web Address
Female Dyspareunia	http://www.vulvodynia.com.au/info/terminology.html
Vulvodynia	http://www.vulvodynia.com/
National Vulvodynia Association	http://www.nva.org
Vulva Pain Foundation	http://www.thevpfoundation.org
Vulvar Vestibulitis	http://www.uihealthcare.org/2column.aspx?id=15592
International Pelvic Pain Society	http://pelvicpain.org
Vaginismus	https://www.vaginismus.com

Strategies and Techniques

GPPPD is not only a disorder that commonly has a physical cause, but it also creates fear that can be of phobic proportions. Most therapy programs to date, with the exception of that in Meana (2015) and our chapter in the first edition of this volume, fail to address this concern. The therapist needs to ask about the level of fear of penetration.

Cognitive-Behavioral Interventions

Provide reassurance. The first intervention is to reassure the woman that the treatment will be pain free and within her control. Women with this disorder often refuse to seek treatment until they are desperate to have a child or the partner is threatening to leave or have an affair. The following are two of our *cardinal rules* for treatment and greatly reassure the woman. First, she should never experience more than tolerable discomfort (not pain) and second, she is always in control of penetration during exercises with the partner. The partner must agree to this second rule. She is in charge of when, how much, how quickly, how much thrusting takes place and so on. There can be absolutely no exceptions. It is also important to reassure the woman that in spite of what she might have been told in the past, this disorder is real and the pain is real. It is not just in her head as a way to avoid sex.

Reduce the impact on the relationship. The impact on the relationship should be discussed early on in treatment. The partner's frustration, anger and other feelings need to be explored or they may reveal themselves in inappropriate ways. For example, one client reported that her boyfriend occasionally made flip remarks about how sexually frustrated he was. These kinds of remarks negatively impact communication and impair trust. Additionally, the male partner may have a sexual problem or have an unconscious need for his partner to be unable to have intercourse.

Explore the meanings. The therapist needs to explore what this problem means to the woman. Some couples have never been able to consummate their relationships, and this is very distressing to them. In other cases women refuse sex and see themselves as bad wives or defective. Additionally, while most treatment approaches focus on the behavioral, the therapist needs to explore every possible cause for the problem, such as sexual trauma or negative sex messages in the family. Possible causes need to be worked through prior to the therapy beginning unless the client would like to start doing homework exercises and work on the issues at the same time. If homework is attempted and the client fails to carry through on the homework, it is possible that her or their fears and anxieties are too strong for homework to begin.

Assign appropriate homework exercises. The classic treatment of vaginismus was through homework to help relax the PC musculature. This treatment should only be undertaken once the medical issues have been ruled out or treated. The woman may work with a sex therapist if the problem is confined to tightening or spasm in the PC musculature. The goal is to help her relax the muscle surrounding the vaginal opening. She is instructed to try to insert one very well lubricated finger very slowly and with no pain. Always suggest using plenty of lubrication. Some women do not like to use their fingers and may purchase vaginal dilators of graduated sizes that can be purchased through medical supply stores or on reputable websites that the therapist has used before. Again, the therapist needs to be careful to prescribe small, gradually increasing steps that are aimed at promoting success. The woman is to stop when resistance is experienced, allow the muscle to relax and try to insert more. In the first few exercises, insertion may be minimal or just involve challenging the pubococcygeus muscle. The woman is to focus on relaxing the muscle and read, listen to music or watch TV while doing the exercises with herself. Once she can insert one finger comfortably, she can then move the finger in and out, which challenges the PC muscle. Insertion during these exercises may last for 10–15 minutes. Once the woman can insert one finger comfortably and move it in and out, she then repeats the same exercise but tries to insert two fingers, beginning with one and then adding the second. Then, when she can insert two fingers with no movement and no pain, she begins to move the two fingers in and out.

The woman can now bring her partner into the exercises. She can have him watch her demonstrate the progress she has made or move to the next exercise. The man is instructed that his role in the couple exercises is to assist by inserting an object or his finger as directed by the woman. They must agree that she is always in charge of the penetration exercises. She is to lubricate herself well and hold his finger while inserting it slowly. The exercises described previously are then repeated with the male partner: one finger with no movement, one finger with movement, two fingers with no movement, two fingers with movement. Some women can do these exercises fairly quickly; others will take more time. The level of fear usually increases sharply when the partner is involved so there may be some difficulty, which requires backing up in the sequence of exercises. It is absolutely essential that they both understand that they should not attempt intercourse until told to do so.

Once the partner can insert two fingers or a dildo the size of a penis and move it in and out without any pain, the couple is ready to transition to intercourse. This portion of the exercise needs to be rehearsed by discussing it early in the conjoined sessions. The woman needs to be reassured by her partner that she can control penetration. Also, she needs to know that she can stop whenever she wishes. The partners always start with the penetration portion of the exercises in gradual increments and slowly proceed to penetration. They may initially use vaginal dilators or the partner's finger. Doing so is done carefully and with the woman always in control of the process. When she feels ready for penetration, she moves on top of her partner and very slowly inserts his penis as much as she is comfortable, usually superficially in the beginning. When penetration occurs, she is to remain still, with no movement, in order to relax the PC muscle. Once she feels ready, she begins to add movement while he remains still. This exercise is continued with more and more movement until the problem is fully resolved and a variety of positions can be enjoyed.

During the last phase of the treatment of vaginismus, men want to move and have an orgasm. The therapist must insist that the woman is in control until the problem is resolved and the women needs to understand that he will need stimulation to orgasm in most cases or else his frustration and anger will become a problem. During this phase of therapy, the woman may stop at some point because the muscle has not yet fully relaxed and ask for some sexual stimulation for herself if desired and stimulate the man manually to orgasm should he so desire. We advise the therapist also consult the *The V Book: Doctor's Guide to Complete Vulvovaginal Health* by Elizabeth Stewart and Paula Spencer (2002).

Meana (2015) has provided an excellent outline of treatment. During the initial stages of treatment the therapist needs to do the following:

- Provide education, goal setting and anxiety reduction.
- Reinforce help-seeking.
- Validate and demystify the pain.
- Discuss the role of anxiety.
- Provide exercises for the woman to engage in genital self-exploration.
- Expand the sexual repertoire of the couple and deemphasize intercourse.
- Emphasize affection and sensuality, often using sensate focus.

During the core phase of treatment the therapist needs to do the following:

- Arrange for a gynecological consultation with the right physician.
- Coordinate treatment with a physical therapist if necessary.

Enhance sexual interactions for the couple by encouraging them to set aside quality time, learn to build desire and arousal, enhance self-perceptions of desirability, engage in directed masturbation and practice nonpenetration forms of sensual and sexual activity. Facilitate communication to help all these tasks work.

Meana (2015) also discusses individual proclivities that need to be addressed during treatment. The main issues are to address the tendency toward hypervigilance and catastrophizing the pain through the use of cognitive reframing and challenging old sexual schemas about sex and pain. The other main task is to help the couple learn how to increase affectional, sensual or sexual activity by expanding the range of their physical interactions and learning how to effectively communicate their physical needs, wants and desires as well as fears and feedback needed to avoid pain. Interestingly, although GPPPD usually has a biomedical basis, the same treatment elements that are used in treating absent/low sexual desire are often used for this disorder.

Medical Treatments

The medical treatments for GPPPD are varied, depending on the practitioner and the geographic location. The sophistication of the medical practitioner is extremely important. It is advisable to work to create a treatment team of gynecologists who are specialists in pelvic pain disorders and physical therapists who are familiar with the treatment of GPPPD and pelvic floor disorders that contribute to the pain. The first line of defense is often a prescription for the woman to apply topical ointments to reduce localized pain in the affected areas. These ointments are typically forms of anesthetic agents that are intended to reduce superficial pain. Oral medications, mostly tricyclic antidepressants, are often used because some of these medications serve to reduce neuropathic pain. Other prescription drugs, sometimes with anticonvulsant properties, are used to reduce neuropathic pain. It should be noted that some of these medications are used in very high doses and cause a variety of side effects, including fatigue. Some physicians familiar with the treatment of vestibulitis will perform an outpatient procedure called vestibulectomy, which involves surgically removing the painful tissue. Typically, surgery is used only after the other medical treatments have failed.

Mindfulness-Based Treatments

Mindfulness treatments can be efficacious in treating pain and can help the woman deal with GPPPD although the empirical data are thus far somewhat inclusive. Rosenbaum (2013) recommends the following:

- The woman attends to perceptions, feelings, attitudes and thoughts.
- She learns to recognize how negative cognitive judgment of feelings can be detrimental to treatment and can intensify pain.
- The woman learns to accept feelings and perceptions (pain, anxiety, shame, sadness and frustration) without judgment
- The woman recognizes that thoughts and sensations may be simply observed rather than followed.

The following articles discuss mindfulness techniques: Brotto (2012), Rosenbaum (2013) and Sommers (2012).

References

American Psychiatric Association. (2013). *Diagnostic and statistical manual of mental disorders* (5th ed.). Arlington, VA: Author.

Bader, M.J. (2002). *Arousal: The secret logic of sexual fantasies*. New York: St. Martin's Press.

Barbach, L. (2000). *For yourself: The fulfillment of female sexuality.* New York: Signet.

Barbach, L. (2001). *For each other: Sharing sexual intimacy.* Garden City, NY: Penguin Putnam.

Basson, R., Althop, S., Davis, S., Fugl-Meyer, K., Goldstein, I., Leiblum, S., et al. (2004). Summary of recommendations on sexual dysfunction in women. *Journal of Sexual Medicine, 1,* 24–34.

Brotto, L. (2012). Non-judgmental, present-moment, sex . . . as if your life depended on it. *Sexual and Relationship Therapy, 26*(3), 215–216.

Eichel, E.W., Eichel, J.D.S., & Kule, S. (1988). The technique of coital alignment and its relation to female orgasmic response and simultaneous orgasm. *Journal of Sex and Marital Therapy, 14*(2), 129–141.

Friday, N. (1973). *My secret garden: Women's sexual fantasies.* New York: Pocket Books.

Graham, C.A. (2010). The DSM-5 diagnostic criteria for female orgasm disorder. *Archives of Sexual Behavior, 39,* 256–270.

Graziottin, A., & Leiblum, S.R. (2005). Biological and psychosocial pathophysiology of female sexual dysfunction during the menopausal transition. *Journal of Sexual Medicine, 2, Suppl 3,* 133–145.

Harlow, B.L., Wise, L.A., & Stewart, E.G. (2001). Prevalence and predictors of chronic lower genital tract discomfort. *American Journal of Obstetrics and Gynecology, 185,* 545–550.

Heiman, J.R., & Meston, M. (1997). Empirically validated treatment for sexual dysfunction. *Annual Review of Sex Research, 8,* 148–194.

Hite, S. (1976). *The Hite report.* New York: Macmillan

Hucker, A., & McCabe, M.P. (2013). An online, mindfulness-based cognitive-behavioral therapy for female sexual difficulties: Impact on relationship functioning. *Journal of Sexual Medicine, 40*(6), 561–576. doi:10.1080/0092623X.2013.796578

Komisaruk, B., Beyers-Flores, C., & Whipple, B. (2006). *The science of orgasm.* Baltimore, MD: The Johns Hopkins University Press.

Kaplan, H.S. (1979). *Disorders of sexual desire.* New York: Brunner/Mazel.

Kilmann, P.R., Boland, J.P., Norton, S.P., Davidson, E., & Caird, C. (1986). Perspectives of sex therapy outcome: A survey of AASECT providers. *Journal of Sex and Marital Therapy, 12,* 116–138.

Laan, E.H. (2011). Can we treat anorgasmia in women? The challenge to experiencing pleasure. *Sexual & Relationship Therapy, 26,* 329–341.

LoPiccolo, J., & Stock, W.E. (1986). Treatment of sexual dysfunction. *Journal of Consulting and Clinical Psychology, 54,* 158–167.

McCabe, M.P. (2015). Female orgasmic disorder. In K.M. Hertlein, G.R. Weeks, & N. Gambescia (Eds.), *Systemic sex therapy* (2nd ed.) (pp. 171–190). New York: Routledge.

McCabe, M.P., & Giles, K. (2012). Differences between sexually functional and dysfunctional women in psychological and relationships domains. *International Journal of Sexual Health, 24,* 181–194.

Meana, M. (2009). Painful intercourse: Dyspareunia and vaginismus. In K. Hertlein, G. Weeks, and N. Gambescia (Eds.), *Systemic sex therapy* (pp. 237–262). New York: Routledge.

Meana, M. (2012). *Sexual dysfunction in women.* Cambridge: Hogrefe Press.

Meana, M. (2015). Painful intercourse: Genito-pelvic pain/penetration disorder. In K.M. Hertlein, G.R. Weeks, & N. Gambescia (Eds.), *Systemic sex therapy* (2nd ed.) (pp. 191–210). New York: Routledge.

Rosenbaum, T. Y. (2013). An integrated mindfulness-based approach to the treatment of women with sexual pain and anxiety: Promoting autonomy and mind/body connection. *Sexual and Relationship Therapy, 28*(1–2), 28–28. doi:10.1080/14681994.20 13.764981

Sommers, F. G. (2012). Mindfulness in love and love making: A way of life. *Sexual and Relationship Therapy, 28*, 84–91.

Staples, J., Rellini, A. H., & Roberts, S. P. (2012). Avoiding experiences: Sexual dysfunction in women with a history of sexual abuse in childhood and adolescence. *Archives of Sexual Behavior, 41*, 341–350.

Stewart, E., & Spencer, P. (2002). *The V book: A doctor's guide to compete vulvovaginal health*. New York: Bantam.

ter Kuile, M. M., & Reissing, E. D. (2014). Lifelong vaginismus. In Y. M. Binik & K. S. K. Hall (Eds.), *Principles and practice of sex therapy* (pp. 177–194). New York: Guilford Press.

van Lankveld, J. J., Granot, M., Weijmar S., Binik, W., Wesselmann, Y., Pukall, U., & Achtrari, C. (2010). Women's sexual pain disorders. *The Journal of Sexual Medicine, 7*(1), 615–631.

10

THE NEW SENSATE
FOCUS TECHNIQUE

Sensate focus was introduced by Masters and Johnson (1970) and refined by Kaplan (1974). This cognitive-behavioral treatment approach incorporates psychoeducation about the sexual response and a series of incremental physical exercises performed outside of the therapeutic setting. In principle, sensate focus is a form of in vivo desensitization intended to promote relaxation, communication, attention to physical sensations and the physical and emotional connection between partners. At the time, it was an innovative psychological approach to the treatment of sexual problems. Sexual functioning is now viewed, to a large extent, as more complex than previously understood; however, this primarily behavioral method continues to be a fundamental element of most sex therapy treatments.

Sexual problems are affected by the interaction of numerous systems involving the partners, their relationship and familial and contextual influences on the couple system as described in the Intersystem Approach. Additionally, current treatments now commonly merge physiological (medical) and psychological methods in order to provide the most efficacious treatment outcome (Abdo, Afif-Abdo, Otani, & Machado, 2008; Lieblum, 2007). Moreover, many treatment modalities are beginning to recognize the interactional dynamics of the couple and family systems, and the cultural factors influencing the partners (Hall & Graham, 2012). Thus, current therapies, while incorporating sensate focus techniques, are considerably more comprehensive than originally stipulated by Masters and Johnson (1970) and Kaplan (1974).

In order to face the challenges of sex therapy today, we have developed a systemic approach that easily encompasses the medical/behavioral models that continue to dominate the field. We believe that in many cases sexual problems originate within the couple, become rooted in their dynamics and are maintained by the couple's beliefs and behaviors. Accordingly, sensate focus homework exercises must concentrate on the couple rather than on one partner (Weeks, 2005). The couple struggles with the sexual problem and needs to work together to remedy it. The process of sex therapy, in our view, permits the couple to grasp and practice systemic techniques. We believe couples want to understand the treatment process and will be more likely to cooperate if the underlying principles are explained and make sense to them. Gradually, the partners learn to understand their roles in creating barriers to intimacy rather than focusing on a symptomatic partner. Over time, they recognize their own sensual preferences and dislikes and communicate in a mutual fashion about them. Ultimately, partners collaborate to build a mutually satisfying and flexible sexual relationship.

We have elected to review our application of sensate focus in one chapter rather than repeat the general principles throughout the text. The exercises presented in this chapter can be used in treating almost every type of sexual dysfunction (Weeks & Gambescia, 2015). For more detailed or specific applications of sensate focus, readers are directed to examine our publications that focus on erectile dysfunction (Weeks & Gambescia, 2000), hypoactive sexual desire (Weeks, 1987, 1995; Weeks & Gambescia, 2002) and a review of assignments used to treat specific sexual dysfunctions (Gambescia & Weeks, 2006). *Systemic Sex Therapy* (Hertlein, Weeks, & Gambescia, 2009) also provides an overview chapter of sex therapy, reviews when to use sensate focus and explores sensate focus within the context of sex therapy in general.

The Role of Cognitive-Behavioral Homework

Many of our clients report that they feel powerless with respect to owning and controlling their sexual feelings. Often, they believe the misguided notion that sexual gratification is something that happens to them. During the process of relationship/sex therapy, such misconceptions are corrected and the couple learns to take responsibility for their own sensual and sexual relationship. In time, they understand that pleasurable sexual intimacy is carefully created, fostered and nurtured.

The systemic treatment of sexual dysfunctions is accomplished through a combination of techniques, psychoeducation, bibliotherapy, guided imagery and cognitive restructuring (Lieblum, 2007; Weeks & Gambescia, 2002; Weeks & Gambescia, 2015). Many of these procedures occur in the therapist's office: providing accurate information about sexual anatomy and physiology, correcting irrational thinking, dispelling sexual myths and others. Partners learn to recognize and stop negative thoughts, substitute positive cognitions and integrate various relaxation techniques or mindfulness therapy techniques that can be used in sexual situations (Kozlowski, 2013; Lazarus, 1965; Wolpe, 1958).

The most practical use of psychotherapy, however, is to extend the learning experience beyond the therapy hour and the boundaries of the office (Gambescia & Weeks, 2006). Through sensate focus assignments, partners can practice skills or follow instructions they have learned in the office and experience sensual and sexual touch within a familiar, relaxed, comfortable environment. The therapist prescribes detailed cognitive and sensual behavioral homework that incorporates sensual touch, a focus on the present, nonjudgmental communication and eventually sexual touch. Each assignment involves small incremental steps that help to build confidence, competence and an increased sense of efficacy in overcoming the sexual problem.

Promoting Compliance

The idea of homework may have onerous connotations to one or both partners. As they discuss their reactions to the concept, various alternative terms may emerge until there is agreement about the nature of the tasks and what they are called. Ultimately, the couple must understand that homework is not something that the therapist imposes on disinclined partners. Instead, it is a systemic process in which the therapist selects broad parameters and *the couple* is helped to design each step with the therapist's oversight. Compliance is encouraged through this collaborative process and by providing a rationale for assignments. Clients want to know how a particular activity will help them (Weeks & Gambescia, 2000, 2002). This collective approach encourages couples to take ownership of their therapy and responsibility for factors that promote improvement.

Pessimism and Skepticism

Sexual dysfunctions produce stress, worry and unhappiness for the individual and the partner (Chevret, Jaudinot, Sullivan, Marrel, & De Gendre, 2004; Hart & Schwartz, 2010; Rosen & Althof, 2008). Couples often attempt to solve their sexual problems on their own using information they have found on the Internet or from books. By the time they present for treatment, the partners are often frustrated and pessimistic that any treatment can help them, particularly psychotherapy. They have doubts that just talking about a sexual problem will produce results. It is important for the therapist to anticipate skepticism and normalize their fears. For instance, it is helpful to point out that their feelings of hopelessness are natural given the amount of energy they have put into correcting the situation. The couple's efforts should be reinforced before proceeding to explain how sex therapy can help them to understand the genesis of the sexual problems and the ways of treating it. They also need to understand that they are correct in their assumption that just talking about the problem will not produce the change desired. The role of homework must be clearly described as integral to successful resolution of most problems.

Commitment

It is essential for the therapist to continually assess the level of commitment of each partner in two general areas: (1) to their relationship and (2) to the process of therapy. One or both partners may be ambivalent, tenuous or unequally committed. The couple will need to make their relationship a priority and agree to work together constructively in the office and at home. As expected, commitment is a necessary condition for successful completion of the homework exercises. Devoted partners encourage each other when progress is slow, issues become painful and the tendency is to give up. Ultimately, commitment is an important factor in overcoming skepticism and pessimism. This process is also helpful in preventing relapse (Weeks & Fife, 2014).

Partners who are locked in conflict and cannot cooperate with each other will need some marital work before attempting sex therapy (Gambescia & Weeks, 2006). This contraindication for sex therapy must be explained to the partners, particularly those who are impatient and want to proceed directly with sex therapy. The therapist must help the couple understand the systemic premise that sexual difficulties are embedded within their relationship dynamics (Weeks & Hof, 1987; Weeks & Gambescia, 2000, 2002). When the couple is ready, they will work to resolve the relationship issues that would interfere with successful treatment of sexual problems. Once they are able to work together and support each other, treating the sexual problems will be possible.

The Systemic Perspective

When Masters and Johnson (1970) and Kaplan (1974) pioneered the idea of sensate focus, they were not thinking systemically. Their therapeutic concentration was on the symptomatic partner rather than the couple. In effect, the nondysfunctional partner served as a surrogate cotherapist at home in helping the sexually dysfunctional partner. We believe that sexual problems are best understood and treated by viewing the reciprocal role of each partner within the greater context of their relationship; emotional and physical intimacy is a mutual process (Weeks, 1987, 1995). Our experience has been that sexual difficulties negatively impact intimacy patterns. The most common of these difficulties is that over time the couple becomes avoidant of sexual interactions and often any physical interactions. By the time couples seek treatment, both partners have a sexual problem in the broadest sense and the treatment must focus on the ailing relationship and their physical avoidance of each other. Moreover, the chronic nature of sexual problems can produce emotional and sexual disconnection due to frustration, anger and disappointment. A typical scenario is the partner who develops absent/low sexual desire in response to a man with recurrent erectile dysfunction, or in response to a partner who avoids sex due to a fear of failure.

Often, in the initial phases of treatment, partners are frustrated and want to blame the other or view the other as the cause for the problem. They are often unaware that the fundamental difficulty resides within the relationship. Through the guidance of the systemically oriented therapist, partners gradually accept that the development, maintenance and/or treatment of sexual dysfunctions must involve both partners as a couple system. For instance, they learn that blaming is an ineffective method of problem resolution because it misses the point, systemically speaking. Eventually, they realize the broader systemic understanding that the behavior of each mutually affects the other; problems are shared and solutions require a joint approach rather than a one-sided focus.

Sensate Focus Exercises

Sensate focus offers a structured, gradual and flexible approach to the treatment of sexual dysfunctions. In addition, when it is not essential to solving sexual problems, this method can be beneficial in facilitating many aspects of the couple's emotional, intimate and overall sexual relationship. The exercises are designed for the partners to focus on the sensual aspects of intimacy rather than on sexual performance (Kleinplatz, 1996). Partners are required to concentrate on their own varied wants, needs and sensual experiences. They are instructed to maintain a focus on the present situation rather than past grievances or future goals. During the exercises, the couple is encouraged to communicate wishes, desires, likes and dislikes about touch, sensual and sexual interactions. The therapist suggests that all communications are positively stated and coaches the couple on this process in the session. Using sensate focus exercises, the couple creates constructive mutual experiences and enjoys positive anticipation for future sensual and sexual activity.

Understanding Sensate Focus

Sensate focus exercises were originally designed with the express purpose of helping couples to enjoy pleasurable sensory experiences and to overcome the destructive impact of sexual anxiety. In the preliminary version of sensate focus, however, there was little elaboration about technique and other elements we believe are essential for the therapist to comprehend (Masters & Johnson, 1970). For instance, a major and often unacknowledged element is the powerful benefit in articulating what is desired or perhaps disliked during sexual intimacy. Through guidance and coaching, partners learn to communicate, often for the first time, without embarrassment (Maurice, 1999). Sensate focus looks like an easy exercise to implement from the therapist's perspective. It usually appears to be something the couple thinks will be easy to implement. These assumptions can be misleading. Sensate focus exercises are not easy to design and implement, and couples often acknowledge avoidance of the exercise at first, feelings of awkwardness or difficulty in expression of their needs.

Another factor that the therapist must appreciate is the strong relationship between anxiety and sexual performance. Couples in sex therapy obsess and worry about their sexual problems. The performance anxiety that is experienced by the couple can usually be related to attaining a particular behavior or a particular feeling state. Further, the anticipation of a problem (anticipatory anxiety) and the self-monitoring that occurs during sexual activity interferes with pleasure and perpetuates the problem. This contagious process adds to the anxiety experienced by both partners in intimate situations. They agonize about functioning (performance anxiety) or the impression that they are not feeling the right feelings, such as more desire (response anxiety); however, it is not these anxieties alone that produces the sexual difficulty, but rather the dysfunctional thinking associated with it (see Gambescia, Sendak, & Weeks, 2009). "Am I going to lose my erection?" "Why can't I feel desire or more desire?" Performance, anticipatory and response anxieties have a detrimental effect on most sexual functioning, including the ability to feel desire (Weeks & Gambescia, 2002). The goal of treatment, therefore, is to eliminate or significantly reduce all forms of sexual anxiety.

The theoretical foundation of the original concept of sensate focus is systematic desensitization, a treatment designed to reduce anxiety (Wolpe, 1958, 1992). As stated, sensate focus is a specific application of systematic desensitization in which partners are helped to overcome anxiety and negative associations to sexual intimacy (Lazarus, 1965). The couple is gradually and judiciously exposed to situations that once made them anxious. Simultaneously, they are exposed to exercises designed to minimize anxiety. Once anxiety is lowered, the couple progresses to a slightly more difficult experience or one that would have produced much anxiety in the past, thus interfering with performance. Over time and after repeated trials, partners are no longer anxious about the whole spectrum of sensual or sexual touching.

In order to promote desensitization, the exercises must allow the couple to experience sensual (and eventually sexual) behaviors in a relatively anxiety-free context. Therefore, the blueprint of the exercises must carefully fit the situation. Additionally, the process must be gradual and measured. That is, each exercise must be designed to be small enough so that it is experienced as an accomplishment, not a failure or simply something the partners are already capable of doing. Because the emphasis is on experiencing a sensual connection rather than sexual performance, success is much more likely. Progressively, the partners learn to relax in intimate situations, moving from dysfunction to satisfying intimacy.

Sensate focus exercises, in our opinion, are designed to interrupt the cycle of avoidance (negative reinforcement), which is destructive to relational/sexual satisfaction. This feature is often undervalued or not mentioned in many applications of sensate focus. Women who lack desire eventually consider physical touch to be a prelude to sexual interaction; thus, they evade affectional and sensual contact. Before long, the partners cease touching, cuddling and other forms of physical affection. Merely doing sensate focus exercises is a success because it breaks the cycle of avoidance of physical interaction. An issue with the use of sensate focus that we have noted is the inaccurate presumption by the therapist that the couple is ready to start with what the therapist considers to be an advanced sensate focus rather than with smaller, nonerotic incremental exercises (Kaplan, 1975). In the next session, we talk about this issue but also move beyond it and discuss sensual touch for erotic stimulation.

Currently, mindfulness practices are emerging as fundamental elements of sex therapy. Mindfulness is regarded at the state of experiencing the present moment without making judgments about the experience (Kozlowski, 2013). Two practices are central to mindfulness sex therapy: a present-centered emphasis (on the here and now) and a process-absorbed focus (the opposite of having a goal). While these elements are often discussed in traditional sensate focus treatment, they are at the core of the mindfulness approach to sensate focus. Sommers (2013) proposes a sensory check list that helps each partner increase awareness of sensory experiences (vision, hearing, smell, taste, touch). He uses labels such as gradual, graduated or homeplay to give life to the positive aspects of the reciprocal touch exercises. This means each exercise builds on the last in small increments. Also, he does not impose a time limit so that the giver can decide when he or she is tired of giving, a noteworthy departure from traditional sensate focus. Weiner, Cannon, and Avery-Clark (2014) distinguish between sensate focus and erotic touch in that sensate focus involves touching for one's own interest, curiosity and exploration, but not for pleasure or arousal and not for the partner's pleasure or arousal. Our view of sensate focus incorporates the aforementioned principles and expands the practice to gradually include erotic touch.

Nine Functions of Sensate Focus

Properly implemented, the sensate focus exercises accomplish multiple purposes and objectives. These objectives must be communicated to the couple in order to help them become aware of what they are doing and why. The partners will appreciate knowing the principles behind each exercise as well as the richness of an assignment, which appears so simplistic on the surface. Of course, partners do not need to be informed about all nine functions, but only about those that are relevant to the particular exercise being prescribed. As a result, the partners can expect that if they carry out a particular assignment, they will achieve certain experiences and goals.

The therapist and clients must keep in mind that each exercise represents a step within a continuum from simple to complex and from affectional to sensual to sexual. Each successive codesigned exercise is based on the couple's ability to start in a particular place and to move forward at a successful and comfortable pace. The nine functions of sensate focus are as follows:

1. To help each partner become more aware of his or her own sensations. Couples in sex therapy become so focused on solving a particular sexual dilemma that they worry about nothing but performance whenever they want to be intimate. Instead of experiencing pleasurable feelings, they think about negative experiences in the past or anticipate a failure when trying to be sexual. Eventually, the partners suppress and lose touch with their own sensuality and the pleasurable aspects of physical intimacy that they can experience. This negative process in interrupted through the first objective of sensate focus. The individual partners are directed to focus on *his or her own* pleasurable experiences of being touched. The therapist asks them straightforwardly to think about what they feel in the moment and not worry about anything else. This simple directive gives partners the opportunity to freely explore their own feelings of being touched without worrying about the sexual problem or what the other person might want or feel. We have found that couples have more difficulty with this instruction than expected. They might complain that they do not want to be selfish or that the homework is overly simplistic. In actuality, they often need several trials to successfully complete portions of the assignment that involve concentrating on their own pleasure.

2. To focus on one's own needs for pleasure and worry less about the problem or the partner. The second purpose of sensate focus emerges from the first. Our clients become so distracted by intrusive antisexual thoughts (negative relational/sexual thoughts and cognitive distractions) that they fail to enjoy being touched and later sensual and sexual pleasure. These cognitions are sometimes about the sexual experience of the partner and how he or she will be disappointing the partner. The goal of much of their sexual activity is about pleasing the partner. The partner with the identified problem focuses too much on the other and not enough on himself or herself and what he or she needs in order to feel as much sensation and pleasure as possible. Each partner's own needs, wants and desires need to be freely expressed, keeping the focus on each person's reactions or experiences. Focusing on oneself and one's partner at this stage of treatment is impossible. The partner without the identified problem may feel it is his or her task to help the partner perform as that person wishes. This partner is so focused on the solution to the problem that he or she gains little to nothing from touching or attempting to be sexual. This is why the partners take turns in touching each other. This second function of sensate focus helps the partners to censor thoughts that distract them from their own enjoyment. We often incorporate cognitive techniques such as thought stopping and thought substitution in order to promote pleasurable sensations (Beck 1976, 1995). The couple must be helped to understand that worry, anxiety and trying to take care of the partner actually create distance between them and preclude mutually enjoyable touching, sensual and sexual experiences.

3. To communicate sensual and sexual needs, wishes and desires. Although communication is an important mediator of both sexual and relationship satisfaction (Byers, 2005; Mark & Jozkowski, 2013), most couples we have treated fall short in this domain. Typically, the partners are too inhibited to ask for what they actually want, and thus have not developed a feeling of being physically proficient with each other. Past physical interactions have contributed to feelings of incompetence, awkwardness or embarrassment with respect to articulating their emotions. In order to improve the overall quality and satisfaction of the couple's sexual life, they need to learn how to communicate with each other; consequently, verbalizing sensual needs, wishes and desires is a prerequisite to moving to the physical portions of the assignments. Two basic instructions are given to the couple. They are told to *notice* and *verbalize* what they like and need in order to keep the feelings pleasurable. Couples will require a significant amount of encouragement, praise and patience in getting started with this task. Through successful completion of this third objective, the partners develop an awareness of their own needs and learn that they can become masterful in providing and receiving the pleasure they seek.

Sensate focus exercises provide an ideal setting for this communication to be practiced. Exercises begin in small incremental steps; therefore, it is easier for the couple to discuss preferences during nongenital stimulation. The couple should be asked how they feel about communicating with each other in this way. It is also essential to have them consider the reasons for failing to communicate needs and preferences in the past. The therapist should also have the partners discuss the impact of overt and covert messages they received in their families of origin on present sexual communication, taking care of one's needs and sexual beliefs. Each time an exercise is prescribed, the therapist must ask about the couple's communication. It would be a major mistake to assume the couple suddenly gains this skill after the first exercise. Competent communication is shaped and reinforced over many trials (Bandura, 1969). Sometimes the couple will experience a successful week and subsequently forget the lessons of the prior week. Tracking this aspect of treatment requires great consistency on the part of the therapist.

4. To increase awareness of the partner's sensual and sexual needs. Many of our clients are unable to talk to each other about sensual and sexual preferences or they believe that such discussions are unnecessary. We have often heard the mythological notion that the partner should know what is desired without being told. A particularly dangerous variation is the linking of love with telepathic abilities; if the partner really loved the other, he or she would know what to do. This belief can only lead to anxiety, anger, disappointment, irritation and so on. Additionally, the couple feels chronically frustrated and helpless because they believe that the other person does not care about them. In reality, important information about preferences or needs was never communicated.

Reciprocity is a key element of this fourth function of sensate focus. Each partner is encouraged to ask for what he or she wants and also notice or ask about what is pleasurable for the other. Sensitivity to the partner is promoted, thereby enhancing the mutuality of the experience for both. The couple becomes more aware and appreciative of the positive sensual and sexual aspects of being together rather than focusing on problems. This interactional process heightens mutual sexual and sensual sensitivity.

5. To expand the repertoire of intimate touching, sensual and sexual behaviors. Our experience in working with hundreds of couples has shown that sexual behavior tends to become highly patterned over time. Inevitably, couples settle into a limited repertoire with little variety and experimentation. The fifth goal of sensate focus is for the couple to be experimental and creative, and to try new ways of touching each other, including sensual and sexual behaviors. This objective occurs naturally as the partners enhance their sensory awareness and develop a better understanding of their affectional, sensual and sexual needs. The therapist might say, "Try as many things as you can think of to give yourself and your partner pleasure. Be creative. Think about what you would like. Tell your partner, and listen carefully to what your partner tells you." The impact of the exercise is to help the couple explore an extensive menu of physical pleasure. They can now spontaneously select from a wide variety of experiences that they know will be pleasurable and have permission to try opening up to new activities. The therapist must follow up in the next session by encouraging the couple to discuss the new behaviors they have attempted, how each partner felt and whether they are ready to move to the next exercise.

6. To learn to appreciate foreplay or touching as an end in itself rather than a means to an end. Couples in sex therapy often truncate foreplay because so much of their concentration has been on solving a sexual problem. Additionally, U.S. men and women tend to approach foreplay, or non-goal-oriented sex, very differently. Generally, men fail to appreciate the role of foreplay as an end in itself rather than a prelude to intercourse or some other mutually agreed upon form of sexual expression. For example, many of the men with Erectile Disorder will experience just enough stimulation to obtain an erection that they think will allow for penetration and then immediately attempt penetration. The problem with this strategy was discussed in Chapter 6. Women tend to want more touching, holding, affection and sensuality in their lives. Unfortunately, it is all too common that men give affection in order to obtain sex and women give sex in order to obtain affection. This exchange is likely to have a destructive outcome. During the sensate focus process, couples are prohibited from having intercourse or engaging in any other form of sexual expression that was not part of the exercise. In this way, they begin to discover the value of non-goal-oriented touching and later non-goal-oriented sexual expression. This sixth function of sensate focus is designed to break the formulaic affection/sex exchange approach to sex mentioned earlier, thereby freeing the couple to explore and negotiate the type of pleasurable touching they wish to share. The couple begins to appreciate foreplay or nonsexual pleasure as a goal in itself. It is not connected to a pressure-filled script that any foreplay must and should lead to intercourse.

7. *To create positive relational experiences.* Unlike past encounters, which have been negative in terms of effect or outcome, sensate focus exercises are experienced positively particularly if they are well designed, well timed and well sequenced. The therapist wants to help the couple generate as many positive physical and communicative interactions as possible. Gottman (1994) has empirically shown that the happiest or most satisfied couples are those who experience quantitatively the most positive interactions. The positive relational outcome constitutes the seventh goal of the sensate focus exercises. Affirming interactions create positive anticipation, promote a good feeling about the relationship and help the couple believe that they are moving in the right direction, in general.

8. *To build sexual desire.* Typically, sex therapy clients present for treatment after their sensual and sexual relationship has deteriorated significantly. Often, they report diminished sexual desire and a global avoidance of physical interactions. The therapist must inquire about the level of desire prior to treatment, at the beginning of treatment and throughout the duration of treatment. Through sensate focus, performance and response anxieties (anxiety over not feeling the anticipated or so-called correct feeling) are gradually removed from sensual and sexual touch. The couple can enter a touching experience anticipating a positive outcome because each encounter is enjoyable in itself and not linked to a performance or response goal. This eighth objective involves enjoying the positive rewards of sensate focus, specifically, increases in sexual desire and willingness to be together physically. When the couple recounts an exercise in session, each partner evaluates the other for levels of interest and enthusiasm. Frequently the partners will interpret enthusiasm about the exercises as a measure of sexual desire. The sensate focus exercises are not *the* treatment for absent/low desire, interest or arousal. They are one element of a larger treatment program designed to help the couple reconnect with reduced anxiety.

9. *To enhance the level of love, caring, commitment, intimacy, cooperation and sexual interest in the relationship.* The last objective of sensate focus results from the couple's commitment to their relationship and to the process of therapy. The couple entered treatment despite significant pessimism and had participated actively in the homework exercises. Throughout the duration of treatment, beginning with sensate focus, they prioritized their relationship. Although they may have entered therapy thinking that just one person had a problem, they learned to appreciate how the problem had impacted their

relationship and how their relationship may have contributed to the problem (Weeks & Gambescia, 2000, 2002, 2015). The therapeutic process opened far more exploration than the couple had anticipated. Working together, with each partner taking responsibility for their part, provided a powerful message for them regarding the *strength of their relationship*. Couples will begin to discern this positive message as the therapy proceeds.

On the other hand, if one partner is reluctant or refuses to engage in the exercises, it could indicate a lack of interest in the other. This fact is especially true when one partner gets ahead of the other or when one is stuck or resistant. The therapist must help the couple to see explicitly that disinterest in the process might reflect a lack of commitment to the therapeutic process and in some cases to a lack of commitment to the relationship. If treatment is going well, the therapist validates the couple for working hard but especially for their commitment to each other. Couples enjoy hearing that they are making progress and they like to be praised for their commitment and hard work. The progress made in the sensate focus exercise may be dismissed as unimportant by the couple if they fail to appreciate how much progress they have made because the process is so incremental. The therapist needs to point out the purpose of the exercises and validate their progress. Most importantly, for this particular function of the exercise, it is important for the therapist to validate the love, caring and commitment of the partners.

Readiness for Sensate Focus Assignments

When using sensate focus, it is helpful to remember it is a tool for the couple. As we all know, couples will only use tools if they are ready. Part of being prepared to engage in the sensate focus exercises involves having motivation and a positive attitude about wanting to do the exercise. In order to determine a couple's readiness, the therapist describes what is involved in the sensate focus, noting each partner's reactions. Additionally, the therapist will want to inquire directly to determine if the couple is prepared to proceed to the systemically oriented sensate focus exercises.

- Do the two of you believe that you are ready for assignments that involve physical touch?
- Physical touch can be sensual and/or sexual. What does it mean for the two of you to be *sensual* with each other?
- What does it mean for the two of you to be *sexual* with each other?
- How are the two concepts, sensual and sexual, alike or different?
- In what ways do the two of you think you are sensual/sexual beings?
- What does it mean to experience pleasure from being touched?
- What does it mean to experience sensual/sexual pleasure?
- What do the two of you like most/least about being sexual?

- What does it mean to actually communicate your sensual/sexual feelings and wants?
- Do you think it will be difficult to communicate about touch, sensual and sexual wants? Why? Why not?
- Can the two of you think of any negative consequences of experiencing sensual/sexual pleasure or becoming more intimate as a couple?
- Can the two of you think of any ways that you might avoid these exercises?

If the attitude is generally positive, the therapist can proceed with the exercise. However, if one or both partners expresses hesitation, ambivalence or negative attitudes about the exercises, it is necessary to process those feelings first.

Structure and Application of Sensate Focus

A word of caution is necessary regarding the structure and application of sensate focus exercises. Some authors have presented a variety of predetermined formats involving sizeable progressions or steps (Kaplan, 1975; Masters & Johnson, 1970; Weiner, Canon, Avery-Clark, 2014). Typically, these protocols involve large progressions and/or predetermined exercises; this is ineffective at best and often detrimental. For example, Kaplan (1975) discussed Pleasuring I and II. She even provided a sample script of what a therapist might say to the couple for these exercises. In Pleasuring I, she assumed the couple would be able to remove all clothing and get into bed in order to touch each other in nonsexual ways. This kind of exercise is far beyond what many couples can do and would set them up to fail, reject the exercise or terminate treatment prematurely. Therapists who accept this kind of staging process and prescribe steps that are too large or do not fit the specific situation may actually cause damage to the couple. The couple is being given an exercise that is far beyond their capacity and will lead to failure. For example, one couple had not touched each other nor had any physical relations for years. They were told they would need to begin the process of becoming physically reconnected. They agreed to sit in the living room fully clothed and hold hand while watching TV for 15 minutes three times a week. The husband was phobic about any kind of touching. The first week went well, but he still felt some anxiety. They decided to do the same exercise the second week. Things were going well until the wife decided to interlace their fingers. When she attempted to do so, the man jumped up and ran from the room saying, "Why would you do such a thing?" This type of exercise is not to be found in the literature on sensate focus nor are fine graduations of the exercise ever mentioned. We think of sensate focus in terms of major stages but within each stage there may be fine graduations. We sometimes think of these exercises as 1.1, 1.2, 1.3, 2.1, 2.2, etc. with as many exercises as needed to reduce anxiety.

For sensate focus to be successful, the exercises must be constructed in several graduated increments and designed according to the specific needs of the couple as they progress through treatment. Every assignment is created assidu-ously and modified as necessary. All pressure and anxiety must be removed from the touching, sensual or sexual situation to ensure a positive outcome. Desensitization to sexual anxiety is gradual and systematic; thus, treatment requires a series of many steps that are based on the successful completion of the last. The therapist needs to continually assess the type of physical interaction and communication that produce successful completion of each step.

The specific assignments are practiced at home at least three times per week. Repetition provides plentiful opportunities to gradually reduce anxiety, change behavior and break old habits that contributed to sexual difficulties. Therapy sessions, therefore, should occur on a weekly basis in order to monitor and mod-ify the assignments and the therapist must be available for clarification between sessions if necessary (Gambescia & Weeks, 2006). It is important for partners to understand that sensate focus permits occasions and opportunities for them to rebuild their physical, sensual and sexual relationship. The therapist might suggest that the partner who has been passive in the past take the initiative to begin the exercise and decide which role he or she defines as the active role. Some couples like to do the exercises spontaneously. Others will prefer to put the times or days on a calendar. We often suggest picking five times to schedule the exercise with the goal of doing three. This gives them an out for two of the sessions when they aren't in the mood. Also, couples often need prompting to relax and enjoy the unhurried pace rather than accelerating the process.

The couple completes only the required behavioral increment each time; thus, the burden of responsibility and resulting performance pressures are elimi-nated (Wincze & Carey, 2001; Gambescia & Weeks, 2006). Writing some notes for the couple to review often helps them control the pace. The therapist must be mindful that couples will sometimes go beyond the limits of the assignment. In such instances, the rationale for pacing and structured exercises must be clarified.

Another way of thinking of the exercises is that the therapist provides a gen-eral guideline or shell for the exercises and asks the couple to fill in the details. For example, the therapist might suggest that the couple is ready for gentle back touch. The couple can decide who initiates it, how much clothing is on, where it takes place, how long it lasts and so on. Once they have all the elements in place, the therapist summarizes the exercise and asks how they feel about it. One other point that should be mentioned is that the communication that is to take place during the exercise is to always be positive unless something hurts. The couple is asked is avoid saying what they don't like and think about what they do like or want and to express that thought.

Using Metaphors

We have found that prescribing any homework assignment is useful if it can be combined with a skill or a metaphor that is congruent with how the client thinks about change. For example, teachers will understand the use of homework as a metaphor for doing the assignment, clients in construction will understand metaphors about blueprints and about creating a foundation from the ground up, people in highly structured professions such as the military will understand metaphors about the need to follow a rigid plan that has been proven successful in order to accomplish a mission and so on. We call this *metaphoric isomorphism*. In other words, one task is parallel to another and there is a sense of confidence and competence in one area that can be transferred to the other area. One case illustrates this point well. In order to conserve space we will just focus on the male partner. The couple consisted of a man in his 70s and a partner in her early 60s. He had been married three times, had one long-term unmarried relationship and had been with the current partner for 2 years. His partner had been married twice. She initiated the therapy. They reported being highly compatible and each one said they had finally found the partner for whom they had been searching all their lives. The one area that was missing was sex. The man had low interest in sex, felt sexually illiterate and reported that he was embarrassed that he did not know how to please his partner. She would sometimes stimulate him to orgasm and he would then ask her if she wanted to be stimulated rather than pick up on the obvious cue that she was sexually interested. She reported having had healthy sexual relationships but found herself in relationships that did not work for other reasons.

The man had had multiple successful careers. One career was useful in creating a homework metaphor. Beginning at the age of 5 his mother decided he was going to become a successful pianist. She insisted that he practice 7 days a weeks for a minimum of 5 hours a day. His mother was extremely controlling, his father was mostly absent physically and emotionally and his life became one of studying the piano for many years. His parents ignored his needs, wants, desires and feelings and he felt his childhood was lost. As an adult he found it difficult to express his needs and feelings. The therapist knew that his study of piano might provide a metaphor that would be isomorphic with doing the homework. The therapist, however, had to be careful. He did not like the way his mother controlled his homework, but he saw that practice or homework had lead him to great achievements. The therapist described his homework as self-determined and fun homework. Some therapists have even called this homework sex games. The homework the partners decided to do first was a simple backrub in the living area of the house. It was clear that he was uncomfortable with this assignment and doubted his ability to do it successfully although he said he wanted to be successful. As he discussed his piano career, the therapist asked him how he expressed emotion through music. His response was that he had to learn how to find and be sensitive to the feelings inherent in the music. He also talked about the fact that as a pianist he had to learn how to "get on the other side of the piano," to think about how the listener heard the music. The therapist then suggested that the exercise was much like music. He needed to find the music in giving and receiving touch and he had to get on the other side of the piano, which meant to think about how his partner would feel. These instructions appeared to lead to a trance like state of intense concentration on his part. After a couple of minutes, he smiled and said, "I know how to do this." By making the exercise isomorphic with the musical skill he had acquired he felt confident he could accomplish the task.

Proscribing Intercourse

At the outset, the couple is instructed to avoid intercourse and any activity that is sexual. The rationale for this proscription must be explained to the couple. In effect, avoiding all sexual activity helps to create a nondemand atmosphere, removes performance pressure and deescalates anxiety. The couple should be reminded that repeated pleasurable encounters will eventually lead to an improved physical relationship. Most couples report a sense of relief when they discuss their feelings about not having sexual activity initially. They have grown weary of attempting performance-oriented sex only to have a problem.

Creating a Sensual Environment

A critical element of sensate focus is the practice of taking responsibility for creating a private, relaxing, physical environment that will foster sensual intimacy. We usually recommend a location that is initially outside the bedroom because of the negative associations to this physical setting. Additionally, the situation must be free from interruptions. Time together in a relaxed manner is the priority. At our suggestion our clients often plan pleasant music, massage oil, scented candles, controlled lighting, comfortable temperatures and so on. The use of recreational drugs is prohibited. Although we do not recommend alcohol, a small amount can promote relaxation, if desired. The couple selects convenient times that are sufficient and unhurried, yet not too long. Each partner functions as a giver and a receiver with each assignment—but not simultaneously. We have found that it is prudent to establish ahead of time the order of who goes first before the couple tries the exercises for the first time. Subsequently, they can alternate to preserve a balance.

Touching and Sensual Pleasuring

The first broad category phase of sensate focus begins with a series of graduated exercises involving touching and later sensual touch. The couple must be prepared and must comprehend that touch and sensual pleasuring does not involve sexual interaction of any type. As mentioned earlier, the goal is to promote self-awareness, help the partners reconnect with sensual feelings as the process unfolds and encourage the couple to have a series of positive interactions with each other.

We often begin by asking the couple to describe the kinds of touching that they find to be mutually enjoyable, such as cuddling or holding hands. Determine the style of contact that has been positive historically and avoid areas that have been problematic in the past. The couple and therapist discuss pragmatic aspects such as whether clothing is to be worn, the specific activities that will be performed, the location and other aspects. Some couples literally have not touched each other for months or even years. Clearly, the touching and later sensual touching will need to be broken down into small, comfortable units commensurate with their tolerance for physical contact. The therapist stresses that both partners must be comfortable with the starting point and progression of each exercise and suggests various kinds of touch involving the hands, feet, scalp and face.

It is important to be very clear in giving the instructions for each assignment. The following statement is typical of how we might set up this exercise, regardless of the amount of contact: "Your first task will be to do a touching exercise. It is not a sexual exercise; instead the focus is on having a touching or sensual experience." It is necessary to have the couple discuss their ideas and feelings about what constitutes comfortable, anxiety-free touching. "You will need to set aside about 10–20 minutes for the main part of this experience. However, for the first few exercises it may be 10 minutes with a total of 5 minutes for each to give and receive. The duration of the time is set by you with me guiding you to be conservative in helping to design the exercises. During each exercise each partner takes turns touching the other in a way that feels pleasant and relatively free of anxiety. The touch can resemble a gentle massage (of the specific body parts that were determined to be touched in session). Each partner will have a specified number of minutes to be the giver and the receiver. Rather than touching each other at the same time, they are told to take turns. By taking turns they will be able to focus either on what they are feeling or on what the other person would like to receive from them. The goal of this exercise is not to get sexually stimulated; however, if that happens just take note of it." The therapist should help the couple discuss how they would feel if either or both became aroused. They need permission to anticipate the possibility but not to act on their arousal during the exercise. For example, sometimes in the later stages of sensate focus a man might get a partial to full erection, but the therapist has prohibited intercourse. The couple wonders what they should do if an erection occurs. The therapist can talk in advance about viewing an erection as something that does not need to be used, but as a sign of success that treatment is working and a compliment to one's partner. Explanations might vary depending on the couple's worldview.

A note of caution applies to couples who are too damaged, anxious or insecure to begin the exercises with sustained physical touch of any kind. Sometimes we recommend they walk together holding hands, as tolerated, taking note of the sensual aspects of the walk (smells, sounds, touching the other's hand, etc.). Another suggestion is to simply sit together on a sofa or outdoors without touch (with music or just listening to nature) as an initial step. If they can tolerate this activity, they can move to minimal touch. Conversation, if any, should involve neutral or positive comments about the experience. Sensate focus should be designed to begin with the smallest, least threatening or anxiety-provoking initial increments.

Occasionally, the couple selects a starting point that might be too advanced for their level of intimacy tolerance, such as reciprocal facial touch. It is useful to remember that couples often undervalue the powerful impact of sensate focus and want to push the pacing because of their frustration and need to achieve their goal. Gentle redirection with validation from the therapist can reinforce the principles of sensate focus and the need for limited exposure, tiny increments, repeated trials and small successes.

During the initial steps or progressions of touching and sensual pleasuring, the giver listens carefully to what the receiver wants while the receiver takes in as much pleasurable sensation as possible and is asked to concentrate only on what is feeling good. The receiver becomes an active participant, directing the giver by communicating what is enjoyable in order to maintain pleasurable sensations. Communicating will give the partners practice in learning how to ask first for pleasant touch, then sensual touching and later for sexual touching and activities. After a few successful trials, the couple is instructed to be creative and experimental, to ask for different kinds of touch in order to experience various sensations. The receiver is not to worry about the giver but to focus on two thoughts: put himself or herself in a *mental loop* and think of only what is feeling good in each moment and consider what he or she would like in order to keep the sensations pleasant or pleasurable. This sounds like an easy exercise to do, but we have found that couples need a lot of practice before everything begins to flow, especially the communication. Couples often have deeply held beliefs and prohibitions about any form of communication about physical/sexual expression using words.

The therapist encourages positive anticipation. The therapist might say, "It would be better if you did not just make this a cold and clinical exercise. Try to get in the mood by thinking positive thoughts, remembering past pleasant experiences together and saying things to each other during the day to create a positive mood." Thought stopping and thought substitution are also suggested: "Take note of any negative thoughts or feelings that occur during this exercise but do not dwell on them. Instead, think about pleasurable aspects of sensual touching. We will discuss any negative reactions in session. If you find yourself thinking about problems you have experienced in the past, stop these thoughts immediately and focus on your own pleasure. You will succeed to the extent that you are able to give each other and yourself pleasant touch or pleasurable sensual feelings." Readers will note that the couple is being asked to engage in some cognitive therapy during the exercise. During the session, the therapist might explore the kinds of negative cognition they might have had and help them develop positive counterthoughts.

Typically, the couple begins each therapy session by reporting about the completed homework exercises. Each encounter should be thoroughly debriefed in order to move on to designing the next assignment. In general, we are interested in what the couple enjoyed best and least, if the exercises went smoothly and how much anxiety was experienced and if there were any problems for either partner. In contemplating the next assignment, the therapist considers developing a hierarchy of anxiety-provoking behaviors and the importance of small steps in order to ensure that these behaviors can be completed with little to no anxiety. With each successive assignment, the partners discuss where they would like to start and the therapist makes sure the partners are comfortable with the plan. The therapist uses behaviorally objective language so that the couple knows exactly what is expected. The following questions are typical of what we ask in the follow-up:

- How did the exercise go? (Start with an open-ended question to see what the couple thought was most significant.)
- How many times were you able to do it?
- Who initiated the exercises? How did you decide?
- Was the experience pleasant or pleasurable? In what ways?
- On a scale from 1 to 10 how much anxiety did you experience during each exercise? If you felt anxiety, were you able to control or stop it?
- What did you like most about it?
- What was it like to create a sensual environment?
- Were your ideas about a comfortable setting alike or different?
- Was there anything you did not like?
- What was it like when you were the receiver?
- What was it like being on the giving end?
- Did you let your partner know what felt good? How?
- Did you let your partner know what you wanted? In what way? If not, what prevented you?
- How did it feel to communicate your wants?
- Did you feel your partner gave you enough feedback about what he or she felt and what he or she wanted?
- Did you feel turned on during the exercise?
- Were you able to stay focused on just the touching or sensual experiences and not think about the problem you have been experiencing?
- Did you notice that you were avoiding the exercise?
- Was it easy or difficult to find time?
- Were you able to stop the self-monitoring we talked about?
- Were you able to stop any negative thoughts that occurred to you?
- Do you feel ready to move on to another exercise that is a bit more difficult or do you think you need to stay at this level another week?

The therapist may design other questions depending on the material presented or queries targeted toward the specific problem at hand.

The touching and sensual pleasuring exercises are broken down into small behavioral units depending on the couple's weekly report. The process could take 1, 2, or several weeks, depending on where they started and the progress made in being free of anxiety while doing different touching exercises, communicating with each other, feeling free to ask for what they want and so on. Sometimes the couple will need to remain on the same exercise for 2 or 3 weeks or take a step back. Setbacks are to be expected and the couple must be encouraged to view these instances as opportunities for growth. It is important not to rush this process, especially when the couple is trying to achieve the end goal of the therapy too quickly.

Another of many couples we have treated had not been physically intimate with each other for a number of years. When asked where they thought they could start, they were not sure. The therapist suggested that perhaps they start with giving each other a hand massage for 5 minutes while fully clothed in the living room. This example shows that the predetermined formats described earlier for Pleasuring I and II exercises Kaplan (1975) would have been unthinkable for such a couple.

Sensual Pleasuring with Erotic Stimulation

Once the couple has progressed to the point of being able to give each other a full-body nongenital massage, they can advance to the next series of assignments. The second general category of sensate focus exercises incorporates breast and genital stimulation although the prohibition against intercourse is still in effect. The intent is to help the couple enjoy sexual stimulation as a goal in itself within an anxiety-free environment. Each exercise begins with nonsexual touching and gradually progress to include prearranged touch that provides genital sensation. The therapist must take the same precautions in formatting graduated assignments that are built upon the successful completion of the last exercise. The therapist must remind the partners to focus on the pleasurable sensations and interrupt any negative cognition that may emerge by taking note of negative cognitions for later discussion in the session. Later, the therapist can focus on addressing the sensations being experienced and validate their success.

Over time and after successful trials, the couple is encouraged to allow the sexual sensations to build to whatever level is desirable. The duration and arousal that accompany genital and breast stimulation may lead to noncoital orgasm, but is not necessary. In fact, noncoital orgasm is never stated as a goal; prescribing a particular goal state (i.e., orgasm or erection) can increase performance anxiety. Although orgasm is acceptable, if desired, men should be cautioned to orgasm only if they have an erection. To ejaculate without a firm erection may help to create ED through simple classical conditioning. *The therapist must be careful to never prescribe any kind of sexual goal, but to say that when the conditions are right, nature will take over and things will work as expected.* The therapist can repeat that it is our unrealistic expectations leading to anxiety that are the main cause of most sexual problems.

Moving through these steps may take several trials and weeks. Once again the couple is asked to engage in the exercises three times during the week with the expectation that the couple will perceive their progress in these exercises as below average, average or above average. The couple should complete three exercises unless there is a good reason not to. One example of an acceptable excuse would be if one partner reports too much anxiety. Couples will require encouragement during the process as well as reminders about the reasons for gradual steps. Progress is closely monitored with a review at the beginning of each session. At the end of each session, another homework assignment is given to promote further success, feelings of competence, connection between partners and success in reducing anxiety with behaviors that would have evoked considerable anxiety prior to therapy.

Transitioning to Intercourse

Once the couple has successfully completed several successful trials of sensate focus with erotic stimulation, they can progress to sexual intercourse if desired. As with other stages of sensate focus, intercourse can be dissected into many steps such as outer course (rubbing the genitals together without penetration, degree of penetration or penetration without thrusting, penetration without orgasm).

Nondemand intercourse, by definition, does not require any particular type of performance; thus, if intercourse is desired without orgasm, it should be acceptable. If a partner does not want to have intercourse, he or she should be free of the demand and the value of the intimate encounter should not be diminished. Prior sensate focus exercises have taught the couple to experience their sexuality in a variety of ways. Intercourse is just one way of expressing their sexual feelings; it is not the ultimate goal of sex (Gambescia & Weeks, 2006).

Many couples, particularly men, have been taught to believe that coitus alone is the crucial objective of sexual expression. This sort of singular goal-oriented thinking can make transitioning to intercourse difficult. The therapist must anticipate that unrealistic notions about performance and sexual desire might continue even if they have been discussed previously. These ideas must be processed as they emerge. Also, the couple must comprehend that sexual desire can fluctuate, is not necessarily synchronous and need not be present at the beginning of sexual activity (Weeks & Gambescia, 2002; Basson, 2000). Desire can emerge as the individuals relax and begin to experience pleasure from intimate touch. Men must be careful not to assume an erection will occur immediately but will be a progressive process of getting and losing the erection until it is completely firm. This fact is especially true for older men. Sometimes women also expect the man to immediately have an erection with the slightest touch and they assume that if he doesn't, he must not find her attractive.

If the couple decides to have intercourse, instruct them to focus on the sensations, positive thoughts, fantasies and other techniques that have helped to make the experience pleasurable. Reinforce that they should not worry about what they think they *should* feel but on what they *do* feel. They can enjoy the fact that they are doing something that brings them closer and builds positive experiences (Gambescia & Weeks, 2006).

Maintaining a concentration on current sensations should replace the goal orientation that accompanies many sexual problems (Lousada & Angel, 2011). Additionally, negative judgments, so common in our couples, about the self or the partner are to be interrupted and replaced with positive observations. Taking a positive stance regarding the self and relationship will reinforce the mindfulness principles they have learned. Sensate focus reinforces and validates empathy, compassion, affection and connection (Lazaridou & Kalogianni, 2013).

Conclusion

Sensate focus is recognized as a practical treatment for many sexual difficulties (Maurice, 1999; Weeks & Gambescia, 2015); however, information regarding appropriate implementation of the exercises is often omitted from the description of the exercises. Frequently, therapists make the erroneous assumption that the technique is simple; therefore the couple should know how to use it. In clinical supervision, we often hear reports of therapeutic disasters resulting from incorrect usage of sensate focus. We believe that the proper application of sensate focus can make the difference between therapeutic success and failure. This simple yet powerful method can increase the sense of cohesion, love, caring, commitment, cooperation and intimacy between partners—provided it is implemented properly and in a collaborative way with the couple.

We have devoted this chapter to the discussion of many aspects of sensate focus, including structuring the exercises, timing, pacing, function, selection of activities and structure. Moreover, we have also emphasized the use of sensate focus in a systemic or balanced way. Each partner has a contribution to the development and/or maintenance of the sexual problem and will need to work collaboratively to resolve it. We are guided by systemic principles that recognize the need for both partners to actively participate in treatment.

Sensate focus facilitates the communication of touching and sensual and sexual preferences and dislikes, a difficult endeavor for most sex therapy clients. This method also reduces sexual anxiety and helps couples attain a greater degree of emotional and physical closeness. We have found that both partners benefit equally from the experience. Thus, we are constantly thinking about the reciprocal (systemic) nature of the problem and how the exercises give each partner mutual benefit. Sensate focus keeps both partners interested, motivated and satisfied with the progress of therapy because they are always gaining something for themselves while seeing improvement in the sexual relationship.

References

Abdo, C. H., Afif-Abdo, J., Otani, F., & Machado, A. C. (2008). Sexual satisfaction among patients with erectile dysfunction treated with counseling, sildenafil, or both. *Journal of Sexual Medicine, 5*(7), 1720–1726.

Basson, R. (2000). The female sexual response: A different model. *Journal of Sex & Marital Therapy, 26*(1), 51–65.

Bandura, A. (1969). *Principles of behavior modification.* New York: Holt, Rinehart & Winston.

Beck, A. T. (1976). *Cognitive therapy and the emotional disorders.* New York: International Universities Press.

Beck, J. (1995). *Cognitive therapy: Basics and beyond.* New York: Guilford Press.

Byers, E. (2005). Relationship satisfaction and sexual satisfaction: A longitudinal study of individuals in long-term relationships. *The Journal of Sex Research, 42*(2), 113–118.

Chevret, M., Jaudinot, E., Sullivan, K., Marrel, A., & De Gendre, A. S. (2004). Impact of erectile dysfunction on sexual life of female partners: Assessment with the index of sexual life (isl) questionnaire. *Journal of Sex and Marital Therapy, 30*(3), 157–172.

Gambescia, N., Sendak, S. K., & Weeks, G. (2009). The treatment of erectile dysfunction. *Journal of Family Psychotherapy, 20*(2), 221–240.

Gambescia, N., & Weeks, G. (2006). Sexual dysfunction. In N. Kazantzis & L. L'Abate (Eds.), *Handbook of homework assignments in psychotherapy: Research, practice, and prevention* (pp. 351–368). Norwell, MA: Kluwer Academic Publishers.

Gottman, J. (1994). *What predicts divorce: The relationship between marital processes and marital outcomes.* Hillsdale, NJ: Lawrence Erlbaum.

Hall, K., & Graham, C. (Eds.). (2012). *The cultural context of sexual pleasure and problems.* New York: Routledge.

Hart, T., & Schwartz, D. (2010). Cognitive-behavioral erectile dysfunction treatment for gay men. *Cognitive and Behavioral Practice, 17,* 66–76.

Hertlein, K. M., Weeks, G. R., & Gambescia, N. (Eds.). (2009). *Systemic sex therapy.* New York: Routledge.

Kaplan, H. (1974). *The new sex therapy.* New York: Brunner/Mazel.

Kaplan, H. (1975). *The illustrated manual of sex therapy* (2nd ed.). New York: Brunner-Routledge.

Kleinplatz, P. (1996). The erotic encounter. *Journal of Humanistic Psychology, 36*(3), 108–123.

Kozlowski, A. (2013). Mindful mating: Exploring the connection between mindfulness and relationship satisfaction. *Sexual and Relationship Therapy, 28*(1–2), 92–104.

Lazaridou, A., & Kalogianni, C. (2013). Mindfulness and sexuality. *Sexual and Relationship Therapy, 28*(1–2), 29–38.

Lazarus, S. S. (1965). The treatment of a sexually inadequate man. In L. P. Ullmann & L. Drasner (Eds.), *Case studies in behavior modification* (pp. 243–260). New York: Holt, Rinehart & Winston.

Lieblum, S. R. (2007). Sex therapy today: Current issues and future perspectives. In S. R. Lieblum (Ed.), *Principles and practice of sex therapy* (4th ed.) (pp. 3–25). New York: Guilford Press.

Lousada, M., & Angel, E. (2011). Tantric orgasm: Beyond Masters and Johnson. *Sexual and Relationship Therapy, 26*(4), 389–402.

Mark, K., & Jozkowski, K. (2013). The mediating role of sexual and nonsexual communication between relationship and sexual satisfaction in a sample of college-age heterosexual couples. *Journal of Sex & Marital Therapy, 39*(5–6), 410–427.

Masters, W. H., & Johnson, V. (1970). *Human sexual inadequacy.* Boston: Little, Brown.

Maurice, W. (1999). *Sexual medicine in primary care.* St. Louis, MO: Mosby.

Rosen, J., & Althof, S. (2008). Impact of premature ejaculation: The psychological, quality of life, and sexual relationship consequences. *Journal of Sexual Medicine, 6,* 1296–1307.

Sommers, F. G. (2013). Mindfulness in love and love making: A way of life. *Sexual and Relationship Therapy, 28*(1–2), 84–91.

Weeks, G. R. (1987). Systemic treatment of inhibited sexual desire. In G. Weeks & L. Hof (Eds.), *Integrating sex and marital therapy: A clinical guide* (pp. 183–201). New York: Brunner/Mazel.

Weeks, G. R. (1995). Inhibited sexual desire. In G. Weeks & L. Hof (Eds.), *Integrative solutions: Treating common problems in couples therapy* (pp. 215–252). New York: Brunner/Mazel.

Weeks, G. R. (2005). The emergence of a new paradigm in sex therapy: Integration. *Sexual and Relationship Therapy, 20*(1), 89–104.

Weeks, G. R., & Fife, S. T. (2014). *Couples in treatment: Techniques and approaches for effective practice* (3rd ed.). New York: Routledge.

Weeks, G. R., & Gambescia, N. (2000). *Erectile dysfunction: Integrating couple therapy, sex therapy, and medical treatment.* New York: W. W. Norton.

Weeks, G. R., & Gambescia, N. (2002). *Hypoactive sexual desire: Integrating sex and couple therapy.* New York: W. W. Norton.

Weeks, G., & Gambescia, N. (2015). Couple therapy and treatment of sexual problems: The Intersystems Approach. In A. Gurman, J. Lebow, and D. Snyder (Eds.), *Clinical handbook of couple therapy* (5th ed.) (pp. 635–658). New York: Guilford Press.

Weeks, G. R., & Hof, L. (1987). *Integrating sex and marital therapy.* New York: Brunner/Mazel.

Weiner, L., Cannon, N., & Avery-Clark, C. (2014). Reclaiming the lost art of sensate focus: A clinician's guide. *Family Therapy Magazine, 13*(5), 46–48.

Wincze, J. P., & Carey, M. P. (2001). *Sexual dysfunction: A guide for assessment and treatment* (2nd ed.). New York: Guilford Press.

Wolpe, J. (1958). *Psychotherapy by reciprocal inhibition.* Stanford, CA: Stanford University Press.

Wolpe, J. (1992). *The practice of behavior therapy* (4th ed.). Boston, MA: Allyn & Bacon.

11

FACTORS THAT COMPLICATE TREATING SEXUAL DISORDERS

Introduction

In sex therapy practice, individuals or couples request treatment for a specific problem or condition. Often, the problem is stated in the initial contact or during the first session. Once the therapist begins to address the presenting problem, however, other factors can arise that obscure assessment and treatment. Factors that complicate treatment often involve faulty communication or misinformation, thereby intensifying the presenting problem. In this chapter we review some of the common factors that can interfere with treatment, including sexual ignorance, faulty cognitions, and sexual guilt and shame.

Sexual Ignorance

Sexual ignorance is a major contributor to many sexual disorders. Masters and Johnson (1970) were the earliest sexuality researchers to note the striking connection between the lack of sexual information and consequential sexual problems. Zilbergeld (1999) also identified the destructive effects of sexual ignorance and misinformation on sexual enjoyment and functioning. He proposed that a performance-based goal-oriented model of normalcy is particularly damaging to sexual intimacy. By focusing on performance and the solitary goal of orgasm, men and women subscribe to a myth that fails to recognize the sensual and intimate nature of physical touch, nondemand stimulation and overall intimacy.

Sexual Mythology

The greatest source of sexual misinformation and ignorance is the mythology associated with sex. Sexual myths are misguided beliefs, misconceptions and distortions that promote unrealistic standards and rigid expectations about sex. These beliefs originate within culture, religion, the family of origin and other contextual sources and become woven into the fabric of the individual's sexual script. Mythological beliefs perpetuate sexual fear, shame, embarrassment and unrealistic expectations regarding sexual intimacy and can contribute to sexual dysfunction (Adams, Dubbert, Chupurdia, & Jones, 1996).

Common sexual myths target penis size, erectile capacity, orgasmic synchronicity and the decline in sexual enjoyment with aging (see, for example, Hinchliff & Gott, 2008). The list is exhaustive and an Internet search reveals numerous sites that offer help to individuals troubled by sexual problems that are maintained by mythological beliefs. These sites are both humorous and informative:

- http://www.cracked.com/photoplasty_994_27-sex-myths-you-need-to-stop-believing
- http://afterhours.lifehacker.com/10-stubborn-sex-myths-that-just-wont-die-debunked-by-1522576378
- http://www.askmen.com/top_10/dating/top-10-myths-about-sex.html
- https://www.psychologytoday.com/blog/fulfillment-any-age/201207/6-myths-about-female-sexuality-and-why-theyre-wrong
- http://abcnews.go.com/Health/Wellness/14-sex-myths-busted/story?id=24520345

See Peterson and Peterson (2007) for a more complete listing of current sexual myths.

Faulty Cognitions

Acceptance of sexual mythology can interfere with the cognitive understanding of normal sexuality, sexual enjoyment and prevention of sexually transmitted illnesses. It can also interfere with physical health and relationship satisfaction. Furthermore, sexual misinformation causes increased sexual anxiety and sexual guilt (Mosher, 1979) and directly contributes to faulty automatic cognitions (Bancroft & Janssen, 2000). These faulty cognitions promote even more anxiety (Rosen, Leiblum, & Spector, 1994).

Depending on the individual's culture, religion and psychological disposition, faulty cognitions can present in a variety of ways. Religiously based negativism regarding sex can interfere with sexual fantasy and significantly contribute to sexual guilt and shame (Ellison, 2011). Consequently, sexual desire is interrupted and limitations are placed on a range of sexual behavior, such as masturbation. Another source of misinformation involves the distortion about the prevalence of sexual dysfunction. For women, the faulty belief that sexual problems are common will interfere with sexual enjoyment and satisfaction (Chang, Klein, & Gorzalka, 2013). Women who anticipate sexual problems may monitor themselves more for those problems, become more anxious and actually experience sexual dissatisfaction. The effect would be similar to a self-fulfilling prophecy.

East Asian women (compared to Caucasian women) were found to demonstrate more sexual conservatism and sexual guilt and experienced significantly less sexual arousal (Woo, Brotto, & Gorzalka, 2011). They experienced automatic thoughts reflecting sexual guilt about feeling desire and initiating sexual activity. Understandably, in treating East Asian woman with interest and arousal problems, one of the key elements of treatment should be a thorough examination of their beliefs about sex and sexual guilt.

Sexual Guilt, Anxiety and Shame

Problematic sexual cognitions contribute to numerous sexual disorders such as erectile dysfunction (Gambescia & Weeks, 2015) as well as the lack of sexual desire (Weeks & Gambescia, 2015). A study by Nobre and Pinto-Gouveia (2009) supports the position of the other authors that early maladaptive cognitive schemas, resulting from family dysfunction, might have a negative impact on sexual functioning. These core or nuclear schemas generally persist throughout a person's life. Men with sexual dysfunctions reported earlier maladaptive schemas involving beliefs about their dependence and incompetence, feeling disconnected and rejected, lacking in autonomy and inability to perform well, having impaired limits in areas such as responsibility and goal setting, being other directed and experiencing hypervigilance and inhibition (Nobre & Pinto-Gouveia, 2009). These findings were supported in another study that found that men and women with sexual dysfunctions demonstrated faulty cognitions regarding incompetence, powerlessness and feeling like a failure (Gomes & Nobre, 2012). From a treatment perspective, the clinician would need to identify the specific cognitions regarding the client's sexual problem and later thoroughly explore the client's early maladaptive schemas. The exploration and cognitive revision of this early maladaptive schema is a new and important concept for the treatment of all sexual problems.

In the accompanying edited volume by Hertlein, Weeks, and Gambescia (2015), the various authors use illustrations from clinical practice to demonstrate how anxiety is related to a variety of sexual disorders and how guilt restricts the expression of sexual feelings and behaviors. It may be the case that specific sexual myths and cognitive schemas are more closely linked to one type of problem than another, but research has yet to examine this possible relationship. In fact, recent clinical research on the negative impact of sexual mythology and sexual dysfunction has been sparse; however, clinical experience often supports the existence of this particularly destructive mechanism.

Dealing with Sexual Mythology

The best way to counter faulty beliefs and cognitions (and reduce the related sexual anxiety) is through psychoeducation and cognitive therapy techniques. Distorted information must be unlearned and replaced with factual information. For instance, if the client believes that penis size is related to sexual satisfaction, this thought can be countered with information about the range of normal penis size, coital positioning (Pierce, 2000), the importance of clitoral stimulation and the value of expanding the sexual repertoire. Another example involves commonly held faulty beliefs about sex and aging: "I am too old to have sex" or "I should not need sex now that I am old." These thoughts can be countered with factual information that many older adults continue to enjoy sexual activity throughout their life spans (Fisher, 2010; Lindau et al., 2007). Sexual thoughts related to guilt over sexual desire ("I am bad/wrong for wanting sex") must be stopped and replaced with cognitions less reflective of guilt. Therapists, then, need to address mythology, misinformation and core cognitive schemas with couples while considering which strategies are most appropriate for dealing with these anxiety-provoking views.

Dealing with Common Intimacy Fears

There are many ways a therapist might become aware that fears are impacting the course of treatment. In some cases, clients will not complete the homework assigned to them. Although this might happen on occasion in any treatment, repeated noncompliance with homework might signal to the therapist that there is an issue or fear preventing further growth. Additionally, there are couples who miss appointments or attend scheduled appointments so erratically that it is difficult to move forward when sessions are spent reviewing what has transpired within the last few weeks. Because of the nature of sex therapy and because of the momentum gained from the progressive weekly assignments, it is imperative that the therapist address attempts to sabotage treatment. An effective way to do this might be to meet with the clients to discuss the fears that prevent other couples from completing treatment as prescribed or attending therapy on a regular basis. It is important to normalize that these fears are common, and that they are part of the process of treatment rather than an indication to stop treatment. Many couples presenting with a sexual problem have developed a pattern of sexual avoidance. Sexual avoidance is self-perpetuating because it is negatively reinforced. Negative reinforcement means they are either anxious or fearful about trying to have sex; by finding reasons to avoid sexual interactions, they reduce their fear and anxiety. The reduction of fear and anxiety is a reward, or a reinforcer. Specific fears and suggestions for how to manage them are detailed in the following subsections.

Fear of Intimacy

A general rule of sex therapy is that couple therapy must be completed or at least well underway to completion prior to attempting sex therapy. Couples who have significant relational problems will not be able to successfully engage in sex therapy because the wish to connect and cooperate with each other is essential. For example, couple work is important prior to sex therapy in instances in which there are underlying fears of intimacy. Underlying fears about intimacy prevent partners from achieving emotional, intellectual and/or sexual intimacy. Sexual problems are often an expression of one or more of these underlying fears. Without decreasing or diminishing the intensity of these fears, progress in the couple's sexual relationship will be limited. In fact, in most cases the authors have treated, the couple cannot make any progress in sex therapy until the fears have been addressed.

Sternberg (1986) defined intimacy as the sense of closeness, a feeling of being connected or bonded, a sense of welfare for the other, having high regard for the other, perceiving the other as trustworthy and giving emotional support freely to the other, among other meanings. Another study focused on how intimacy is experienced by men, including feeling as if one could be oneself with the partner, feeling accepted by one's partner and feeling a level of trust with one's partner that differed from trust with a friend (Patrick & Beckenbach, 2009). The literature has a large body of theoretical and empirical/assessment work on intimacy. Prager (2013) discussed major intimacy dilemmas that can interfere with a couple's relationship and potentially affect sexual intimacy. Men for example, can have sex without intimacy but find it more difficult to have intimacy without sex (Patrick & Beckenbach, 2009). Weeks and Hof (1987) and Weeks and Fife (2014) suggested that a bulk of couple/sexual pathology results from problems in the area of intimacy. This awareness is rarely mentioned in texts on couple or sex therapy. Moreover, what sometimes appear to be problems in the areas of commitment and passion are often directly linked to or result from problems in the area of intimacy. For example, the person who is labeled commitment phobic is often just reacting to an underlying fear of intimacy that makes it difficult to commit. The assumption of Weeks and Fife's (2014) theory regarding intimacy is that everyone who enters a relationship has some underlying or unconscious fears of intimacy. For most partners, these fears are not powerful and they do not contribute to relational and/or sexual problems; however, for other partners, these fears may be more intense and can exert a destructive force in the sexual relationship as well as in the overall relationship. The concept that intimacy is a root cause of marital/sexual pathology is one that is almost never found in the marriage and family therapy literature (Weeks & Fife, 2014). It would be impossible to catalog all the possible underlying fears of intimacy. Fortunately, a few of these fears are fairly common and are described next, along with examples of how each fear might impact the couple's sexual relationship or lead to sexual problems.

Descriptions of the fears, as well as a discussion of the implications of the fears, are summarized in Table 11.1.

TABLE 11.1 Fears of Intimacy

Underlying Fears of Intimacy	Description	Implications for the Relationship
Fear of Rejection/ Abandonment	Usually grounded in one's family of origin: perhaps parents ignored, rejected or abandoned their child. This fear manifests in the adult child's intimate relationships.	The individual will avoid being close or intimate with his/her partner.
Fear of Dependency	A fear of becoming controlled or reliant on someone else. Can result in a loss of autonomy, self-control and independence.	Act as if they do not need anyone and make every effort to maintain their independence. Sexually he or she will avoid intimacy that shows any needs or vulnerability.
Fear of Anger	A fear that one will lose control over his or her anger and hurt another or that anger will be expressed toward him or her.	Not hearing partner's anger can result in impaired communication or avoidance of discussing intimate topics; not expressing one's anger verbally may prevent the development of intimacy.
Fear of Feelings	The most common cause is one's family of origin having an excess of out-of-control feelings or being devoid of feelings.	Can result in avoidance of feeling anything, thus any intimate contact would be avoided since it arouses feelings.
Fear of Losing Control	The fear has two levels: first, that someone else is going to take control of them, and second that there will be a loss of self.	Due to culture's strong belief that our bodies are our own and each of us has control over our body, sex is a part of oneself over which only the individual has control. A person may overcontrol sex in order to compensate for a lack of control in other parts of the relationship.

Fear of Anger

Some individuals are afraid of their own anger or of being the recipient of anger from others, especially a partner. The suppression or avoidance of anger causes them to suppress angry feelings and turn off many other feelings as a result. When interacting in an intimate relationship, conflict and anger inevitably arise. Individuals who fear anger suppress all feelings and deeper interactions because of the anticipated negative consequences. Sex is one way of interacting intimately; thus, the partner may begin to avoid sex. Sometimes these individuals perceive sex as an area where they may be criticized or where their feelings may be aroused and their anger may surface.

An example of fear of anger is Rich, a man who recently lost all sexual interest. The therapist ruled out any medical issues but found that he was experiencing posttraumatic stress disorder (PTSD) from the Vietnam War where he had been a sniper. Additionally, the therapist learned that the client felt his anger was out of control early in his life. When he was younger, if he became angry, he would start a physical fight and often injure the other person. Rich entered the Army as soon as legally permissible and learned to channel his aggression more appropriately by becoming an expert sniper. Further, Rich married someone who could vacillate between being passive to aggressive. He could relate to the passive side because he had learned to be passive but felt anger when his wife was assertive. After an extended assessment, the therapist realized that Rich was carrying a good deal of anger and resentment toward his wife although he did his best to hide these feelings from himself. Rich was overcontrolling his anger, which then led to resentment. His chronic resentment later led to the suppression of his sexual desire. Rich needed to do family-of-origin work about coping with anger in the family, deal with his PTSD and work on viewing anger and conflict as healthy and productive rather than destructive. The therapist also learned that the immediate predisposing factor to his loss of desire occurred when his business failed. Rich was also angry with himself for not making the business work. The therapist had multiple issues to manage with Rich in individual therapy before he was ready to begin working through the impact of these issues on his sexual desire.

Fear of Feelings

Some individuals actually have a fear of feeling or experiencing their own feelings, often a result of observing feelings that were out of control in their family. In one case, a woman watched her father suffer from bipolar disorder. She witnessed severe mood swings and erratic behavior in her father and assumed from an early age that feelings cause people to lose control over their lives. Further, she assumed that the feelings that would get stirred up during sex would cause her to become emotionally out of control. She controlled her feelings by suppressing them whether they were pleasant or unpleasant. Several other clients reported seeing parents who were feeling depressed much of the time. Others may have seen two parents whose moods led to disengagement or habitual conflict. The internalized message was that feelings eventually only have bad consequences and so it is preferable not to feel at all.

Anthony suffered from such a fear. In therapy he presented with an inability to orgasm. The therapist realized that Anthony avoided expressing feelings because an orgasm is an intense emotion. The therapist did a genogram with Anthony and learned that his mother was bipolar. Anthony grew up in fear of her irrational moods and could remember that he made the decision that feelings would never rule his life. Thus, he learned to turn off all feelings. He lacked sexual desire but he still had sex because he considered it an obligation. He wanted to be a good husband but could not release his feelings through the experience of orgasm. The therapist helped Anthony understand his mother's illness, how he had reacted to her and interpreted her behavior and how the fear of feelings had continued into adulthood, affecting his choice of a partner and how he expressed himself sexually.

Fear of Losing Control

Intimate relationships are replete with dynamics involving power and control. These dynamics can surface as disagreements about money, domestic responsibilities, childcare and sex. Losing control is always a complex situation with multiple levels of etiology; nonetheless, in a relationship loss of control has two major presentations. The first is simply being told what to do by a partner and the other is actually being controlled behaviorally. In the first instance, the common response is to fight back, creating overt conflict in the relationship. The second and deeper problem is when one partner tries to dictate feelings and thoughts, often in an indirect way, which causes distress for the partner receiving the messages. The therapeutic challenge is to determine why a person would select a controlling partner in the first place. Often, there is an unconscious wish to be controlled, or ambivalence about control. They wish to be controlled yet rebel against it. The next therapeutic objective is to assess the underlying dynamics, address the presentations and help the couple gain or regain a more workable distribution of power. One common presentation of struggles over power and control is the complaint of absent/low sexual desire, where the controlled partner develops strategies to protest by losing interest in sex. Although a passive strategy, it is highly effective because it calls attention to the dynamic. The person who lacks desire is in control of sexual frequency and will avoid sex in order to maintain control in one area. The lack of desire for sex is a metaphor for maintaining control over at least one aspect of one's life.

Marilyn and Oscar presented with absent/low desire on Marilyn's part. She said she would sometimes have sex with Oscar because it was her duty, but she had never really felt the desire for sex after being in the relationship for a few months. Oscar wanted them to come to therapy because of this problem but he did not want to push Marilyn to do anything she did not want to do. He had been taught to respect women, be overly pleasing and not to violate a woman's sexual boundaries. The therapist began to explore Marilyn's history and found that she was the good kid in the family. Her parents pressured her to conform to how they wanted her to be and they would strongly disapprove of any act that went against them. Marilyn had never been encouraged to develop her own sense of self or autonomy. She believed she was simply an extension of her parents, always trying to please them to gain love and approval. They were much alike in doing what their parents told them was right. As the woman she believed it was her duty to please Oscar in all respects. She felt guilty when she did not respond to his sexual advances. Like many men and women we have seen with lack of desire, the person with the symptom is trying to find someplace that is his or her own, a place over which the person has complete control and self-determination. In our culture, we believe we control our bodies and our sexuality. It is one place that is sacred to the extent that it is acceptable to have control over one's sexuality. Of course a person can have sex or be forced to have sex, but they cannot be forced to want to want it or to have desire. Marilyn had unconsciously chosen sex as the one place where she could draw the line and unconsciously express her desire for autonomy. The therapist worked with Marilyn to help her understand how her parents had not supported her development as an autonomous person. Her role was to please her parents and later to please others. She needed to move past the belief that the only way to gain love, as her parents defined it, was to please others. The therapist used a combination of family-of-origin work, insight and cognitive therapy to help Marilyn accomplish these goals, understand their dynamic and learn why she and Oscar had chosen each other. Neither one would strongly challenge the other because of unconscious collusion to protect each other and the desire to avoid any conflicts. They were taught to be people pleasers, which involved suppressing their needs and not challenging others. Both partners needed to work on self-differentiation; learn to be more assertive with each other; own their own needs, wants and desires; and allow each other to be more autonomous.

Fear of Rejection/Abandonment

Fear of rejection or abandonment may have significant implications for treatment. There are several ways in which this fear can be realized. In some cases, rejection by the family of origin as a child can create a fear of abandonment within the individual's adult couple relationship. In other cases, the fear of rejection is prompted by the history of the couple's relationship, particularly if there has been a pattern of being traumatically abandoned. Investigating the family of origin through the use of focused genograms is one of the best ways to uncover a history of rejection or abandonment. The client's interpretation of what happened in the family will usually reveal whether he or she felt neglected, unwanted or physically/emotionally abandoned.

Mack presented a tragic picture of feeling abandoned. The therapist had discovered that Mack had always believed his wife would eventually leave him; thus, he was unconsciously afraid to form a close bond to her. The therapist challenged fear of abandonment and Mack told the following story: When he was five and playing with his younger brother at the top of a set of stairs in their home, Mack's brother accidentally fell down the stairs and almost died. The parents dealt with this problem by sending Mack to live with relatives without any explanation because they were convinced that Mack had pushed his brother. Further, Mack's parents only saw him occasionally. The lesson that Mack learned was that the ones who love you would inevitably reject you. The therapist suggested some family-of-origin work with Mack. His parents had explained to him that they loved both of their children but felt because Mack was bigger, he might accidentally push his brother down the stairs again. Mack had always assumed that his parents had just arbitrarily decided to abandon him and had no idea why he had been sent away. The parents admitted to overreacting to the situation by sending him away and explained that the cost of supporting him and making trips to see him were beyond their budget. Thus, they sent money to the relatives but only visited when they had the money to do so. This knowledge changed Mack's view of his parents and he began to work through his feelings of abandonment with his parents and how he had carried that fear to his marriage.

Mack's fear of abandonment also carried over to his sexual relationship. He viewed being sexual as a way to become close to his wife; therefore, part of his overall way of maintaining distance was to remain emotionally and sexually distant from his wife. His wife, Carolyn, also carried unconscious fears of abandonment. She had grown up in a family with a mother who had a dismissive attachment style. Carolyn expected very little from her marital relationship: the mere fact that Mack wanted to marry her was enough. The prospect of emotional closeness was not something they expected. The sexual symptom was the tip of the iceberg. The therapist was able to help them see that the symptom had much deeper roots. The resolution of the sexual symptom could not be accomplished without changing the deeply embedded problems within each partner.

Fear of Dependency

In a context where each person is responsible for his or her piece of the problem, it may be difficult for each/one partner to trust the other to do his or her part in providing for the partner's needs. By the time couples come to therapy, there have been a series of disappointments regarding each other's ability to fulfill the other's need. The partner wants to be dependent on the other to fulfill his or her needs but believes being too dependent will only lead to failed expectations, disappointment and hurt. The fear of dependency can emerge in a number of ways. In the family of origin the child may be encouraged to be dependent but is then constantly disappointed that the parents do not meet his or her needs. In order to avoid disappointment the child learns to be independent or even counterdependent (being completely self-sufficient). Other families discourage dependency. They expect their children to learn to take care of themselves, including filling all their own emotional needs. Many of these individuals equate dependency with weakness or personal failure. The fear of dependency can be expressed sexually. In order for many sexual needs to be fulfilled, the partners must depend on the other to be sensitive, aware and willing to meet the partner's needs.

Blake and Mary entered treatment because she had lost her feeling of desire for Blake soon after they began to date. Blake wanted her to initiate sexual activity because he could not guess when she was interested or receptive to sex. She agreed that the problem was entirely hers and she should be the one to always initiate sex. Blake added that because Mary was never interested he did not want to initiate and be rejected. Initially, it appeared that the problem was Mary's but when the therapist learned that Blake had never initiated sex, the picture changed because Blake's contribution was also problematic. Since Blake never began sexual activity, Mary concluded that he did not desire her. The therapist then began to explore their individual histories. Blake's mother had died at childbirth. The therapist wanted to know more about how his mother's death had affected him. Blake's father was wealthy, never remarried and hired nannies to care for Blake. At an early age the father had played a game with Blake where his father bent Blake's toes back until he cried and then told him that if he cried, it meant he was a weak person. His father would often repeat the phrases that "life was tough" and "every man for himself." Blake was also told that women would be attracted to him if he was highly successful and that a successful man simply attracts women who want to have sex with him. Further, his father would often bring one or two new women into the home and sleep with them, and they would never be seen again. In fact, Blake said his father's idol in life was Hugh Hefner. Further, Blake's father told him specifically that a real man never had to ask for sex; to do so meant he was weak and a failure. The therapist realized that Blake's behavior was actually counterdependent. He avoided being reliant on anyone and acted as if he could handle all of life's issues completely on his own. He had replicated his father's exact behavior. After his mother died, his father never depended on anyone emotionally. He had hundreds of liaisons with women but it was obvious to Blake later in life that his father was either hiring expensive escorts or using women. Blake expected his wife to pursue him emotionally and sexually, which proved that he could live without her emotionally and sexually.

The therapist worked with Blake to understand his fear of being dependent and how that fear had been instilled in him from an early age. As Blake started to understand this pattern of counterdependency, the therapist could then coach him on ways to identify and express his needs to his wife. Without going into Mary's history to show the complimentary dynamics, it was clear she was a dependent personality. She was pursuing someone who was a distancer in order to prove she was worthy of love.

These short case studies are illustrative of the common fears of intimacy. We demonstrated how one partner's fears can interfere with the couple's sexual life. Many times, both partners demonstrate common fears and they can compound each other by triggering fears in each other. Specifically, when one partner manifests a strong fear of intimacy, there is likely to be another fear in the other partner that may not be evident overtly. Additionally, the sexual problem being expressed by one partner (and his or her underlying fear) may serve to mask the underlying fears of the other. Any experienced couples clinician has noted that when one spouse gets better, the other often gets worse. When the partner with the overt problem improves, the other partner's pathology manifests itself in some way in order to maintain homeostasis within the couple system. The most common way this presents is an unconscious attempt to sabotage improvement in the partner with the problem. The Intersystem therapist should not wait for this to happen. Rather, understanding the systemic and interlocking nature of the pathology, the therapist will want to assess for fears of intimacy in the nonsymptomatic partner. If this attempt is unsuccessful, the problem in the nonsymptomatic partner will most likely appear later in treatment. As systems thinkers, we need to remain attentive to the idea that both partners are struggling and will need to work together to resolve the problem.

References

Adams, S. G. J., Dubbert, P. M., Chupurdia, K. M., & Jones, A. J. (1996). Assessment of sexual beliefs and information in aging couples with sexual dysfunction. *Archives of Sexual Behavior, 25*(3), 249.

Bancroft, J., & Janssen, E. (2000). The dual control model of male sexual response: A theoretical approach to centrally mediated erectile dysfunction. *Neuroscience and Biobehavioral Review, 24*(5), 571–579.

Chang, S., Klein, C., & Gorzalka, B. (2013). Perceived prevalence and definitions of sexual dysfunction as predictors of sexual function and satisfaction. *Journal of Sex Research, 505*(5), 502–512.

Ellison, D. (2011). Religious negativism and fantasy guilt. *The Family Journal, 19*(1), 101–107.

Fisher, L. L. (2010). *Sex, romance, and relationships: 2009 AARP survey of midlife and older adults* (Publication No. 19234). Washington, D.C.: AARP.

Gambescia, N., & Weeks, G. (2015). Systemic treatment of erectile disorder. In K. Hertlein, G. Weeks, & N. Gambescia (Eds.), *Systemic sex therapy* (2nd ed.) (pp. 72–89). New York: Routledge.

Gomes, A., & Nobre, P. (2012). Early maladaptive schemas and sexual dysfunction in men. *Archives of Sexual Behavior, 41*(1), 311–320.

Hertlein, K., Weeks, G., & Gambescia, N. (2015). *Systemic sex therapy.* New York: Routledge.

Hinchliff, S., & Gott, M. (2008). Challenging social myths and stereotypes of women and aging: Heterosexual women talk about sex, *Journal of Women & Aging, 20*(1–2), 65–81. doi:10.1300/J074v20n01_06

Lindau, S. T., Schumm, P., Laumann, E. O., Levinson, W., O'Muircheartaigh, C. A., & Waite, L. J. (2007). A study of sexuality and health among older adults in the United States. *New England Journal of Medicine, 357*, 762–774.

Masters, W. H., & Johnson, V. E. (1970). *Human sexual inadequacy.* Boston, MA: Little, Brown.

Mosher, D. L. (1979). Sex guilt and sex myths in college men and women. *Journal of Sex Research, 15*(3), 224–234.

Nobre, P. J., & Pinto-Gouveia, J. (2009). Cognitive schemas associated with negative sexual events: A comparison of men and women with and without sexual dysfunction. *Archives of Sexual Behavior, 38*(5), 842–851. doi:10.1007/s10508-008-9450-x

Patrick, S., & Beckenbach, J. (2009). Male perceptions of intimacy: A qualitative study. *Journal of Men's Studies, 17*(1), 47–56. Retrieved from http://ezproxy.library.unlv.edu/login?url=http://search.proquest.com/docview/222600699?accountid=3611

Peterson, F. L., & Peterson, C. C. (2007). A healthcare professional's guide to contemporary sexual myths. In L. VandeCreek, F. L. Peterson, & J. W. Bley (Eds.), *Innovations in clinical practice: Focus on sexual health* (pp. 323–326). Sarasota, FL: Professional Resource Press/Professional Resource Exchange.

Pierce, A. P. (2000). The coital alignment technique (CAT): An overview of studies. *Journal of Sex and Marital Therapy, 26*(3), 257–68.

Prager, K. (2013). *The dilemmas of intimacy: Conceptualization, assessment, and treatment.* New York: Routledge.

Rosen, R. C., Leiblum, S. R., & Spector, I. (1994). Psychologically-based treatment for male erectile disorder: A cognitive-interpersonal model. *Journal of Sex & Marital Therapy, 20*, 67–85.

Sternberg, R. (1986). A triangular theory of love. *Psychological Review, 93*(2), 119–135.

Weeks, G., & Fife, S. (2014). *Couples in treatment* (3rd ed.). New York: Routledge.

Weeks, G., & Gambescia, N. (2015). Definition, etiology, and treatment of low/absent sexual desire. In K. Hertlein, G. Weeks, & N. Gambescia (Eds.), *Systemic sex therapy* (2nd ed.) (pp. 125–151). New York: Routledge.

Weeks, G., & Hof, L. (1987). *Integrating sex and marital therapy: A clinical guide.* New York: Brunner/Mazel.

Woo, J. S., Brotto, L. A., & Gorzalka, B. B. (2011). The role of sex guilt in the relationship between culture and women's sexual desire. *Archives of Sexual Behavior, 40*(2) 385–394.

Zilbergeld, B. (1999). *The new male sexuality* (rev. ed.). New York: Bantam.

12
PRINCIPLES OF HOMEWORK

Introduction

Many of the cognitive and behavioral assignments we design in session must be practiced outside of the therapy office in order for lasting change to occur. The purpose of this chapter is to discuss the benefits of using at-home exercises as an adjunct to sex therapy. Homework is generally defined as an activity that is to be carried out after the therapy session: it is therapist directed or structured, related to practicing activities learned during the session and expected to have a therapeutic effect. It is often used to effect change in clients' attitudes, skill sets, feelings and cognitions (McCarthy, 1985). Often, we hear that clients and therapists dislike the term homework because it conjures up unpleasant memories of school assignments. Regardless of the terminology used, cognitive and behavioral assignments provide numerous opportunities (trials) for the client or couple to practice (shape) new cognitions and behaviors. Additionally, homework assignments are often prescribed for specific sexual problems. We have found that homework requires understanding of various principles and strategies in order to be implemented properly. See Gambescia and Weeks (2007) for a complete discussion of the various techniques and implementation of the assignments.

Homework

Homework exercises contain several core elements as discussed in *Handbook of Homework Assignments in Psychotherapy* (Kazantzis & L'Abate, 2007). First, they should be relevant to the sexual/relational issues and within the ability level of the client or couple. Homework must be discussed and practiced in session and assignments must be clearly described and accompanied by written directions.

Finally, the process of homework requires a strong therapeutic relationship, trust, collaboration and a clear statement of commitment (Kazantzis & L'Abate, 2007). Charlton and Brigel (1997) suggested that homework assignments in sex therapy should have components that attend to both emotions and behaviors. Gambescia and Weeks (2007) believed that the therapist should play a "directive role in session and beyond the therapy hour through the judicious use of assignments to be performed at home" (p. 354). As a way to facilitate homework assignments, Gambescia and Weeks (2007) advised that the therapist work with couples to address their concerns related to homework completion. In many cases, these concerns relate to fear of failure and uncertainty about what to expect during the homework. The therapist should talk with the couple about their reactions to doing homework and may find it valuable to relabel homework as tasks or exercises. As with any other assignment in treatment, couples are more likely to comply if they feel that they have a vested interest in the process. The couple needs to understand the reason for the homework and be able to link the completion of the assignment to reaching their treatment goals.

Each homework assignment is tailored specifically to the couple, considering their strengths and readiness to do the work. The creation of the exercises is always done collaboratively, meaning that the clients are co-creators of the homework. The therapist can suggest beginning with an exercise with a particular goal and describe the type of exercise that is normally done. In short, the therapist presents a shell or template for the exercise. The couple is then asked to consider what they think they can successfully do and to work out the particulars. For example, a couple that has not engaged in any touching or affection might be told they need to find some pleasant way to reconnect physically a few times a week. They can then decide on the content of the activity, how long it lasts, who initiates it, where they do it and so on. In one case, a couple decided they would exchange a closed-mouth kiss when the husband left and came home each day. They also agreed to sit next to each other in the living room while watching TV, hold hands when out in public and briefly cuddle at night. They agreed that either could initiate the activity and that the duration would be short, with the exception of sitting together. Further, they agreed that if something made them uncomfortable, they would talk about it when it happened.

Common Structural Elements

Panchana and Sofronoff (2005) and Tompkins (2004) suggested that although tailoring homework assignments to couples in sex therapy is important, there are also common structural elements that have been identified by many authors. For example, Gambescia and Weeks (2007) suggested that homework compliance is increased when the therapist and couple negotiate when the homework is to be scheduled, identify who will initiate the homework, and clearly understand what they are supposed to do within the homework. These authors considered some of the basic structural elements to be time, place, duration and determining who is to do what.

Assign Relevant, Acceptable and Appropriate Homework

The couple should view the assigned homework as relevant to their presenting problem and to meeting their goal. It should be a task that they deem as sexually acceptable. For example, the therapist would not prescribe an assignment he or she knows the couple has an aversion to doing. In addition, both the therapist and the client should agree that the homework is appropriate to meeting their goals. The therapist should discuss any emotional reaction to the homework after assigning it, rather than after the clients fail to complete it. The couple's initial emotional reaction to a homework assignment is a good indication of their readiness to do it or their resistance to it.

We have provided a list of books, videos, websites and reputable adult stores in Chapter 13. Whenever a couple is asked to read a particular book, watch a video or use other resources, the therapist should ask them how they feel about each activity, as described earlier. A classic example is when the therapist suggests buying a vibrator when treating anorgasmia. This suggestion can stir powerful feelings in both partners and may need to be processed thoroughly and slowly.

Make Sure the Homework Is Appropriate for the Couple's Age, Abilities and Lifestyle

The homework should match the clients' physical abilities and be considerate of their resources—including free time, schedules and finances. Typically, the couple is asked to do the homework assignment three times during any given week. The couple must be ready (state of willingness) to begin the homework and have the time available to devote to its completion. Suggesting that an economically strapped couple go on a second honeymoon for a week or buy an expensive vibrator merely sets them up for failure. The therapist should always ensure that the couple is capable of doing the homework, paying particular attention to any physical limitations based on health, age or ability to access the required resources.

Assign Simple, Clear Homework with Specific Instructions

It may be helpful to develop assignments with the clients and to take a collaborative attitude in designing the homework. Give the couple the parameters of the exercise and ask them to think about how and when they would like to do it. This gives them a sense of ownership in their therapy.

Start Small and Build on Successes

Begin with simple homework exercises and work toward more difficult, complex or challenging ones as defined by the couple. Make the assignments so incremental that the couple should be successful in completing them.

Make Assignments Single Focused and Specific

Make sure the assignment is specific and directs either behavioral or attitudinal changes. Do not allow ambiguity or veiled references to muddy the focus of the assignment. The language used in making the assignment should be direct, clear, concise and understandable to the couple. Get the couple to focus on only one step at a time. The first task of the therapy is to obtain a baseline of the couple's sexual behavior by having them closely monitor what happens during a sexual interaction. The next step might be for the couple to engage in some touching behavior in the living room and the next phase might be touching each other fully clothed in bed. This sequence of exercises helps the couple to reconnect physically through specific steps.

Ensure Understanding

Ask the couple to write down the homework or repeat it back. Make sure they both agree to do the homework and understand the purpose of the exercise before they leave the session. For high-conflict couples or those believed to have little motivation to complete the homework, create a homework contract. Review the terms of the contract with each partner and have each sign it. Make three copies, giving one to each partner and placing the third in their chart. We believe doing so is helpful and appropriate, but creating a contract does not guarantee homework completion. The purpose of the contract is to have a written statement of what the couple agreed to but may fail to do. We can then shift attention away from the homework to personal or relational issues that might be preventing them from carrying out the assignment. The fact that the homework is in writing means that neither one can claim they misunderstood, misinterpreted or simply forgot that the homework was given. In order to understand what contributed to not doing the homework, our view is to discuss the couple's relational issues first, as well as their readiness for change and emotions about doing the homework.

Obtain an Investment

Ask clients how they feel about the assignment, what problems they might have doing it, and in some cases, how they might sabotage the exercise. It might help to phrase the assignment as a win–win. The assignment is a win–win because if they are successful in doing it, they have progressed one more step; if they fail to do it and we process it and learn from it, we have removed a barrier to them achieving their goal. Ask the partners what they think the exercise will offer them individually and as a couple. For example, the exercise might be designed so that each one is to do something different. For one partner, the goal may be therapeutic; for the other, is the goal may be simply pleasurable. Make sure partners feels their role in the homework is important, enjoyable and worthwhile.

Build in Contingency Plans and Offer Flexibility

Part of ensuring buy-in is giving the couple options in completing the assignment. Planning for the unforeseen lets the couple know their therapist understands and appreciates the complexity of their lives and, more importantly, emphasizes the process that they will become more physically or emotionally connected with each other, which is the most important outcome. Completing the prescribed assignment exactly as described is of secondary importance.

Offer Support

The therapist can tell clients to call if they have questions or experience confusion about the homework assignment as they undertake it. Most couples will not need this step, but if they do, it can almost always be handled quickly. The partners will also feel that the therapist cares about their treatment more if this offer is made. Our experience has been that very few couples call for clarification and if they do, the phone calls are very brief. If it is obvious they need more time, then they can come back to a session earlier or not attempt the homework and stay on their regular schedule of appointments.

Case Illustration

In one instance, a couple had not experienced cuddling or physical intimacy for the 2 years since the discovery of the wife's two affairs. The couple received treatment for several months for the factors that made their marriage vulnerable to infidelity and they were again committed to the marriage. They were ready to resume physical intimacy and decided (on their own) to begin by touching and cuddling for a few minutes three times per week. Because the husband was hypersensitive to rejection when his wife withdrew from physical advances, he was encouraged to talk about feeling rejected in a way that she could hear him. Still, it was difficult for her to engage in nondemand physical touch. The therapist and couple decided that the first step would be for them to take a walk while holding hands. After completing that assignment several times, they were ready to cuddle on the sofa for 10 minutes or until one became uncomfortable. It was important for them to both have an understanding that the activity was to be self-contained without an expectation of anything more. The therapist suggested they plan the activity ahead of time and flip a coin to determine who would initiate. After several months and many graduated increments, they moved to nondemand sensual touch. As the exercises become more sexual and complex, the details that needed to be covered increased and the incremental advances were carefully planned in session and discussed afterward. The assignments were always intended to produce success, not failure. The object of the homework was to help them slowly reach their goal of sexual intimacy by keeping anxiety low, success high and by explaining that each link in the chain was a step toward their goal. Eventually, they were able to gradually reintegrate sexual intimacy into their relationship.

Processing an Assignment

The discussion or processing of an assignment can be just as valuable as the assignment itself; therefore, there are some key issues that need to be considered when addressing homework. One issue is to regularly follow up. Always follow up on the exercise at the beginning of the next session. The more consistently therapists review homework, the more seriously the clients will take and undertake it. In reviewing homework, keep in mind the three A's. First, *ask* for details. Get a specific description of what happened each time from each partner. Forewarn clients they will be asked about all of their homework and to keep mental or written records in order to give the therapist an accurate report. Some sex therapists encourage their clients to get a calendar with big spaces for writing or a dated journal where they record the efforts. This information will enable the therapist to gauge their progress and design the next exercise. Next, *address* efforts. Some couples may have difficulty with even the most basic exercise. Be sure to stay positive and validate whatever efforts they made in completing the homework. Look for any positive changes observed in their attitudes or behaviors, giving consistent praise and encouragement. Be sure to stay balanced if it appears that one partner has had more success in homework completion than the other; focus on the teamwork nature of the exercises and pay attention to the process by which they undertook the homework as well as the outcome. Finally, *anticipate* incompletion. If the partners fail to do the exercise, then process the reasons why and either proceed with the same exercise or work through their resistance. Some of the resistance might be related to fears (for a detailed discussion of complicating factors, see Chapter 11 in this volume). For some couples, relational issues such as couple conflict will prevent them from being successful in completing the homework. These must be worked on first. Other clients may have anticipated that any attempt to connect physically would result in anger, disappointment, a sense of failure or any other negative feelings that have been associated with sexual interaction in the past, and therefore avoided doing the assignment. If that is the case, then work through their fears as you encourage their efforts to try the homework again.

Reading Assignments

Another form of homework is to provide educational material, resource lists, bibliotherapy, directions or other information to the client or couple. They must be ready for and express interest in receiving this additional information. As stated previously, reading assignments can feel like homework, so there might be automatic internalized resistance to doing work outside of the therapy session. Often, the therapist prepares handouts for use in specific situations. The publication *Innovations in Clinical Practice: Focus on Sexual Health* (VandeCreek, Peterson, & Bley, 2007) provides several handouts for use in sex therapy for both the therapist and the client. Client handouts are designed to help clients examine attitudes and beliefs, become better educated on a topic or practice different skills. Therapists can use handouts to assist in assessment and treatment planning. An example is Peterson's (2007) handout representing a sexual identity cube. It depicts a 3in × 3in × 3in cube with three planes: one describes a client's sexual orientation (heterosexual, bisexual, homosexual), another plane describes gender (male, transgender, female), and a third plane identifies the client's sex role (masculine, androgynous, feminine). This tool helps the therapist better identify a client's perception of his or her sexuality.

Another example would be Bley's (2007a, 2007b) handouts that guide sensate focus activities and pelvic floor exercises. These handouts describe in brief and concise terms how to implement the exercises. The traditional sensate focus handout guides the couple through three stages of activities: nongenital pleasuring, nongenital and genital pleasuring and intercourse pleasuring. However, our conceptualization of sensate focus might not employ the use of handouts because the specific directions are considerably more incremental than prior conceptualizations of sensate focus.

Additionally, we commonly supply handouts of resources for purchasing vibrators, finding erotica, explaining the various medical modalities for treating erectile disorder, finding resources for transgender clients, using bibliotherapy related to specific sexual issues and so on.

Regardless of the subject, handouts and reading assignments augment treatment, increase learning, provide psychoeducation and alleviate distress and anxiety.

References

Bley, J. W. (2007a). Kegel exercises (pelvic floor exercises). In L. VandeCreek, F. L. Peterson, & J. W. Bley (Eds.). *Innovations in clinical practice: Focus on sexual health* (pp. 321–322). Sarasota, FL: Professional Resource Press/Professional Resource Exchange.

Bley, J. W. (2007b). Sexual pleasuring (sensate focus exercises). In L. VandeCreek, F. L. Peterson, & J. W. Bley (Eds.). *Innovations in clinical practice: Focus on sexual health* (pp. 317–320). Sarasota, FL: Professional Resource Press/Professional Resource Exchange.

Charlton, R.S., & Brigel, F.W. (1997). Treatment of arousal and orgasmic disorders. In R.S. Charlton (Ed.), *Treating sexual disorders* (pp. 237–280). San Francisco, CA: Jossey-Bass.

Gambescia, N., & Weeks, G. (2007). Sexual dysfunction. In N. Kazantizis & L. L'Abate (Eds.), *Handbook of homework assignments in psychotherapy: Research, practice, and prevention* (pp. 351–369). Norwell, MA: Kluwer Academic Publishers.

Kazantzis, N., & L'Abate, L. (2007). *Handbook of homework assignments in psychotherapy: Research, practice, and prevention.* Norwell, MA: Kluwer Academic Publishers.

McCarthy, B. (1985). Use and misuse of behavioral homework exercises in sex therapy. *Journal of Sex and Marital Therapy, 11*(3), 185–191.

Panchana, N.A., & Sofronoff, K. (2005). Sexual problems. In N. Kazantzis, F.P. Deane, K.R. Ronan, & L'Abate. *Using homework assignments in cognitive behavioral therapy* (pp. 307–327). New York: Routledge.

Peterson, F. (2007). The complexity of sexual diversity: Sexual identity cube and self-awareness exercise, In L. Vandercreek, F. Peterson, & J. Bley (Eds.), *Innovations in clinical practice: Focus on sexual health.* Sarasota, FL: Professional Resource Press.

Tompkins, M.A. (2004). *Using homework in psychotherapy.* New York: Guilford Press.

VandeCreek, L., Peterson, F., & Bley, J.W. (Eds.). (2007). *Innovations in clinical practice: Focus on sexual health.* Sarasota, FL: Professional Resource Press/Professional Resource Exchange.

13

PSYCHOEDUCATION IN SEX THERAPY

Introduction

Psychoeducation is commonly used in sex therapy and is considered to be one of the most effective evidence-based practices in psychotherapy (Lukens & McFarlane, 2004). It is a form of education that is provided by the therapist that integrates factual information about a variety of topics with psychological education. It is used as an adjunct to sex therapy and may include information about sexual functioning and relationship information, such as communication techniques. In this chapter we focus on various areas of psychoeducation concentration.

Bibliotherapy

The use of bibliotherapy as an accessory to psychotherapy has been well documented in the sex therapy literature (see, for example, Weeks & Gambescia, 2002). Bibliotherapy involves using selected reading material to assist clients in solving particular issues that are relevant to them. In sex therapy, bibliotherapy serves as a form of psychoeducation, providing accurate information that replaces mythological thinking. Furthermore, the acquisition of new material engenders innovative thoughts or actions in our clients. Bibliotherapy takes many forms. It could involve reading books or Internet-based material (such as YouTube & Ted Talks), viewing videos, watching selected television shows or any other form of media that would be considered psychoeducational. Bibliotherapy accomplishes much and is not limited to the following:

- Helping to dispel misinformation
- Reducing anxiety
- Providing accurate information

- Offering couples new perspectives
- Fostering attitudinal change
- Supporting the use of new behaviors
- Suggesting new thoughts, ideas and viewpoints
- Giving permission to try forbidden behaviors
- Promoting communication about sex

Couples in sex therapy often feel they are the only ones with the type of problem they have. They feel alone and isolated, and may overpathologize their situation. They also feel embarrassed, confused, hopeless and ashamed that they must reveal such intimate details to a stranger. Bibliotherapy has the potential to open the communication around the couple's problem area. Reading about a particular topic can help desensitize a couple to discussing topics. For example, most couples do not want to discuss their sexual fantasies. After reading one or more books on sexual fantasies, couples are usually much more open to discuss the topic. The mere fact that someone is writing about their problem has the effect of helping normalize their behavior. They no longer feel alone in having the problem and may gain some useful insight and information about the nature of their problem. This normalizing function will help the couple to see that many individuals go through similar issues and have dealt with these issues successfully.

Table 13.1 lists some bibliotherapy resources that can be helpful to the client and or therapist in sex therapy. Although this list is far from exhaustive, we believe that these resources are a basic starting point for therapists looking to assign readings to their clients or to read themselves. These books cut across a wide variety of presenting problems and issues specific to sex therapy. We have categorized the references for easier access.

TABLE 13.1 Sexuality Books Bibliography

Adolescents and Young Adults	Bell, R. (1998). *Changing Bodies, Changing Lives: A Book for Teens on Sex and Relationships* (3rd ed.). New York: River Press.
	Corinna, H. (2007). *S.E.X.: The All-You-Need-to-Know Progressive Sexuality Guide to Get You Through High School and College.* New York: Marlowe & Company.
	Pardes, B. (2007). *Doing It Right: Making Smart, Safe, and Satisfying Choices about Sex.* New York: Simon Pulse.
Aging	Block, J. D., & Bakos, S. C. (1999). *Sex over 50.* Paramus, NJ: Reward Books.
	Duffy, M. (Ed.) (1999). *Handbook of Counseling and Psychotherapy with Older Adults.* Hoboken, NJ: John Wiley & Sons.

(Continued)

TABLE 13.1 Continued

	Gross, Z. H. (2000). *Seasons of the Heart: Men and Women Talk about Love, Sex, and Romance after 60.* New York: New World Library.
	Price, J. (2011). *Naked at Our Age: Talking Out Loud about Senior Sex.* Berkeley, CA: Seal Press.
	Seiden, O. (2007). *Sex in the Golden Years: The Best Sex Ever.* Parker, CO: Thornton.
Asexuality	Bogaert, A. (2012). *Understanding Asexuality.* Lanham, MD: Rowman & Littlefield.
BDSM	Brame, G. G. (2000). *Come Hither: A Commonsense Guide to Kinky Sex.* New York: Fire-side.
	Miller, P., & Devon, M. (1995). *Screw the Roses, Send Me the Thorns.* Fairfield, CT: Mystic Rose Books.
	Ortman, D., & Sprott, R. (2013). *Sexual Outsiders: Understanding BDSM Sexualities and Communities.* Latham, MD: Rowman & Littlefield.
	Wiseman, J. (1996). *SM 101: A Realistic Introduction.* San Francisco, CA: Greenery Press.
Children	Harris, R., & Emberley, M. (1994). *It's Perfectly Normal: Changing Bodies, Growing Up, Sex, and Sexual Health.* Somerville, MA: Candlewick Press.
Compulsivity (Sexual)	Carnes, P.J. (2001). *Out of the Shadows.* Center City, MN: Hazelden.
	Carnes, P., & Adams, K. (2002). *Clinical Management of Sex Addiction.* New York: Routledge.
	Corley, M., & Schneider, J. (2002). *Disclosing Secrets: When, to Whom, and How Much to Reveal.* Wickenburg, AZ: Gentle Path Press.
	Goodman, A. (1998). *Sexual Addiction: An Integrated Approach.* Madison, CT: International Universities Press.
	Kasl, C.D. (1990). *Women, Sex and Addiction: A Search for Love and Power.* New York: Harper Collins.
	Maltz, W., & Maltz, L. (2008). *The Porn Trap: The Essential Guide to Overcoming Problems Caused by Pornography.* New York: HarperCollins.
	Sbraga, T., & O'Donohue, W. (2004). *The Sex Addiction Workbook: Proven Strategies to Help You Regain Control of Your Life.* Oakland, CA: New Harbinger.
Culture	Hall, K., & Graham, C. (Eds.). (2012). *The Cultural Context of Sexual Pleasure and Problems.* New York: Routledge.
Disability	Katz, A. (2012). *Prostate Cancer and the Man You Love: Supporting and Caring for Your Partner.* New York: Rowman and Littlefield.
	Kaufman, M., Silverberg, C., & Odette, F. (2007). *The Ultimate Guide to Sex and Disability: For All of Us Who Live with Disabilities, Chronic Pain and Illness.* San Francisco, CA: Cleis Press.

(Continued)

TABLE 13.1 Continued

Fantasy	Bader, M.J. (2002). *Arousal: The Secret Logic of Sexual Fantasies.* New York: St. Martin's.
	Friday, N. (1973). *My Secret Garden: Women's Sexual Fantasies.* New York: Pocket.
	Friday, N. (1975). *Forbidden Flowers: More Women's Sexual Fantasies.* New York: Pocket Books.
General Sexuality	Barbach, L. (2000). *For Yourself: The Fulfillment of Female Sexuality.* Garden City, NY: Penguin Putnam.
	Barbach, L. (2001). *For Each Other: Sharing Sexual Intimacy.* Garden City, NY: Penguin Putnam.
	Comfort, A. (2009). *The Joy of Sex: The Ultimate Revised Edition.* New York: Harmony Press.
	Joannides, P. (2012). *The Guide to Getting It On! A Book about the Wonders of Sex* (7th ed.). Waldport, OR: Goofy Foot Press.
	Nelson, T. (2008). *Getting the Sex You Want.* Beverly, MA: Fair Winds Press.
History	Faucault, M. (1990). *The History of Sexuality: An Introduction.* New York: Vintage.
Infidelity	Carlson, J., & Sperry, L. (Eds.). (2010) *Recovering Intimacy in Love Relationships: A Clinician's Guide.* New York: Routledge.
	Glass, S.P. (2004) *Not Just Friends.* New York: Free Press.
	Snyder, D., Baucom, D., & Gordon, K. (2007). *Getting Past the Affair: A Program to Help You Cope, Heal, and Move On—Together or Apart.* New York: Guilford Press.
	Spring, J., & Spring, M. (1997). *After the Affair: Healing the Pain and Rebuilding Trust When a Partner Has Been Unfaithful.* New York: Harper Paperbacks.
	Spring, J. (2005). *How Can I Forgive You? The Courage to Forgive, The Freedom Not To.* New York: Harper Paperbacks.
	Weeks, G., Gambescia, N., & Jenning, R. (2003). *Treating Infidelity: Therapeutic Dilemmas and Effective Strategies.* New York: W.W. Norton.
LGBT	Alexander, M., & Rose, M. (2010). *The Color of Sunlight.* Lexington, KY: CreateSpace.
	Beemyn, G., & Rankin, S. (2011). *The Lives of Transgender People.* New York: Columbia University Press.
	Berzon, B. (2004). *Permanent Partners: Building Gay & Lesbian Relationships That Last.* New York: Plume Books.
	Bigner, J., & Wetchler, J. (2004). *Relationship Therapy with Same-Sex Couples.* New York: Routledge.
	Brown, M., & Rounsley, C. (2003). *True Selves: Understanding Transsexualism—For Families, Friends, Coworkers, and Helping Professionals.* San Francisco, CA: Jossey-Bass.
	Garber, M. (1995). *Vice Versa: Bisexuality and the Eroticism of Everyday Life.* New York: Simon & Schuster.

(Continued)

TABLE 13.1 Continued

	LaSalla, M. (2010). *Coming Out, Coming Home: Helping Families Adjust to a Gay or Lesbian Child*. New York: Columbia University Press.
	Lev, A. I. (2004). *Transgender Emergence*. New York: Haworth Press.
	Newman, F. (1999). *The Whole Lesbian Sex Book: A Passionate Guide for All of Us*. San Francisco, CA: Cleis Press.
Love & Sex	Mitchell, S. A. (2002). *Can love last? The Fate of Romance over Time*. New York: Norton.
	Morin, J. (1995). *The Erotic Mind*. New York: Harper Collins.
	Perel, E. (2006). *Mating in Captivity*. New York: Harper Collins.
	Tiefer, L. (1995). *Sex Is Not a Natural Act & Other Essays*. Boulder, CA: Westview Press.
Men	Kerner, I. (2008). *Passionista: The Empowered Woman's Guide to Pleasuring a Man*. New York: HarperCollins.
	Zilbergeld, B. (1999). *The New Male Sexuality*. New York: Bantam.
Pain	Wise, D., & Anderson, R. (2008). *A Headache in the Pelvis: A New Understanding and Treatment for Prostatitis and Chronic Pelvic Pain Syndromes* (5th ed.). Occidental, CA: National Center for Pelvic Pain Research.
Paraphilia	Laws, R. D., & O'Donahue, W. T. (2008). *Sexual Deviance: Theory, Assessment, and Treatment by Laws* (2nd ed.). New York: Guilford Press.
Pharmacology	Crenshaw, T. L., & Goldberg, J. P. (1996). *Sexual Pharmacology: Drugs That Effect Sexual Function*. New York: W.W. Norton.
Polyamory	Anapol, D. (2010). *Polyamory in the 21st Century*. United Kingdom: Roman & Littlefield.
	Barker, M., & Langdridge, D. (Eds.). (2010). *Understanding Non-Monogamies*. London: Routledge.
	Bergstrand, C., & Sinski, J. (2010). *Swinging in America: Love, Sex, and Marriage in the 21st Century*. Santa Barbara, CA: Praeger.
	Block, J. (2008). *Open: Love, Sex and Life in an Open Marriage*. Berkley, CA: Seal Press.
	Easton, D., & Liszt, C. (1997). *The Ethical Slut: A Guide to Infinite Sexual Possibilities*. San Francisco, CA: Greenery Press.
	Hardy, J. (1997). *The Ethical Slut: A Practical Guide to Polyamory, Open Relationships & Other Adventures*. Berkley, CA: Celestial Arts.
	Ravenscroft, A. (2004). *Polyamory: Roadmaps for the Clueless & Hopeful*. Santa Fe, NM: Crossquarter Publishing Group.
	Savage, D. (2013). Festival of dangerous ideas. https://www.youtube.com/watch?v=C-laWOpXxC8

(Continued)

TABLE 13.1 Continued

Research	Janssen, E. (Ed). (2007). *The Psychophysiology of Sex*. Bloomington: Indiana University Press. Komisaruk, B., Beyer-Flores, C., & Whipple, B. (2006). *The Science of Orgasm*. Baltimore, MD: The Johns Hopkins Press. Michael, R., Gagnon, J. H., Laumann, E., & Kolata, G. (1995). *Sex in America: A Definitive Survey*. New York: Warner Books.
Sex Therapy	Binik, Y.M., & Hall, S.K. (2014). Introduction: The future of sex therapy. In Y.M. Binik and K.S. Hall (Eds.), *Principles and Practice of Sex Therapy* (5th ed.) (pp. 1–16). New York: Guilford Press. Hertlein, K.M., Weeks, G.R., & Gambescia, N. (Eds.) (2015). *Systemic Sex Therapy* (2nd ed.). New York: Routledge. Kleinplatz, P. (Ed.). (2012). *New Directions in Sex Therapy: Innovations and Alternatives* (2nd ed.). New York: Brunner-Routledge. Levine, S.B., Risen, C., & Althof, S. (Eds.). (2010). *Handbook of Clinical Sexuality for Mental Health Practitioners* (2nd ed.). New York: Routledge.
Tantra	Carrellas, B. (2007). *Urban Tantra*. New York: Crown.
Technology	Hertlein, K.A., & Blumer, M. (2014). *The Couple and Family Technology Framework: Intimate Relationships in a Digital Age*. New York: Routledge.
Trauma	Johnson, S. (2005). *Emotionally Focused Couple Therapy with Trauma Survivors: Strengthening Attachment Bonds*. New York: Guilford Press. Maltz, W. (2012). *The Sexual Healing Journey: A Guide for Survivors of Sexual Abuse* (3rd ed.). New York: Harper-Collins.
Women	Foley, S., Kope, S.A., & Sugrue, D.P. (2011). *Sex Matters for Women: A Complete Guide to Taking Care of Your Sexual Self* (2nd ed.). New York: Guilford Press. Hall, K. (2004). *Reclaiming Your Sexual Self: How You Can Bring Desire Back into Your Life*. New York: Wiley. Kerner, I. (2004). *She Comes First: The Thinking Man's Guide to Pleasuring a Woman*. New York: HarperCollins. Meston, C., & Buss, D. (2009). *Why Women Have Sex: Understanding Sexual Motivations from Adventure to Revenge (and Everything in Between)*. New York: Henry Holt. Mintz, L. (2009). *A Tired Woman's Guide to Passionate Sex*. Avon, MA: Adams Media.

Videos/Multimedia

Videos, DVDs, and multimedia can provide a great deal of psychoeducation for clients struggling with sexual issues. Most of the videos listed give tips and suggestions to couples on how to enhance their lovemaking. Many of these videos can be ordered through a variety of websites. Table 13.2 provides a list of some of the better resources for couples in sex therapy. This list reflects a few of the more traditional video selections assigned by therapists.

TABLE 13.2 Sexual Enhancement Videos

Video/Title Series Name	Publisher/Producer	Where to Get It
Better Sex Video Series	Sinclair Institute	Advertised on the Better Sex Website at http://www.bettersex.com/Adult-Sex-Education/movie-collections/sp-better-sex-video-series-6-volume-collection-2313.aspx
Sex Essentials Series	Victory Multimedia	Advertised on the Sex Essentials website at http://www.seductivesexpositions.com
Loving Sex Series	Alexander Institute	Advertised on the Loving Sex website at http://www.lovingsex.com/collections/loving-sex
Becoming Orgasmic DVD	Sinclair Institute	Advertised on the Sinclair Institute website at http://www.sinclairinstitute.com/index.php/becoming-orgasmic.html
Great Sex for a Lifetime	Sinclair Institute	Advertised on the Sinclair Institute website at: http://www.sinclairinstitute.com/index.php/better-sex-for-a-lifetime-8-dvd-set.html
Guide to Great Sex for Couples over 40	Sinclair Institute	Advertised on the Sinclair Institute website at http://www.sinclairinstitute.com/index.php/couples-guide-to-great-sex-over-40-set.html
The Big O	Sinclair Institute	Advertised on the Sinclair Institute website at http://www.sinclairinstitute.com/index.php/the-big-o-guide-to-better-orgasms.html
Female Masturbation Series	Welcomed Consensus	Advertised on the Welcomed Consensus website at http://www.welcomed.com/videos/video_fm.html
Deliberate Orgasm	Welcomed Consensus	Advertised on the Welcomed Consensus website at http://www.welcomed.com/videos/video_do.html
Loving with Passion	Body, Mind, & Intimacy	Advertised on the Amazon website at http://www.amazon.com/Loving-With-Passion-Sexual-Positions/dp/B0009A40MK

(Continued)

TABLE 13.2 Continued

Video/Title Series Name	Publisher/Producer	Where to Get It
Better Sex Video Series for Black Couples	Sinclair Institute	Advertised on the Better Sex Website at http://www.bettersex.com/Adult-Sex-Education/movie-collections/sp-the-better-sexvideo-series-for-black-couples-vol-1-2-set-282.aspx
Complete Guide to Sexual Positions	Pacific Media	Advertised on the Amazon website at http://www.amazon.com/Complete-Guide-Sexual-Positions-Assorted/dp/B00014NFDY
101 Love Positions	Body, Mind, & Intimacy	Advertised on the Amazon website at http://www.amazon.com/101-Love-Positions-Sexual/dp/B00009K45X
Creative Positions for Lovers: Beyond the Bedroom	Sinclair Institute	Advertised on the Sexuality Resources website at https://sexualityresources.com/product/creative-positions-lovers-beyond-bedroom

Internet Resources

There are also several major Internet sites that refer people to further information on books and films among other resources. These sites are major national organizations, research institutes or clearinghouses for information. The authors selected the following websites, but the Kinsey Institute has one of the most comprehensive collections of psychoeducational sexuality topics. The links to sexuality resources include but are not limited to the following:

- American Association for Marriage and Family Therapy
- American Association of Sexuality Educators, Counselors, and Therapists
- Foundation for the Scientific Study of Sexuality
- Sexuality Information and Education Council of the United States
- LGBT World
- The Kinsey Institute
- National Council on Family Relations
- SexandRelationships.com
- Sinclair Intimacy Institute
- Society for Sex Therapy and Research
- Women's Sexual Health Foundation

Other Internet Sources

An Internet search of universities and private practices revealed a rich volume of helpful references, books and other media related to sexuality and sexual health. The therapist should review these websites for accuracy before providing them to clients. We are listing a few websites known to the authors for examples:

- The website for the group Sex Therapy in Philadelphia provides a list of books for clients on a range of topics. The topics covered on this site include communication, divorce, infidelity, sexual addiction, sexual orientation and gender, masturbation, sexual toys and others.
  http://www.sextherapyinphiladelphia.com/recommended-books
- The Institute for Sexual and Marital Therapy provides a book list on their webpage under the link Online Store. These books are recommended by the website authors and include areas related to human sexuality, sexual dysfunction, relationship issues and information specifically geared toward men and women.
  http://www.sexualtherapy.com/Bookstore.html
- Robert Birch offers a site that is devoted to sexual enrichment. This site is designed to enhance the sexual pleasure of adults and includes adult erotica, information about sexual techniques and resources for clients.
  http://www.oralcaress.com
- The Sexual Trauma and Recovery website offers readings, self-administered questionnaires and other resources related to sexual compulsivity.
  http://starhealing.org/

Some clients lack the basic terminology or language of sexuality. They do not know the names of various parts of the sexual anatomy or the proper terms for various behaviors. This may result in communication problems and embarrassment in discussing some topics, because the clients may use slang or other idiosyncratic references to behaviors with no common meaning. In some cases, partners will not bring up a topic of concern due to their inadequate terminology. These clients can be directed to sites that will help them learn more about the language of sex, such as the following:

- University of Hawaii AIDS Educational and Training Center
  http://www.hawaii.edu/hivandaids/links_sex.htm
- Farlex Dictionary of Sexual Terms and Expressions
  http://www.sex-lexis.com
- My Pleasure
  http://www.mypleasure.com/education/glossary/a.asp
- The Sex Dictionary
  http://www.thesexdictionary.com

Many Internet sites are new and others seem to disappear. Recommended websites must be matched to the individual's tolerance of the material. As of the publication of this book, we have found numerous websites directed to a particular group or activity:

- http://sexetc.org (for teens)
- http://www.apa.org/pi/aging/resources/guides/sexuality.aspx (sexuality and aging)
- http://www.dcfukit.org (for men who have sex with men)
- http://mybeautifulsexlife.com (general sexuality)
- www.sexualityresources.com (for women: A Woman's Touch)
- http://www.ifeelmyself.com/public/main.php (female orgasm)
- http://literotica.com (erotica)
- http://www.nsvrc.org/about/national-sexual-violence-resource-center (sexual violence)
- http://healthystrokes.com (masturbation)

The Internet has become a major and readily available source of practically free information. As stated, the therapist might search the Web to find a factually based website that addresses the client's need for information and then direct the client to it. More technologically sophisticated clients can be asked to do their own search following the guideline to search for websites that are professional organization or university based. These sites will usually be up to date and contain factual information. The therapist needs to follow up to find out which websites the client visited and what they learned. The Internet can also provide an overwhelming amount of sexually stimulating photographs and film clips for couples who are simply interested in something to arouse them. Couples who are interested in sadomasochism (S&M) or bondage and discipline (B&D) may find little in the local bookstore, but a search on the Internet will offer up plenty of material.

In conclusion, psychoeducational material is an invaluable resource for couples. The therapist should become familiar with the basic information in this chapter by reading or skimming the books, watching the videos and visiting a variety of websites. The bookstore at an AASECT conference gives the therapist an opportunity to view much of this material as well as see many of the sexual enhancement products (lubricants, sex toys, etc.) that are mentioned in another chapter. We assume therapists have attended a Sexual Attitude Readjustment workshop (SAR) at a national conference or one offered privately in order to become desensitized to the vast spectrum of sexual behavior, language and images they will encounter in their clients and in the media with which they should be familiar.

References

Lukens, E.P., & McFarlane, W.R. (2004). Psychoeducation as evidence-based practice: Considerations for practice, research, and policy. *Brief Treatment and Crisis Intervention, 4*(3), 205–225.

Weeks, G.R., & Gambescia, N. (2002). *Hypoactive sexual desire: Integrating sex and couple therapy*. New York: W.W. Norton.

14

PHYSICAL/MEDICAL ISSUES IN SEX THERAPY

Introduction

Sexuality is an integral part of one's self-definition, enjoyment of life and sense of well-being; nonetheless, sexual expression can be unfavorably impacted by changes in bodily function that result from chronic illness, aging, trauma or disability. Historically, treating sexual problems within populations affected by such changes has been underemphasized in the clinical literature. More recently, however, increasing attention to the physical issues that impact sexual health and satisfaction has been noted in the medical and sex therapy literature (Gomez & Andrianne, 2014; Hughes & Lewinson, 2014). It has also been addressed in the family therapy literature under the context of medical family therapy (Hughes, Hertlein, & Hagey, 2011). Unfortunately, although the goals of medical and sex therapy are similar in clients with physical issues, the two domains have had little overlap in clinical literature and practice (see Moser & Devereux, 2012). It is our position that sex therapists become important collaborators with medical practitioners in the treatment of medically related sexual issues. For several reasons, we believe that sex therapists will see an increasing number of referrals for treatment of sexual issues among the aging, chronically ill, disabled or differently abled clients.

First, thanks to medical advances, people are living longer with chronic illnesses, particularly HIV, cancer and diabetes. Second, the aging of the baby boomers has resulted in enlarged greater prevalence of couples over age 50 that are committed to remaining as sexually active as they were decades ago. Third, advocates for disabled individuals have been vocal in demanding that society view this cohort as sexual beings with a right to sexual pleasure, resulting in more willingness on the part of the disabled to seek help when they face sexual difficulties. Finally, as research continues to demonstrate the need for and effectiveness of sex therapy (Mona, Syme, & Cameron, 2013), physicians are gaining greater awareness about addressing these issues in medical practice and also collaborating with a sex therapist.

It is essential that sex therapists have at least a basic understanding of the ways in which medical problems can impact sexual functioning and satisfaction and some basic knowledge of treatment issues within these populations from an Intersystem perspective. This chapter provides specific treatment strategies to counter the most commonly occurring sexual dysfunctions related to particular health conditions. We discuss four facets of medical difficulties that must be understood in treatment planning: (1) how the specific medical problem affects sexual functioning, (2) the client's perception of and beliefs about the problem, (3) the partner's perceptions of the problem and how it affects his or her sexuality, and (4) the individual's or couple's resiliency and ability to adapt to change.

Sexuality and Clients with Physical Illness

Numerous body systems are involved with sexual functioning. These include but are not limited to the skeletal, muscular, cardiovascular, digestive, endocrine, neurological, respiratory, immune, reproductive and integumentary (skin, hair, nails) systems. Damage or disease to any or all of these systems and the psychological stress of having a chronic illness can create conditions that result in or exacerbate existing sexual problems (Enzlin, 2014).

Neurological Ailments

Maladies such as Parkinson's disease, multiple sclerosis, stroke and other neurological disorders (disease/injury of the nervous system) can directly affect the physiological response involved in sexual functioning.

Multiple sclerosis. For instance, with multiple sclerosis (MS), demyelination of the brain and spinal cord can result in decreased libido, numbness or abnormal sensations in the genitals, erectile dysfunction or loss of vaginal lubrication and difficulties with orgasm (Celik et al., 2013). Sexual functioning in MS women is associated with enhanced disability, pain, duration of the disease and degree of concomitant depression (Gumus, Akpinar, & Yilmaz, 2013). Medical and psychological treatments must be consistently focused on the numerous gradual changes in sexual function over time, and the impact of the disease on the woman's sexual schema, her partner and sexual compensations.

Cerebral palsy. Other neurological conditions, such as cerebral palsy, may involve various problems or challenges with sexuality. These difficulties result from the direct effect of the disease on sexual functioning. Additionally, there may be an indirect effect on the sexual experience due to the social aspects of sexual interaction, such as sexual knowledge and comfort (Wiegerink, Roebroeck, Bender, Stam, & Cohen-Kettenis, 2011). If sexual difficulties exist in an individual with a neurological illness, the therapist should be aware that the medical aspects of the disorder can be compounded by psychogenic factors such as stress, worry and anxiety related to having a chronic illness. In some cases sexual symptoms can also result from a failure to adapt the sexual repertoire to changes in physical ability. Even when neurological disease does not directly cause a sexual dysfunction, motor system changes such as tremors, rigidity and spasms can make certain sexual acts more awkward and potentially painful.

Parkinson's disease. A disheartening aspect of Parkinson's disease is sexual dysfunction due to the complex interplay between its impact on the motor and nonmotor aspects of functioning and the resulting psychological distress and sexual dissatisfaction (Meco, Rubino, Caravona, & Valente, 2008). Anticipatory anxiety in such situations can fuel the loss of desire, creating a self-fulfilling belief that spirals into further sexual difficulty.

Stroke. Empirical data validate our clinical observation that individuals who have had mild strokes experience decreased participation in sexual activities. Additionally, they report the need for more psychoeducation on the potential for sexual changes post stroke and adaptation to these changes (Seymour & Wolf, 2014). Sex therapists should always be part of the rehabilitation team for stroke survivors because these clinicians worry about the effect of stroke on intimate relationships and sexual needs of the partner. Additionally, stroke survivors require help with the emotions that result from the impaired ability to physically engage in sex as they once did (Rosenbaum, Vadas, & Kalichman, 2014). More severe strokes, of course, profoundly impact sexual positioning and movement during sex. Readers are referred to Mona, Syme, and Cameron (2013) for a discussion of the common difficulties and a model of care experienced by individuals and couples affected by stroke regarding their sexuality and sexual health.

Cardiovascular Illness

The prevalence of cardiovascular disease increases with age and can directly contribute to sexual difficulties associated with aging (Lewis et al., 2010). A notable example is Erectile Disorder (ED). The empirically significant relationship between medical conditions and ED is well documented (Kloner & Schwartz, 2011), especially as the man ages. Additionally, organic ED is regarded as a known marker for cardiovascular diseases, diabetes and morbidity (Chung, Chen, Lin & Lin, 2011). Although often asymptomatic, cardiovascular disease may eventually produce difficulties such as labored breathing, chest pains and irregular heartbeat (Wylie & Kenney, 2010). Moreover, medications used to treat cardiovascular illnesses, such as beta-blockers and thiazide diuretics, can also adversely impact sexual functioning (Simopoulos & Trinidad, 2013). Medical/sexual myths and fears complicate the client's expectations about living with cardiovascular illness and will adversely affect a client's sexual function.

Women with cardiovascular disease are often found to avoid sexual intercourse with their partners, even though having intercourse is safe among patients with stable cardiovascular disease (Assari, 2014). We have noted that avoidance of sex can occur with men too although it is not as prevalent. It is essential that all healthcare professionals, including the sex therapist, discuss sexual aspects of treatment to allay fears about sexual functioning.

Cancer

Having cancer and receiving cancer treatment will often impact the sexual relationship, sometimes long after the cancer is successfully treated. Much of the attention of the medical team, cancer patient and loved ones is primarily focused on survival. Nonetheless, sexuality eventually becomes a topic of concern for the person suffering with cancer and his or her partner. Unfortunately, healthcare providers often overlook sexual issues even if the person's body will become disfigured from the cancer and/or from the treatments used to eradicate the cancer. The cancer diagnosis can cause psychological damage, trauma and fear. Additionally, treatments can impact the person's self-esteem and sexual relationship, and potentially interfere with sexual capacity (Brotto & Kingsberg, 2010). Avoiding discussions about sexual issues related to cancer will engender fear and/or embarrassment in the client and partner. In this section we briefly review a few of the forms of cancer that will impact sexuality. The therapist is advised to become familiar with all of the issues involved in diagnosis, treatment, reactions in the client and relational worries and concerns.

Prostate cancer. Prostate cancer is particularly distressing for men because of the real possibility of losing either sexual functioning or one's life. To those who face this disease, deciding about treatments can be overwhelming. Many of the treatments will alter sexual functioning; thus, deciding about treatment is a difficult trade-off, and we have worked with men who have said they would rather die than lose their sexual capacity. While newer, nerve-sparing surgical procedures may result in greater restoration of erectile capacity, it is estimated that 40%–73% of men having a radical prostatectomy regain full erectile functioning within 12 months (Ficarra & Novara, 2011). In our practice, men who undergo the nerve-sparing procedure often return to normal functioning but only after a significant period of time. During this period, they wonder if they have lost the ability to have an erection permanently. They need to be reassured that normal functioning or near-normal functioning will return, and they are encouraged to find other means of sexual expression until that time. Additionally, the use of erection-enhancing medications has been shown to be effective with the majority of postoperative men (Cakar, Karaca, & Uslu, 2013; Zelefsky et al., 2014), and thus should be discussed with the man and his partner.

Breast cancer. Breast cancer is very common and enhanced treatments have greatly increased the survival rates of women (Siegel, Naishadham, & Jemal, 2013). Nonetheless, the quality of life issues related to body image and sexuality often interfere with recovery and psychological adjustment in breast cancer survivors. Likewise, women may feel less feminine after breast surgery, particularly mastectomy, because the sensitive tissue of the breast and nipples has been removed and reconstructed. We often help these women mourn the loss of their sexual selves and help them reformulate a changing sexual schema. See Pillai-Friedman and Ashline (2014) for an in-depth discussion that deals specifically with sexual loss and grief after breast cancer treatment. Another article addresses research on sexual difficulties after cancer in neglected sexual minorities such as lesbian and bisexual women (Boehmer, Ozonoff, Timm, Winter & Potter, 2014). In this study, minority women demonstrated lower sexual frequency and scored lower on desire and ability to reach orgasm and higher on pain compared to control subjects.

Cancer treatments and sexuality. Oncology is a branch of medicine that deals with the detection and treatment of cancers. Medical oncology is a cancer treatment that uses chemotherapy (the use of drugs to kill cancer cells) or other medications. Surgical oncology focuses on the diagnosis and removal of the tumor and surrounding tissue during an operation. Radiation oncology specializes in treating cancer with radiation therapy to kill cancer cells.

All of these forms of treatment have a variety of side effects. For instance, radiation can produce fatigue, nausea, diarrhea and other conditions that reduce sexual desire. If the tissue targeted includes the genitalia, inflammation and irritation may make sexual activity painful. Pelvic radiation may also change the shape and mucosal layer of the vagina, leading to dyspareunia (painful sex). Irritation of the prostate gland or urethra from radiation, as well as scar tissue after healing from treatment, can cause painful ejaculation or ED.

It is not uncommon for women to report a number of sexual problems after receiving chemotherapy for cancer treatment. These effects are exacerbated when radiation is also used. A number of studies confirm that problems with dyspareunia (painful coitus); vaginal dryness; decreased sexual desire; and difficulties of sexual arousal, hot flashes and sleep disturbances are a consequence of the cancer treatment process for women (Demirtas & Pinar, 2014).

Tamoxifen, a specific hormone, is used to treat breast cancer that has spread to other parts of the body in men and women or early breast cancer in women who have already been treated with surgery, radiation and/or chemotherapy. Tamoxifen may also result in diminished desire and arousal for both men and women. For women, this treatment has been linked to vaginal dryness, pruritus and pain and discomfort during intercourse (Baumgart, Nilsson, Evers, Kallak, & Poromaa, 2013).

Men receiving medical treatment for prostate cancer report an overall reduction in quality of life and sexual functioning. As discussed earlier, radical prostatectomy, radiation and chemotherapy can all contribute to neurovascular injury of the penis and supporting structures, local inflammatory changes, atrophy of the smooth muscle supporting the corpora cavernosa and so on (Chung & Gillman, 2014). The therapist is responsible for helping the man and his partner review the various treatments and related side effects and make informed decisions based on accurate information. Additionally, postsurgical recovery will involve the use of erection-enhancing medications and devices, all of which should be reviewed by the treatment team, including the sex therapist.

The clinician will need to research the type of treatment used for each type of cancer in order to develop a more complete picture of the predictable side effects. Once the side effects are understood, the therapist can help the client and the couple to deal with the short-term effects and learn how to live with long-term impact of the illness. The following pamphlets can provide information about the different forms of cancer and treatment:

*   *Coping with Appearance Changes due to Breast Cancer: Tips to Help Improve Your Body Image.* The University of Texas MD Anderson Cancer Center, 2012.
*   *Renewing Intimacy and Sexuality after Gynecologic Cancer.* Gynecologic Cancer Foundation, 2012.
*   *Sexuality and Cancer: A Guide for Patients and Their Partners.* The University of Texas MD Anderson Cancer Center, 2008.
*   *Sexuality for the Man with Cancer.* American Cancer Society, 2006.
*   *Sexuality for the Woman with Cancer.* American Cancer Society, 2007.

Diabetes

The most common form of diabetes, Type II diabetes mellitus, is a lifelong (chronic) disease in which there are high levels of glucose in the blood because the pancreas cannot make enough insulin or the body does not utilize insulin efficiently. Over time, the high glucose levels in the blood can damage the nerves and small blood vessels of the eyes, kidneys and heart and lead to atherosclerosis, or hardening of the arteries, that can cause heart attack and stroke (Vafaeimanesh, Raei, Hosseinzadeh, & Parham, 2014). This disease is also associated with older age as well as clinical depression associated with diabetes-related complications (Rutte et al., 2014).

Sexual dysfunction is highly prevalent in men and women with Type II diabetes mellitus; therefore, addressing sexual dysfunction in diabetes care is critical (Meeking, Fosbury, & Cummings, 2013). Diminished sexual desire may exist in individuals with diabetes as a general loss of energy, which reduces sex drive. Although less common, the loss of bladder control from nerve damage negatively impacts one's sense of sexual attractiveness. Some diabetic women may experience more difficulty reaching orgasm. Additionally, physical complications of diabetes, such as the greater occurrence of genitourinary infections, may also impact sexual functioning by increasing chances for sexual pain or discomfort and reducing desire to engage in sexual acts.

Occasionally, ED is the first warning sign of diabetes, due to the slow but negative impact on the vascular and nervous systems of the genitals (Maiorino, Bellastella, & Esposito, 2014). The importance of conducting a thorough Intersystem assessment (individual biological aspect of the problem) for all sexual problems is underscored by the fact that many men who present for ED treatment may not have had the requisite medical screening/testing. Without a screening, the therapist cannot rule out diabetes as a factor in the etiology of a client's sexual problems.

Sexuality and Disability

Individuals with physical disabilities have become a significant subgroup, comprising 10% of the world's population (as discussed in Mona, Syme, & Cameron, 2013). As such, these individuals cannot be regarded simply as a minority group with a medical disability. They must be viewed within all domains of the Intersystem in order to provide comprehensive and integrative care. People with disabilities have biological and psychological issues, relational concerns and families of origin who have influenced their life schemas. These individuals also interact with complex cultural, religious and environmental factors of their own.

Sexual difficulties have been described in many medical conditions, including spina bifida, spinal cord injuries, neuromuscular diseases, arthritis, epilepsy, spinal cord injury and traumatic brain injury (Moreno, Arango-Lasprillab, Gan, & McKerral, 2013). In all of these disorders the neurological aspects of sexuality have been compromised. Many with these disabilities experience cognitive, behavioral and physical changes that directly or indirectly affect sexual functioning. These changes can interfere with the ability to develop and maintain relationships, the expression of sexuality and one's ability to give and receive affection and love (Moreno et al., 2013).

For instance, traumatic brain injury frequently results in changes in sexual arousability; for men it affects erectile function and for women it changes genital sensation and lubrication (Julia & Othman, 2011). However, the likelihood of whether one will lose all genital sexual function depends on the location of the injury and its severity.

For some, sexual problems may result from their response to societal views of individuals with disabilities as unappealing or asexual, often discouraging them from dating and forming intimate relationships (Olkin, 1999). This view can become internalized and the person comes to believe the societal view is correct. It is essential that therapists assess a client's self-image and understanding of his or her sexual problem. According to Gill and Hough (2007), women with a disability report that feeling attractive and desirable is more important to their sexual well-being than their genital functioning. If an individual with a disability does not feel attractive or desirable, such feelings can reduce the instances in which the partner with the disability initiates sex or responds to a partner's invitations. Consequently, a negative self-image diminishes opportunities for intimate relationships and sexual activity, which in turn reinforces the client's belief that he or she is undesirable. The therapist must help persons with disabilities know that they can be valued and desired in a relationship, have a right to their own sexual pleasure and, regardless of physical limitations, can give pleasure to another. In short, a person with a disability is not necessarily sexually disabled.

Nonetheless, special consideration must be placed on understanding the nature and etiology of a client with a disability or physical limitation. The effect of the disability may be a mix of psychological reactions and having to deal with physical restrictions. Individuals with life-long disabilities may have different issues than those who face a recent or adult-onset disabling event. For instance, those with life-long disabilities may have experienced a lack of sex education and socialization during adolescence, resulting in sexual dysfunctions that center on anxiety, lack of interpersonal skills or lack of exposure to potential partners and formative sexual experiences (Altuntug, Ege, Akın, Kal, & Sallı, 2014). Such anxiety, lack of early experiences and so on can impact a current sexual relationship by reducing sexual communication and feelings of sexual competence, impairing sexual performance and inhibiting the desire to form intimate relationships. Clients who have a physical disability from a recent or adult-onset disabling event may carry issues such as grief, impaired sexual functioning and a disrupted sexual self-image. Therefore, learning ways to find sexual pleasure that go beyond what might be considered typical sexual behavior and adopting an image of oneself as a person who can be sexually desired and can show a desire for others is necessary.

Sexuality and Aging

Changes in sexual desire and behavior are normal throughout the life cycle. With aging individuals, the therapist must be mindful that intimacy and connection are just as important later in life as they were in the earlier years. Also, the most important predictor of sexual interest and activity in a person's later years is frequency of sexual activity earlier in life (Schick et al., 2010). Additionally, many couples remain sexually active throughout life, provided they have good physical and mental health, positive attitudes toward sex and a healthy partner (DeLamater, 2012). At the same time, sexual arousal is noted to decrease with age in women, going from 15% between ages 20 and 40 to nearly 70% in woman age 60 to 69 (Palacios, Castaño, & Grazziotin, 2009).

In fact, a sizable number of men and women engage in partnered and solo sexual activities even in the eighth and ninth decades of life (Lindau et al., 2007). In sexually active older couples, DeLamater (2012) also found a higher quality of relationship satisfaction and less depression in couples who remained sexually active.

Health Issues

Sexual behaviors diminish with age but surprisingly less than expected (Lindau et al., 2007). When sexual frequency diminishes with age, it is often due to lack of desire (usually resulting from medications), ill health, ED in men, hormonal changes linked to menopause or lack of a partner. Often, couples vary the type of sexual activity they employ, usually in response to an age-related medical condition. Intercourse is often replaced by outercourse (noncoital sex) in order to compensate for erectile difficulties, vaginal atrophy or other physiological consequences of disability or disease (Degauquier, Absil, Psalti, Meuris, & Jurysta, 2012). Additionally, companionship rather than sexual attraction becomes a motivating reason for sexual relations. More than ever, communication is an important component of sexual activity in order to discuss concerns and changes in stimulation required in order to facilitate pleasurable sensations. As a general rule, partners prefer more physical and mental stimulation as they age.

Because the incidence of physical illnesses increases with age, sexual dysfunction in the elderly can sometimes signal the presence of underlying mental or physical disease processes. Physical changes associated with aging include heart disease, high blood pressure and diabetes, as well as the effects of treatment for these health problems. The clinician should inquire and gather a list of the medications a client is currently taking, he or she needs to determine which class the medication is in. For instance, Lexipro is in the SSRI (selective serotonin re-uptake inhibitor) antidepressant class and Xanax is an antianxiety agent. Clinicians can also read the following for more detailed information:

- "Sexual Pharmacology: Love Potions, Pills, and Poisons" (Verhulst & Reynolds, 2009)
- "The Interplay between Mental and Sexual Health" (Phelps, Jones, & Payne, 2015)
- "Recognizing and Reversing the Sexual Side Effects of Medications" (Segraves & Ballon, 2010)

Some clients may not recall all of their medications or dosages, so we recommend that they compile a list of medications, dosages and duration when they return home and bring their prescription information to the following session.

Men

Physiologically, as men get older, they may experience a host of sexual changes related to erectile capacity, sensitivity, tumescence and refractory period. ED is so common it is almost normative. The International Consultation Committee for Sexual Medicine on Definitions/Epidemiology/Risk Factors for Sexual Dysfunction produced a meta-analysis of published works regarding male sexual dysfunction. The committee found the prevalence of ED ranged from 20% to 40% among men between ages 60 and 69, and increased to 50%–100% in men 70 years and older (Lewis et al., 2010).

Women

The major issue facing older women is the impact of menopause on sexuality. The biological changes associated with menopause can result in interest/arousal difficulties, vaginal dryness and sexual pain. The loss of estrogen during menopause can trigger hot flashes and vaginal atrophy (deterioration of vaginal tissue), making arousal physiologically more difficult although local estrogen treatment as well as more sexual activity can help with this issue (Pandit & Ouslander, 2010). Additionally, low androgen levels in women may decrease sexual desire and pleasure. However, some of our clients have noted that menopause gives them a more relaxed approach toward sex, enhancing their enjoyment and satisfaction as the risk of unwanted pregnancy ends.

Sexual Scripting

As at any other age, sexual scripting influences our view of ourselves as sexual persons. Sexual scripts are blueprints and guidelines for how we define sexual expression, orientation, behavior, attraction, desires and self-definition (Kimmel, 2007; Zilbergeld, 2005). It is important that the therapist help the older individual or couple review their sexual script, consider how it has changed over the years and consider and accept what it is now. Reevaluation of the sexual script should be a part of every sexual assessment.

Changing Roles

An elderly partner's poor health status may contribute to a sexual difficulty in the relationship. The stress of caretaking for one's partner may negatively impact sexual desire due to fatigue, worry, anxiety and perhaps even resentment toward the partner. We believe that when partners can show that they care for one another intimately and are able to openly express their affection and sexual desires, there is a lowered risk of developing more complex sexual issues (see, for example, Weeks, Gambescia, & Jenkins, 2003).

Partner Availability

Another important issue for aging individuals is partner availability, and a great deal of research has determined that there is a use it or lose it phenomenon: infrequent sexual activity increases the likelihood of erectile and lubrication difficulties. Aging singles living in residential care facilities are most at risk because of their extremely limited ability to meet new partners and engage in sexual behavior. Staff members often discourage intimate expression between residents. This is especially heartbreaking when one partner is in an assisted care portion of the facility and the other is continuing to live in the residence. Further, society tends to view the elderly as sexually dead. Because of these issues, assessment should include the client's internalization of social messages or the client's ability to challenge stereotypes successfully. Conflicts between the client's or couple's sexual values and the sexual norms of the dominant culture may result in sexual difficulties (Syme, 2014). When social norms do not permit the elderly to share affection or present themselves as sexual beings, there can be negative impacts on sexual function and overall relationship satisfaction.

Sexually Transmitted Illnesses

Aging persons are at risk of acquiring sexually transmitted infections (STIs), particularly in view of the fact that they often remain sexually active. Individuals over 50 constitute 11% of new AIDS cases and are more likely to be diagnosed late in the course of the disease, according to the 2013 Centers for Disease Control fact sheet, *HIV among Older Americans*. Older individuals acquire syphilis, gonorrhea and other STIs but at lower rates than younger persons (Johnson, 2013). Older persons might not have received psychoeducation about STIs or might believe they are not at risk. Often, they fail to use barrier forms of protection because they need not worry about an undesired pregnancy. If there has been loss of a spouse, the remaining spouse may reenter the dating scene and often have unprotected sex. Physicians hardly ever discuss STIs with older patients. Also, the symptoms of STIs can be similar to those of other illnesses that commonly affect older adults, including malaise, loss of appetite and swollen glands. The therapist must include assessment for STIs in the overall evaluation for this population.

Sexual Assessment

A review of current health status and medical history should highlight the organic basis of sexual difficulties and indicate the client's general capacity to engage in sexual activities. After attending to the medical aspects of aging (such as illness and medications), clinicians need to assess how clients view their age and sexuality. What is the client's or couple's sexual script? Does he or she ascribe to contextual conditions that stigmatize sexuality in older people? Assessment should also include the level of sexual satisfaction as well as relational satisfaction. Essential content areas should be environmental, cultural, religious and any other sociocultural factor that can affect sexual satisfaction. Older couples are often capable of sharing sexual pleasure in spite of illness and medications if they have a positive view of themselves sexually and can communicate about sex. Others might need more help in accepting the realities of aging and modifying their sexual scripts, expanding the sexual repertoire, improving communication and so on.

Treatment Strategies for Special Populations

The therapist is required to attend to the ways in which illness, disability or aging can impact an individual's sense of self and sexual identity. Additionally, all of the physical factors mentioned earlier will alter the couple's sexual relationship. The therapist can help the couple utilize coping mechanisms to foster an enjoyable sex life and expand the definition of sex in order to successfully adapt to their particular physical problems or limitations.

Keeping a Systemic Focus

Many of the treatments for the special populations in this chapter are discussed in other sections of this book, particularly the treatment section. In general, we address all facets of the Intersystem Approach, beginning with issues that arose within the families of origin, the actual physical issues of each partner and the psychological strengths and vulnerabilities of each partner. Fastidious attention is directed to the level of satisfaction and adaption in the relationship, including sexual satisfaction. Finally, the contextual factors of the Intersystem are addressed, such as finances, physical surroundings, daily hassles, culture, ethnicity, religion and so on.

Collaborate with Medical Providers

With nearly all of the specific populations under consideration in this chapter, it is important to collaborate with the clients' medical team. The therapist's goal in working with each client's physician is to understand the unique nature of the client's illness or disability and its impact on sexual functioning in order to better determine the client's goals for sex therapy. In situations where consultations with physicians are not possible, review the relevant resources provided in Table 14.1 to get a general understanding of the issues facing the client who suffers from specific disorders or diseases.

TABLE 14.1 Internet Resources for Specific Physical issues

Topic	Web address
American Cancer Society: Sexuality for Men and Their Partners	http://www.cancer.org/docroot/MIT/MIT_7_1x_SexualityforMenandTheirPartners.asp
American Cancer Society: Sexuality for Women and Their Partners	http://www.cancer.org/treatment/treatmentsandsideeffects/physicalsideeffects/sexualsideeffectsinwomen/index
Sexual Activity and Heart Disease or Stroke	http://216.185.112.5/presenter.jhtml?identifier=4714.asp
Sexual Dysfunction in Women: Sex Isn't Working for Me. What Can I Do?	http://www.aafp.org/afp/2000/0701/p141.html
Age Page: Sexuality in Later Life	http://www.nia.nih.gov/health/publication/sexuality-later-life
Why Safe Sex is a Menopause Priority	http://www.regardinghealth.com/nam/RHO/2004/06/Article.aspx?bmkEMC=14610
Sexual Health and Aging: Keep The Passion Alive	http://www.mayoclinic.com/health/sexual-health/HA00035
Sex, Romance, and Relationships: AARP Survey of Midlife and Older Adults	http://www.aarp.org/relationships/love-sex/info-05-2010/srr_09.html
The National Multiple Sclerosis Society	http://www.nationalmssociety.org
Sexual Health Network: A Better Way to Test for STDs	http://www.sexualhealth.com

To coordinate with physicians, it will be necessary to obtain release of information permissions. Working with the client's physician lets the client know that you are serious about getting all the information needed to help them. Some clients experience sexual side effects from drugs but are not aware of it. Therapists may need to collaborate with the physicians in order to change the pharmaceutical treatments in a way that may minimize the negative sexual effects. Physicians are sometimes not aware that a patient is having a sexual difficulty because clients are embarrassed to tell the doctor.

At a minimum, the physician and/or therapists should counsel clients about timing sexual activity with prescription use, especially medications that may blunt desire, interfere with arousal or inhibit orgasm. It will be important to understand how the client experiences the medication (drowsiness, loss of focus, sexual difficulties, etc.) and encourage the client to strategize with the prescribing physician about ways to work within the constraints of the medication's effects. In addition to drugs prescribed to treat physical ailments, clinicians should take into account that many different classes of drugs can have significant sexual side effects. We only give examples of a few groups since an extensive list can be found in our companion volume *Systemic Sex Therapy* (Hertlein, Weeks, & Gambescia, 2015) in the chapter "The Interplay between Mental and Sexual Health" (Phelps, Jones, & Payne, 2015). The most common offenders in clinical practice appear to be the antidepressants, particularly the serotonin-based types, because they can inhibit desire and orgasm. Antihypertensive drugs, used to treat high blood pressure, come in various types and can affect all aspects of the sexual response, including arousal. Antipsychotics are used to treat psychoses and other problems such as anger outbursts in lower doses; these medications can cause erectile or ejaculatory problems. The list is exhaustive and the therapist must have all information about prescribed, over-the-counter, herbal, recreational and other drugs, doses and duration of use.

Finally, therapists may need to work with physicians when a client's sexual difficulties can be treated medically, such as in the use of prosexual medications to enhance erections (Bitzer, Platano, Tschudin, & Alder, 2008); however, medical interventions work best when combined with psychotherapy (see Gambescia & Weeks, 2015). In the case of ED, there is often a combined psychogenic and organic etiology that must be treated concurrently. For women, pharmaceutical interventions to restore sexual interest, arousal or orgasmic capacity has not been approved by the FDA (Food and Drug Administration); nonetheless, off-label medications are sometimes prescribed, such as Wellbutrin (Bupropion). In our experience, pharmaceutical agents to enhance sexual interest, desire and arousability in women have yielded mixed results and are not currently recommended.

Psychoeducation

The best way to approach treatment is to inquire about sexual ability and disability. The therapist might be unfamiliar with the challenges of specific disabilities and the client is often the best source of education. Frank, direct questions can be asked to ascertain the level of sexual function. Sometimes clients with known disabilities do not consider themselves sexually disabled. It is incumbent upon the therapist to read about and investigate the particular disability in order to best help the client.

A major component of psychotherapy for specific medical populations involves psychoeducation for the therapist about the particular issues a client may be experiencing. The therapist might be uncomfortable or unfamiliar with the information. It is incumbent upon the therapist to increase knowledge and control his or her own anxiety, especially with this group of individuals who may have been traumatized by societal views of their situations. Next, investigate how the client has adapted to the illness or disability by exploring his or her sexual knowledge, comfort and degree of trauma due to marginalization and stigmatization. Basic psychoeducation is, therefore, an important element of treatment for the client as well as therapist.

Physical realities. Discuss modifiable risk factors such as smoking, alcohol consumption, lack of exercise and eating habits that can interfere with sexual activity. Therapists should counsel clients on how to reduce their risks of becoming overly fatigued through managing stress and achieving a balance in work/leisure life. The therapist helps explain the links between lifestyle and sexual function in order to promote acceptance and change in these areas.

Physical issues related to an illness or disability, such as loss of bladder and bowel control, can be addressed through psychoeducation. If the therapist is unfamiliar with these issues, it is essential for him or her to consult with the medical treatment team and investigate accurate resources in order to help partners accommodate to their specific disability. For clients with painful sex, the client must discuss the etiology of the pain as well as the meaning or interpretation of the pain. Treatment might involve instructing clients on the use of lubricants and dilators and encouraging the practice of relaxation techniques. Recommendations regarding using pillows, bolsters or cushions can promote comfort for clients with surgery wounds, back injuries, spastic limbs and other conditions. A useful website for many aspects related to sexuality and disability is www.high10yourlife.com, provided by a certified sexuality educator who conducts explicit educational sex and relationship workshops for all disabled people who wish to heighten their sensuality and intimacy. Also, she recommends furniture, sexual enhancers and other objects that sensitively address the specific needs of those with disabilities in search of direct and honest psychoeducation. Finally, http://mitchelltepper.com/media/publications is another valuable website addressing all areas of sexuality and disability.

Reducing Anxiety, Misinformation and Myths

As stated, we investigate cognitions and feelings regarding myths related to aging, illness and disability. In addition to bibliotherapy, we use cognitive and behavioral therapy, specifically cognitive restructuring. It is important to address performance anxiety, suggest relaxation techniques and employ mindfulness practices. We help the partners to increase and expand their sexual repertoire within the limits of their physical problems. This involves thinking about sex as more than goal-oriented penetrative sex. Often, we suggest numerous forms of noncoital sex. Enhancing communication skills is especially useful but challenging because most people have difficulty feeling comfortable and entitled to ask for what is needed and pleasurable and to redirect the partner with concrete feedback. Discussing the illness or disability openly in session may be the only place where the couple communicates about their real sexual limitations and their stress and anxiety about sex.

Connected with anxiety surrounding sexual activity may be a host of myths, such as the false belief that sexual acts could be fatal or make the illness worse. Faulty beliefs and a lack of practical knowledge about sex and illness or disability also limit sexual satisfaction. Although individuals may have basic sex information, therapists would be wise to dispel myths and assess the accuracy of the clients' beliefs about sexuality and ability, illness and aging. The therapist must listen carefully for sexual misinformation, elicit information about what is pertinent to their situation and give corrective information. A technique we use is to ask each partner to list the maladaptive beliefs they have about their sexuality and their physical situation. The therapist might add to the list with information acquired during sessions. Sometimes clients need help in understanding why certain beliefs are nonfactual. As stated, cognitive restructuring is necessary to address and change each belief. This involves addressing inaccurate beliefs about the illness or disability and correcting inaccurate information about sexuality within the client's or couple's physical circumstances. You may need to explore these beliefs from a psychodynamic perspective if they are core beliefs or otherwise related to other core aspects of the person's self-identity. This exploration could involve an examination of the client's psychosexual development and how these early life experiences are continually functioning in the background of awareness. These very early experiences may still be affecting how a client interprets and responds to his or her current situation. In many cases, the client has adopted ideas about what it is like to be chronically ill and disabled from watching other members of his or her family struggle with illness. Sometimes, the client has learned about how people who are disabled or ill manage their sex lives from the implicit and/or explicit messages received from other family members, friends or the media.

Addressing Relationship Issues in the Context of Illness

As we suggested earlier, aging, illness and/or disability may have changed the client's level of desire. Level of desire, especially a discrepancy in desire, should be closely examined. Attempts should be made in therapy to reconcile these differences in the couple. The desire discrepancy may have predated the physical problem or be compounded by it. The therapist will need to perform a complete sex history for the couple and also explore the impact of the illness on the couple and sexual dynamics. For example, one partner may become the caretaker to the other, thus creating a parent-child relationship, as it is sometimes called. This type of relational dynamic is part of a much larger dynamic that affects more than the sexual relationship. It could be understood that desire and activity are two different phenomena. One partner may please the other sensually or sexually without having sexual desire just because he or she wants to give the other a gift.

Attending to Sexual Scripting

The sexual self of the client must be explored prior to and during the exploration of the sexual problem. How has the physical issue impacted sexual desire, attractiveness, interest and so on? How has it impacted the partner and how is the couple compensating sexually? Sometimes an individual will have incorporated a negative self-image and might not be communicating with his or her partner about feelings, attitudes and beliefs. The psychotherapy will investigate the client's early learning about sex, the impact of this learning on his or her sexual script, and the perceived effects of physical issues on the client's and couple's sexuality. An individual might need permission and time to mourn the loss of sexual functioning, express anger, rage, embarrassment, fears and so on. Some of our clients are not partnered and will need to discuss their concerns about dating and sexual expectations. We reduce reluctance to dating by allowing for discussion of expectations and by reinforcing the notion that dating can be treated as an opportunity to spend time with another person without pressures related to sex. Some individuals may have developed a virtually phobic avoidance of trying to develop a relationship. The therapist will need to process their avoidance feelings and their negative beliefs about their sexuality and value in a relationship. The development of a more positive sexual self-image can occur through cognitive interventions discussed previously.

Expanding the Sexual Repertoire

Throughout the chapter, we have discussed expansion of the sexual repertoire. In general, this means that the couple is helped to appreciate pleasurable activities as a goal state. Each activity can be enjoyed and valued as an expression of pleasure, intimacy, caring and so on depending on the *meaning* of sex for the individual or couple. A sexual act that does not culminate in penetration or orgasm need not be viewed as falling short of a goal. In fact, the pressure to experience goal-oriented penetrative sex is discouraged in all of our clients; instead, they are helped to be mindful of the sensations they are feeling in the moment, and to communicate these feelings to the partner, if partnered. Sometimes, expansion involves exploring new positions, techniques and devices or sexual aids. It is often necessary to include psychoeducation to dispel myths and cognitive work to reduce the exclusive focus on intercourse and coital orgasm as the only real way to have sex. Thus, the focus of sexual intimacy is on pleasure over performance.

Many clients have internalized the belief that good sex is about a particular type of performance that their illness or disability makes impossible. The goal of sex needs to be reconfigured to represent giving and receiving (if partnered) sensual pleasure regardless of the desired outcome. Once clients accept this as the goal of sex, anxiety will be reduced and the therapist can then help them determine the most effective ways for them to experience pleasurable sensations through psychoeducation and sensual touch exercises (see the discussion of sensate focus in Chapter 10 in this text). Support an attitude of trial and error, with an emphasis on the pursuit of pleasurable activities. Couples who are looking for easy answers or for the therapist to simply tell them what to do will be disappointed. Emphasize creativity in an effort to inspire them to find their own solutions. Table 14.2 provides some factually based resources about sexuality that will help correct myths and misinformation and supply scientifically based information for clients who have a variety of disabilities.

TABLE 14.2 Sexuality Resources for Physical Disabilities

Source	Authors/Editors
The Illustrated Guide to Better Sex for People with Chronic Pain	Robert W. Rothrock, PA-C, and Gabriella D'Amore, PA-C
MS and Intimacy: Managing Specific Issues	Tanya Radford
Sexual Concerns When Illness or Disability Strikes	Carol L. Sandowski, M.S.W., A.C.S.W.
The Sexual Politics of Disability: Untold Desires	Tom Shakespeare, Dominic Davies, and Kath Gillespie-Sells, Editors
Sexuality after Spinal Cord Injury: Answers to Your Questions	Stanley H. Ducharme and Kathleen M. Gill
Sexuality and Spinal Cord Injury	Sylvia Eichner McDonald, Willa M. Lloyd, Donna Murphy, and Margaret Gretchen Russert
Choices: A Guide to Sex Counseling with Physically Disabled Adults	Maureen E. Neistadt, M.S., O.T.R./L., and Maureen Freda, O.T.R./L
Providing Comprehensive Sexual Health Care in Spinal Cord Injury Rehabilitation: Continuing Education and Training for Health Care Professionals	Mitchell S. Tepper
Sexual Function in People with Disability and Chronic Illness: A Health Professional's Guide	Marca L. Sipski and Craig J. Alexander
Sexuality and Chronic Illness: A Comprehensive Approach	Leslie R. Schover, Ph.D., and Søren Buus Jensen, M.D.
The Ultimate Guide to Sex and Disability: For All of Us Who Live with Disabilities, Chronic Pain, and Illness	Miriam Kaufman, M.D., Cory Silverberg, and Fran Odette

Enhance Couple Communication

The onset of illness, disability, or age-related decline may significantly influence couple dynamics, producing impaired communication, changes to sexual intimacy, unwelcome role changes and role strain and challenges in adapting to the new situation (Dankoski & Pais, 2007). The more functional partner might feel guilt about having sexual feelings toward someone who is ill or in pain from a disability. These are issues that couples may be very reluctant to discuss, particularly in the presence of the partner with the illness or disability. Sometimes it will be necessary to meet with each partner individually to get a sense of what they are experiencing and help them develop a plan for discussing their concerns in the couple session. We often prescribe incremental sensate focus assignments to be performed at home with the stipulation that the partners communicate about what they are feeling. This exercise will also reveal underlying obstacles to the couple having better sexual expression. Additionally, accessing the client's sense of humor, fun and creativity will afford a sense of empowerment to keep the focus on sexual enjoyment, not dysfunction.

Attend to Issues in the Therapist

As stated, the therapist must be informed about and prepared to discuss accurate information in a relaxed yet direct manner. Many health and mental health practitioners have circumvented the critical discussions involving sexual needs and proceeded with treatment as though sex is unimportant in illness, aging and disability. Clients may not have ever been asked directly about their levels of sexual interest, activity and desire to improve their sexual lives. Therapists need to understand how countertransference factors can hamper treatment and increase embarrassment, stigmatization and vulnerability in the client. Additionally, older clients may be reluctant to discuss sexual problems with a therapist who is the same age as their child or grandchild. Individuals with a disability may be highly sensitive to a perceived lack of empathy from therapists without a disability. The therapist must firmly believe in the client's right to sexual pleasure and ability to have a satisfying sexual and intimate relationship.

Finally, therapists may experience multiple countertransference issues with this population. Therapists may fall prey to the cultural stereotype that chronically ill, older couples or individuals with disabilities are not sexually interested or active. Therapists may also have fears of their own about illness, disability and death or may be having trouble coping with one of these problems in their own families or relationships. The idea that they may someday be like the people they are treating may arouse so much fear and anxiety that therapists block any discussion that gets to the depth of the client's current despair and hopelessness. If a sex therapist is avoiding taking these kinds of referrals or working with them to sort out the issues mentioned here, that therapist may be experiencing a countertransference issue. The therapist must be open to his or her own vulnerability in order to help those in such a vulnerable position. If the therapist has difficulty accessing the client's painful emotions or avoiding subjects, it is essential that the therapist seek supervision or psychotherapy.

Another issue that arises in considering populations with disabilities is the use of sexual surrogates. The movie *The Sessions* (Levine, 2012) sensitively portrayed a sex surrogate working with a man with a severe physical disability. Although surrogacy is often considered with abled and disabled individuals, the use of surrogates remains a controversial topic and has professional, legal, ethical and financial concerns (Rosenbaum, Aloni, & Heruti, 2013). Apparently, surrogate partners work to help clients build communication skills and self-confidence, and assist clients in becoming more comfortable with physical and emotional intimacy. Unfortunately, empirical data about the efficacy of surrogacy are unavailable. Currently, sex surrogacy is illegal in most states; nonetheless, there is an association that certifies surrogates who are trained and work in conjunction with sex therapists. See www.surrogatetherapy.org for more detailed information.

References

Altuntug, K., Ege, E., Akın, B., Kal, H.H., & Sallı, A. (2014). An investigation of sexual/reproductive health issues in women with a physical disability. *Sexuality & Disability, 32*(2), 221–229. doi:10.1007/s11195-014-9342-z

Assari, S. (2014). Intercourse avoidance among women with coronary artery disease. *Journal of Sexual Medicine, 11*(7), 1709–1716. doi:10.1111/jsm.12459

Baumgart, J., Nilsson, K., Evers, A.S., Kallak, T.K., & Poromaa, I.S. (2013). Sexual dysfunction in women on adjuvant endocrine therapy after breast cancer. *Menopause, 20*(2), 162–168. doi:10.1097/gme.0b013e31826560da.

Bitzer, J., Platano, G., Tschudin, S., & Alder, J. (2008). Sexual counseling in elderly couples. *Journal of Sexual Medicine, 5*(9), 2027–2043. doi:10.1111/j.1743-6109.2008.00926.x

Boehmer, U., Ozonoff, A., Timm A., Winter, M., & Potter, J. (2014). After breast cancer: Sexual functioning of sexual minority survivors. *The Journal of Sex Research, 51*(6), 681–689. doi:10.1080/00224499.2013.772087

Brotto, L.A., & Kingsberg, S. (2010). Sexual consequences of cancer survival. In S. Levine, C. Risen, & S. Althof (Eds.), *Handbook of clinical sexuality for mental health professionals* (pp. 329–347). New York: Routledge.

Cakar, B., Karaca, B., & Uslu, R. (2013). Sexual dysfunction in cancer patients: A review. *Journal of Balkan Union of Oncology, 18*(4), 818–823.

Celik, D.B., Poyraz, E.C., Bingol, A., Idiman, E., Ozakbas, S., & Kaya D. (2013). Sexual dysfunction in multiple sclerosis: Gender differences. *Journal of Neurological Sciences, 324,* 17–20.

Centers for Disease Control and Prevention. (2013). *HIV among older Americans.* Retrieved from http://www.cdc.gov/hiv/risk/age/olderamericans

Chung, S.D., Chen, Y.K., Lin, H.C., & Lin, H.C. (2011). Increased risk of stroke among men with erectile dysfunction: A nationwide population-based study. *Journal of Sexual Medicine, 8*(1), 240–246.

Chung, E., & Gillman, M. (2014). Prostate cancer survivorship: A review of erectile dysfunction and penile rehabilitation after prostate cancer therapy. *The Medical Journal of Australia, 200*(10), 582–585.

Dankoski, M.E., & Pais, S. (2007). What's love got to do with it? Couples, illness, and MFT. *Journal of Couple & Relationship Therapy, 6*(1/2), 31–43.

Degauquier, C., Absil, A.S., Psalti, I., Meuris, S., & Jurysta, F. (2012). Impact of aging on sexuality. *Revue Medicale de Bruxelles, 33*(3):153–63.

DeLamater, J. (2012). Sexual expression in later life: A review and synthesis. *Journal of Sex Research, 49*(2–3), 125–141.

Demirtas, B., & Pinar, G. (2014). Determination of sexual problems of Turkish patients receiving gynecologic cancer treatment: A cross-sectional study. *Asian Pacific Journal of Cancer Prevention, 15*(16), 6657–6663.

Enzlin, P. (2014). Sexuality in the context of chronic illness. In Y. Binik and K. Hall (Eds.), *Principles and practice of sex therapy* (5th ed.) (pp. 436–457). New York: Guilford Press.

Ficarra, V., & Novara, G. (2011). Radical prostatectomy. *Critical Reviews in Oncology/Hematology, 78,* S8–S9.

Gambescia, N., & Weeks, G. (2015) Systemic treatment of erectile disorder. In K.M. Hertlein, G.R. Weeks, & N. Gambescia (Eds.), *Systemic sex therapy* (2nd ed.) (pp. 72–89). New York: Routledge.

Gill, K.M., & Hough, S. (2007). Sexual health of people with chronic illness and disability. In L. VandeCreek, F.L. Peterson, & J.W. Bley (Eds.), *Innovations in clinical practice: Focus on sexual health* (pp. 223–245). Sarasota, FL: Professional Resource Press/Professional Resource Exchange.

Gomez, F., & Andrianne, R. (2014). Normal ageing of the male and female genitourinary tract. *Revue Medicale de Liege, 69*(5–6), 343–348.

Gumus, H., Akpinar, Z., & Yilmaz, H. (2013). Effects of multiple sclerosis on female sexuality: A controlled study. *Journal of Sexual Medicine, 11*(2), 481–486. doi:10.1111/jsm.12397

Hertlein, K.M., Weeks, G.R., & Gambescia, N. (Eds.). (2015). *Systemic sex therapy* (2nd ed.). New York: Routledge.

Hughes, A., Hertlein, K.M., & Hagey, D. (2011). A MedFT-informed sex therapy for treating sexual problems associated with chronic illness. *Journal of Family Psychotherapy, 22*(2), 114–127. doi:10.1080/08975353.2011.577689

Hughes, A.K., & Lewinson, T.D. (2014). Facilitating communication about sexual health between aging women and their health care providers. *Qualitative Health Research, 16.* doi:1049732314551062

Johnson, B.K. (2013). Sexually transmitted infections and older adults. *Journal of Gerontological Nursing, 39*(11), 53–60. doi:10.3928/00989134-20130918-01

Julia, P., & Othman, A. (2011). Barriers to sexual activity: Counseling spinal cord injured women in Malaysia. *Spinal Cord, 49*(7), 791–794. doi:10.1038/sc.2011.4

Kimmel, M. (2007). *The sexual self: The construction of sexual scripts.* Nashville, TN: Vanderbilt University Press.

Kloner, R., & Schwartz, B. (2011). Clinical cardiology: Physician update: Erectile dysfunction and cardiovascular disease. *Circulation, 123*(1), 98–101.

Levine, J., Nemeth, S., Lewin, B. (Producers), & Lewin, B. (Director). (2012). *The sessions* [Motion picture]. United States: Fox Searchlight Pictures.

Lewis, R.W., Fugl-Meyer, K., Corona, G., Hayes, R.D., Laumann, E.O., Moreira Jr., E.D., Rellini, A.H., & Segraves, T. (2010). Definitions/Epidemiology/Risk factors for sexual dysfunction. *Journal of Sexual Medicine, 7*(4), 1598–1607.

Lindau, S.T., Schumm, P., Laumann, E.O., Levinson, W., O'Muircheartaigh, C.A., & Waite, L.J. (2007). A study of sexuality and health among older adults in the United States. *New England Journal of Medicine, 357,* 762–774.

Maiorino, M.I., Bellastella, G., & Esposito, K. (2014). Diabetes and sexual dysfunction: Current perspectives. *Diabetes, Metabolic Syndrome and Obesity, 7,* 95–105.

Meco, G., Rubino, A., Caravona, N., & Valente, M. (2008). Sexual dysfunction in Parkinson's disease. *Parkinsonism and Related Disorders, 14,* 451–456.

Meeking, D.R., Fosbury, J.A., & Cummings, M.H. (2013). Sexual dysfunction and sexual health concerns in women with diabetes. *Practical Diabetes, 30*(8), 327–331.

Mona, L., Syme, M., & Cameron, R. (2013). Sexuality and disability: A disability-affirming approach to sex therapy. In Y. Binik and K. Hall (Eds.), *Principles and practice of sex therapy* (5th ed.) (pp. 457–481). New York: Guilford Press.

Moreno, J.A., Arango-Lasprilla, J.C., Gan C., & McKerral, M. (2013) Sexuality after traumatic brain injury: A critical review. *NeuroRehabilitation, 32*(1), 69–85.

Moser, C., & Devereux, M. (2012). Sexual medicine, sex therapy, and sexual health care. In P. Kleinplatz (Ed.), *New directions in sex therapy* (2nd ed.) (pp. 127–140). New York: Routledge.

Olkin, R., (1999). *What psychotherapists should know about disability.* New York: Guilford Press.

Palacios, S., Castaño, R., & Grazziotin, A. (2009). Epidemiology of female sexual dysfunction. *Maturitas, 63*(2), 119–123. doi:10.1016/j.maturitas.2009.04.002

Pandit, L., & Ouslander, J. (2010). Managing postmenopausal vaginal atrophy. *Harvard Women's Health Watch, 17*(7), 4–5.

Phelps, K.W., Jones, A.B., & Payne, R.A. (2015). The interplay between mental and sexual health. In K. Hertlein, G. Weeks, & N. Gambescia (Eds.), *Systemic sex therapy* (2nd ed.) (pp. 255–275). New York: Routledge.

Pillai-Friedman, S., & Ashline, J.L. (2014). Women, breast cancer survivorship, sexual losses, and disenfranchised grief: A treatment model for clinicians. *Sexual and Relationship Therapy, 29*(4), 436–453.

Rosenbaum, T., Aloni, R., & Heruti, R. (2013). Surrogate partner therapy: Ethical considerations in sexual medicine. *Journal of Sexual Medicine, 11*(2), 321–329.

Rosenbaum, T., Vadas, D., & Kalichman, L.J. (2014). Sexual function in post-stroke patients: Considerations for rehabilitation. *The Journal of Sexual Medicine, 11*(1), 15–21. doi:10.1111/jsm.12343.

Rutte, A., van Splunter, M.M., van der Heijden, A.A., Welschen, L.M., Elders, P.J., Dekker, J.M., Snoek, F.J., Enzlin, P., & Nijpels, G. (2014). Prevalence and correlates of sexual dysfunction in men and women with type 2 diabetes. *Journal of Sex & Marital Therapy, 1,* 1–10.

Schick, V., Herbenick, D., Reece, M., Sanders, S., Dodge, B., Middlestadt, S.E., & Fortenberry, J.D. (2010). Sexual behaviors, condom use, and sexual health of Americans over 50: Implications for sexual health promotion for older adults. *Journal of Sexual Medicine,* (Suppl 5), 315–329.

Segraves, R.T., & Ballon, R. (2010). Recognizing and reversing the sexual side effects of medications. In S. Levine, C. Risen and S. Althof (Eds.), *Handbook of clinical sexuality for mental health professionals* (2nd ed.). New York: Routledge.

Seymour, L.M., & Wolf, T.J. (2014). Participation changes in sexual functioning after mild stroke. *Journal of Occupation, Participation and Health, 34*(2), 72–80. doi:10.3928/15394492-20131217-01.

Siegel, R., Naishadham, D., & Jemal, A. (2013). Cancer statistics, 2013. *CA: A Cancer Journal for Clinicians, 63*(1), 11–30.

Simopoulos, E. F., & Trinidad, A. C. (2013). Male erectile dysfunction: Integrating psychopharmacology and psychotherapy. *General Hospital Psychiatry, 35*(1), 33–38.

Syme, M. L. (2014). The evolving concept of older adult sexual behavior and its benefits. *Generations, 38*(1), 35–41.

Vafaeimanesh, J., Raei, M., Hosseinzadeh, F., & Parham, M. (2014). Evaluation of sexual dysfunction in women with type 2 diabetes. *Indian Journal of Endocrinology & Metabolism, 18*(2), 175–179. doi:10.4103/2230-8210.129107

Verhulst, J., & Reynolds, J. K. (2009). Sexual pharmacology: Love potions, pills, and poisons. *Journal of Family Psychotherapy, 20*(4), 319–343.

Weeks, G., Gambescia, N., & Jenkins, R. (2003). *Treating infidelity.* New York: W. W. Norton.

Wiegerink, D., Roebroeck, M., Bender, J., Stam, H., & Cohen-Kettenis, P. (2011). Sexuality of young adults with cerebral palsy: Experienced limitations and needs. *Sexuality and Disability, 29*(2), 119–128.

Wylie, K., & Kenney, G. (2010). Sexual dysfunction and the ageing male. *Maturitas, 65*(1), 23–27.

Zelefsky, M. J., Shasha, D., Branco, R. D., Kollmeier, M., Baser, R. E., Pei, X., Ennis, R., Stock, R., Bar-Chama, N., & Mulhall, J. P. (2014). Prophylactic sildenafil citrate improves select aspects of sexual function in men treated with radiotherapy for prostate cancer. *Journal of Urology, 192*(3), 868–874. doi:10.1016/j.juro.2014.02.097

Zilbergeld, B. (2005). *Better than ever: Love and sex at midlife.* Norwalk, CT: Crown House.

15

DIVERSITY IN SEXUAL EXPRESSION

Introduction

This chapter presents an overview of some of the diverse and less common expressions of sexuality the clinician is likely to encounter in sex therapy practice. As such, some clients will fall outside of the range of mainstream sexual disorders defined in the *DSM-5* (American Psychiatric Association, 2013). The clinician should be prepared, comfortable and competent in helping clients who might appear to be *gender diverse*, or not conforming to gender-based expectations of society, including transgender, transsexual, intersex, cross-dresser, gay, lesbian, bisexual, kinky and so on. Therapists should not presuppose that gender-diverse clients are pursuing treatment of their specific gender/erotic/sexual preference or orientation but instead might want help with other personal or relational issues.

The (heterosexual) therapist should never assume that a client is heterosexual. Some clients will not immediately disclose their sexual identity or preferred form of sexual expression; therefore, inquiry is necessary about sexual orientation/identification and preferred ways of expressing their gender, sexuality and eroticism. A matter-of-fact approach is most useful when asking about whether clients choose to express their sexuality in a heterosexual/homosexual relationship that is monogamous or whether they have other preferences. Asking these questions demonstrates openness to alternative forms of sexual expression.

We anticipate that this chapter will facilitate a process of self-exploration and formal education for therapists regarding the specific practices and experiences of *all* clients. This process involves *being* with these clients, accepting them for their choices, supporting them in their challenges and promoting a safe environment for their explorations of intimacy.

ative expression, *queer* as a reclaimed self-label is now an
ı sets its subject apart from all forms of heteronormative sex-
Additionally, queer denotes a broad area of gender noncon-
:ts binary groupings (gay or straight, male or female) or other
ations such as LGBT (lesbian, gay, bisexual, transgender). The
definition anu ᵤse of the term has changed considerably; contemporary usage
is intentionally ambiguous in order to embrace all forms of gender diverse
expression, disrupt societal norms and expand the boundaries for gender and
sexual identification. According to Iasenza (2010) the word queer speaks to
"the potential fluidity and multidimensionality of same and other sex/gender
experience in all people" (p. 292).

Although increasingly visible, queer individuals may still remain socially
isolated because of sexual practices that are viewed as outside the accepted
norm. Mental health professionals and sex therapists are expected to demonstrate competence when dealing with queer clients through education,
tolerance, acceptance and recognition of positive aspects of queer identities
(as discussed in Brooks & Inman, 2013). Thus, therapists will incorporate the client's self-described identity into assessment, treatment planning and therapeutic
interventions. Following clients' leads in choosing language to describe their
identities reinforces their sense of belonging to a group and prevents injury to the
therapeutic alliance.

Kinky Clients

The meaning and definition of kink is specific to the individual or partners
engaging in this form of erotic activity. While most therapists are likely to
encounter clients who engage in a variety of nonstandard erotic behaviors
ranging from consensual to pathological, they are often uninformed and ill
prepared to help kinky clients. Therapists can be repulsed or alarmed by
descriptions of sexual behaviors that eroticize power, pain and fear (Kelsey,
Stiles, Spiller, & Deikhoff, 2012) and may follow societal trends that pathologize unconventional behavior (Yost, 2010) or suspect that the kinky client
might have a history of childhood abuse. Nonetheless, although these individuals often view their own behavior as atypical, many report that they engage
in safe, satisfying and consensual activities (Stiles & Clark, 2011). According
to Nichols (2006), kinky erotic activities include one or more of the following
characteristics:

- Role-playing of fantasy sexual scenarios
- Hierarchical power structure
- Intense stimulation usually associated with physical or emotional pain

- Forms of sexual stimulation involving sensory confusion, deprivation, restraint and so on
- Using favored objects and materials as sexual enhancers
- Fetishistic sexual practices

Treatment Implications

Each therapist faces a challenge to question and understand the countertransference feelings that can be triggered by kinky clients and overcome hesitancy in order to clarify facts and contexts. There is an additional responsibility to determine if practices are safe, consensual and psychologically fulfilling (Kelsey, Stiles, Spiller, & Deikhoff, 2012). It is important for therapists to note that the kink lifestyle may not come up as a presenting problem in treatment, but instead may be a background issue (Lawrence & Love-Crowell, 2008). Another therapeutic task is to help promote an understanding of what the sexual/erotic practices actually mean to the client or partners and how they feel about them. Finally, the degree of compulsivity and risk to the individual or partners must be ascertained (Nichols, 2006). The therapist is reminded that kinky practitioners were found to have rather healthy psychological characteristics, specifically those who enjoy bondage and discipline (BD), dominance and submission (DS), and sadism and masochism (SM) (BDSM). In a recent study, kink practitioners were found to be more extraverted; open to new experiences; less sensitive to rejection; more securely attached; able to communicate needs, desires, and boundaries; and open to taking more risks (Wismeijer & van Assen, 2013). In addition, therapists who are more successful with kink clients are those who approach such clients with a nonjudgmental attitude, are knowledgeable about kink practices, have an understanding about sexual minorities and do not pathologize this group (Lawrence & Love-Crowell, 2008).

Kink Resources

Comprehensive websites on kink, power exchanges, fetishes, sexuality and relationships for all genders and orientations can be found in Table 15.1.

TABLE 15.1 Kink Resources

- Bean, J. (1994). *Leathersex: A Guide for the Curious Outsider and the Serious Player.* San Francisco, CA: Daedalus.
- Brame, G.G., Brame, W.D., & Jacobs, J. (1996). *Different Loving: The World of Sexual Dominance and Submission.* New York: Villard Books.

(Continued)

TABLE 15.1 Continued

- Califia, P. (2001). *Sensuous Magic: A Guide to S/M for Adventurous Couples.* San Francisco, CA: Cleis Press.
- Easton, D., & Lizst, C.A. (1995). *The Topping Book: Or, Being Good at Being Bad.* San Francisco, CA: Greenery Press.
- Miller, P., & Devon, M. (1995). *Screw the Roses, Send Me the Thorns: The Romance and Sexual Sorcery of Sadomasochism.* Fairfield, CT: Mystic Rose Books.
- http://www.KinkAcademy.com
- http://www.Kink.com
- http://www.FetLife.com

Lesbian, Gay and Bisexual Clients

In this section, we focus explicitly on same-sex sexuality, that is, lesbian women and gay men. Prior to Kinsey's studies in 1948 and 1953, respectively, public and scientific communities viewed sexual behavior as falling within immutable binary categories: heterosexual or homosexual. Kinsey argued that people experience same and other gender attraction and behaviors, of varying intensity, at different times over the lifespan. Some individuals are comfortable and verbal about their external and internal sexual/erotic lives and experience congruity between their declared and actual sexual/erotic orientation. In many instances, clients assert a self-labeled sexual orientation, such as lesbian or gay; however, it is not necessarily correlated with same-sex behavior, fantasy and attractions (Diamond, 2014). Additionally, a person's sexual self-identification might be more fluid, occurring within a range of fantasy and/or behavior. Thus, assessment should advance beyond one's stated sexual identification in order to grasp the operating forces of the client's sexual world. Some lesbians have sex with men or fantasize about it and some heterosexually identified men may have an active sex life with men.

Many people in same-sex relationships identify as *bisexual* (attraction to partners of both genders) or *pansexual* (someone who is not limited in sexual attraction with regard to biological sex, gender identity or gender expression). Lev and Nichols (2015) emphasize that much of the research on homosexuality has ignored the fact that one partner might identify as homosexual and the other as bisexual, overlooking significant differences in community, affiliation, identity and other relational dynamics. Additionally, some lesbian and gay couples may have one or more transgender members.

LGB Issues

As stated earlier in the chapter, multiple overlapping groups of minority sexual orientations and gender identities celebrate a sense of connection rather than imposed categorical restrictions; nonetheless, the inclusive labeling can create more anxiety and confusion among those who are outside of the queer communities, and even for those within. Queer individuals are stigmatized, marginalized and oppressed, and many have internalized negative messages from their families of origin, peers, the media and society at large (Mena & Vaccaro, 2013). Lesbians, gays and bisexuals encounter bias, prejudice and lack of support for their partnerships, as well as legal issues that include rights of survivorship, insurance benefits and beneficiaries, power of attorney and so on. Some of the ongoing stressors include the current debates around same-sex marriage, resurgence of reparative therapy and the impact of the HIV-AIDS pandemic (Rutter, 2012).

It is difficult to determine the number of people who identify as lesbian, gay, bisexual and so on because some continue to identify as heterosexual while having sex with members of the same biological gender. Many more people are attracted to and aroused by various queer identities, even if only through fantasy or in secrecy. Numerous research efforts have attempted to measure the prevalence of issues raised by Kinsey, such as the disparity between sexual attraction and actual sexual behavior. One study that focused on sexual behavior determined that about 7% of adult women and 8% of men identify as gay, lesbian or bisexual; yet the proportion of Americans who have had same-gender sexual interactions at some point in their lives is higher (Chandra, Mosher, Copen, & Sionean, 2011).

Treatment Issues

Many heterosexual therapists unintentionally embrace heteronormative assumptions, privileges and identities, including the belief that gender-diverse identities and behaviors reflect psychopathology. In 1973 the *Diagnostic and Statistical Manual of Mental Disorders* (American Psychiatric Association, 1973) removed homosexuality as a disease, yet *homophobia* (an irrational fear or intolerance of homosexuality) and *heterosexism* (the systemic process that privileges heterosexuals and oppresses homosexuals) continue to influence the therapeutic process (McGeorge & Stone Carlson, 2011), particularly if the clinician is unaware of heteronormative biases.

Many same-sex couples enter sex therapy carrying the poisonous effects of homophobia. Secrecy, shame and other byproducts of familial and societal prejudice, once introjected, can inhibit sexual expression in our LGB clients and contribute to emotional or relational damage. Iasenza (2004) recommends a multicontextual approach that includes obtaining an expanded sexual history, including systemic issues in childhood, adolescence and adulthood, and also inquiring about community contact, societal influences, and current sexual functioning. This in-depth sexual history may then be utilized to identify the resources, talents and competencies clients already possess that can be applied to help resolve their presenting sexual problem (Iasenza, 2004).

Therapist Competency

Uninformed therapists fail to ask the questions that fully elucidate the client's sexual behaviors, influences and identities, thereby confounding treatment. Therapists might also assume that kinky, queer, and nonmonogamous behaviors and identities are at odds with one's idealized self-image. This is not always the case, and therapist heteronormativity can cause clients to feel further marginalized or stigmatized. Furthermore, therapists should observe for countertransference and projection, particularly noting any reactivity to hearing about sexual acts between homosexually identified clients (Rutter, 2012). McGeorge and Stone Carlson (2011) recommend that heterosexual therapists investigate their heteronormative assumptions, including formative societal and familial messages about sexual orientation, normativity, and healthy sexuality and also be keenly aware of the ways in which they have benefited from living in a heterosexist society.

Assumptions about the sex lives of particular groups, such as the belief that lesbian couples suffer from the lack of desire and eventually succumb to a phenomenon called lesbian bed death, will obstruct treatment efficacy. Two recent studies offer credible evidence that most lesbian couples regularly engage "in a range of nongenital and genital sexual behaviors with their partners" as frequently as heterosexual women (Cohen & Byers, 2014, p. 899) and are very much alive in terms of a wide range of sexual activities and sexual satisfaction. In another study, lesbian women experienced orgasm more frequently than did either heterosexual or bisexual women (Garcia, Lloyd, Wallen, & Fisher, 2014). Therefore, therapist competency involves staying current on the literature in the field.

Another form of proficiency is the art of learning from clients about preferred terminology, practices and beliefs. Competency involves training, supervision and consultation with colleagues and other mental health professionals who specialize in working with gender-diverse individuals, couples and families. At times, personal psychotherapy is indicated for therapists to examine their own conscious or unrecognized prejudices, reactivity and countertransference issues. Also, maintaining a list of helpful websites, organizations, books, videos and other resources for psychoeducation is indispensable (see Table 15.2).

TABLE 15.2 LGB Resources

- http://www.ipgcounseling.com/resources/lgbtq-bdsmkink-polyamory-websites
- http://www.ipgcounseling.com/resources/lesbiangaybisexualqueer-library
- American Psychological Association (2012). "Guidelines for Psychological Practice with Lesbians, Gay, and Bisexual Clients." *Journal of the American Psychological Association, 67*(1), 10–42.

(Continued)

TABLE 15.2 Continued

- GLAAD: *Ally's Guide to Terminology*: http://www.glaad.org/sites/default/files/ allys-guide-to-terminology_1.pdf
- TrevorProject.org: *Crisis Intervention and Suicide Prevention for LGBTQ Youth*
- GLSEN: *Gay, Lesbian, Straight Education Network*
- Leight, A.K. (2013). *Sex Happens: The Gay Man's Guide to Creative Intimacy*. Minneapolis, MN: Langdon Street Press.
- Newman, F. (2004). *The Whole Lesbian Sex Book*. San Francisco, CA: Cleis Press.
- StraightforEquality.org: contains workplace and healthcare trainings

Nonmonogamous Intimate Relationships

We have long known that human exceptions to lifelong monogamy, such as infidelity, are common. Researchers have demonstrated monogamy to be culturally bound rather than a universally natural state (Fisher, 2014; Hua 2008; Coontz, 2006; Barash & Lipton, 2002). Experiments challenging the social construct of monogamy are not new (e.g., the Oneida community), but in the past several decades popular willingness to investigate new, consensually nonmonogamous (CNM) frameworks for intimate relationships is growing, and more crystallized knowledge and guidance for those interested is available (see Table 15.3). Any assumptions that a clinician would be unlikely to encounter CNM clients are misguided; substantial minorities of heterosexual and lesbian couples and a majority of gay male couples have some sort of agreement permitting exceptions to monogamy, and one estimate claims more than half a million openly polyamorous families are in the United States (Graham, 2014).

Types of Consensual Nonmonogamy

In CNM, the partners themselves best elucidate their intimate relational boundaries; CNM vocabulary is not reliably consistent. That said, the following are some commonly repeated definitions from which to explore clients' relationships.

Swinging, Open Relationship, "Monogamish" or Nonmonogamous

Generally speaking, a dyad allows but restricts extradyadic sexual intimacy with agreements or rules that the couple negotiates internally. These preserve some elements of monogamy, usually the exclusivity or specialness of emotional or romantic intimacy, within the dyad (Savage, 2012; Wosick, 2012). The labels a couple chooses for this arrangement may largely be a matter of age or preferred subculture.

Polyamory

Literally meaning "many loves," polyamory denotes that romantic and emotional intimacies are expressed and shared with more than one partner, but may or may not be restricted, for one partner. A polyamorous (or poly) individual may have multiple simultaneous romantically and/or sexually intimate relationships, or may just be inclined to allow them if they have not yet formed. Polyfidelity is a subset of polyamory, denoting a mutually committed group of three, four or more people in which each individual is intimately linked to each other person in the group.

Rules and Agreements

Those in CNM relationships often negotiate agreements of varying specificity, restrictiveness and rigidity about accepted behaviors. Usually, but not always, these agreements prioritize a primary partner over secondary partners, seeking to codify and operationalize the specialness of the primary partner; such agreements may be written, verbal, case by case or some combination thereof (Wosick, 2012).

Common foci for rules and agreements include sexually transmitted infection (STI) risk reduction (e.g., testing status and use of nonpermeable barriers), restricted behaviors (e.g., "no sleeping over," "no oral"), restricted locations or times (e.g., "not in our bed," "only on business trips," "we always spend Sundays together") and restricted participants (e.g., "only women," "no mutual friends," "only the two of us together with another"). Disclosure to children, families of origin, friends and colleagues must be negotiated. Couples may also codify the level of internal disclosure they are comfortable with, possibly agreeing to a highly trusting don't ask, don't tell arrangement, mandatory pre-approval of partners or some other negotiated disclosure of the details of their extradyadic encounters.

The most common area for couples to agree to restrict is extradyadic emotional intimacy: "don't fall in love" (Wosick, 2012). In practice, emotional intimacy can be harder to predict or control, and can become a source of conflict or necessitate a renegotiation of relationship agreements. Clients who exercise a previously agreed-upon veto power over a secondary relationship may cause injury to their relationship by breaking their partner's heart (Veaux & Rickert, 2014). Some poly individuals practice nonhierarchical relationships, in which no one partner has de facto authority to enforce rules on others.

What Works, What Doesn't

There is no universally prescribable framework for CNM other than honesty. Beyond honesty clients are required to determine for themselves what works for them. High self-differentiation, high self-worth and tolerance for uncertainty are likely protective factors for CNM clients (Veaux & Rickert, 2014).

Experienced CNM participants recommend agreements that, rather than restricting connections with secondary partners, instead emphasize nurturing connections between primary partners, preserving specialness without objectifying secondary partners (Easton & Hardy, 2009; Veaux & Rickert, 2014).

Peer-reviewed research of CNM is thus far sparse and conducted on self-selecting samples that validate its viability. STI risk-reduction behaviors are more common in consensually nonmonogamous relationships than in those with nonconsensual infidelity (Conley, Moors, Ziegler, & Karathanasis, 2012). Convenience samples report levels of need fulfillment and relationship satisfaction in CNM partners (Mitchell, Bartholomew, & Cobb, 2014); one study asserts greater intimacy levels than in monogamy (Morrison, Beaulieu, Brockman, & Beaglaoich, 2013). A 15-year qualitative study of children in polyamorous households found their families were no more pathological than families with monogamous, serially monogamous, de facto polygamous or polygamous members (Goldfeder & Sheff, 2013). The question of whether individuals exist on a continuum of orientation (rather than preference) for monogamy or nonmonogamy is open and worthy of further exploration.

Countertransference Issues

Zimmerman (2012) emphasized the importance of clinicians recognizing that the current paradigm of monogamy is socially constructed, historically recent and heterocentric. The idea of humans as biologically monogamous is supported neither by science nor casual observation. Clinicians are obligated to examine and challenge ideas such as these:

- Attitudes and reactivity toward the concept of multiple concurrent sexual and/or romantic partners
- Snap, pathologizing judgments (such as intimacy issues) (Brandon, 2011)
- Assumptions about a correct model for intimate relationships
- Assumptions about jealousy as either inherently positive or inherently negative
- Assumptions of promiscuity in CNM individuals
- Assumptions that if a CNM client presents for treatment, the problem is non-monogamy (Graham, 2014; Zimmerman 2012).
- Attitudes about sexual purity, squeamishness around STI potential and stigmatic concepts about infections that are transmitted sexually versus otherwise
- Attitudes toward the purpose and boundaries of sexual pleasure

Because social sanction for CNM is low, clients themselves may be prone to mis-identify nonmonogamy as their primary problem. Sex-positive therapy is critical, and clinicians have the duty to pursue education about CNM relationships, now readily available in multiple books, articles and websites (see Table 15.3)

TABLE 15.3 Nonmonogamy Resources

https://www.morethantwo.com
http://www.lovemore.com/polyamory/
Anapol, D. (2010). *Polyamory in the 21st Century.* United Kingdom: Roman & Littlefield.
Barker, M., & Langdridge, D. (Eds.). (2010). *Understanding Non-Monogamies.* London: Routledge.
Block, J. (2008). *Open: Love, Sex and Life in an Open Marriage.* Berkeley, CA: Seal Press.
Bergstrand, C., & Sinski, J. (2010). *Swinging in America: Love, Sex, and Marriage in the 21st Century.* Santa Barbara, CA: Praeger.
Easton, D., & Hardy, J. (2009). *The Ethical Slut: A Practical Guide to Polyamory, Open Relationships & Other Adventures.* Berkeley, CA: Celestial Arts.
Hardy, J. (1997). *The Ethical Slut: A Practical Guide to Polyamory, Open Relationships & Other Adventures.* Berkeley, CA: Celestial Arts.
Ravenscroft, A. (2004). *Polyamory: Roadmaps for the Clueless & Hopeful.* Santa Fe, NM: Crossquarter Publishing Group.
Savage, D. (2013). https://www.youtube.com/watch?v=C-laWOpXxC8
Veaux, F., & Rickert, E. (2014). *More Than Two: A Practical Guide to Ethical Polyamory.* Portland, OR: Thorntree Press.

Transgender

Gender, often used as one of the world's clearest examples of a binary (male/female), is in fact incredibly complex biologically and across cultures and history. *Gender identity* refers to the subjective experience of one's own gender. *Gender expression* refers to the ways in which one presents gender externally. Both of these can differ from the biological sex or gender we are assigned at birth. When a person is *transgender*, his or her gender identity differs from the assigned gender. *Cisgender* refers to the opposite (and much more common) experience: one's assigned gender at birth aligns with one's gender identity (GLAAD, 2014).

A person's gender expression is not necessarily tied to gender identity or assigned gender. Those who cross-dress, for instance, may have a gender expression that differs from their gender identity (a cisgender male may sometimes cross-dress as a female); cross-dressing is not the same thing as being transgender. The word transvestite, though still in use in the *DSM-5*, is considered outdated (GLAAD, 2014). *Transsexual* is another term growing out of favor, but which some people who want to or have made a medical transition from male to female (MTF) or from female to male (FTM) may prefer; therapists should follow clients' leads in self-labeling. Some individuals identify as genderqueer (a nonspecific and nonbinary gender identity) (GLAAD, 2014), gender atypical, gender nonconforming or androgynous. *Intersex* refers to those born with ambiguous genitalia (Lev & Sennott, 2012).

Gender identity (the subjective experience of one'
sexual orientation, which refers to the gender of '
and/or romantically attracted to. A transgender or
attracted to men, women, both, neither (asexua)'
A FTM transgender person who is attracted to '
because he is a male who is attracted to women.

Clients who are transgender may choose to transition t~
affirm socially (living, dressing, and/or presenting as their affirm~
changing names and pronouns), medically (hormonal therapy and/or ge~.
reassignment surgery), both or neither.

Gender Dysphoria

Gender dysphoria is the marked incongruence between one's gender identity and
one's biological or assigned gender, which is experienced as distressful to the
individual. Additionally, it causes impairment in social, school/occupational, or
other important areas of functioning (American Psychiatric Association, 2013).
This condition is not transient; the individual is symptomatic for greater than
6 months and it sometimes persists for their lifespan; many, if not most transgender individuals' dysphoria begins in early childhood. Previously referred to
as *Gender Identity Disorder* in *DSM-IV* (American Psychiatric Association, 1994),
the new diagnosis shifts the focus to distress as the clinical problem, rather than
identity. Individuals are required to have a diagnosis in order to get insurance
coverage for medical treatments such as hormone therapy and gender reassignment surgery (American Psychiatric Association, 2013).

Transgender Issues

Transgender people are frequently judged, discriminated against and harassed,
and they are disproportionately targets of extreme and gruesome violence and
murder (National Coalition of Anti-Violence Programs, 2013). They are often
rejected by their families of origin and face *transprejudice* in many facets of life,
including school, work, religion, the legal system and other public institutions.
Transgender individuals have been historically marginalized and pathologized
by the mental health community (American Counseling Association, 2010).

Treatment Implications

Transgender clients are often wary of mental health professionals and may
have even encountered clinicians who have attempted to change their gender identity. Many transgender clients have internalized shame, profound body
image issues particularly concerning their genitalia and confusion over gender-
role behavior (Lev & Sennott, 2012). If a transgender client is transitioning

ly, hormone therapy and surgical treatments can impact his or her sex ositively, negatively or in mixed ways.

Some healthcare providers require a referral from a psychotherapist before allowing a transgender person to begin medical transition, and some do not. The World Professional Association for Transgender Health (WPATH) Standards of Care have been updated to no longer require psychotherapy as a precursor for medical transition (WPATH, 2012), and in many major cities clients will not need clearance from a psychotherapist, but some medical professionals in underserved areas may still require it. Clients may seek therapy for any number of reasons: to obtain such a referral; to process distress and decision making; for assistance with family and relational discord over their gender identity and transition process; or for the same reasons gender-conforming people do— concerns about sexual practices, sexual gratification and sexual intimacy (Lev & Sennott, 2012).

Transgender clients are an extremely vulnerable group with a high rate of trauma (National Coalition of Anti-Violence Programs, 2013), suicide attempts and suicide, particularly in younger persons. The data are somewhat varied but the rate of suicide attempts is reported to be as high as 41% for trans men and 18% for trans women (Maguen & Shipherd, 2010). Transgender clients suffer from numerous issues in addition to those mentioned previously, including psychiatric comorbid factors (e.g. depression and substance abuse), a history of forced sex, gender-based discrimination and gender-based victimization (Clements-Nolle, Marx, & Katz, 2006).

Therapist Competency

It is necessary to assume a nonjudgmental and nonpathologizing position that is sensitive to transgender clients and their partners, particularly when uncomfortable dealing with gender nonconformity. Countertransference can block treatment or, even worse, damage a client's sexuality and self-esteem (Lev & Sennott, 2012). It is critical that therapists recognize and challenge internalized prejudice and discrimination against transgender individuals and rely on approaches supported by research and best practices (American Counseling Association, 2010). Consulting with and seeking supervision from experienced transgender-affirming clinicians is also recommended. Other considerations for transgender clients are the use of sensitive intake paperwork (providing nonbinary gender options and space to denote preferred pronouns), offering private and/or unisex restrooms and being aware of the physical safety of their transgender clients by allowing them to choose whom they disclose to.

Gender assumptions are deeply built into our understanding of the world and our language; it takes effort and flexibility to adjust to new understandings about gender. Using the client's preferred pronouns (especially when they choose neutral pronouns such as they/them) may be a challenge at first but is a

TABLE 15.4 Transgender Resources

- World Professional Association for Transgender Health: http://www.wpath.org
- Transline: transgender medical consultation service for healthcare providers: http://project-health.org/transline
- http://web.mit.edu/trans
- http://www.glaad.org/transgender/trans101
- http://www.hrc.org/resources/category/transgender
- http://community.pflag.org/transgender
- http://mazzonicenter.org/publications
- Angello, M. (2013). *On the Couch with Dr. Angello: A Guide to Raising and Supporting Transgender Youth*. West Yorkshire, England: Mira Publishing.
- Butt, R. (2013). *Now what? For families with Trans and Gender-Nonconforming Children*. Indianapolis, IN: Dog Ear Publishing.
- Ehrensaft, D. (2011). *Gender Born, Gender Made: Raising Healthy Gender-Nonconforming Children*. New York: The Experiment.
- Krieger, I. (2011). *Helping Your Transgender Teen: A Guide for Parents*. New Haven, CT: Genderwise Press.
- Lev, A.I. (2004). *Transgender Emergence: Counseling Gender Diverse People and Their Families*. New York: Routledge.
- Teich, N.M. (2012). *Transgender 101: A Simple Guide to a Complex Issue*. New York: Columbia University Press.

---

critical competency for alliance building, and apologizing for errors is recommended. Therapists must apply self-compassion in concert with compassion for their transgender client's distress and life challenges, while seeking ongoing education to increase their understanding. Some educational resources are listed in Table 15.4.

Paraphilias

Sexual behavior is extremely diverse, ranging from the playful to the harmful. Many kinky clients engage in consensual paraphilias. A paraphilia is generally defined as an atypical sexual interest or practice. The professional literature has used a number of definitions but the most recent is "any intense and persistent sexual interest other than sexual interest in genital stimulation or preparatory fondling with phenotypically normal physiologically mature consenting human partners" (American Psychiatric Association, 2013, p. 685). The *DSM-5* (American Psychiatric Association, 2013) distinguishes between paraphilia and paraphilic *disorder* in that the disorder causes distress or impairment to the individual; a paraphilia does not. Additionally, a paraphilic disorder entails personal harm or another person's psychological distress, injury or death, or a desire for sexual behaviors involving unwilling persons or persons unable to give legal consent (American Psychiatric Association, 2013). A number of the common paraphilias are listed in Table 15.5.

TABLE 15.5 *DSM-5* Paraphilias

Voyeurism	Spying on others in private activities
Exhibitionism	Exposing the genitals
Frotteurism	Nonconsensual touching or rubbing against another person
Sexual Masochism	Eroticized humiliation bondage or suffering
Sexual Sadism	Inflicting humiliation bondage or suffering on others
Pedophilia	Sexually arousing fantasies, sexual urges or behaviors involving children
Fetishism	Using nonliving objects or having a highly specific focus on nongenital body parts
Transvestitism	Sexually arousing cross-dressing

There is a lack of clinical literature and research on the assessment and treatment of paraphilias, and the research focuses mainly on offenders (Balon, 2013). Of the 547 paraphilias listed by Aggrawal (2009), the eight listed in Table 15.5 are discussed in detail in the *DSM-5* because they are the most common, noxious (a term used in the *DSM-5*) and potentially harmful to others when nonconsensual (American Psychiatric Association, 2013).

Individuals who engage in consensual paraphilias will not likely enter psychotherapy because the paraphilic activity is not causing personal or interpersonal distress. For instance, many who practice varieties of BDSM do so for their own personal/interpersonal/erotic satisfaction. However, some individuals with paraphilic disorders may enter treatment because of personal or interpersonal embarrassment, discomfort, guilt, shame, distress and so on. For instance, a male college student sought treatment because he was unable to give up his attraction to pregnant women. He spent countless hours looking at images of pregnant women and masturbating to these images. Even if not masturbating he looked for opportunities to view pregnant women clothed or unclothed.

Another source of personal distress is sexual dysfunction that is powered by paraphilic fantasy. For instance, a paraphilia can be the underlying cause of the lack of desire or erectile disorder. The individual's fantasies cannot be experienced with the primary partner or may be so divergent from the actual sexual partner that arousal is difficult or impossible. Also, fetishistic sexual fantasies are often atypical, potentially causing shame and embarrassment in the person with the fetish and disinterest in the sexual partner.

Treatment Implications

As a precondition in conducting any sex history, detailed information is gathered about sexual fantasies with all sexual disorders, particularly those that may result from hidden arousal patterns. When dealing with clients with paraphilias that are not consensually engaged, therapists should be prepared to use a number of different treatment options because one treatment might not work consistently. The final alternative is to consult a specialist in dealing with fetishes, often a forensic sex therapist, if unfamiliar with treating paraphilias. For a more detailed discussion of the assessment and treatment of paraphilias, see Fedoroff (2010). When paraphilias are safe, and consensually explored, therapists must be aware of and challenge countertransference.

Asexuality

As evidenced in Kinsey's "Category X," a small minority of the population has consistently expressed a lack of sexual attraction to others (Van Houdenhove, Gijs, T'Sjoen, & Enzlin, 2014). Today, this increasingly visible minority are sometimes identifying as asexual, denoting an ego-syntonic (in harmony with one's self-esteem) lack of sexual attraction. Asexual identity can be complex and may challenge the therapist's assumptions about sexuality.

Is Asexuality an Orientation?

The asexual community, mainly coalescing online around the Asexual Visibility & Education Network (AVEN), largely supports the classification of asexuality as an orientation rather than a disorder (AVEN, 2014a). Many have experienced a lifelong lack of sexual attraction (Brotto & Yule, 2011), although self-identification as asexual also allows for acquired lack of attraction (AVEN, 2014b). Just as homosexuality and heterosexuality are conceptualized as existing on a continuum, so do asexual individuals conceptualize their level of sexual attraction toward others. The question of how low a person's level of sexual attraction must be to qualify as asexual is thus far subjective.

Asexual research subjects clarify that they do not experience aversion or anxiety regarding partnered sexual activity, but instead find it uninteresting or "boring" (Prause & Graham, 2007). It is critical to understand that asexuality is not an absolute lack of sexual desire, arousal or interest; self-reported masturbation rates among asexual men and women are consistent with the general population (Brotto & Yule, 2011). The difference, rather, is that asexual desire is "not oriented toward another person" (Van Houdenhove et al., 2014, p. 180). Initial research into a biological basis for asexuality has found that these individuals lack desire for any person (Yule, Brotto, & Gorzalka, 2014); however, research data about asexuality are scarce.

Distinguishing from the Lack of Sexual Interest/Arousal or Desire

One critical difference cited between asexuality and the lack of sexual interest/ arousal or desire is distress: people who lack sexual interest or arousal are often (but not always) distressed by it. Conversely, only a minority (10%) of self-identified asexual individuals report that their lack of sexual attraction to others distresses them (Brotto, Knudson, Inskip, Rhodes, & Erskine, 2010). Because distress is subjective and possibly relational, further research is needed to clarify the sources of distress in interest/arousal and desire disorders and its absence in asexuality.

Current thinking also posits that those with low/absent sexual interest/desire still experience sexual attraction, without interest or desire, whereas, those who are asexual may experience desire, but without attraction to another person (Van Houdenhove et al., 2014). A study using vaginal pulse amplitude measures found no psychophysiological arousal dysfunction in asexual women (Brotto & Yule, 2011).

Assessment and Treatment Issues

Asexual identity can be complex; individuals may place themselves on continua that separate *romantic* attraction from *sexual* attraction (AVEN, 2014b; Steelman & Hertlein, in press). A number of resources regarding asexuality are listed in Table 15.6.

Relational issues in discordant asexual/sexual couples may require negotiation of consensual but unilaterally desired sexual interaction (Brotto & Yule, 2011); a subset may resolve this discordancy with consensual nonmonogamy (Scherrer, 2010). Brotto et al. (2010) discovered a substantial portion of their (small) asexual sample satisfied criteria for Schizoid Personality Disorder and noted that AVEN members sometimes discuss potential overlap with the Asperger's community.

Steelman and Hertlein (in press) propose the structure of relational treatment with an asexual individual should be flexible to allow for different roles in treatment, allowing for focus on the individual or the couple, and using one member of the couple as a cotherapist. Phases of treatment include joining and then moving onto clarifying the couple's sexual and romantic typologies. Therapists then challenge assumptions associated with being in a couple (i.e., what is the expected behavior for a couple?). The final phase is to develop an agreed-upon definition of how affection is expressed in the relationship.

TABLE 15.6 Asexuality Resources

- AsexualVisibility & Education Network (AVEN): http://www.asexuality.org
- Decker, J.S. (2014). *The Invisible Orientation*. New York, NY: Carrel Books
- Tucker, A. (Director) (2011). *(A)sexual* [Documentary film]. United States

Countertransference Issues

When working with asexual clients, therapists are obligated to monitor their own assumptions about healthy sexuality, sexual attraction, interest and desire. Furthermore, they should be aware that self-identified asexual individuals do not report feeling emotionally closer to their partner after sex and are not distressed by their lack of sexual attraction (Prause & Graham, 2007). Suppositions about the inseparability of sexual and romantic attraction must also be explored and challenged, both in the clinician and the client. Competency includes education about the varied continua of sexual and romantic expression, and potential barriers that might arise due to rigid beliefs about sexual normativity. Moreover, the clinician is required to be open to and supportive of complex identities the asexual clients might affirm.

Tantric Sex

We include a brief description of Tantra because it is a sexual practice as well as a philosophy related to eroticism, sex and intimacy. It is unlikely that the sex therapists will encounter couples whose presenting problem is the practice of Tantra; however, some clients may incorporate tantric exercises in lovemaking and therapists should be familiar with its basic principles.

Tantra refers to the broad body of knowledge that integrates sexuality and spirituality. Tantric principles originate from Hindu writings that incorporate sexual rituals, disciplines and meditations utilizing breathing, movement, sound, visualization and touch. Its practice is over 2,000 years old and has become increasingly popular in Western culture (Muir & Muir, 1989). In Tantra, the ultimate goal or purpose of sex is not simply to achieve orgasm but rather sexual and spiritual intimacy. Other principles of tantric practice include the idea that both men and women can experience multiple and extended orgasms and that an orgasm can include diverse affective states (Lousada & Angel, 2011). We have noted that among the general population, the commonly held belief is that Tantra is an esoteric form of sexuality that is only designed to create more intense or extended orgasms. This belief underrepresents the numerous facets and benefits of tantric practice

Therapeutic Application

Tantric methods can be helpful in the therapeutic setting as an adjunct to other sex therapy techniques (see Barratt & Rand, 2007). Tantra affirms the holistic naturalness of sexual expression, enabling a therapeutic focus far greater than anatomical and physiological functions. As with mindfulness techniques, Tantra facilitates understanding and honoring mind-body interconnectedness and integrates sexuality with emotional and spiritual connectedness. Similarly,

TABLE 15.7 Tantra Resources

- Anand, M. (1989). *The Art of Sexual Ecstasy*. New York: Tarcher/Putnam.
- Carrellas, B. (2007). *Urban Tantra: Sacred Sex for the Twenty-First Century*. Berkeley, CA: Celestial Arts.
- Kuriansky, J. (2002). *The Complete Idiot's Guide to Tantric Sex*. Indianapolis, IN: Alpha.
- Macleod, Don, & Macleod, Debra. (2008). *The Tantric Sex Deck: 50 Paths to Sacred Sex & Lasting Love*. San Francisco, CA: Chronicle Books.
- Richardson, D. (2003). *The Heart of Tantric Sex: A Unique Guide to Love & Sexual Fulfillment*. Hants, UK: O Books.
- www.tantra.com
- www.secretgardenpublishing.com
- http://www.davidyarian.com/tantra-and-ecstatic-sexuality-resources.htm

---

mindfulness therapy incorporates an awareness of one's thoughts, feelings and sensations in the present moment, without judgment (Sipe & Eisendrath, 2012). Tantra recognizes that erotic life and emotional life are inseparable, enabling clients to have a more complete sensual experience that embodies passion and emotion. For clients with trauma histories, tantric practice goes beyond sensate focus to help them release somatic blockages and emotional inhibitors. For conflicted clients, tantric practice helps them to overcome internalized scripts of shame/guilt/fear/anxiety about body functioning. Finally, the practice of Tantra offers individuals and couples new ways of communicating that can deepen empathy and understanding. A list of resources regarding tantric sex appears in Table 15.7.

In sum, tantric practices encourage an emotional connection to the partner, sensuality as a goal in itself and the lack of a performance orientation (Lousada & Angel, 2011). Additionally, mindfulness exercises intentionally advocate compassion, affection, receptivity and nonjudgmental interactions (Kozlowski, 2013). Existential approaches, which can also be incorporated in treatment, inspire an understanding of the multiple meanings of sex within the internal and wider existent worlds of the partners (Barker, 2011). Each of these modalities directly or indirectly supports our Intersystem Approach, enriches our therapeutic strategies and is well tolerated by our clients.

Therapist Competency with Diversity in Sexual Expression

Countertransference Issues

Given the strong reactions that people in society have to nonconforming types of sexuality, it is not only important to understand the experience of the client(s) who may have been stigmatized, marginalized and subjected to discrimination and violence. Equally important is the fact that therapists are also the products of their society and may therefore be prone to a range of countertransference reactions. It is surprising how little attention has been given to this issue in the literature. Since countertransference usually derives from unconscious beliefs, the insidious nature of the process must be carefully monitored during the course of therapy.

We have underscored the importance of therapist awareness and competency in working with all of the diverse groups mentioned in this chapter. In a recent article, Pillai-Friedman, Pollitt, and Castaldo (2014) proposed that therapists are responsible to do *more* than the required work for sex therapy certification, starting with participation in specialized experiential education that exposes, analyzes and addresses negative feelings and attitudes about all areas of sexual functioning, especially nonconforming expressions of sexuality. The next step is focused didactic education of both scholarly and popular works on diverse sexual practices. Finally, focused supervision is recommended to develop the necessary skills, which will take therapists to greater levels of proficiency and self-understanding. To the extent possible, educational, experiential and supervisory methods may be used to prevent countertransference.

Not all cases of countertransference can be prevented. How is a therapist to know if he or she is playing out countertransference? We believe some of the following may be indicators of countertransference:

- Overidentification with the client's sexual identity or expression
- Underidentification or rejection/judgment of the client's sexual identity or expression
- A feeling of discomfort in working with the client
- Avoiding or dreading working with the client
- A feeling of disgust or repulsion regarding the client's sexual identity or expression
- Feeling distracted during the session
- Trying too hard to be understanding and empathetic to the client
- A recognition that the therapist is not reacting in the same manner (feeling, attitudes, cognitions, behaviors) that are typical in other sex therapy cases

Thus, we have an ongoing, ethical responsibility to remain educated, informed and self-aware in working with all aspects of sexual expression.

Recognizing Transference Issues

Often, in search of a safe psychotherapeutic environment, many clients seek treatment with openly LGBT therapists; however, therapy's effectiveness is not necessarily determined by presumed similarities between client and therapist. A better way to evaluate competence is to openly discuss similarities and differences and incorporate such discussions for the purpose of relationship building in the psychotherapeutic process.

As with any client, queer clients will experience transference feelings toward the therapist. Some of these feelings might be universal, such as feeling loved, understood, misunderstood and eroticized. Other transference reactions might be about being uncomfortable with the straight therapist. The client might be suspicious, defensive, frightened or awkward because of the differences in gender presentation between himself or herself and the therapist. Clinicians should expect that gender-diverse clients might hold their own set of prejudices about gender-conforming therapists and might expect heteronormative assumptions and privileges to be operating in the therapist.

The reverse may also be true. Assume the therapist is openly gay or lesbian and the client is heterosexual. The client may assume the therapist will not be able to understand him or her. The client may also assume that the therapist may somehow, explicitly or implicitly, suggest he or she experiment with homosexual behavior. A client with mixed feelings about his or her sexual orientation may see the therapist as a warm and open person, but also begin to sexualize the therapist as a potential love object.

In cases of transference and countertransference any numbers of permutations are possible. One might assume it is somewhat unorthodox to even mention these concepts in a book dealing with a systemic approach to sex therapy because the early systems thinkers so assiduously avoided anything that was associated with psychoanalytic and psychodynamic concepts. Putting therapeutic camps aside, some concepts are useful irrespective of the general theoretical framework, and the Intersystem Approach is an inclusive rather than exclusionary frame.

References

Aggrawal, A. (2009). *Forensic and medico-legal aspects of sexual crimes and unusual sexual practices*. Boca Raton, FL: CRC Press.

American Counseling Association. (2010). Competencies for counseling with transgender clients. *Journal of LGBT Issues in Counseling, 4*(3/4), 135–159.

American Psychiatric Association. (1973). *Diagnostic and statistical manual of mental disorders* (2nd ed.). Arlington, VA: Author.

American Psychiatric Association. (1994). *Diagnostic and statistical manual of mental disorders* (4th ed.). Arlington, VA: Author.

American Psychiatric Association. (2013). *Diagnostic and statistical manual of mental disorders* (5th ed.). Arlington, VA: Author.

American Psychological Association. (2012). Guidelines for psychological practice with lesbian, gay, and bisexual clients. *Journal of the American Psychological Association, 67*(1), 10–42.

Asexual Visibility & Education Network [AVEN]. (2014a). AVENwiki: Sexual Orientation. Retrieved from http://www.asexuality.org/wiki/index.php?title=Sexual_orientation

Asexual Visibility & Education Network [AVEN]. (2014b). General FAQ. Retrieved from http://www.asexuality.org/home/?q=general.html

Balon, R. (2013). Controversies in the diagnosis and treatment of paraphilias. *Journal of Sex & Marital Therapy, 39*(1), 7–20.

Barash, D.P., & Lipton, J.E. (2002). *The myth of monogamy: Fidelity and infidelity in animals and people.* New York: Henry Holt.

Barker, M. (2011). Existential sex therapy. *Sexual and relationship therapy, 26*(1), 33–47.

Barratt, B.B., & Rand, M.A. (2007). On the relevance of tantric practices for clinical and educational sexology. *Contemporary Sexuality, 41*(2), 7–12.

Brandon, M. (2011). The challenge of monogamy: Bringing it out of the closet and into the treatment room. *Journal of Sexual and Relationship Therapy, 26*(3), 271–277.

Brooks, L., & Inman, A. (2013). Bisexual counseling competence: Investigating the role of attitudes and empathy. *Journal of LGBT Issues in Counseling, 7*(1), 65–86.

Brotto, L.A., Knudson, G., Inskip, J., Rhodes, K., & Erskine, Y. (2010). Asexuality: A mixed-methods approach. *Archives of Sexual Behavior, 39*, 599–618.

Brotto, L., & Yule, M.A. (2011). Physiological and subjective sexual arousal in self-identified asexual women. *Archives of Sexual Behavior, 40*, 699–712.

Chandra, A., Mosher, W.D., Copen, C., & Sionean, C. (2011). *Sexual behavior, sexual attraction, and sexual identity in the United States: Data from the 2006–2008 National Survey of Family Growth.* National Health Statistics Reports (No. 36). Hyattsville, MD: National Center for Health Statistics.

Clements-Nolle, K., Marx, R., & Katz, M. (2006). Attempted suicide among transgender persons: The influence of gender-based discrimination and victimization. *Journal of Homosexuality, 51*(3), 53–69.

Cohen, J.N., & Byers, E.S. (2014). Beyond lesbian bed death: Enhancing our understanding of the sexuality of sexual-minority women in relationships. *The Journal of Sex Research, 51*(8), 893–903. doi:10.1080/00224499.2013.795924

Conley, T.D., Moors, A.C., Ziegler, A., & Karathanasis, C. (2012). Unfaithful individuals are less likely to practice safer sex than openly nonmonogamous individuals. *The Journal of Sexual Medicine, 9*(6), 1559–1565.

Coontz, S. (2006). *Marriage, a history: How love conquered marriage.* New York: Penguin Books.

Diamond, L.M. (2014). *I was wrong! Men are pretty darn sexually fluid, too.* Austin, TX: Society for Personality and Social Psychology Preconference on Sexuality.

Easton, D., & Hardy, J. (2009). *The ethical slut: A practical guide to polyamory, open relationships & other adventures.* Berkeley, CA: Celestial Arts.

Fedoroff, J.P. (2010). Paraphilic worlds. In S.B. Levine, C. Risen, & S. Althof (Eds.), *Handbook of clinical sexuality for mental health professionals* (2nd ed.) (pp. 401–424). New York: Routledge.

Fisher, H. (2014). *10 facts about infidelity.* Retrieved from http://ideas.ted.com/2014/01/23/10-facts-about-infidelity-helen-fisher

Garcia, J.R., Lloyd, E.A., Wallen, K., & Fisher, H.E. (2014). Variation in orgasm occurrence by sexual orientation in a sample of U.S. singles. *Journal of Sexual Medicine, 11*, 2645–2652.

GLAAD. (2014). GLAAD media reference guide: Transgender issues. Retrieved from http://www.glaad.org/reference/transgender

Goldfeder, M., & Sheff, E. (2013). Children of polyamorous families: A first empirical look. *Journal of Law and Social Deviance, 5*, 150–243.

Graham, N. (2014). Polyamory: A call for increased mental health professional awareness. *Archives of Sexual Behavior, 43*(6), 1031–1034.

Hua, C. (2008). *A society without fathers or husbands: The Na of China.* Brooklyn, NY: Urzone, Inc.

Iasenza, S. (2004). Multicontextual sex therapy with lesbian couples. In S. Green & D. Flemons (Eds.), *Quickies: The handbook of brief sex therapy* (pp. 15–25). New York: W.W. Norton.

Iasenza, S. (2010). What is queer about sex? Expanding sexual frames in theory and practice. *Family Process, 49*(3), 291–308.

Kelsey, K., Stiles, B., Spiller, L., & Diekhoff, G. (2012). Assessment of therapists' attitudes towards BDSM. *Psychology and Sexuality, 4*(3), 255–267. doi:10.1080/194198 99.2012.655255

Kinsey, A., Pomeroy, W., & Martin, C. (1948). *Sexual behavior in the human male.* Philadelphia, PA: W.B. Saunders.

Kinsey, A., Pomeroy, W., Martin, C., & Gebhard, P. (1953). *Sexual behavior in the human female.* Philadelphia, PA: W.B. Saunders.

Kozlowski, A. (2013). Mindful mating: Exploring the connection between mindfulness and relationship satisfaction. *Sexual and Relationship Therapy, 28*(1–2), 92–104.

Lawrence, A.A., & Love-Crowell, J. (2008). Psychotherapists' experience with clients who engage in consensual sadomasochism: A qualitative study. *Journal of Sex & Marital Therapy, 34*(1), 67–85. doi:10.1080/00926230701620936

Lev, A.I., & Nichols, M. (2015). Sex therapy with lesbian and gay male couples. In K. Hertlein, G. Weeks, & N. Gambescia (Eds.), *Systemic sex therapy* (2nd ed.) (pp. 213–234). New York: Routledge.

Lev, A.I., & Sennott, S. (2012). Understanding gender nonconformity and transgender identity: A sex positive approach. In P.J. Kleinplatz (Ed.), *New directions in sex therapy* (pp. 321–336). New York: Routledge.

Lousada, M., & Angel, E. (2011). Tantric orgasm: Beyond Masters and Johnson. *Sexual and Relationship Therapy, 26*(4), 389–402.

Maguen, S., & Shipherd, J.C. (2010). Suicide risk among transgender individuals, *Psychology & Sexuality, 1*(1), 34–43.

McGeorge, C., & Stone Carlson, T. (2011). Deconstructing heterosexism: Becoming an LGB affirmative heterosexual couple and family therapist. *Journal of Marital & Family Therapy, 37*(1), 14–26.

Mena, J.A., & Vaccaro, A. (2013). Tell me you love me no matter what: Relationships and self-esteem among GLBQ young adults. *Journal of GLBT Family Studies, 9*(1), 3–23.

Mitchell, M.E., Bartholomew, K., & Cobb, R.J. (2014). Need fulfillment in polyamorous relationships. *Journal of Sex Research, 51*(3), pp. 329–339.

Morrison, T.G., Beaulieu, D., Brockman, M., & Beaglaoich, C.O. (2013). A comparison of polyamorous and monoamorous persons: Are there differences in indices of relationship well-being and sociosexuality? *Psychology & Sexuality, 4*(1), 75–91.

Muir, C., & Muir, C. (1989). *Tantra: The art of conscious loving.* San Francisco, CA: Mercury House.

National Coalition of Anti-Violence Programs. (2013). *Lesbian, gay, bisexual, transgender, queer, and HIV-affected hate violence in 2012.* New York: New York City Gay & Lesbian Anti-Violence Project.

Nichols, M. (2006). Psychotherapeutic issues with "kinky" clients: Clinical problems, yours and theirs. *Journal of Homosexuality, 50*(2/3), 281–300.

Pillai-Friedman, S., Pollitt, J.L., & Castaldo, A. (2014). Becoming kink-aware: A necessity for sexuality professionals. *Sexual and Relationship Therapy*, published online. doi:10.1080/14681994.2014.975681

Prause, N., & Graham, C.A. (2007). Asexuality: Classification and characterization. *Archives of Sexual Behavior, 36,* 341–356.

Rutter, P.A. (2012). Sex therapy with gay male couples using affirmative therapy. *Sexual & Relationship Therapy, 27*(1), 35–45.

Savage, D. (2012). *Meet the monogamish.* Retrieved from http://www.thestranger.com/seattle/SavageLove?oid=11412386

Scherrer, K.S. (2010). Asexual relationships: What does asexuality have to do with polyamory? In M. Barker & D. Langdridge (Eds.), *Understanding non-monogamies* (pp. 154–159). New York: Routledge.

Sipe, W., & Eisendrath, S. (2012). Mindfulness-based cognitive therapy: Theory and practice. *Canadian Journal of Psychiatry, 57*(2), 63–69.

Steelman, S., & Hertlein, K.M. (in press). Asexuality: A primer for MFTs. *Journal of Family Psychotherapy.*

Stiles, B., & Clark, R.E. (2011). BDSM: A subcultural analysis of sacrifices and delights. *Deviant Behavior, 32,* 158–189.

Van Houdenhove, E., Gijs, L., T'Sjoen, G., & Enzlin, P. (2014). Asexuality: Few facts, many questions. *Journal of Sex & Marital Therapy, 40*(3), 175–192.

Veaux, F., & Rickert, E. (2014). *More than two: A practical guide to ethical polyamory.* Portland, OR: Thorntree Press.

Wismeijer, A.J., & van Assen, A.M. (2013). Psychological characteristics of BDSM practitioners. *The Journal of Sexual Medicine, 10*(8), 1943–1952.

Wosick, K. (2012). *Sex, love, and fidelity: A study of contemporary romantic relationships.* Amherst, NY: Cambria Press.

World Professional Association for Transgender Health [WPATH]. (2012). Standards of care for the health of transsexual, transgender, and gender-nonconforming people. *International Journal of Transgenderism, 13*(4), 165–232.

Yost, M. (2010). Development and validation of the attitudes about sadomasochism scale. *Journal of Sex Research, 47,* 79–91.

Yule, M.A., Brotto, L.A., & Gorzalka, B.B. (2014). Biological markers of asexuality: Handedness, birth order, and finger length ratios in self-identified asexual men and women. *Archives of Sexual Behavior, 43*(2), 299–310.

Zimmerman, K.J. (2012). Clients in sexually open relationships: Considerations for therapists. *Journal of Feminist Family Therapy, 24*(3), 272–289.

16

ETHICS IN SEX THERAPY

Introduction

Rigorous professional and ethical standards apply to traditional psychotherapy. Sex therapists, however, have unique considerations beyond standard ethical issues, primarily because of the nature of their work. This chapter reviews specific obligatory concerns in sex therapy treatment, such as the responsibility of the therapist to understand his or her own ethical vulnerabilities that could obstruct treatment and a safe environment for the therapeutic work involving sexuality. Some of these issues involve the person of the therapist while others affect the way a case is identified, assessed and treated.

The Process and Structure of Treatment

Client Identification

There are several issues that sex therapists should consider throughout the process of treatment, including client identification, problem definition and goal setting (Kleinplatz, 2015). Client identification can be particularly complicated in sex therapy cases for several reasons. First, the couple coming to seek treatment is composed of two individuals who often have independent agendas and may try to build an alliance with the therapist in order to implement their agenda. For example, one couple came to treatment to address absent/low sexual interest in the wife. During the assessment, it became clear that her lack of desire was complicated by several factors, including physiological limitations (a back injury that compromised her ability to feel sensations), difficulty in being able to communicate her needs to her partner without feeling blamed and depression. Her hope was that therapy would "convince" her partner that he bore some responsibility for the sexual problems they were having, most notably related to his blameful attitude toward her and the disruption in their communication. His agenda in treatment was to "get help for her," not acknowledging any responsibility for his part in the treatment process. In this way, the husband viewed the sex therapy process as one by which he would function as a cotherapist in order to be of assistance to his partner rather than as a full participant in treatment.

The identified client is the symptom bearer in a couple or family system. This person is often a scapegoat whose symptoms distract the observer (the therapist) from the larger systemic family issues and dynamics. When a couple presents with a sexual or relational problem, even if one partner is the identified client, the couple is the focus of treatment; thus, if a client is partnered, the Intersystem view is that the couple is the identified client. Even when the therapist works mostly with one individual, the therapeutic effects will be experienced throughout the client/family system. Therefore, determining who is the identified client has significant implications for goal setting, intervention development and implementation and ultimately treatment compliance (Weeks & Gambescia, in press).

Clients may agree in session to treatment goals proposed by the therapist but secretly disagree individually or unconsciously collude to disagree. For example, in the case described earlier, if the therapist outlines treatment goals that engender both partners to be active in the treatment process, the therapist may be viewed by the husband as siding with the wife's agenda, thereby accepting no responsibility. The end result may be a premature termination or sabotaging interventions. For this reason, it is crucial that the therapist address the question of client identification *early* in the treatment process to avoid complications later in treatment.

A therapeutic reframe is often helpful in client identification because the couple is helped to understand the situation from another viewpoint, particularly when they are embedded in the cycle of a larger system, their partnership. If carefully constructed and presented, the reframe aids the partners in changing their view or meaning of a particular symptom (her problem) to one that is shared by the couple (their problem). If the reframe is successful, it will diffuse anger and promote empathy. The therapist must carefully reframe the problem in a way that includes the needs of both partners. The reframe allows for both partners to accept responsibility for the problem and its resolution (Weeks & Gambescia, in press). Therapy should not proceed beyond this point until the partners agree on their problem and goal of treatment based on a systemic frame of the problem.

Furthermore, what is in the best interest for the couple's relationship may contradict one or both agendas of the individuals within the couple (Hill & Coll, 1992; Weeks, Odell, & Methven, 2005). In the case described earlier, it seemed clear that each partner wanted to put the responsibility for the problem on the other. Blaming the other partner, however, is not likely to resolve the problem between the two. In this way, the therapist's agenda (preservation of the couple relationship) may be different than each individual's agenda. The therapist will need to proceed slowly and cautiously until both partners are ready to accept personal responsibility and until there is agreement between the agenda of the couple and that of the therapist.

Problem Definition

Couples often request treatment for a sexual problem or disorder. Frequently, the problem is mentioned during the initial contact. Once they enter treatment, however, the therapist becomes aware that the definition of the problem expands from the sexual symptomology to that of communication patterns, an individual's physical diagnoses or the messages received from one's family of origin related to sexuality or other issues. Consequently, in many sex therapy cases, clients and therapists can have difficulty clarifying the problem to be solved. The conceptualization of the problem ultimately guides treatment goals and interventions. As stated, it can take time and numerous conversations to agree about problems and implement proper treatment. Diagnosing or labeling too quickly, without a deeper understanding of the problem, hinders the clinician from further exploring the behavior (Kleinplatz, 2012). Further, labeling of the problem as a disorder may also be counterproductive to treatment because it can stigmatize or traumatize a client who already may feel ashamed or abnormal. It is incumbent upon the therapist to investigate all facets of the sexual problem or any consensual sexual behavior (including behavior not within the scope of the presenting problem) without bias or judgment. For instance, one couple presented for treatment because of the woman's recent lack of interest in sex. The therapist discovered that the couple had an agreement about consensual polyamory in which they engaged in sex with others under certain circumstances. The wife was upset that the husband had violated their agreement by having sex with another woman without telling her. His disclosure was upsetting to the wife and interfered with her trust and feelings of desire for her husband.

Goal Setting

Goal setting in sex therapy is an ethical issue because the direction of treatment can be influenced by the therapist's values, the values of the couple and societal norms. Which perspective takes priority and why? Inherent in the therapist-client relationship is the reality of a therapist's power. Regardless of the therapeutic stance or the therapist's intention, the client often ascribes greater power to the therapist. The therapist needs to be mindful of the values that are implicitly and explicitly imposed on the treatment process, particularly related to the development and implementation of goals. The therapist may find himself or herself advocating a certain position, set of attitudes or values and in fact be creating greater difficulty for clients. Too often clinicians impose their unstated goals of eliminating the symptom on the client, without asking about the client or couple's goals of treatment. Some clients seek outcomes from treatment that might not be aligned with those of the therapist; thus, limiting the possibilities of treatment does not honor the client(s) (Kleinplatz, 2012).

Another ethical issue arises for sex therapists in terms of goal setting when there are a variety of ways to conceptualize the problem (Kleinplatz, 2015). Sexual issues and relationship issues coincide, leaving the sex therapist with the task of determining whether improvement within the sexual relationship will lead to improvements within the dyadic relationship, or whether changes to the dyadic relationship will improve the sexual problem. Some couples will accept the notion that improvements within their relationship are necessary preconditions to moving ahead with sex therapy. Others, however, despite the therapist's beliefs regarding the etiology of the problem, are clear that the problem is only sexual and want to proceed immediately with sex therapy treatment. In such cases, the sex therapist needs to balance how to represent the feasibility of the client's goals while still engendering hope and confidence in the therapeutic process.

Range of Sex Therapy Practice

A sex therapist uses techniques in a specialized way and has knowledge of sexual functioning and dysfunction that implies a specific set of training, supervision and clinical experience. According to AASECT (American Association for Sexuality Educators, Counselors and Therapists) (2014), certified sex therapists are "licensed mental health professionals, trained to provide in-depth psychotherapy, who have specialized in treating clients with sexual issues and concerns. In the absence of available licensure, they are certified, registered, or clinical members of a national psychotherapy organization. Sex therapists work with simple sexual concerns also, but in addition, where appropriate, are prepared to provide comprehensive and intensive psychotherapy over an extended period of time in more complex cases." (See http://www.aasect.org/certification-types-distinguishing-sexuality-educators-counselors-and-therapists.) AASECT is the only certifying agency in the United States and worldwide.

Before advertising oneself as a sex therapist, a rigorous postgraduate training program must be completed. One example is the Council for Relationships Postgraduate Sex Therapy Program in Philadelphia, PA (http://councilforre lationships.org/professional-education/sex-therapy/), although there are others listed on the website. Applicants to this program are preselected only if adequately trained and experienced in individual and couple therapy. The process of sex therapy certification includes hundreds of hours of education, supervision with a certified AASECT supervisor, hundreds of clinical hours of sex therapy cases and numerous hours of values training such as a SAR (Sexual Attitude Reassessment). See the AASECT website for more details. Also, there is a rigorous recertification process, which involves demonstration of specified hours of ongoing continuing education.

For the sake of clarification, AASECT offers *certification* as a sex therapist; it is not a licensing agency. Sex therapy is an advanced specialty. The therapist must first be licensed as a physician, psychiatrist, psychologist, marriage and family therapist, social worker, counselor, nurse or other.

If you are not a certified sex therapist, be clear with your clients that, while you understand that sexual dysfunctions and problems are common, you are not certified to provide treatment and refer them to the appropriate referrals in your area. Unfortunately, we have had the experience of treating a number of couples who previously sought sex therapy from a therapist who alleged to be a sex therapist but lacked the skills, knowledge and certification to practice ethically and/or effectively. In most of these cases, the clients were the same or worse than when they started appropriate sex therapy. At the very least, they were now more skeptical and pessimistic that they could be helped to overcome their sexual problems because they had already experienced failure at the hands of someone they presumed knew how to practice sex therapy.

Referrals and Consultations in Sex Therapy

The number of qualified or certified professionals in sex therapy is actually small compared to the general population. In cases where a sex therapy referral is needed, the general therapist can visit the AASECT website (www.aasect.org). However, due to the low number of Certified Sex Therapists the client may need to commute some distance to find a qualified person. The Society for Sex Therapy and Research (http://www.sstarnet.org) is another professional association that specializes in sex therapy and research. It is not a certifying agency like AASECT, but many of their members are experts in the sex therapy field, although not all of them are certified. Some are researchers and others are prominent authors. Many of their members also have membership in AASECT, AAMFT (American Association of Marriage and Family Therapy), and other professional associations for couple and sex therapy.

Collaboration

Sex therapists are almost always in a position of having to deal with multiple factors in the etiology of a sexual problem. They cannot work in isolation but need to think of treatment in interdisciplinary terms. This fact requires the sex therapist to have many other professional resources with whom they can collaborate closely:

- Gynecologists and urologists
- Primary care physicians/internal medicine specialists/psychiatrists
- Pain management physicians
- Psychologists
- Physical therapists
- Clergy
- Specialists in the treatment of sexual compulsivity, disability, transgender issues and other subspecialists familiar with specific populations

The sex therapist will probably need to provide some education to other professionals about the nature of sex therapy and the fact that multiple etiologies may be involved and interact with each other. The professionals mentioned above usually have very limited training in treating sexual disorders. The sex therapist is at the hub of treatment, coordinating the goals and interventions of the other professionals. Unfortunately, some professionals do not understand the value of a collaborative relationship or want to take control of treatment despite of the fact that the problem is outside their scope of practice. Building a therapeutic team that works collaboratively is an essential part of being effective as a sex therapist.

Identifying Ethical Dilemmas in Sex Therapy

Gender Bias

The therapist must always be sensitive to gender biases operating in their clients and themselves. Although gender preconceptions are common in individual therapy, they are especially robust in couple therapy because of the possibility for triangulation based on gender. We often hear from individual and partnered clients as well as therapists that they *prefer* a male or female therapist for some specific reasons, often related to family-of-origin issues; thus, gender bias can be operative in the selection of a therapist even prior to the initial session. Often one partner can feel "outnumbered" simply because of the gender of the therapist. Other unconscious factors can be activated by the gender of the therapist such as expectations and feelings (based on social, cultural, etc. introjects) that emerge in the clients in the therapy setting.

Therapists are also subjected to gender biases related to social, political and other characteristics that are consciously or unconsciously tied to gender. For example, gender biases can affect the selection criteria of the diagnosis. As a result of the publication of the *DSM-5* (American Psychiatric Association, 2013), there has been debate over the disorders of sexual desire and how the diagnostic criteria are now different for men and women. Women are viewed as sexually passive, receptive and responsive while men are depicted as more determined, initiative and desirous of sexual activity (Spurgas, 2013). Thus, the definition of sexual desire may be driven by recent findings on the sexual response of women, but is also a result of heteronormative notions about healthy sexuality (Spurgas, 2013). Additionally, research designs, treatment goals and medications are marketed based on sociocultural notions and expectations of gender-based normative assumptions of the sexual response. Spurgas (2013) notes that diagnostically, men are typified with more performance-related problems such as erectile dysfunction, while women stereotypically psychologically block sexual enjoyment (p. 1). Therapists who have different standards of pathology for men and women are essentially reinforcing, consciously or unconsciously, heteronormative preconceptions about sex. This idea is not new. Previous accounts of gender biases in sex therapy exist:

• The presence of a double standard in mental health based on the sex role differences ascribed to sex role stereotyping and how one is adjusted to one's environment (Rieker & Carmen, 1983).
• "The diagnosis of sexual dysfunction, which appears at first to be objective and factual, is based in part on a complex chain of values and beliefs" (Brown & Sollod, 1988, p. 389).
• Healthy women were considered more submissive, less adventurous, more suggestive, less competitive, less illogical and less objective (Broverman, Vogel, Voverman, Clarkson, & Rosenkrantz, 1972).

Gender biases also have implications for problems that are not major sexual disorders. Hecker, Trepper, Wetchler and Fontaine (1995) found that if a therapist believes that men tend to engage in infidelity more often than women, and is seeing a couple where a woman has engaged in infidelity, the therapist might view the women as more pathological because it does not fit the norm. Hertlein (2004) investigated therapists' biases in the treatment of Internet infidelity cases. Although most therapists overtly reported that their treatment would not differ depending on the gender of the identified client, the data as a whole indicated the opposite.

There is the potential for sex therapists to be unaware that they are reinforcing gender role stereotypes. For example, a sex therapist may place a greater value on the man achieving orgasm in the relationship than the woman, stemming from the belief that this is more important to men. In this instance, the first interventions might be designed to manage the man's issue within treatment and give less priority to the woman's problems and goals (Handy, Valentich, Cammaert, & Gripton, 1985). Kleinplatz (2015) advises that sex therapists should conduct balanced assessments, which give equal airtime to the interests of both parties.

Another byproduct of gender biasing is the inadvertent circumvention of the underlying couple dynamics. As we have stated previously in this book, underlying feelings of resentment, fear of intimacy, fear of commitment and other relational issues will influence how a couple presents for therapy, their identification of the presenting problem, the selection of the identified client and so on. Moreover, a sexual disorder in one partner might be a reflection of a sexual problem in the other. Couples do not often state this at the beginning of therapy; consequently, it is up to the therapist to investigate this very common yet unstated phenomenon. See McCabe and Goldhammer (2012).

Religious Issues in the Therapist and Client

Religion is closely tied to culture, race, ethnicity and the self-identification of the therapist and client. Religious principles are deeply embedded in the value system of the therapist and clients; therefore, these values can affect the conceptualization of a sex therapy case and the treatment plan. See Hall and Graham (2012) for a more detailed discussion of cultural issues. Therapists cannot select clients who share their religious belief system; therefore, therapists must be comfortable in dealing with all aspects of a client's reality, particularly religion. The therapist can unintentionally view the client's sexual behaviors through a judgmental lens due to the unrecognized influence of religious values on treatment. For example, marital and family therapists with strong religious beliefs were found to demonstrate lower levels of comfort working with lesbian and gay male clients (Green, Murphy, & Blumer, 2010). In another study, therapists were offered strategies to assist them in their efforts to support the integration of sexual orientation and religion for lesbian and gay clients who are coming out (Bowland, Foster, & Vosler, 2013).

We are continuing to see attention to religion and sexuality in the clinical literature. Additionally, we have noted that religious biases are sometimes noted in postgraduate clinical clergy trainees and supervisees. In one instance, a training therapist admitted that he felt that homosexuality was "wrong." This example reinforces that the therapist is responsible to examine any prejudice, religious or otherwise, that would create an unsafe environment for conducting psychotherapy (Hertlein, 2011; Iasenza, 2010). This process can be accomplished through additional supervision, experiential exercises and personal psychotherapy.

Research emphasizes the importance of understanding that therapist religiosity can be a factor in hindering a therapeutic relationship and inadvertently harming the client. Therapists who indicated that they were highly religious rated clients in vignettes regarding sexual behavior as more pathological than therapists who indicated lower levels of religiosity (Hecker, Trepper, Wetchler, & Fontaine, 1995). Therapists also regarded single persons engaging in intercourse with multiple partners as more pathological than married persons engaging in sex with the same frequency. Hertlein and Piercy (2008) also found that more religious therapists were more likely to view clients in Internet infidelity scenarios as sex addicted and viewed the problem the couple was facing as more severe than therapists with lower levels of religiosity. Thus, more religious therapists found the presenting problems to be more damaging to the relationship. These examples are presented as a warning about the potential for therapists to unconsciously interject a religious bias into sex therapy. The examples are not intended as a criticism of more religious therapists, just as a cautioning for all therapists.

Secrets in Therapy

There can be times when ethical issues related to secrets in sex therapy may emerge. This situation is especially prone to happen when one partner is seen individually or communicates something to the therapist outside the session. For example, in one case, a client who called for treatment admitted to the therapist that she noted her orgasm problems began as a result of a fight she and her partner had, while her partner believed the problem to be related to the medication she was taking. Neither one wanted the other to know about their thoughts regarding the etiology of the woman's lack of interest in sex. In another case, a client admitted to having an affair and therefore knew that the sexual problems he was having were specific to his partner rather than generalized. The therapist, in each example, was confronted with the dilemma of how to conduct therapy when there is an active affair or how to proceed in the best interest of the couple. Each of these scenarios must be managed delicately by a therapist to avoid becoming triangulated within the client system (Weeks, Gambescia, & Jennings, 2003).

Schneider and Levinson (2006) outlined the ethical issues specifically related to the disclosure of secrets in treatment. Three considerations for therapists to consider are (1) what happens if the secret is revealed, (2) what happens if the secret is not disclosed and (3) the effect on the therapist/therapeutic process if the secret is not disclosed. Therapists must also make a decision as to whether to see each member of the couple together or separately, or a combination of the two.

Weeks, Odell, and Methven (2005), Weeks, Gambescia, and Jennings (2003), and Weeks and Fife (2014) provide an extensive discussion of the rules of confidentiality in treatment. The rule they suggest is based on the idea that confidence will be maintained if there are individual sessions intermixed with the sex/couple therapy as long as the information about various problems or secrets does not interfere with the progress of treatment. In some cases, individual therapy may be needed at either the client's or the therapist's request. If there is a secret preventing progress, the partner in the individual sessions is requested to reveal the secret to his or her partner. If that partner fails to do so, the therapist may unilaterally terminate therapy by telling the couple there is an individual issue that is preventing progress, but not reveal the content of the secret. At this point, the other partner knows there is a secret and will choose whether to pursue learning what it might be. In fact, partners often know the nature of the secret but do not want to deal with it until they realize they cannot develop a better relationship as long as they deny it. The use of this strategy is vastly more complex than described here. For readers searching for more options in dealing with secrets such as incest, past and present infidelity, addictions, negative thoughts they do not want to share with the partner that they think would be hurtful and so on, readers should carefully examine the texts mentioned previously.

Boundaries in Sex Therapy

In addition to the countertransference issues discussed in other areas of this chapter, we feel it is essential for the therapist to clearly monitor and delineate the boundaries between the client and the therapist because boundary violations can occur without the therapist's full awareness. For instance, the therapist might collude with one partner without realizing. Also the therapist might set up an idealistic goal that is not the goal requested by the couple. Also therapists can circumvent some of the feelings that clients wish to discuss in therapy due to their own discomfort. In all of these examples, a boundary violation can indirectly occur (see Ravella, 2007).

The therapist must be ethical, resolute and vigilant in looking for potential areas in which boundary violations can occur. Physical violations can arise in many ways: The therapist can accidentally see a client in a situation outside of the therapy session. Additionally, the therapist can violate a time boundary by allowing a session to go on too long because of a particularly positive feeling about a client. Another potential area for boundary violation is revealing intimate facts about oneself to the client in order to help the client feel more comfortable, when, in fact, the therapist is attempting to manage his or her own anxiety. Although this might seem like we are stating the obvious, the therapist must be particularly mindful about protecting private facts about a client or couple in treatment. For instance, many of us teach in postgraduate programs and present case material during class or at sex therapy clinical conferences. This is a particularly delicate area and, if the case is presented for teaching purposes, identifying information must be changed in order to protect the confidentiality of clients. Finally, the use of emails for discussion of personal material is not advised, particularly in sex therapy cases. The Internet is not a safe place for conducting email psychotherapy or protecting confidentiality. Furthermore, another boundary is being violated if the client sends long emails and expects the therapist to read them without discussion of the fee for this sort of service. It is prudent to utilize email for scheduling purposes only. Finally there's the issue of gift giving. This is particularly difficult because a small gift might be an expression of gratitude; however, it could reflect a lot more than an innocent feeling. The therapist must carefully decide if and when to except a gift from the client and to be sure that the meaning of the gift is thoroughly discussed and understood.

Erotic transference can present a challenge for the client and therapist in all therapies, particularly sex therapy. In this area, the therapist needs to be particularly clear about boundaries, yet considerate and compassionate. First, the therapist must always dress professionally and appropriately. Dress details are often discussed in codes of ethics of professional associations. Essentially, the therapist should never dress in a manner that can be misinterpreted by the client. Additionally, the therapist must be careful to use humor judiciously and not to speak in innuendo because an unclear communication can leave room for an inaccurate interpretation.

Also, the therapist must be keenly aware of the line that can be crossed in both the acceptance and expression of positive emotions toward the client. Although it is expected that the client is appreciative of the therapist's caring and nonjudgmental attitude, any discussion beyond this topic should be carefully monitored and circumvented. A general rule is this: if the therapist must set a limit, it is important to attend to the client's feelings. In one situation, the therapist needed to set boundaries on a client's discussion of the sexual activity that he particularly enjoyed. It became apparent to the therapist that the client was engaging in needless discussion of particular behaviors. Processing of this topic, although difficult and sensitive, was helpful in that it set a clear message about boundaries and provided an opportunity for the client to reflect about how he comes across when talking to others about sexuality.

For a more detailed discussion of professional boundaries in clinical sexuality, see Plaut (2010) and Weeks, Gambescia, and Jennings (2003). Sex therapists must be particularly knowledgeable about their own areas of vulnerability to boundary violations. Furthermore, they should engage in self-care through maintenance of a balanced lifestyle in which affirmation can come from a number of different sources, not just from therapy clients.

Managing Ethical Dilemmas

Managing ethical dilemmas in sex therapy can be an overwhelming experience for the therapist (see Watter, 2012). Often, it is best to consult with colleagues when there is an ethical question or issue. There are several opportunities for the sex therapist to obtain consultation. The therapist can, for example, obtain supervision or consultation from another certified sex therapist in his or her local area. AASECT provides a directory of certified sex therapists in each state on their website. In cases where there is not a certified sex therapist to be found locally, the therapist might also seek consultation from their already established clinical supervisor. Such a supervisor, while not a specialist in sex therapy, can provide consultation related to the relational dynamics and interventions, shed light on potential etiology and discuss other general psychotherapy techniques and approaches. Finally, the therapist can seek consultation from other therapists in the area working with the same issues, thereby developing supportive and collaborative networks. Most sex therapists are also members of the American Psychological Association or the American Association for Marriage and Family Therapy (AAMFT), and others must belong to some professional organization and be appropriately licensed in their field. As members of professional organizations, they have access to legal and ethical counsel from attorneys who work for the organizations.

Organizations and Guidelines for Ethical Issues in Sex Therapy

All therapists have a responsibility to be familiar with the ethical codes and standards that include the range or scope of practice and the professional organizations to which they belong. AASECT publishes a code of ethics for the practice of sex therapy and sex education (see the website at http://www. aasect.org/code-ethics). This document establishes guidelines for the code of conduct in the areas of competence and integrity, ethical and moral standards, protection of the consumer, welfare of students and trainees and welfare of research participants. We also strongly believe that because sex therapy also involves couple therapy, the sex therapist should be a well-trained couple's therapist and a member of the American Association of Marriage and Family Therapists (AAMFT) and should be familiar with their code of ethics (see http://www.aamft.org/iMIS15/AAMFT/Content/legal_ethics/code_of_ethics.aspx). Similarly, the Society for the Scientific Study of Sexuality has published an ethics statement that advises all members to follow the ethics guidelines of their disciplines (Society for the Scientific Study of Sexuality, 2014).

Sex Therapy Surrogates

We decided to include the topic of sexual surrogacy in this chapter because it can present an ethical dilemma for the therapist, and it is no longer a hidden subject. In fact, discussions of sexual surrogacy occur regularly among therapists on the AASECT listserv and the topic has been popularized through popular films such as *The Sessions* in 2013 (see www.foxsearchlight.com/thesessions). The term *surrogate* in sex therapy refers to an individual who will engage in intimate sexual behaviors with a client.[1] The sexual surrogate's focus is commonly in building skills for emotional and sexual intimacy as well as social skills, relaxation and sexual touching. It involves a combination of coaching and experiential work (Freckelton, 2013). In most circumstances, sexual surrogates are professionals who are enlisted to help clients overcome sexual anxieties, ignorance or dysfunction. Sexual surrogates often undertake significant training, are sometimes certified in their profession and work closely with sex therapists. In fact, sexual surrogates have their own professional organization, the International Professional Surrogates Association (IPSA), with its own code of ethics that can be viewed online at http://www.surrogatetherapy.org/code-of-ethics/, although there are others. IPSA (2014) describes surrogate partner therapy as a program focused on increasing the client's knowledge, skills, and comfort. The organization further discusses that the end of therapy occurs mutually between the client, surrogate partner and the clinician when the goals have been met (IPSA, 2014).

According to IPSA (2014), the legal status of surrogate partner therapy is undefined throughout many parts of the United States and other countries. The code of ethics proposed by IPSA seeks to reassure the community of the responsibility and professionalism in the work conducted by surrogate therapists; however, it fails to establish a guideline on the advancement of the professional relationship to a personal relationship (Freckelton, 2013). Sexual surrogate partner therapy remains an area of significant controversy within the general community and within the health professions because of the lack of empirical knowledge about its effectiveness (Freckelton, 2013).

Summary

Sex therapists, as well as all therapists, must be keenly aware of their strengths, limitations and degree of balance in their lives. A work–life balance, in particular, should be maintained in order for the therapist to have the personal strength and endurance to address the difficult, sensitive and edgy topics that can come up in sex therapy. It is extremely important for sex therapists to attend workshops and conferences annually because of the many changes in the diagnostic criteria for sexual disorders, and in the new and emerging ways in which individuals are expressing themselves sexually. In addition to educational workshops, sex therapists should engage in experiential workshops often, perhaps more often than therapists in general practice, because of the sensitivity of sexual material dealt with daily and the propensity for ethical issues.

In our clinical practices, many of us work daily with issues of sexual compulsivity, infidelity, pessimism over having a healthy sexual life, physical sexual pain and other extremely charged sexual issues. It is incumbent upon the therapist to create balance within the clinical practice—limiting the numbers of infidelity clients, for instance—in order to preserve therapist integrity and strength. Sex therapists need to create a supportive environment for themselves. This means having access to other therapists for consultation and perhaps supervision. Additionally, therapists must always be mindful of conditions such as burnout and compassion fatigue, which interfere with developing and maintaining positive coping skills needed to mediate the perceived stressors of work (Thompson, Amatea, & Thompson, 2014). Mindfulness is another antidote to burnout. Therapists who have higher levels of mindfulness are more able to handle emotional exhaustion than clinicians who tend to hold their emotions internally without a mechanism for release (Thompson, Amatea, & Thompson, 2014). We need to take the advice we offer to our clients regarding our own self-care.

Note

1. Sexual surrogates differ from facilitated sex in that facilitated sex refers to the assistance required by a disabled individual to assist with the preparation to participate in sexual activity, including positioning and removal of attire. Unlike in sexual surrogacy, the sexual facilitator does not participate in sexual activity.

References

American Association of Sexuality Educators, Counselors and Therapists [AASECT]. (2014). AASECT home page. Retrieved from http://www.aasect.org

American Psychiatric Association. (2013). *Diagnostic and statistical manual of mental disorders* (5th ed.). Arlington, VA: Author.

Bowland, S.E., Foster, K., & Vosler, A.N. (2013). Culturally competent and spiritually sensitive therapy with lesbian and gay Christians. *Social Work, 58*(4), 321–32.

Broverman, I., Vogel, S., Voverman, D., Clarkson, F., & Rosenkrantz, P. (1972). Sex-role stereotypes: A current appraisal. *Journal of Social Issues, 28,* 59–78.

Brown, R., & Sollod, R. (1988). Ethical and professional issues in sex therapy. In R. Brown & J. Field (Eds.), *Treatment of sexual problems in individual and couples therapy* (pp. 387–408). Costa Mesa, CA: PMA Publishing.

Freckelton, I. (2013). Sexual surrogate partner therapy: Legal and ethical issues. *Journal of Psychiatry, Psychology, and Law, 20*(5), 643–659. doi:10.1080/13218719.2013.831725

Green, M.S., Murphy, M.J., & Blumer, M.L. (2010). Marriage and family therapists' comfort working with lesbian and gay male clients: The influence of religious practices and support for lesbian and gay male human rights. *Journal of Homosexuality, 57*(10), 1258–73. doi:10.1080/00918369.2010.517072

Hall, K., & Graham, C. (Eds.). (2012). *The cultural context of sexual pleasure and problems,* New York: Routledge.

Handy, L., Valentich, M., Cammaert, L., & Gripton, J. (1985). Feminist issues in sex therapy. *Journal of Social Work & Human Sexuality, 3*(2–3), 69–80.

Hecker, L.L., Trepper, T.S., Wetchler, J.L., & Fontaine, K.L. (1995). The influence of therapist values, religiosity and gender in the initial assessment of sexual addiction by family therapists. *American Journal of Family Therapy, 23*(3), 261–272.

Hertlein, K.M. (2004). *Internet infidelity: An examination of family therapist treatment decisions and gender biases* (Unpublished doctoral dissertation). Virginia Tech, Virginia.

Hertlein, K.M. (2011). Therapeutic dilemmas in treating internet infidelity. *The American Journal of Family Therapy, 39*(2), 162–173. doi:10.1080/01926187.2010.530927

Hertlein, K.M., & Piercy, F.P. (2008). Therapists' assessment and treatment of Internet infidelity cases. *Journal of Marital and Family Therapy, 34*(4), 481–497.

Hill, D., & Coll, H. (1992). Ethical issues in marital and sexual counseling. *British Journal of Guidance & Counseling, 20,* 75–89.

Iasenza, S. (2010). What is queer about sex? Expanding sexual frames in theory and practice. *Family Process, 49*(3), 291–308.

International Professional Surrogates Association [IPSA]. (2014). IPSA home page. Retrieved from http://www.surrogatetherapy.org

Kleinplatz, P.J. (2012). Advancing sex therapy or is that the best you can do? In P.J. Kleinplatz (Ed.), *New directions in sex therapy: Innovations and alternatives* (2nd ed.) (pp. 101–118). New York: Routledge.

Kleinplatz, P.J. (2015). The current profession of sex therapy. In K.M. Hertlein, G.R. Weeks, & N. Gambescia (Eds.), *Systemic sex therapy* (2nd ed.) (pp. 17–31). New York: Routledge.

McCabe, M., & Goldhammer, D. (2012). Demographic and psychological factors related to sexual desire among heterosexual women in a relationship. *Journal of Sex Research, 49*(1), 78–87. doi:10.1080/00224499.2011.569975

Plaut, M. (2010). Understanding and managing professional-client boundaries. In S. Levine, C.B. Risen, & S.E. Althof (Eds.). *Handbook of clinical sexuality for mental health professionals* (2nd ed.) (pp. 21–38). New York: Brunner-Routledge.

Ravella, D. (2007). Ethics in sex therapy. In L. VandeCreek, F. Peterson, Jr., & J. Bley (Eds.), *Innovations in clinical practice: Focus on sexual health* (pp. 63–72). Sarasota, FL: Professional Resource Press/Professional Resource Exchange.

Rieker, P.P., & Carmen, E.H. (1983). Teaching value clarification: The example of gender and psychotherapy. *American Journal of Psychiatry, 140*(4), 410–415.

Schneider, J., & Levinson, B. (2006). Ethical dilemmas related to disclosure issues: Sex addiction therapists in the trenches. *Journal of Sexual Addiction and Compulsivity, 13,* 1–39.

The Society for the Scientific Study of Sexuality [SSSS]. (2014). SSSS home page. Retrieved from www.sexscience.org

Spurgas, A.K. (2013). Interest, arousal, and shifting diagnoses of female sexual dysfunction, or: How women learn about desire. *Studies in Gender and Sexuality, 14*(3), 187–205. doi:10.1080/15240657.2013.818854

Thompson, I.A., Amatea, E.S., & Thompson, E.S. (2014). Personal and contextual predictors of mental health counselors' compassion fatigue and burnout. *Journal of Mental Health Counseling, 36*(1), 58–77.

Watter, D.N. (2012). Ethics and sex therapy: A neglected dimension. In P.J. Kleinplatz (Ed.), *New directions in sex therapy: Innovations and alternatives* (2nd ed.) (pp. 85–99). New York: Routledge.

Weeks, G., & Fife, S. (2014). *Couples in treatment.* New York: Routledge.

Weeks, G., & Gambescia, N. (in press). Couple therapy and the treatment of sexual problems: The Intersystem Approach. In A. Gurman, J. Lebow, & D. Snyder, *Clinical handbook of couple therapy* (5th ed.). New York: Guilford Press.

Weeks, G., Gambescia, N., & Jennings, R. (2003). *Treating infidelity: Therapeutic dilemmas and effective strategies.* New York: W.W. Norton.

Weeks, G.R., Odell, M., & Methven, S. (2005). *If only I had known: Avoiding common mistakes in couples therapy.* New York: W.W. Norton.

ABOUT THE AUTHORS

Gerald R. Weeks, PhD, ABPP, CST, is professor in the Program in Marriage and Family Therapy at the University of Nevada-Las Vegas. He is the founder of the Intersystem Approach to Therapy and the Intersystem Approach to Sex Therapy. He is a licensed psychologist, approved supervisor and clinical fellow of the American Association of Marriage and Family Therapy (AAMFT), and is a diplomate (board certified) and senior examiner of the American Board of Family Psychology of the American Board of Professional Psychology. Dr. Weeks is also a clinical member, certified sex therapist, and approved supervisor of sex therapy of the American Association of Sex Educators, Counselors and Therapists (AASECT). He is also a diplomate of the American Board of Sexology. In 2009 he became the sixteenth member in the history of AAMFT to receive the Outstanding Contribution to Marriage and Family Therapy and in 2010 he received the Family Psychologist of the Year award from Division 43 of the APA. He has published 20 books across a broad spectrum of topics, including some of the major contemporary professional texts in the fields of individual, sex, marital and family therapy. Some of his books are widely used in marriage and family therapy programs. Dr. Weeks has lectured extensively throughout North America, Australia and Europe on sex, couple and psychotherapy. Dr. Weeks has more than 30 years' experience in practicing and supervising sex, couple and family therapy.

Nancy Gambescia, PhD, CST, is director of the Postgraduate Program in Sex Therapy at the Council for Relationships, Philadelphia, PA. The program is one of very few in the United States that provides AASECT-approved postgraduate training is sex therapy. She is also a clinical associate in psychiatry at the Perelman School of Medicine at the University of Pennsylvania. Dr. Gambescia has over 30 years' experience in teaching, supervising and working with individuals and couples. Dr. Gambescia is a clinical fellow and approved supervisor in the American Association of Marriage and Family Therapy (AAMFT). She is also a clinical member, certified sex therapist, and approved supervisor of sex therapy of the American Association of Sex Educators, Counselors and Therapists (AASECT). Dr. Gambescia is a member of the Society for Sex Therapy and Research (SSTAR) and a certified sexologist and diplomate of the American Board of Sexology. She has coauthored six books that emphasize the Intersystem Approach to couple and sex therapy and has written numerous journal articles and textbook chapters that focus on relationship and sexual issues. She has presented at a number of refereed and invited lectures and workshops in the United States and Europe on couple and sex therapy.

Katherine M. Hertlein, PhD, is professor and program director of the Marriage and Family Therapy Program at the University of Nevada-Las Vegas. She received her MA in marriage and family therapy from Purdue University-Calumet and her PhD in human development with a specialization in marriage and family therapy from Virginia Tech and is an AAMFT approved supervisor. Across her academic career, she has published over 50 articles, six books, and over 25 book chapters. She has coedited a book on interventions in couple's treatment, interventions for clients with health concerns and a book on infidelity treatment. Dr. Hertlein has also produced the first multitheoretical model detailing the role of technology in couple and family life, published in her latest book, *The Couple and Family Technology Framework*. She presents nationally and internationally on sex, technology and couples. Dr. Hertlein has won numerous awards, including the 2008 and 2014 Greenspun College of Urban Affairs Outstanding Teaching Award, the 2010 Greenspun College of Urban Affairs Outstanding Research Award, the 2013 Supervisor of the Year Award from the Nevada Association for Marriage and Family Therapy, the 2013 Outstanding Mentor Award from UNLV's Graduate and Professional Student Association, the 2014 Nevada System of Higher Education's Regents' Rising Researcher Award, and the 2014 Barrick Scholar Award from the University of Nevada-Las Vegas.

INDEX

AAMFT *see* American Association
for Marriage and Family Therapy
(AAMFT)
AASECT *see* American Association of
Sexuality Educators, Counselors, and
Therapists (AASECT)
abandonment 184–5
absent/low sexual desire 96–105;
asexuality and 246; bibliotherapy on 98;
cognitive work on, conducting 100–1;
communication and, promoting 102–3;
defining 97–8; diagnosing 50, 96–7;
education on 98; fear of losing control
and 183–4; Female Sexual Arousal/
Interest Disorder related to 97–8;
homework for 104–5; intimacy fears
associated with 102; Male Hypoactive
Sexual Desire Disorder related to 97;
medical issues associated with 103–4;
negative sexual thoughts associated
with 50–1; other sexual disorders and,
assessment for 103; pessimism and 99;
reframes for 102; relationship, addressing
concerns in 99; response anxiety and,
reducing 99–100; sexual fantasies and,
increasing of 101–2; sexual person
and, defining oneself as 101; skepticism
and 99; strategies for 98–105; in *Systemic
Sex Therapy* 99, 104; techniques for
98–105; treatments for 97; *see also* sexual
desire
acceptable homework 191

acquired DE 121
acquired PE 59
acquired sexual disorders 18–19
ADD 101
addiction 27, 54–5
ADHD 101
affection, sexual 34–5
age-related ED 217
age-related FSAD 57
aging 215–19
AIDS 218, 235
American Association for Marriage and
Family Therapy (AAMFT) 2, 204, 258,
265
American Association of Sexuality
Educators, Counselors, and Therapists
(AASECT) 206; certified sex therapists
257–8, 264; sex therapy, educational and
supervisory standards for certification
in 2–3; sexual enhancement products
206; sexual surrogacy 265; vibratory
technology 139
American Cancer Society 213
American Physical Therapy Association 145
American Psychiatric Association 75
American Psychological Association 265
anger 182
anorgasmia 132, 137
anticipation, positive 169–70
antidepressants 117
anxiety: absent/low sexual desire, reducing
response to 99–100; asexuality and

245; DE and reducing 125; disorders associated with 24, 178; factors complicating treating sexual disorders 178; PE and 59; physical/medical issues for special populations for reducing 222–3; sensate focus technique for 157; sexual performance and 157; special populations, reduction of 222–3; *see also* performance anxiety
appropriate homework 111–12, 137–41, 191
Arousal: The Secret Logic of Sexual Fantasies 135
arthritis 214
asexuality 245–7
Asexual Visibility & Education Network (AVEN) 245–6
assessment: of asexuality 246; behavioral 76; of DE 120–3, 125; of ED 55; FOD, therapist questions for 60–1; of GPPPD 62–3; for other sexual disorders 103; of PE 58–9, 59–60; physiological 76–7; psychological 77–80; of sex addiction 54–5; of sexual disorders 32–3; treatment and, overlapping of 83; *see also* intersystem assessment of sexual disorders; sexual assessments
assumptions 47–8
attachment 68
attachment theory 7–8
Attachment Theory and Sexuality 3–4
attraction 69, 246
attributional strategy 5–7
AVEN *see* Asexual Visibility & Education Network (AVEN)
aversion 245
avoidance 157–8

backward conditioning 119
B&D *see* bondage and discipline (B&D)
BDSM *see* bondage, discipline, sadism, masochism (BDSM)
behavioral assessment 76
Betty Dodson with Carlin Ross website 134
bibliotherapy 98, 108, 137, 197–202
biological factors 142
biological status 8–9
biomedical basis of GPPPD 148–9
biphasic assessment process 33–5
Birch, Robert 205
bisexual 234

BISF-W *see* Brief Index of Sexual Functioning for Women (BISF–W)
BMSFI *see* Brief Male Sexual Function Inventory (BMSFI)
bondage, discipline, sadism, masochism (BDSM) 28, 36, 233, 244
bondage and discipline (B&D) 206, 233
boundaries 46, 263–4
breast cancer 24–5, 212
Brief Index of Sexual Functioning for Women (BISF–W) 80
Brief Male Sexual Function Inventory (BMSFI) 79

cancer 24–5, 211–13
cardiovascular illness 210–11
caretaking 217
Centers for Disease Control 218
cerebral palsy 209–10
certified sex therapists/therapy 2–3, 257–8, 264; *see also* therapist
changing roles 217
chemotherapy 213
Cialis 110
cisgender 240
clear homework 191
client identification 254–6
clinical interview 49
clinical judgment 26
Clinician's Guide to Systemic Sex Therapy, A 16
clitorodynia 145
CNM *see* consensually nonmonogamous (CNM)
code of ethics of AAMFT 265
cognitive-behavioral homework 153–4
cognitive-behavioral interventions 146–9
cognitive-behavioral therapy 134–5
cognitive work 100–1, 109–10
collaboration 219–21, 258–9
comfort 44–5
commitment 4, 155, 162–3
communication 160; absent/low sexual desire and, promoting 102–3; physical/medical issues for special populations 226; skills in 35; special populations 226
compliance 154
confidentiality 45, 262–3
congruence 5–6
consensual BDSM 28
consensually nonmonogamous (CNM) 237–9
consensual sexual masochism 28

consultations 258–9
contextual factors 12–13, 43–4
contingency plans 193
control, fear of losing 183–4
cooperation in relationships 162–3
Coping with Appearance Changes due to Breast Cancer: Tips to Help Improve Your Body Image 213
Council for Relationships Postgraduate Sex Therapy Program 257–8
countertransference issues 239–40, 247–9
couples Intersystem Approach 1–3
couples therapy 1–3
cross-dressing 28
culture 68

Dapoxetine 117
DE *see* Delayed Ejaculation (DE)
definition 5
Delayed Ejaculation (DE) 18, 21, 120–8; acquired 121; assessment for 120–3; contributory factors associated with 122; *in DSM-5* 21; fantasies and 126–7; fetishes and 126–7; intergenerational factors for 124; lifelong 121; pharmacological agents for 121–2; phenomenological study of 124; relationship issues and 123–4; strategies for 124–8; techniques for 124–8; treatment techniques for 124–5; underreporting 121
dependency 185–7
depression 24
Derogatis Interview for Sexual Functioning (DISF) 79
Derogatis Sexual Functioning Inventory 78
desensitization 157
diabetes 213–14
diagnosis: of absent/low sexual desire 50, 96–7; of dyspareunia 143; of ED 55, 106; of Female Sexual Interest/Arousal Disorder 25, 50, 56–7; of FOD 131; of GPPPD 62, 142; of PE 58–9; of sexual disorders 16–29; of vaginismus 141–3
Diagnostic and Statistical Manual of Mental Disorders (DSM-5): DE in 21; desire disorders in 96; ED in 20–1; female genital arousal in 28; FOD in 22, 131; GPPPD in 22; limitations of 22–6; Male Hypoactive Sexual Desire Disorder in 20; paraphilia in 243–4; PE in 21; penetration in 115; in sex therapy, role

in 17; sexual addiction in 54; sexual compulsivity in 54; sexual desire in 259; sexual disorders in, classification and criteria for 16–18; sexual dysfunction in, diagnostic criteria for 16; Sexual Interest/Arousal Disorder in 19–20; sexual problems not currently in 27–9; specifiers of 18–19; T and Z codes in, relational diagnosis through the 26; transvestite in 240
directed masturbation (DM) 134–5
disabilities 214–15
disorder *vs.* problem 23–4
DM *see* directed masturbation (DM)
dominance and submission (DS) 233
DS *see* dominance and submission (DS)
DSM-5 see Diagnostic and Statistical Manual of Mental Disorders (DSM-5)
DSM-IV 241
DSM-IV-TR: FSAD in 56; Male Orgasmic Disorder in 121; Partner Relational Problem in 29; SAD in 53; sexual addiction in 54; sexual compulsivity in 54; sexual disorders in, classification and criteria for 16–18; sexual dysfunction in 79
dyadic issues 9–11
dysesthetic vulvodynia 144
dyspareunia 18, 144–5; cancer and 212; diagnosis of 143; GPPPD and 62, 141–2; pelvic radiation and 212; prevalence of 142

early ejaculation *see* Premature Ejaculation (PE)
East Asian women 178
eating disorders 24
ED *see* Erectile Disorder (ED)
ejaculation 113; *see also* Delayed Ejaculation (DE); Erectile Disorder (ED); Premature Ejaculation (PE)
elderly 216
electromyography (EMG) 77
EMG *see* electromyography (EMG)
epilepsy 214
Erectile consistency 113
Erectile Disorder (ED) 18–21, 55–6, 106–7; age-related 217; assessment for 55; cardiovascular illness and 210; diabetes and 214; diagnosis of 55, 106; in *DSM-5* 20–1; etiology of 55–6; final issues in 115; GPPPD and 115; HSDD and 25; manual stimulation

and 114; medical issues and 24; PE and 115–16; performance anxiety and 56, 114; prevalence of 20–1; prosexual medications for 221; psychological consequences of 24, 106; relational problems and 25; sensual touch and 111–12; sexual dysfunction in both partners and 89–90; strategies for 107–15; symptoms of 20, 106; techniques for 107–15; therapist questions for 56; treatment for 91–2, 107, 110–11
Erectile Dysfunction *see* Erectile Disorder (ED)
erections *see* Delayed Ejaculation (DE); Erectile Disorder (ED); Premature Ejaculation (PE)
erotic stimulation 171–2
erotic transference 264
ESO *see* Extended Sexual Orgasm (ESO)
ethical dilemmas: boundaries as 263–4; gender bias as 259–61; identifying 259–64; managing 264–6; organizations and guidelines for 265; religious issues as 261–2; secrets as 262–3; sex therapy surrogates as 265–6
ethical sex therapy 257–9
ethical treatment 254–7
ethics 254–67
Extended Sexual Orgasm (ESO) 141
extradyadic emotional intimacy 238

family-of-origin influences 11–12
fantasies 101–2, 126–7, 135, 244
Farlex Dictionary of Sexual Terms and Expressions 205
faulty cognition 177–8
FDA *see* Food and Drug Administration (FDA)
fears 183–4; *see also* intimacy fears
feelings 182–3
female genital arousal 28
Female Orgasmic Disorder (FOD) 18, 22, 60–1, 131–41; anorgasmia and 132, 137; assessment of 60–1; diagnosis of 131; *DSM-5,* diagnostic criteria for 22, 131; etiologic factors associated with 60; intergenerational factors and 133; medical issues and 132; medical issues related to 60; orgasm and 132; performance anxiety and 133; prevalence statistics for 131; psychological factors and 133; relational

issues and 133–4; sexual satisfaction and 132; stimulation and 137–8; strategies and techniques for 134–41; symptoms of 131; treatment for 134–5; vibrators and 139–40; websites for 134
Female Sexual Arousal Disorder (FSAD) 18, 56–8
Female Sexual Function Index (FSFI) 80
Female Sexual Interest 18
Female Sexual Interest/Arousal Disorder 17, 50–3, 97–8; diagnosis of 25, 50, 56–7; in *DSM-5* 96; in *DSM-IV-TR* 17; relational problems and 25; sexual dysfunction and, multiple 89
female to male (FTM) 240–1
fetishism 28, 126–7
flexibility in homework 193
focused genital touch 112–13
FOD *see* Female Orgasmic Disorder (FOD)
Food and Drug Administration (FDA) 221
For Each Other 137
foreplay 161–2
For Yourself 137
Foundation for the Scientific Study of Sexuality 204
free form intercourse 114–15
FSAD *see* Female Sexual Arousal Disorder (FSAD)
FSFI *see* Female Sexual Function Index (FSFI)

gay relationships 36
gender: assumptions about 242–3; bias in 259–61; diversity in 231; expression of 69, 240; nonconformity in 28, 232; sexual genogram and questions about 72; *see also* gender identity
gender dysphoria 28, 241
gender identity 28, 240–2; disorders associated with 241 (*see also* gender dysphoria); gender nonconformity and 28; of lesbian, gay and bisexual clients 234; of LGB 234; psychological issues and 42; sex history and 37; sexual assessments on 79
genderqueer person 240–1
gender role stereotypes 260
generalized sexual disorders 18–19
genetic factors 59
genital swelling 28–9
genital touch 112–13

Genito-Pelvic Pain/Penetration Disorder (GPPPD) 18, 22, 61–3, 141–9; assessment of 62–3; biological factors as common cause of 142; biomedical basis of 148–9; diagnosis of 62, 142; in DSM-5 22; dyspareunia and 62, 141–2; ED and 115; individual factors for 142; intergenerational factors for 143; lifelong 142; medical treatments for 149; prevalence of 142; relational causes of 143; relational factors for 143; sexual dysfunction in both partners and 90; sociocultural factors for 143; strategies and techniques for 146–9; symptoms of 22; terminology for describing 143–5; treatment of 63; vestibulodynia and 142; in women 149

gift giving 263–4

goal setting 256–7

Golombok-Rust Inventory of Sexual Satisfaction (GRISS) 79

Good Vibrations 134

Google 46

GPPPD see Genito-Pelvic Pain/Penetration Disorder (GPPPD)

GRISS see Golombok-Rust Inventory of Sexual Satisfaction (GRISS)

Guide to Assessments That Work, A 79

Gurman, Al 2–3

Guttman Scale of Sexual Experience 78

Gynecologic Cancer Foundation 213

Handbook of Couple Therapy 2

Handbook of Homework Assignments in Psychotherapy 189

Handbook of Sexuality-Related Measures 79

health issues 216

Hefner, Hugh 186

heterosexual therapist 231

Hite Report, The 140

HIV 208, 218, 235

homework 190–3; for absent/low sexual desire 104–5; appropriate 111–12, 137–41; case illustration of 193–4; cognitive-behavioral 153–4; processing assignments and 194; reading assignments and 195

homophobia 235

HSDD see Hypoactive Sexual Desire Disorder (HSDD)

Hyperactive Sexual Desire/Sexual Compulsivity 54–5

hypersexuality 27

Hypoactive Sexual Desire Disorder (HSDD) 17, 24; in DSM-IV-TR 17; ED and 25; Intersystem Approach to 3–4; sensate focus technique for 153

identification of client 254–6

IELT see intravaginal ejaculatory latency time (IELT)

IIEF see International Index of Erectile Function (IIEF)

individual problems 25–6

Innovations in Clinical Practice: Focus on Sexual Health 195

Institute for Sexual and Marital Therapy 205

interactional behavior 4

intercourse 167, 172–3

interdependence 5–6

intergenerational factors 43, 124, 133, 143

International Consultation Committee for Sexual Medicine on Definitions/ Epidemiology/Risk Factors for Sexual Dysfunction 217

International Index of Erectile Function (IIEF) 80

International Professional Surrogates Association (IPSA) 266

Internet resources on psychoeducation 204–6

Interplay between Mental and Sexual Health, The 216

interpretation 4–5

intersex 240

Intersystem Approach to sex therapy 1–14; application of 3–8; biological status and 8–9; contextual factors and 12–13; for couples 1–3; development of 3; domains of 8–13; dyadic issues and 9–11; etiology of 8–13; family-of-origin influences and 11–12; for HSDD 3–4; integrational constructs of 3–4; integrative perspective of 2; interactional components of 5–8; intrapsychic components of 4–5; medical status and 8–9; methodology of 2; psychological status and 9; treatment within 8–13

intersystem assessment of sexual disorders 32–64; biphasic assessment process for 33–5; clinical interview for 49; contextual factors and 43–4; intergenerational factors and 43; interviewing for specific 49–50;

Orgasm and Ejaculation Disorders
and 58–63; physiological status and 41;
psychological status and 42; relationship
and 42–3; Sexual Desire Disorders and
50–8; sexual history and 35–41, 44–9
intimacy: concept of 180; defined 180;
extradyadic emotional 238; FSAD and
57; in relationships 162–3; Sternberg's
Triangular Theory of Love and 4;
tolerance to 169; touching and 161;
see also intimacy fears
intimacy fears 102, 179–87; abandonment
as 184–5; anger as 182; dependency as
185–7; feelings as 182–3; losing control
as 183–4; rejection as 184–5
intrapsychic behavior 4
intravaginal ejaculatory latency time
(IELT) 115
investment in homework 192–3
IPSA *see* International Professional
Surrogates Association (IPSA)

kink resources 233–4
kinky clients 232–4
kinky erotic activities 232–3
Kinsey, Alfred 47
Kinsey Institute, The 204
Kinsey's "Category X" 245

lesbian, gay, bisexual, transgender (LGBT)
69, 232, 235, 249
lesbian, gay and bisexual (LGB) 234–7
level of care 162–3
level of love 162–3
Levitra 110
Lexipro 216
LGB *see* lesbian, gay and bisexual (LGB)
LGBT *see* lesbian, gay, bisexual, transgender
(LGBT)
LGBT World 204
lifelong DE 121
lifelong GPPPD 142
lifelong sexual disorders 18–19
love 68, 162–3
low sexual desire *see* absent/low sexual
desire
Lyme's Disease 49

Male Erectile Disorder 18; *see also* Erectile
Disorder (ED)
Male Hypoactive Sexual Desire Disorder
17, 20, 50–3, 97
Male Orgasmic Disorder 18, 121; *see also*
Delayed Ejaculation (DE)

Male Sexual Health Questionnaire
(MSHQ) 80
male to female (MTF) 240
manual stimulation 114
masturbation 126–7, 134–5
McCoy Female Sexuality Questionnaire
(MFSQ) 80
medical issues/problems 87, 103–4,
208–27; aging 215–19; disabilities
214–15; ED and 24; FOD and 60, 132;
physical illness 209–14; sexual function
and 209; sexual satisfaction and 209;
for special populations 219–27; *see also*
physical issues
medical prescriptions 221
medical providers 219–21
medical status 8–9
medical treatments 110–11, 116–17, 149
medications, prosexual 221
men: aging in 217; cardiovascular illness
and 210–11; DE in 120–8; ED in
106–7; PE in 115–20; SAD in 53;
treatment for 106–28
menopause 57, 217
mental loop 169
men who have sex with men (MSM) 115
metaphoric isomorphis 166
metaphors for sensate focus technique
165–7
mild sexual disorders 18–19
mindfulness 149, 158
misinformation 222–3
moderate sexual disorders 18–19
monogamish 237
MS *see* multiple sclerosis (MS)
MSHQ *see* Male Sexual Health
Questionnaire (MSHQ)
MTF *see* male to female (MTF)
multimedia on psychoeducation 202–4
multiple sclerosis (MS) 209
multiple sexual dysfunction in individual
88–9
My Pleasure 205
My Secret Garden: Women's Sexual Fantasies
135

National Council on Family Relations 204
negative sexual thoughts 50–1
neurological ailments 209–10
neuromuscular diseases 214
New Male Sexuality, The 108
nondemand intercourse 172
nongenital touch 112
nonjudgmental therapist 46

nonmonogamous intimate relationships 237–40
normal sexual function 17
normal sexual functioning 17

open relationship 237
organizations for ethical dilemmas 265
orgasm: barriers to 135–7; fear of inability for 183; FOD and 132; psychoeducation about 117–18; stimulation and 140–1
Orgasm and Ejaculation Disorders 58–63; FOD as 60–1; GPPPD as 61–3; PE as 58–60
other clinically relevant problems 87–8
Other Specified Sexual Disorders 18, 24–5, 103; FOD and 60; PE and 116; sexual disorders, co-occurring with 24–5; on triage tree 103

pain 61–2; see also Genito-Pelvic Pain/ Penetration Disorder (GPPPD)
pansexual 234
paraphilias 243–5
paraphilic disorder 243
paraphilic fantasy 244
Parkinson's disease 210
Partner Relational Problem 29
partners 89–91, 218; see also couples therapy
passion 4
PC see pubococcygeus (PC) muscle
PDE-5 (phosphodiesterase type 5) inhibitors 111
PE see Premature Ejaculation (PE)
pelvic radiation 212
penetration 113–15, 148
performance anxiety: ED and 56, 108–9, 114; FOD and 133; PE and 21; see also anxiety
Persistent Genital Arousal Disorder (PGAD) 28–9, 58
pessimism 154
PGAD see Persistent Genital Arousal Disorder (PGAD)
pharmacological agents 121–2
phenomenological study of DE 124
physical illness 209–14; cancer 211–13; cardiovascular illness 210–11; diabetes 213–14; neurological ailments 209–10
physical issues 208–27; aging 215–19; disabilities 214–15; health 24–5; physical illness 209–14; for special populations 219–27; see also medical issues/problems
physical limitations 215

physical realities 222
physiological assessment 76–7
physiological status 41
physiologic factors 20
physiology 24
Pleasuring I and II 164, 171
polyamory 238
positive anticipation 169–70
positive experiences 162
posttraumatic stress disorder (PTSD) 182
prediction 5
Premature Ejaculation (PE) 18–19, 21, 58–60, 115–20, 116; acquired 59; anxiety and 59; assessment of 58–60; behavioral strategies and techniques for 117–20; causes of 116; diagnosis of 58–9; in DSM-5 21; ED and 115–16; genetic factors involving 59; medical treatment for 116–17; performance anxiety and 21; psychological factors involving 59; sexual dysfunction in both partners and 90–1; treatment of 117–18
prescriptions 221
presenting problem 87–8
problem definition 256
problem vs. disorder 23–4
processing assignments 194
proscribing intercourse 167
prosexual medications 221
prostate cancer 211–12
Provoked Vestibulodynia 62
psychiatric disorders 27
psychoeducation 197–206; about orgasm 117–18; bibliotherapy on 197–202; Internet resources on 204–6; multimedia on 202–4; for special populations 221–2; videos on 202–4
psychological assessment 77–80
psychological consequences 24, 106
psychological factors/issues 42, 59, 133
psychological status 9, 42
psychology 24
psychotherapy 154
PTSD see posttraumatic stress disorder (PTSD)
pubococcygeus (PC) muscle 148; see also vaginismus

quality of sex life 78–9
queer clients 232
quiet vagina technique 119–20

range of practice 257–8
reaction time 76–7

readiness for assignments 163–4
reading assignments 195
reassurance 146
reciprocity 161
"Recognizing and Reversing the Sexual
Side Effects of Medications" 216
referrals 258–9
reframes 102
rejection 184–5
relationships 162–3; absent/low sexual
desire, addressing concerns in 99; DE
and problems in 123–4, 127; ED and
problems in 25; Female Sexual Interest/
Arousal Disorder and 25; FOD and
133–4; gay 36; GPPPD, causes of
143; intersystem assessment of sexual
disorders and 42–3; nonmonogamous
intimate 237–40; open 237; orgasms,
barriers to 136–7; overall, between
couple 34; problems in 25–6; sensuality
in 35; special populations, issues with
223
relevant homework 191
religious issues 261–2
*Renewing Intimacy and Sexuality after
Gynecologic Cancer* 213
romantic attraction 246
romantic love 68

SAD *see* Sexual Aversion Disorder (SAD)
sadomasochism (S&M) 206, 233
safe environment 45
SAR *see* Sexual Attitude Readjustment/
Reassessment (SAR)
Science of Orgasm, The 137
secrets 262–3
selective serotonin reuptake inhibitors
(SSRIs) 121, 216
self-awareness 46
self-differentiation 238
self-pleasure 159–60
self-sexuality 46
self-worth 238
sensate focus technique 152–74; for
anxiety 157; application of 164–5;
avoidance and 157–8; cognitive-
behavioral homework as 153–4;
commitment as 155; concept of 157;
desensitization and 157; exercises for
156; functions of 158–63; for HSDD
153; intercourse, transitioning to 172–3;
mindfulness and 158; pessimism and
154; principles of 152; promoting
compliance 154; proscribing intercourse

as 167; readiness for assignments on
163–4; sensual environment, creating
167; for sexual performance 157;
skepticism and 154; structure of
164–5; systemic perspective on 155–6;
understanding 156–8; using metaphors
for 165–7; *see also* sensual pleasuring
sensory defensiveness reduction 125
sensual awareness 159
sensual behavior 161
sensual environment 167
sensuality 35
sensual needs 160–1
sensual pleasuring 169; with erotic
stimulation 171–2; touching and
167–71
sensual touch 111–12, 125–6
serotonergic antidepressants 117
serotonin-based antidepressants 117
Sessions, The 227, 265
severe relational discord 88
severe sexual disorders 18–19
sex addiction 27, 54–5
Sex Dictionary, The 205
sex talk 48
sex therapy: for absent/low sexual
desire 96–105; couples therapy and,
integration of 1–3; *DSM-5,* role in
17; ethics in 254–67 (*see also* ethical
dilemmas); homework in, principles of
189–95; intersystem approach to 1–14;
physical/medical issues in 208–27;
principle of 94–5; process of 94–5;
psychoeducation in 197–206; SAD,
avoiding for 53; sensate focus technique
used in 152–74; sexual expression and,
diversity in 231–50; sexual function
and dysfunction measurements 75–80;
sexual genogram and 66–74; techniques
for 94–5; *see also* treatment
Sex Therapy in Philadelphia 205
sex therapy surrogates 265–6
Sexual Addiction and Compulsivity 54
sexual affection 34–5
sexual arousal 57
sexual assessments 79, 218–19; *see also*
assessment
Sexual Attitude Readjustment/
Reassessment (SAR) 46, 206, 258
sexual attraction 69, 246
Sexual Aversion Disorder (SAD) 17, 53–4
sexual behavior 161
Sexual Bill of Rights 101
sexual compulsivity 27, 54

sexual conservatism 178
sexual desire 160, 178; building 162; changes in 215; communication of 160; domains of 51–3; *in DSM-5* 259; incongruence of, between partners 23–4; levels of 51–3; sexual arousal *vs.* 57; *see also* absent/low sexual desire; Sexual Desire Disorders
Sexual Desire Disorders 50–8, 96; ED as 55–6; Female Sexual Arousal Disorder as 56–8; Female Sexual Interest/ Arousal Disorder as 50–3; Hyperactive Sexual Desire/Sexual Compulsivity as 54–5; Male Hypoactive Sexual Desire Disorder as 50–3; Persistent Genital Arousal Disorder as 58; SAD as 53–4
sexual disorder 18–19; anxiety disorders and 24, 178; assessment of 32–3; depression and 24; determining 32; diagnosis of 16–29; in *DSM-5,* classification and criteria for 16–18; *DSM-IV-TR,* classification and criteria for 16–18; eating disorders and 24; intersystem assessment of 32–64; Other Specified Sexual Disorders, co-occurring with 24–5; physical health issues and 24–5; treatment for, factors complicating 176–87; *see also* sexual disorder diagnosis
sexual disorder diagnosis 16–29; with *DSM-IV-TR* 17–19; Intersystem Approach to 29; *see also Diagnostic and Statistical Manual of Mental Disorders (DSM-5)*
sexual disorder treatments, factors complicating 176–87; anxiety as 178; faulty cognition as 177–8; intimacy fears as 179–87; sexual guilt as 178; sexual ignorance as 176; sexual mythology as 176–7, 179; shame as 178
sexual dysfunction: in *DSM-5* 16; in *DSM-IV-TR* 79; in elderly 216; multiple, in individual 88–9; in *Systemic Sex Therapy* 153; *see also* sexual dysfunction measurements; sexual dysfunction treatment
sexual dysfunction measurements 75–80; behavioral assessment 76; physiological assessment 76–7; psychological assessment 77–80
sexual dysfunction treatment: in both partners 89–91; multiple in individual 88–9; systemic 153
sexual enhancement products 206

sexual expression: asexuality 245–7; diversity in 231–50; factors impacting 208; kinky clients and 232–4; of LGB 234–7; nonmonogamous intimate relationships and 237–40; paraphilias and 243–5; queer clients and 232; tantric sex and 247–8; therapist competency with 248–50; transgender and 240–3
sexual fantasies 101–2
sexual function 17, 209, 213; *see also* sexual function measurements
Sexual Functioning Questionnaire for Heterosexuals 78
sexual function measurements 75–80; behavioral assessment 76; physiological assessment 76–7; psychological assessment 77–80
Sexual Function Questionnaire (SFQ) 80
sexual genogram 66–74; attachment and 68; conceptualization of 67; constructing 69–71; culture and 68; defining 66; function of 66–9; gender expression and 69; LGBT and 69; organization of 70–1; potential questions for 71–2; questions related to 67–8; romantic love and 68; scope of 69; sexual attraction and 69; sexual orientation and 69; sexual timeline and 72–4
sexual guilt 178
sexual history 35–41; assumptions and 47–8; comfort and 44–5; guidelines for taking 44–9; safe environment and 45; self-sexuality and 46; sex talk and 48; shaming and 47; systemic thinking and 48–9; therapist considerations for 45–6
sexual ignorance 176
Sexual Interaction Inventory 78
sexual interest 58, 162–3
Sexual Interest/Arousal Disorder 19–20
sexuality 212–13
Sexuality and Cancer: A Guide for Patients and Their Partners 213
Sexuality for the Man with Cancer 213
Sexuality for the Woman with Cancer 213
Sexuality Information and Education Council of the United States 204
sexually transmitted infections (STIs) 218, 238–9
sexual mythology 176–7, 179
sexual needs 160–1
sexual orientation 47, 69, 241, 245

Sexual Orientation Method and Anxiety
78
Sexual Pain Disorders 18
sexual performance 157
sexual person, defining oneself as 101
*Sexual Pharmacology: Love Potions, Pills, and
Poisons* 216
sexual repertoire 224–5
sexual sadism 28
sexual satisfaction 132, 209
sexual scripting 217, 224
sexual surrogacy 265
sexual thoughts, negative 50–1
sexual timeline 72–4
Sexual Trauma and Recovery 205
SFQ *see* Sexual Function Questionnaire
(SFQ)
shame 47, 178
significant individual psychopathology 88
simple homework 191
Sinclair Intimacy Institute 204
single focused homework 192
situational sexual disorders 18–19
skepticism 154
skin conductance (SC) test 77
S&M *see* sadomasochism (S&M)
Society for Sex Therapy and Research
204, 258
sociocultural factors 143
special populations 219–27; anxiety
reduction in 222–3; communication
in 226; medical providers and,
collaboration with 219–21;
misinformation in 222–3; myths in
222–3; psychoeducation in 221–2;
relationship issues in context of illness
223; sexual repertoire in 224–5; sexual
scripting in 224; systemic focus in 219;
therapist for, issues in 226–7
specific homework 191–2
Spencer, Paula 148
spina bifida 214
spinal cord injuries 214
SSRIs *see* selective serotonin reuptake
inhibitors (SSRIs)
Sternberg's Triangular Theory of Love 3–4
Stewart, Elizabeth 148
stimulation: erotic 171–2; FOD and 137–8;
manual 114
STIs *see* sexually transmitted infections
(STIs)
stop-slow technique 118–19
stop-start and squeeze techniques 118

stroke 210
Structured Diagnostic Method (SDM) 80
Substance/Medication-Induced Sexual
Disorder 18
suicide 242
support for homework 193
surrogate partner therapy 265–6
swinging 237
systemic focus 219
systemic perspective 155–6
Systemic Sex Therapy 16, 64, 91–2;
absent/low desire in 99, 104; medical
prescriptions in 221; pain in 62; sexual
dysfunction in 153; systemic treatment
and 91–2, 95
systemic thinking 48–9, 107–8
systemic treatment 91–4

Tamoxifen 212
T and Z codes, relational diagnosis
through the 26
Tantra 247–8
tantric sex 247–8
Tarlov cysts 28
Ted Talks 197
Theory of Interaction 3–4
therapist 248–50; boundaries of
46; considerations for 45–6;
countertransference issues with 248–9;
heterosexual 231; LGB, competency
of 236–7; nonjudgmental 46; self-
awareness of 46; special populations,
issues in 226–7; transference issues,
recognizing 249–50; transgender,
competency of 242–3; treatment, tasks
in 83; *see also* therapist questions
therapist questions: on ED 56; on FOD
60–1; on FSAD 57–8; on SAD 53–4
tolerance to intimacy 169
topical local anesthetics 117
touch/touching 161–2; genital 112–13;
intimacy and 161; nongenital 112;
progressions of 169; sensual 111–12,
125–6; sensual pleasuring and 167–71
transference issues 249–50
transgender 240–3
transprejudice 241
transsexual 240
transvestite 240
traumatic brain injury 214
treatment: for absent/low sexual desire 97;
asexuality, issues with 246; assessment
and, overlapping of 83; beginning 84–6;

cardinal rules for 146; confidentiality in 262–3; for DE 124–5; for dyspareunia 145; for ED 91–2, 107, 110–11; for FOD 134; general considerations for 75–80; goals of 83; of GPPPD 63; within Intersystem Approach 8–13; for kinky clients 233; of LGB 235; medical 110–11, 116–17, 149; for men 106–28; mindfulness-based 149; for multiple sexual dysfunction in individual 88–9; with paraphilias 244–5; of PE 117–18; for PGAD 58; presenting problem *vs.* other clinically relevant problems 87–8; strategies for 83; systemic 91–4; techniques for 83; therapists tasks in 83; for transgender 241–2; triage tree for 86–7; of vaginismus 143–4, 146–8; for women 89, 131–49; *see also* ethical treatment; sex therapy; sexual dysfunction treatment
Treatment Algorithm 86–7
triage tree 86–7, 103
Type II diabetes mellitus 213–14

uncertainty 238
University of Hawaii AIDS Educational and Training Center 205
University of Texas MD Anderson Cancer Center 213
Unspecified Sexual Disorder 18

vagina 144
vaginal photoplethysmography 76
vaginismus 18, 143–4; defining 62, 143; diagnosis of 141–3; in *DSM-IV-TR* 18;

PC muscle and 143–7; prevalence rates for 142; symptoms of 143; treatment of 143–4, 146–8; in women 143
V Book: Doctor's Guide to Complete Vulvovaginal Health, The 148
vestibulodynia 142
Viagra 110
vibrators 139–40
videos on psychoeducation 202–4
Vietnam War 182
vulva 144
vulvar pain 61–2
vulvar vestibulitis syndrome (VVS) 144–5
vulvodynia 144–5

Weeks, Gerald 1–3
Wellbutrin (Bupropion) 221
Woman's Touch, A 134
Woman's Touch Sexuality Resource Center, A 134
women: aging 217; cardiovascular illness and 211; chemotherapy and 212; disabilities in 215; dyspareunia and 144–5; East Asian 178; FOD in 131–41; GPPPD in 141–9; orgasms in, barriers to 135–6; PGAD in 28; SAD in 53; treatment for 89, 131–49; vaginismus in 143
Women's Sexual Health Foundation 204
World Professional Association for Transgender Health (WPATH) Standards of Care 242

Xanax 216

YouTube 197

Taylor & Francis eBooks

Helping you to choose the right eBooks for your Library

Add Routledge titles to your library's digital collection today. Taylor and Francis ebooks contains over 50,000 titles in the Humanities, Social Sciences, Behavioural Sciences, Built Environment and Law.

Choose from a range of subject packages or create your own!

Benefits for you
- » Free MARC records
- » COUNTER-compliant usage statistics
- » Flexible purchase and pricing options
- » All titles DRM-free.

Benefits for your user
- » Off-site, anytime access via Athens or referring URL
- » Print or copy pages or chapters
- » Full content search
- » Bookmark, highlight and annotate text
- » Access to thousands of pages of quality research at the click of a button.

REQUEST YOUR **FREE** INSTITUTIONAL TRIAL TODAY

Free Trials Available
We offer free trials to qualifying academic, corporate and government customers.

eCollections – Choose from over 30 subject eCollections, including:

Archaeology	Language Learning
Architecture	Law
Asian Studies	Literature
Business & Management	Media & Communication
Classical Studies	Middle East Studies
Construction	Music
Creative & Media Arts	Philosophy
Criminology & Criminal Justice	Planning
Economics	Politics
Education	Psychology & Mental Health
Energy	Religion
Engineering	Security
English Language & Linguistics	Social Work
Environment & Sustainability	Sociology
Geography	Sport
Health Studies	Theatre & Performance
History	Tourism, Hospitality & Events

For more information, pricing enquiries or to order a free trial, please contact your local sales team:
www.tandfebooks.com/page/sales

Routledge
Taylor & Francis Group

The home of
Routledge books

www.tandfebooks.com